LONDON NORTH OF THE THAMES
except the City and Westminster

THE KING'S ENGLAND

Edited by Arthur Mee

In 42 Volumes

ENCHANTED LAND (INTRODUCTORY VOLUME)

Bedfordshire and Huntingdonshire
Berkshire
Buckinghamshire
Cambridgeshire
Cheshire
Cornwall
Derbyshire
Devon
Dorset
Durham
Essex
Gloucestershire
Hampshire with the Isle of Wight
Herefordshire
Hertfordshire
Kent
Lake Counties
Lancashire
Leicestershire and Rutland
Lincolnshire
London North of the Thames

London—The City and
   Westminster
London South of the Thames
Monmouthshire
Norfolk
Northamptonshire
Northumberland
Nottinghamshire
Oxfordshire
Shropshire
Somerset
Staffordshire
Suffolk
Surrey
Sussex
Warwickshire
Wiltshire
Worcestershire
Yorkshire—East Riding
Yorkshire—North Riding
Yorkshire—West Riding

THE KING'S ENGLAND

LONDON NORTH OF THE THAMES

except the City and Westminster

By
ARTHUR MEE

fully revised and rewritten by
ANN SAUNDERS
(Ann Cox-Johnson)

Illustrated with new photographs by
A. F. KERSTING

HODDER AND STOUGHTON
LONDON · SYDNEY · AUCKLAND · TORONTO

Printed in Great Britain
for Hodder and Stoughton Ltd.,
St Paul's House, Warwick Lane, London, EC4P 4AH,
by Richard Clay (The Chaucer Press), Ltd.,
Bungay, Suffolk

INTRODUCTION TO REVISED EDITION

In preparing the new edition of THE KING'S ENGLAND care has been taken to bring the books up to date as far as possible within the changes which have taken place since the series was originally planned. In addition the editor has made his revisions both in text and illustrations with a view to keeping the price of the books within reasonable limits, in spite of greatly increased production costs. But, throughout the book, it has been the editor's special care to preserve Mr Arthur Mee's original intention of providing something more than just another guide book giving archaeological, ecclesiastical, and topographical information.

In the case of every town and village mentioned in the King's England Series, it has been the intention not only to indicate its position on the map but to convey something of its atmosphere. The biographical selections about people who are ever associated with that part of the country in which they lived, or who are commemorated in the parish church—which was such a popular feature of the former edition—have been retained and in some cases supplemented.

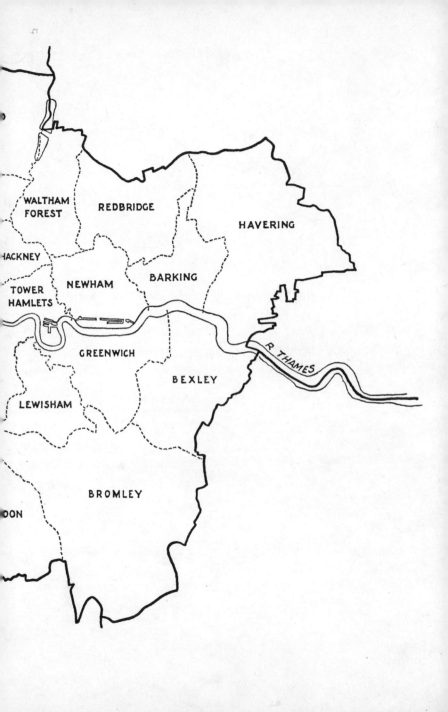

PREFACE

The original London and Middlesex volumes in Arthur Mee's *The King's England* series were written in 1937 and 1940 respectively; they have been reissued, unaltered, many times since in response to a steady demand for the readable and informative accounts of the capital and the county which they provide. But the passing of time, the destruction of war, and the administrative alterations in the boundaries and government of London which took place in 1965, have brought about so many changes that a fresh description has become necessary. Bombs and their resulting fires destroyed or damaged churches, public buildings, and houses alike; modern development has completely changed whole areas, and in 1965 the reorganisation of London so that the whole of the Greater London area was under one central administration meant that the whole of Middlesex and the metropolitan parts of Essex, Kent, and Surrey were engulfed in the capital though retaining their identity as postal areas. Instead of the single square mile of the City or the 117 square miles of Inner London, the metropolis now covers 616 square miles. Instead of the 200,000 citizens who made up the population in Elizabeth I's day, or the 1,000,000 inhabitants shown in the 1811 census, there are now nearly 9,000,000 Londoners.

It was felt that to cover so vast an area, and one so rich in topographical and historical associations, in a single volume, would be unmanageable even if entries were compressed in the most miserly manner, so it was decided to devote three volumes to London, the first dealing with the area north of the Thames, the second with the City and Westminster, and the third with London south of the river. In this first volume, the arrangement is by boroughs, listed in alphabetical order. This arrangement has one great advantage over the single place entry, used in the original Middlesex and Essex volumes, for it makes it possible to link up related areas so that, for example, Harrow, Pinner, and Stanmore can all be considered together and East Ham is no longer divorced from West Ham. Richmond alone is divided by the Thames, and in this volume only the northern bank is described, but an account of the entire borough will be given in the third volume.

This book then covers three originally distinct areas—the six new London Boroughs into which the older Inner London authorities have been incorporated, the whole of Middlesex with its boundaries as revised in 1965, and that part of Essex, a sixth part of the entire county, which has now become a part of London. The Inner London boroughs—Kensington and Chelsea, Camden, Tower Hamlets, Islington, Hammersmith, and Hackney—represent communities engulfed by London's growth from the late 17th through the 18th and 19th centuries. Middlesex, the smallest county in England, barring Rutland, has always had a uniquely close relationship with the capital. From 1132 the City of London has appointed the Sheriff of Middlesex, and in 1965 Middlesex Guildhall was in Westminster. The county has now been divided into the boroughs of Barnet, Brent, Ealing, Enfield, Haringey, Harrow, Hillingdon, Hounslow, and Richmond on Thames. By and large, it was built over later than the Inner London boroughs, the farmlands disappearing from the mid-19th century onwards as London spread out with the growth of the railways. We therefore tend to find an old village centre, such as Hanwell, Hendon, or Pinner, surrounded by areas of development by speculative builders or borough councils.

The same close relationship to the capital is not felt in the five boroughs—Barking, Havering, Newham, Redbridge, and Waltham Forest—which have been carved out of Essex. Once across the Lea, one is on a different, non-London landscape, with heavy industry at Dagenham, part of Epping Forest in Waltham Forest, and an astonishing view across it all from the top of Havering Hill. Hainault Forest has been felled and replaced by the huge Becontree housing estate, one of the LCC's bravest attempts at dealing with an almost insoluble problem, but cows are still grazing on Wanstead Flats, or clattering down the street to stop the early morning traffic in Chingford.

What is surprising is not how much has been altered but how much has remained unchanged. While some old boundaries, such as the Hundred of Gore, have been obliterated or at least fragmented, others, such as Edmonton Hundred, have been renewed. London has advanced inexorably across the green fields, covering them with little houses and gardens, or with blocks of flats, and the villages around which those fields lay should have been annihilated, but they have not. They still flourish, each with its own personality, and that is what this book is trying to do, to show simultaneously the close link between London and its countryside, and the contrast between the capital and the individual villages and townships around it.

This volume is a completely new one and its scope has been

widened, not only geographically to suit London's boundaries, but to include types of buildings and historical details which may have seemed less important a generation ago. The present author hopes, however, that Arthur Mee would approve of the new work; she has tried to retain the spirit of the original even though the style is different and, as Mee did, she has written out of love for London. Mee was writing for the ordinary intelligent person who is interested in the neighbourhood in which he lives, or who wishes to visit another profitably. This book attempts to point out the extraordinary resources, the variety of architectural interest, and the depth of historical associations to be found in every part of London. Its aim is to help and to encourage people to explore on their own, to visit other areas, and to find a fresh delight and interest in what they see.

No topographical work on 20th century London can hope to be properly up-to-date. Even as we go to press the Department of the Environment has announced that the docks nearest to the City are to be closed and the land re-developed; details of the plans are still uncertain and the future of the Covent Garden site is as yet undecided. Future editions will have to record London's latest changes.

Anyone writing about London owes a great deal to those who have written before about this most interesting of cities. The Reverend Daniel Lyson's five volumes on *The Environs of London*, which were published between 1796 and 1811, are invaluable for learning how Middlesex and Essex looked when they were still country places. Of more modern works, I have constantly used Professor Pevsner's *London except the Cities of London and Westminster, Middlesex*, and *Essex* in his *Buildings of England* series, Michael Robbins' excellent and informative *Middlesex* and Ian Nairn's *Modern Buildings in London*. Kenneth Neale's *Discovering London in Essex*, which appeared in 1970, is also interesting. I have throughout relied on the available volumes of the *Survey of London* and the *Victoria County History*, as well as the Royal Commission for Historic Monuments. No one interested in London should be without a copy of the GLC's blue plaque guide—*Commemorative Tablets*.

I have received unfailing and unstinting help and kindness from the librarians and archivists of London's public libraries. They have suggested and made available reading matter, answered innumerable questions, and have checked the final texts. Such errors as remain are not their fault and I can only thank them for their generosity. Dr and Mrs T. A. Heathcote were responsible for the research on, and much of the text for, the sections on Enfield and Hounslow, and Colonel A. V. Murphy undertook the research for the chapter on Richmond. Miss Mercer and the late Miss Darlington, archivists to the Greater London Council, Miss Pollard, reference librarian of Harrow, and Miss Ensing, reference librarian of Kensington and Chelsea, have encouraged me throughout; the Reverend I. W. Harrison of East Ham, Wing Commander Le Conte of Bentley Priory, and Charles Swallow of Harrow School, all gave help and kindness beyond any reasonable request. Mrs Christina Gee, Curator of Keats House, Hampstead, provided reference works constantly, and Miss Jane Osborn of Hodder and Stoughton has been the perfect editor, always hopeful, never impatient. Finally, I should like to thank my family who have worked on this book with me for the last three years. I dedicate it to my children and my nephews—James, Timothy, Matthew, Bevis, Katherine, and Nicholas—who undertook the primary fieldwork on the parks and children's playgrounds of North London.

May, 1970   ANN SAUNDERS

CONTENTS

LIST OF ILLUSTRATIONS

INTRODUCTION

London is an old, proud city. Despite its Celtic name (*Llyn-din*—"river place"), the first permanent settlement was probably made by the Romans, who recognised the advantages of the site—the twin hills, now crowned by St Paul's and Smithfield Market, and the gravel spits along the banks of the Thames which encouraged bridge-building at this, the lowest spannable point.* Within a generation, a sizeable trading town had grown up, linked to the continent by the Thames and soon to be connected with the rest of the island by the network of roads which the Romans began to construct. It was important enough to be one of the objectives of Boadicea's rebellion in AD 61 when 70,000 men, women, and children fell victim to her tribesmen at Colchester, Verulamium (St Alban's), and London. But after the Queen's defeat and death, the cities were soon rebuilt and reinhabited and once again, as Tacitus wrote, London was thronged with merchants. It expanded till it was the sixth largest city in the Roman empire and soon superceded Colchester as the centre of Roman administration. Places of worship, a forum, a palace for the governor of the province, and public baths were all built and the roads ran out from London, traversing the nearby countryside and linking the capital with the farthest parts of the island. Ermine Street ran due north to Lincoln, passing through Edmonton and Enfield, the Silchester Road went westwards along what is now Oxford Street and the Bayswater Road, the line of Watling Street, leading north-west to St Alban's, is followed by the Edgware Road to Brockley Hill, where there were Roman kilns, and the Colchester Road ran out from Aldgate, crossing the Lea at Old Ford, towards where Ilford and Romford now stand. London was the centre where land and water communications, by way of the Thames, met—as they do to this day.

The roads that crossed what were to become Middlesex and Essex passed sites which had been human habitations long before a house was built in London. There was a flint-working factory in Acton, pile-dwellings on the river Lea, an established community at Brentford, and a temple with a village around it where the aeroplanes now fly in and out at Heathrow Airport. The great chalk basin of the

* A full history of the City of London will be attempted in the second volume of this new edition.

Thames Valley, which dips down from the Chilterns and rises again at the North Downs, moulded by volcanic eruption and filled with clay, was chiefly covered by forest, but a forest possible to clear with primitive tools, while the soil beneath was fertile. As Roman rule became more firmly established, so farms and villages grew up in the surrounding countryside, often existing even then to supply the needs of the capital, and yet each possessing its own individuality, its own peculiar characteristics. It is this exchange between the interdependence of London and its countryside, with the simultaneous development of personality in the villages no less than in the capital, which is the central theme of this volume. Harrow is totally unlike Hampstead; Brentford and Uxbridge are both market towns but there all resemblance ends; there is industry in Hayes and in Dagenham but there is no other similarity. It has been the aim of this book to stress the character and uniqueness of each locality, as far as possible.

The Roman army withdrew from Britain in 410 but town life continued in London despite the attacks of the Saxons and other barbarians which began after the exodus of the legions. Civilised existence must have been sadly curtailed but Grim's Dyke was dug at Stanmore during the 5th and 6th centuries and may well mark the limits of London's own *territorium*. In the 8th century, Bede was able to write of London as "the mart of many nations resorting to it by land and sea", and in 886 Alfred rebuilt the city walls as a defence against the Vikings. It was during this period that for a few brief decades a political association of tribes may have come into being, of which now only the name remains—Middlesex, the land of the Middle Saxons. Their history is shadowy enough, but their patronymics are echoed in place-names—Uxbridge and Uxendon take theirs from the Wixan tribe, Ealing from the Geddings, and Enfield was once Eana's clearing in the forest. During the 9th and 10th centuries the administrative units known as hundreds were established; there were six in Middlesex—Gore (covering from Harrow to Hendon), Ossulstone (containing Highgate and Ealing, being divided into two parts), Elthorne (on the extreme west, running from Ruislip to Harmondsworth), Spelthorne (stretching from Bedfont to Hampton), Isleworth (which was sometimes called Hounslow, so its area is indicated), and Edmonton, whose boundaries have been renewed in those allotted to the London Borough of Enfield.

During the 11th century a new court quarter began to grow up at Westminster. Edward the Confessor built both a palace and an abbey there; both were enlarged by ensuing generations till Westminster became the court area, the centre of royal administration and justice, in apposition—sometimes in opposition—to the City. This double centre, this division of the royal from the mercantile power, is a vital fact in London's development and in English history.

When William the Conqueror prevailed at Hastings, he took care not to harm London needlessly. Instead he marched in a wide arc around the city, after burning Southwark on the southern bank of the Thames, laying waste as he went so that London might learn to fear him by example though not from actual bitter experience. When at last the citizens made peace with him and recognised his sovereignty, he confirmed them in all their ancient liberties, but the decreased valuations in Domesday Book for those villages in the Home Counties through which his host had passed, show how dearly they had paid for London's immunity. Middlesex had been worth £909 in King Edward's day; when Domesday was drawn up, its valuation had fallen to £748.

William established his palace and stronghold not in the City itself but on its eastern boundary where he could both guard the citizens against attack by river and himself from the possible uprising of these same citizens—"a vaste and fierce populace". The establishment of comparative peace and order under subsequent rulers gave opportunity for the building of churches, of which the superb carved Norman doorways at Harlington and Harmondsworth, the fonts at Hendon and Hayes, and the entire church at Rainham in Essex, are visible memorials. In 1132, the City of London was granted the right to appoint the Sheriff of Middlesex while the city and the shire had often been grouped together for fiscal purposes.

London itself grew steadily, developing as a great European port, a city of merchants and well-established trade guilds, and above all, a city of churches—more than a hundred in the City alone. Meanwhile agriculture developed in Middlesex and in Essex, and London relied upon the farmers there for meat, vegetables, fruit, and dairy produce, and on the fishermen of Barking for supplies of fish. Fine churches were built at Willesden and East Ham, a small but substantial manor house at Tottenham and a hunting lodge for the Bishop of London at Haringey, and ordinary Londoners relied upon the nearby country areas for recreation as well as for food. The peacefulness of the green fields was disturbed by the bitter battle at Barnet in 1471 which confirmed Edward IV on the throne of England and condemned poor, saintly Henry VI to death. The more momentous battle of Bosworth was fought far away from London in Leicestershire but the change of dynasty which it brought about had astonishing effects on the capital.

The Dissolution of the Monasteries deprived the poor of London of their main sources of charity, emptied buildings of their religious occupants and turned them into tenements, while it enriched the king, his courtiers, and numberless entrepreneurs who realised what a valuable commodity land was. Hampton Court, begun sumptuously enough by Cardinal Wolsey, was enlarged, additions were made to Hanworth and Richmond and a new manor house was built at Chelsea. The nobility and commons followed suit—Lord Arundel built his house at Highgate, Sir John Spencer at Canonbury, Sir Thomas Gresham at Osterley, while others, perhaps less ostentatious but more generous, took over some of the responsibilities of the Church—John Lyon founded Harrow School, Alice Wilkes established almshouses in Finsbury and Thomas Ravenscroft built a grammar school in Barnet.

Agriculture however still flourished. The fields around Heston were golden with the corn that made Queen Elizabeth I's bread and Michael Drayton was able to write in his *Poly-Olbion* of "Peryvale . . . prank'd up with wreaths of wheat". By the early 17th century, the population of the capital was increasing steadily and had probably reached the 200,000 mark. The houses were creeping outside the old city walls and in 1580 Queen Elizabeth had had to issue the first proclamation that no more houses were to be built in the environs of London. The edict was disregarded and the size of London has been a problem ever since. Stow lamented in the year of the queen's death that houses were covering the fields eastwards out of London, and at the same time the docks began to grow up in the Isle of Dogs which had always been a maritime area. Neat walks were laid out across Moor-fields where there had once been a marsh on which the apprentices skated in the Middle Ages, and enterprising citizens took their families for a day's outing to Islington. Despite the unwillingness of Charles I, a new little town was created on old monastic lands around Covent Garden and Bloomsbury by the 4th earl of Bedford, and more country houses inspired by Inigo Jones, such as Forty Hall, or in contrast with his Italianate style, like Cromwell House at Highgate, were built, but the coming of civil war checked development even if it did not end it completely. The king's headquarters were at Oxford, so the western approaches of the city were fortified, and engagements were fought at Brentford and Acton, culminating in a virtually bloodless three-day encounter at Turnham

Green, whence at last the Royalists returned discomfited and inconclusively to the west.

The tragedies of the Plague and Fire of 1665 and 1666 belong to the history of the City but their effects were very much the concern of the surrounding countryside. A whole new court area grew up around Charles II's Court of St James, and less than a generation later, William III's choice of Kensington House as a palace turned that village into a court suburb too. Speculative builders such as Nicholas Barbone, began to develop Holborn, new churches were built to minister to the needs of the growing population, three of the finest of them by Hawksmoor in the East End of London, market-gardening intensified at Fulham and Hammersmith, a new ring-road had to be laid out in 1757 to bring the cattle into Smithfield to feed the population, and the price of hay needed to feed the horses that could not be put out to pasture, rose steadily. At the beginning of the century, the magnificence of Canons at Stanmore and of Wanstead House was celebrated; before the end, Robert Adam was adorning old country houses, such as Osterley and the former convent of Syon, and turning them into exquisite palaces for the very rich. By 1811, the population of London was 1,000,000, that of the whole country 9,000,000; today the population of the Greater London area approaches the latter figure. To house this enormous increase, the suburbs grew up—Willesden, Ealing, and Hackney—and with the coming of the railways and the advent of cheap workmen's fares, they spread farther and farther. Fulham's market-gardens vanished, the slopes around the foot of Harrow Hill were covered with mean building, Golders Green was built by one generation, on either side of the First World War, and Hendon by the next in the 1930s. Throughout the expansion, the determined defence of open spaces by the public and the London County Council—of Hampstead Heath and of Marble Hill at Twickenham, for example—have been sufficient to ensure that London has a greater variety of open spaces than any other city in the world. They vary from the acres of Epping Forest to the single acre of Elm Park at Child's Hill, Hampstead, from the astonishing selection of trees at Stephen's Park, Finchley, to the formal flower-beds of Coronation Gardens, Leyton. The parks are one of London's great glories, and the provision of swings and climbing frames for children within them, one of the GLC's most humane functions.

By 1900, London had grown to such an extent that a new county administration had to be created to attend to the needs of its 117 square miles, but the growth did not stop there. Arterial roads spread out, in the same way that Roman roads had once opened up the countryside, and ribbon development crept along them. The First World War made little physical difference to London, but during the Second whole areas were devastated by fire and bombing. Even while the bombs were falling, plans were being prepared for a new city: *The County of London* by Forshaw and Abercrombie was published in 1943, *The Greater London Region Plan* by Abercrombie in 1944 and *The City of London Plan* by Holden and Holford in 1946. The need for a Green Belt round the metropolis, which had been adopted as early as 1935, was emphasised and its existence has been maintained. New towns—Stevenage, Harlow, Basildon—were created in attempts to deal with London's huge population. In 1960 a Royal Commission decided that a new administration was needed to deal with the 616 square miles. In 1965, the Greater London Council swallowed Middlesex and took over a sixth part of Essex, as well as parts of Kent, Surrey, and Hertfordshire. The London County Council became the Greater London Council while the old borough and urban district authorities were rolled into 32 new London Boroughs. The City of London remains a separate entity.

But in spite of the new administration, motorways, and the sheer mass of the population, the villages of London and Middlesex and Essex have remained villages, surprising and foolish as that statement may seem. Stand beside the dew pond on the top of Barn Hill near Harrow when mist is falling, and ancient Middlesex, populated before London was built, is still there; look across from Dunstan Road in Golders Green to the spire of Harrow Church on the Hill and the gentle vistas which the country once afforded are apparent; survey the Lea Valley from the heights of Mansfield Park and one is astonished by the variety of the landscape. Stand on Highgate Hill on a clear day and one catches the breath as London is revealed, full of buildings and humanity, and intensely alive; stand in the same place on a clear night and watch the lights of the city and sense its variety and fascination and its strength.

How much of that strength is drawn from the countryside around it can never be assessed with precision, but it is safe to say that without the food which the Home Counties supplied in the past, without the land for homes and factories which they provide today, and without the variety and refreshment of landscape, at all times freely given, London could never have become and could not be the city which she is. In 1795, John Middleton wrote in his *View of the Agriculture of Middlesex*:

6

The whole county may be very properly considered as a sort of demesne to the metropolis, being covered with its villas, intersected with innumerable roads leading to it, and laid out in gardens, pastures and inclosures of all sorts for its convenience and support.

Let London be careful how she uses her countryside for it is precious with a significance which can scarcely be put into words but only felt.

This book is an attempt to record how that part of the Greater London area north of the Thames looked in 1970. The author has set out to recall the history, to record the old buildings which are still there to treasure, and to welcome the many fine new ones which have been built. She hopes that it may help residents and visitors to explore and enjoy their own and other areas, that it may encourage them to conserve and to beautify as best they may, and that it may persuade them—should they need persuasion—to be proud to be citizens of London, which is indeed no mean city.

BARKING

BARKING

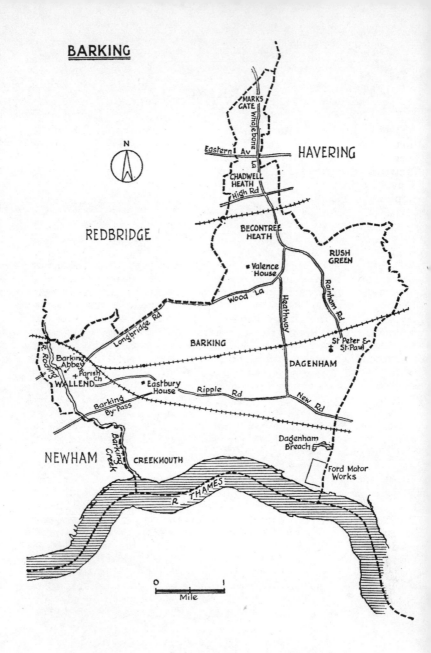

BARKING

The London Borough of Barking consists of the greater part of the former municipal boroughs of Barking and Dagenham, both of which were in Essex. Its southern boundary is the Thames, to the west lies Newham, to the north Redbridge, and to the north and east Havering. It covers 8,877 acres and in 1966 had an estimated population of 171,000.

The creation of this new London borough has reunited parts of the ancient parishes of Barking and Dagenham which once formed the main part of the estate of the Abbey of Barking. This was one of the oldest areas of Anglo Saxon settlements in Essex as the names of *Berecingum* ("Berica's people") and *Daeccanham* ("Daecca's home") denote; evidence of Bronze Age dwellings has been found near Barking Creek, and a strange carved wooden human figure, possibly as old as the 6th century before Christ, was discovered near the Thames, south of Ripple Road. It is now in the Colchester Museum, but a copy can be seen at Valence House (see p. 16). The Romans came and built a road from London to Colchester; one of them died while travelling along it and was buried in a stone coffin by the roadside. His grave was discovered in 1936 and the coffin is now at Valence House.

Barking was famous for its great abbey, dedicated to Our Lady and St Ethelburga, the first abbess. It was founded about 666 by St Erkenwald, Bishop to the East Saxons, for his sister; he founded another for himself at Chertsey. The first three abbesses, Ethelburga, Hildelitha, and Wlfhildis [*sic*], were all canonised, and although the convent was probably destroyed by the Danes in the 9th century, it was restored by Alfred's son, Edward the Elder. Besides Barking, Dagenham, and Ilford, which comprised the manor of Barking, the oldest estate in Essex, the abbey owned properties in London, Middlesex, Buckinghamshire, Bedfordshire, and Surrey. After the Conquest, William stayed in the abbey while the Tower was being built, and he confirmed the abbess in the possession of all her territories. It was she who took precedence over all the other abbesses in England, and the office was held by three queens—by Alftrudis, by Maud, wife to Henry I, and by Maud, wife to Stephen

—by two princesses, the daughters of Henry II and of John, and by Mary Becket, St Thomas's sister. A great church and a fine convent were built and flourished, and served sometimes as a place of detention, for Elizabeth, wife of Robert the Bruce, was kept here from 1306 till 1314, and the little sons of Catherine de Valois, Henry V's widow, and Owen Tudor, came here for about four years on the death of their mother in 1437. The elder boy, Edmund, became the father of Henry VII, and the younger, Jasper, grew up to be the protector of the future Tudor dynasty for he watched over and cherished his nephew and took him away to Brittany when England became dangerous for the boy. The abbesses of Barking were busy ladies, for in addition to their religious and political duties they had to maintain their estates and, as we shall hear, flood damage at Dagenham was a permanent danger.

But, like every other monastery and convent in England, Barking was suppressed by Henry VIII; in 1539, the last abbess, Dorothy Barley, was granted the large pension of 200 marks a year, similar provision was made for her nuns, and the following summer the buildings were pulled down to provide the king with a new house at Dartford and to repair Greenwich Palace. All that remains is the 15th century Curfew or Fire Bell Gate, which now makes an entrance to Barking parish church, St Margaret's. In 1911 the site was excavated and the outlines of the nuns' church, of the cloisters and chapterhouse and refectory and dormitory, can be traced by the grey stones on the green grass. The bare spaciousness of the site swings the spectator's mind back to the calm and purposeful dignity of the life which was once lived here.

We pass under the curfew gate to reach the churchyard, and in the room over the gateway is an early 13th century rood with the figures of Christ, Our Lady, and St John, much worn but still impressive. The church itself is of flint and rag stone with a 13th century chancel and octagonal pillars of the same date in the north aisle while the east chapel on that side may be older still. The arcades were lengthened and the tower added in the 15th century. Stones from the abbey may have been re-used for the repairs of the parish church after 1540. The nave roof is original but the chancel has a stuccoed vault of 1772. The oldest stone in the church is part of a Saxon cross—perhaps the one link with St Erkenwald's settlement—and there is a fragment of a black marble gravestone which came from the abbey with the name of a Norman bishop on it, Maurice. The gravestone of the first vicar here, Martinus, was also recovered from the abbey. He died in 1328 and his memorial is one of those engraved stones which were the forerunners of brasses. It shows him deeply cut in the stone with his curly hair, his embroidered collar and cuffs, and his name and office in bold letters. There is another curious stone from the abbey, deep and hollowed out; it is known as the Nun's Bath, though it is clearly unsuitable for such an office and its purpose is unknown.

The church also contains a 17th century font with a cover painted with flowers, birds and butterflies, a fine 18th century pulpit, an organ case by Byfield and Green, and some really good modern embroidery in the kneelers and altar runner. The south chapel has a screen raised as a fishermen's memorial, with figures of St Nicholas and the three children he saved from death, James and John with their fishermen's nets, St Ethelburga, Elizabeth Fry, and Captain Cook. Of these last two, we shall have more to say.

There are two 15th century brasses of priests in their robes, and another of the same date to Thomas Broke and his wife with their son and daughter. A fourth brass shows John Tedcastell (d. 1596) with his wife, four sons, and five babes in swaddling clothes, who presumably died in infancy. On the chancel wall is an exquisite monument to Sir Charles Montagu (d. 1625); wearing his armour, he sits in a tent guarded by sentries, his page holding a horse nearby and many other tents in the distance. His daughter Elizabeth married Sir Christopher Hatton's heir (see p. 58) and his brother was among those who sentenced Sir Walter Raleigh to death. Among a group of 17th and 18th century busts is Francis Fuller (d. 1636) with three bright shields, John Bennett (d. 1706) in front of the prow of a warship, Orlando Humfreys with four cherubs, John Bamber of 1753, and Sir Crisp Gascoigne, Lord Mayor of London, who died in 1753.

Among the many marriages celebrated in this church is one of particular significance. It was that of Elizabeth Batts and Captain James Cook, and it took place just before Christmas in 1762. They had six children, of whom three died as babies, the other three boys growing up to love the sea. Elizabeth said goodbye to her husband in 1776 and four years later news came to her of his death, which had happened twenty months before in Hawaii. She was to survive him for 56 years, years of great sorrow for her for she outlived all her children and was alone in the world for 40 years. There have been few lonelier lives than that of the bride who stood in this place to marry a sailor who found a continent.

The church stands on the banks of the River Roding and for centuries fishing was Barking's staple industry. A window in the church shows a quay scene, and until the end of the last century when swift railway transport made London able to draw on fish from the east coast ports, Barking was an important fishing centre. A fleet of boats was operated by the Hewett family, who also supplied ice for which they built a huge ice house in Abbey Road and stored it with ice obtained by judicious flooding of the Thamesside marshes in winter. But the decline of the trade was accelerated by a terrible storm off the Dutch coast in December 1863 when some 60 local men were drowned.

There had always been farming in the area—wheat, sheep, and a few cattle—till the late 18th century when there was a gradual change to market gardening, peas, beans, and potatoes for the London market. In 1807, Arthur Young noted that London butchers were paying £10 per acre for grazing land in Barking.

The various manors into which Barking was divided in the Middle Ages—all of them belonging to the abbey—had lovely names—Berengers and Jenkins, Bifrons, Fulks, Porters and Malmaynes and Eastbury. Only one relict remains, Eastbury House, built about 1572 (the date is on a rainwater head), now the property of the National Trust but on lease to the Borough Council who are restoring it and are hoping to use it as an arts centre. It has a massive entrance door, some fine fireplaces, and an oak spiral staircase, the planks of which are dowelled together. This leads up a tower and on to a roof from which one can see for miles. And there is a great painted chamber, the walls of which are covered with seascapes and landscapes, faded but still lovely.

Of modern Barking, the spacious railway station is worth admiring, and the borough serves London well, for it is here that the main outfall of London's drainage is discharged and is carried away by ships to be dumped far out to sea, and Barking Power House provides much of the electricity for lighting the capital. The ancillary trades and industries which grew up around the old fishing port have extended both in kind and magnitude over the last hundred years. Among industries now represented are industrial chemicals, paint, plastics, rubber, timber, electronics, and precision engineering. The town centre, concentrated on East Street, is being comprehensively redeveloped.

Dagenham is full of engineering and technological triumphs from the 18th century onwards, though there is little left of the old village which developed from the cluster of buildings that was once Daecca's home. Almost all that remains is near the church, dedicated to St

Peter and St Paul, which itself has a 13th century chancel. The tower collapsed in 1800, demolishing the nave and south aisle. The church was rebuilt in 1805 with a rather nice tower and classical portico. The combination is perhaps odd, but it is very endearing. Inside is a splendid altar tomb to Sir Thomas Urswyck (d. 1479), Baron of the Exchequer, who helped to set Edward IV on the throne. The brass shows him in judge's robes and his wife in a butterfly head-dress. Nine daughters are below them, one of them in nun's robes; the brass of their four sons was stolen long ago. Sir Thomas was lord of the manor of Marks in north-east Dagenham, and when he died in 1479 an inventory was drawn up of all his property from which we learn that the manor house had twenty rooms, a dairy, and a bake-house, and that there were six books in the chapel, among them a copy of the *Canterbury Tales*. The house was demolished in 1808, but one barn still stands and is in use on Warren Farm.

There is another monument of note in the church, that of another judge, Sir Richard Alibon, who was born here in 1635 and died in 1688. It has been suggested that the bust is sculptured by Van Nost. Alibon was made a judge by James II, the first Roman Catholic to become one for 150 years. He was apparently unlearned in the law and was one of those who tried to convict the Seven Bishops, thereby becoming so unpopular that it was as well he died when he did.

Beside the church is the white gabled vicarage, built in 1665, and the Cross Keys Inn. This was the house of the Comyns family, who were tanners—the almshouses, now demolished, which they founded in the 18th century stood farther up the street—and only became a public house about 1680, changed its name to the Queen's Head about 1708, and became the Cross Keys again a century later. The house originally had a central hall with east and west cross-wings and most of the old hall is still there, a little masked by modern bar arrangements, in this most friendly inn.

The various estates that made up Dagenham have vanished and only the echo of their existence is in the street names which serve to remind us of the past. We have already mentioned Marks, which passed from Sir Thomas Urswyck to Sir Nicholas Bacon and then to his more famous son, Francis, who sold it in 1596 to Sir George Hervey, whose family later took the name of Mildmay. Carew Hervey Mildmay (1690–1784) who was MP for Harwich and private secretary to Bolingbroke, used to entertain splendidly and it needed half-a-dozen coaches to drive his guests to Romford Church. One of his friends was General Oglethorpe of Cranham. In Marks Gate stood a 16th century house called Padnalls; the name was first recorded in 1303, the house was demolished in 1938. Another fascinating name belongs to the manor of Wangey which in the 17th century was the property of another Harvey family, unrelated to those of Marks, one of whom, Samuel, married John Donne's daughter and the poet used to stay with his family at Aldborough Hatch. The manor changed hands again and was bought by the Lethieullier family, one of whom, Smart Lethieullier (1701–60), was a great antiquarian. He purchased the Lordship of the Manor of Barking, was the first to excavate the abbey ruins, and was an early donor to the British Museum.

Parsloes came to be the senior estate, as it were. It passed into secular hands at the Dissolution and was held by three Lord Mayors of London, Sir Martin Bowes, Sir Rowland Hayward, and Sir Edward Osborne. It is of Sir Edward that an almost certainly apocryphal but most romantic story is told. When he was a boy apprentice, he saw his master's little daughter, Anne, fall from the window of their house on London Bridge into the river. He dived in after the child, saved her and when she grew up the two were married. He certainly did marry his master's daughter, and their son, Sir Hewett, was killed in Ireland in 1599 fighting under the Earl of Essex. His son sold Parsloes to William Fanshawe in 1619, whose family held it for almost three centuries. His descendants supported Charles I and suffered for it, but did well after the Civil War, a later William marrying Mary Walter, the daughter of Charles II and Lucy Walter (her brother was the unlucky Duke of Monmouth). Sir Richard Fanshawe was the ambassador to Spain and Portugal who arranged Charles II's marriage with Catherine of Braganza. His wife Anne kept an exciting journal about their embassy which was published earlier this century. The Fanshawes built a fine house which had to be let when they fell into debt in the 1850s and which was finally demolished, being derelict, in 1925. The tenants included Thomas Denman, Lord Chief Justice, and Colonel William Hope, one of the first men to win the Victoria Cross. The estate was taken over by the Essex and London County Councils. Nearly 115 acres were preserved as a park and the rest was built over as part of the Becontree Housing Estate.

The exceptionally fine collection of Fanshawe family portraits and their archives have, however, been most felicitously preserved, for they were presented to the borough by Captain Aubrey Fanshawe, R.N., and are at Valence House; the portraits include works by William Dobson, Jonathan Richardson, and Sir Peter Lely.

Valence is the only remaining manor house in Dagenham. The

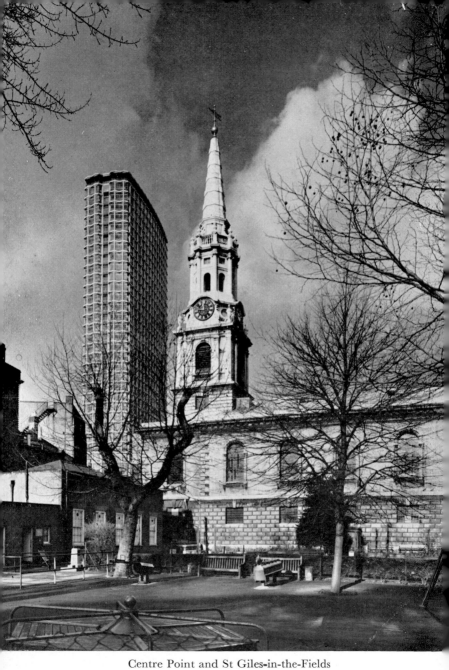

Centre Point and St Giles-in-the-Fields

Church Farm House
Museum, Hendon

The Manor House,
Southall: the main front

first recorded occupant (the land of course belonged to Barking Abbey) was Robert Dyre or Dynes who sold it in 1284 to Sir Thomas Weyland. His widow left it to Agnes de Valence who bequeathed her interest in it to her brother, Aylmer de Valence, the Earl of Pembroke, from whom the property took its name. It passed from hand to hand and was given in 1451 by the Bishop of Worcester to St Anthony's Hospital in London to provide an annual exhibition to Oriel College, Oxford. St Anthony's was one of the mediaeval schools of London and its pupils included Sir Thomas More and Dean Colet. In 1475 Edward IV granted its patronage to the Dean and Canons of Windsor and they continued to own Valence till 1926. At least three manor houses have been built there; the present one was begun in the early 17th century and has been enlarged, reduced, and altered at intervals since. It is now the property of the borough and houses a remarkable and well-displayed local history collection ranging from prehistoric times to the present day, the Fanshawe collection of portraits, furniture lent by the Victoria and Albert Museum and shown to advantage in the panelled rooms, and some fascinating maps. The grounds are agreeable and there are traces of the moat that protected an earlier dwelling.

One other vanished feature in Dagenham's topography must be mentioned—Hainault Forest. It was that part of Waltham Forest which covered northern Dagenham and its name is a corruption of *Hyneholt*, "the (monastic) community wood". Poor widows living in the neighbourhood were allowed a free load of wood from it in winter. The largest tree in it was the Fairlop Oak on the Ilford side (now in Redbridge). It measured 66 feet in circumference and had 17 huge branches. To their shade a benevolent employer, Daniel Day of Wapping, led his workpeople for an annual meal of pork and beans and around this outing a fair grew up. The oak decayed and was blown down in 1820 but the fair went on till 1892 or later though by then the venue was the Bald Hind at Chigwell for the Forest itself had vanished. In 1853, the trees were cut down by order of the Commissioners for Land Revenue, the timber sold for £48,000, the roots grubbed up and the land turned over to agriculture. Men worked by torchlight at night as well as by day and the destruction was complete in little over a year. In 1902, 800 acres were purchased by the London County Council, the Essex County Council, and the local councils, and was turned into a park, called by the old name of Hainault Forest which is today a place of great natural beauty. In 1939, more land was purchased extending the area to 1108 acres. One of the old forest boundary stones is to be seen today in Valence House, others are still in position by Warren Farm, Marks Gate, and in Chadwell Heath High Road.

Perhaps the most exciting story about Dagenham is that of the closing of Dagenham Breach by Captain John Perry in 1720. The story begins much earlier. On the north bank of the Thames lay a rectangular island of some 560 acres of marshland, the River Beam separating it from the mainland on the east side, an inlet of water known as the Gulf or Breach on the west and north. The marshland was vital to local economy for its supply of thatching reeds and for agriculture. A storm, an exceptionally high tide, and a part or the whole of the Level might be flooded. A slight subsidence of the land and the harsh winter of 1376–77 started the trouble and for the next three and a half centuries farmers and landowners large and small were impoverished or ruined by the struggle to keep Dagenham Level from flood waters. In 1409 the abbess of Barking petitioned the king for tax relief, which was granted, for she had spent £2,000 over the previous years in attempts to keep the tide out. A storm on the night of October 29, 1707, tore a 14-foot gap in the river wall and 1000 acres were flooded. By 1713 a huge sum had been paid out uselessly in rates, and two contractors, John Ward and William Boswell, had failed to close the gap. An old warship, the *Lion*, had been scuttled and sunk but the tides had pounded her to pieces and had continued to flow over the land. Then in June 1716 Captain John Perry was appointed. By this time the breach was 400 feet wide. Perry was a skilled naval engineer and had been a most successful adviser to Peter the Great of Russia. He built a dam across the breach on dovetailed wooden piles and stopped the flow on September 4, 1717. Six days later an exceptionally high tide re-opened it and it was not till June 1720 that the flow was effectively staunched. All this time Perry lived on the site in a house that he had had built, known as Breach House. He said that had it not been for the unwavering support given him by the Russia merchants who knew him well he would never have been able to raise the funds to complete the work. Breach House became the meeting place of the Commissioners of the Levels who were responsible for the new river wall. A sheet of water known as the Gulf remained (and still remains); it became a favourite fishing ground and an angling club was formed in 1792 which flourished till the house was demolished 20 years later. Many MPs were members and they had an annual dinner at which whitebait was an essential course on the menu. Indeed the meetings became known as Whitebait Dinners and when the club closed they were transferred to Greenwich. The Gulf was then leased to Richard Webb of Purfleet and he built two cottages in place of Breach House. In 1824 the property was leased to the Fry family and Elizabeth the prison reformer and her children spent many summers there.

Elizabeth Fry was a most remarkable and redoubtable woman. Born in 1780, a daughter of the Quaker family of Gurney, she married at the age of 20. When she was 33 she heard of the appalling conditions in Newgate where 300 women and children were crowded into two wards and two cells with nothing to do, no proper facilities for cleanliness, and neither nightclothes nor bedclothes. They ate and slept, washed and cooked in the same foul place. Even the Governor of Newgate feared to enter but Elizabeth, a tall matronly figure, went in to them constantly and cheered and comforted them and spoke to them of God of whom many had never heard save as an oath. When she left it was to agitate by every means she could think of till a Parliamentary Committee was appointed to investigate conditions. Then she began to visit prisons all over the country, uncovering evils and enforcing redress, and when her husband became bankrupt she stood by him as bravely. She died in 1845 and was buried in the Friends' Burial Ground at Barking.

From the end of the 19th century onwards more and more of Dagenham Marsh was taken over for heavy industry. Samuel Williams, lighterman of London, bought some of the ground and built Dagenham Dock, adding a new jetty in 1911 to fit out the Dreadnought *Thunderer*. She had been built by the Thames Iron-works in West Ham and was the last warship to be launched on the Thames. Between 1929 and 1931, Ford's built their car factory driving in some 22,000 concrete piles to hold up the enormous building on the marshy ground. It was designed by Charles Heathcote and at the time was one of the largest factories in Europe. When labour relationships are untroubled some 1400 cars are produced daily. May and Baker, the pharmaceutical chemists, have built a large factory nearby and have become world famous for their products.

One of the latest developments in the history of Dagenham has been the building of the Becontree Housing Estate. After the First World War there was a serious shortage of housing in or near London. The London County Council bought up 3000 acres in Barking, Dagenham, and Ilford, and in 1921 began to build on it. The plans were by G. Topham Forrest, the LCC's own architect. More than 27,000 houses and cottages were built in all, and though the total effect is monotonous, has no real centre and takes no advantage of the terrain, yet the plan was very good for its time and the houses are pleasant and compact with hospitable porches. There are broad verges to the streets and the residents grow superb roses.

Barking and Dagenham make up an exciting borough between them. They combine much of what is old—the abbey remains, two fine churches, Eastbury Manor House, and Valence House—with the exciting challenges that industry and housing have brought in the 20th century. They are a part of London and yet they are on the edge of the Essex countryside, and they thereby enjoy the best of both worlds.

BARNET

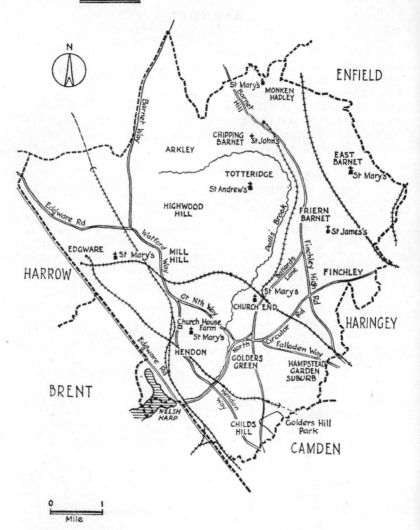

BARNET

BARNET

The London Borough of Barnet is a combination of the former boroughs of Hendon and Finchley, and the former urban districts of Barnet, East Barnet, and Friern Barnet. It includes the villages of Totteridge, Monken Hadley, Mill Hill, and Edgware. It lies to the north-north-east of the Greater London area, with high ground at Barnet, Mill Hill, and Hendon, and is watered by the Dollis Brook, the Mutton Brook, and the Brent. The Borough has a population of approximately 316,000 and covers an area of 22,123 acres (35 square miles).

The Borough of Barnet takes its name from Chipping (or High) Barnet which lies to the north. Until 1965, **Barnet** with Totteridge and Monken Hadley lay within the county of Hertfordshire. The origins of Chipping Barnet are told in its name. The whole area was once a part of the great dense forest that covered Middlesex and beyond. A path led southward down the steep hill to the Dollis Brook and beside it a little village grew up in a burnt clearing—in Anglo-Saxon *bare net*, hence Barnet. To that village King John gave in 1199 the right to hold a market, and so Chipping was added to Barnet for it is derived from the Anglo-Saxon *ceap*, a bargain, as in Cheapside in London. That market became Barnet Horse Fair held in the first week in September, and famous till the First World War for the number and quality of animals which changed hands there. Today there is still a three-day fair, and in 1969 some 300 horses were on view there with plenty of traps, gigs, and chaises for sale as well, besides the more usual swings and roundabouts. The faces of the horse dealers were a study—pure-blooded gypsy or straight out of a Hogarth drawing.

The path through the forest gradually broadened and developed till it became the Great North Road. In coaching days, Barnet was the first stage out from London and its chief inns were the Red Lion, the White Hart, and the Mitre. The first two have been rebuilt but the Mitre remains unaltered, looking as it did in 1660 when General Monk, Cromwell's former lieutenant, stayed there in his march south to put Charles II on the throne of England.

Today, the approach from London is dominated by the parish

church dedicated to St John the Baptist. It is a fine bold building with an impressive west tower and a spire. A church stood here in Norman times but was replaced about 1420 by another built partly at the expense of John Beauchamp, a wealthy maltster of Barnet. In 1875, William Butterfield was called in to enlarge the old church. The exterior he rebuilt, making it more imposing and dressing it in flint with bands of stone and chequerwork, but inside he retained the old nave and the north aisle, adding to them a new longer nave and a south aisle. In one of the spandrels of the old arcade with the clerestory windows above, is a red tablet with yellow letters recording Beauchamp's work, with the date 1453. The corbels that supported the ancient roof are still in place, though the roof has gone. What remains of the old tower is now part of the new nave and one of the old arches leads into the new tower. On these stones are mason's marks and set in the thick walls are two niches, one with a grimacing head in its tracery, the other with carved flowers. The mediaeval chancel has become a vestry and its old piscina is set in the east wall; there is another piscina at the end of the mediaeval north aisle. The vestry has a 15th century doorway with the old door still on its hinges, with an ancient ring and a massive lock. St John's original font is now in St Stephen's Church in Bell's Hill, having been thrown away and then found, after many years, in a garden in Totteridge. The present font has a cover rising nearly 15 feet high, with eight little carved statues.

The 19th century woodwork is particularly interesting and varied. The pulpit is by J. C. Traylen and on it are figures of six missionaries and preachers—Hugh Latimer, John Wesley, Canon Liddon, St Augustine, St Aidan, and St Hugh of Lincoln. The canopy is richly carved and there is more elaborate carving on the choir-stalls, while on 159 pew-ends there are scenes or devices in relief, among them Christ in the Carpenter's Shop, the Good Samaritan, the Stoning of Stephen, and the Vision of Paul.

The new south aisle leads us into the Ravenscroft Chapel in which Thomas Ravenscroft lies on a huge canopied tomb, a dignified figure in ruff and puff sleeves, with much painted heraldry about him and the heads of three angels. He is declared to have been a man of untarnished integrity, of a happy disposition, exceedingly well known for the greatness of his mind. In the wall above the vestry door is a tablet to his wife, who died in 1611, and

> *Whom Nature made a lovely modest maid,*
> *And marriage made a virtuous loving wife.*

The bust of his son, James Ravenscroft, is on the wall of the chapel, with that of his wife, beautifully carved little portraits set in niches. Both the Ravenscrofts were benefactors to Barnet.

Outside the church is a plain cross, raised as a war memorial and to the west stands Barnet Technical College. The college has a fine new building but the site has a long association with education for here was the Queen Elizabeth Grammar School founded in 1573 for the boys of Barnet. The school flourishes today in modern premises in Queen's Road, and the old red-brick building with its octagonal stair-turrets and Great Hall is used for staffrooms and student meetings. In the middle of the hall rises a solid oak post that supports the roof and must often have been used as a whipping post.

Just behind the Technical College are the nine acres of Old Court House recreation ground—the new Court House is southwards, down the hill. The little park has been well landscaped and beyond it, off Wood Street, is Wellhouse Road where, among suburban houses, a wellhouse still marks a spring that Samuel Pepys used to visit for its healthgiving properties. He reached it at seven o'clock on August 11, 1667, after a bitterly cold coach journey, on his way to Hatfield.

Further along Wood Street, there are a number of pretty 18th century houses and cottages, one of which houses a local museum and another a maternity hospital, and beyond are four groups of almshouses. Nearest to the church is Jesus Hospital founded in 1679 by James Ravenscroft for six poor women; the founder's initials are on the gate-piers which are topped with lions. Beyond them in Union Street, surrounding three sides of a green courtyard and screened from the road by fine iron gates, stand the Leathersellers' Almshouses. Originally founded in 1544 by James Hasilwood near St Helen's Bishopsgate in the City of London, they were moved to the purer air of Barnet in 1837, largely at the expense of the Master of the Company, Richard Thornton, and since 1964 have been rebuilt as 19 flats to the design of that fine architect, Louis de Soissons. Nearby are houses for six elderly couples built in 1873 but supported by lands left in 1558 by Eleanor Palmer, and a red-brick group of dwellings for six old ladies founded under the will of John Garrett who died in 1728.

Wood Street leads on to Arkley on the way to St Albans, and there the Gatehouse public house marks the site of a former toll-gate and can be recommended for its hospitality, while to the east of the road, Arkley windmill still stands, now in the grounds of a private house, but opened occasionally to the public in aid of the local church fête.

If we follow the Great North Road which runs to the right of St John's Church, we pass on our right the Hyde Institute founded in 1888 by Miss Julia Hyde who left £10,000 for the purpose; it is now part of the public library system. A mile along the road, there is a broad green with a grey stone obelisk upon it. The stone, erected in 1740 by Sir Jeremy Sambrook who lived at Gobions near North Mimms, marks the supposed site of the death of the Earl of Warwick at the battle of Barnet fought in a heavy mist before dawn on the morning of Easter Sunday, April 14, 1471. The battle lasted some three or four hours but by ten o'clock news had been brought to London and the bells of the City were ringing out for Edward IV, because Warwick the Kingmaker, who had turned his coat to support Henry VI, was lying dead, with some 1500 men from the two armies beside him, on Hadley Green and the ground beyond, called Deadman's Bottom to this day. Edward and his men refreshed themselves in Barnet and gave thanks to God, possibly in St John's Church, and then marched on to London where the gates were opened to him. Henry VI was deposed, paraded through the streets, and murdered on May 21.

Today **Hadley Green** is one of the prettiest pieces of Georgian development to be found near London. Among the 17th and 18th century houses that border it, are the Wilbraham Almshouses, redbrick cottages built in 1612, and a white house, now marked by a blue plaque, where the missionary and traveller David Livingstone stayed in 1857 and wrote his *Missionary Travels and Researches in South Africa* before returning there in 1858.

On the corner of the Green, screened by trees, is the parish church of St Mary the Virgin. A church existed in the 12th century, but the present building was erected in 1494—the date is over the west door, a curious half-eight being used to represent a four—of flint and ironstone with white stone dressings. On top of the tower is a copper beacon or cresset, set up *not* as an Armada warning but during the 18th century, possibly to celebrate the recovery of George III from his illness, and last lit in rejoicing at the Coronation of Queen Elizabeth II (1953).

Inside are a nave, two aisles, a chancel, and two side chapels, dedicated to St Anne and St Catherine. Squints pierce the buttresses between the chancel and the chapels so that mass could be celebrated simultaneously at all three altars. On the capitals of the pillars is the crest of the Goodyere family—a partridge with an ear of wheat in its beak. It was John Goodyere, the lord of the manor, who, dying in

1504, left money "to the making of [the] first floure of the stepull in the said church of hadlegh as moch as it will cost the making of carpentry". His memorial, a brass, has disappeared, but his wife can still be seen in her long robe and elaborate headdress.

Hadley Church contains one of the finest collections of small brasses to be seen in the county. There is William Turnour (d. 1500) with his wife and four children and, lacking their inscriptions so that they cannot be identified, are two 15th century ladies and a 16th century man and his wife. In addition to the brasses there is a fine monument by the sculptor Nicholas Stone to Sir Roger and Lady Wilbraham who endowed the almshouses on the Green. Sir Roger died in 1616, having been Solicitor General of Ireland. His monument, which cost £50, shows busts of himself and Lady Wilbraham while underneath kneel three pretty daughters with long hair. In the corner of the chancel is another monument to Henry Carew (d. 1620) and his mother, Lady Alice Stamford (d. 1573); his family became lords of the manor after the Abbot of Walden in Essex had been forced to surrender the ownership at the Reformation.

St Mary's also possesses an exceptionally fine collection of 16th and early 17th century communion plate—a silver gilt flagon, patten and cups—so valuable and so large that a good part of it is on loan to the British Museum.

Beyond the church are 200 acres of Hadley Common which was originally a part of Enfield Chase, the King's own hunting ground.

Totteridge. If we return to Chipping Barnet and make our way towards London, the road follows for some distance the course of the Dollis Brook. On either side of the stream the fields, in which there are plenty of wild flowers, are preserved as an open space. At Whetstone, Totteridge Lane runs away to the west and along it are many fine houses, several of them such as Garden Hill and Southernhay dating from the 18th century when Totteridge provided a pretty country retreat for well-to-do men who still needed to be within easy reach of London. The largest house of all, Copped Hall, where Lord Lytton lived and Cardinal Manning was born, has, however, been demolished.

The parish church, dedicated to St Andrew, stands at a sharp bend in the road—a bend caused by the boundary of the mediaeval manor house which stood very much where Southernhay stands today. The church which existed in the 16th century, was rebuilt in 1790 and is of plain brick with a weatherboarded bell-turret of 1706 which was retained from the old church. Inside, there is a simple aisleless nave; the apse has an unusual and attractive domed wooden-ribbed roof. The pulpit is a 17th-century one from Hatfield. The church possesses four paintings, two by Benjamin West, the American who became President of the Royal Academy—they are *St John on Patmos* and *The Woman of the Apocalypse*—another by the parson-painter, the Reverend Matthew Peters, R.A., and a lovely group of the *Madonna and Child with Peter and Paul* by Lorenzo Lotto. This was given by Lord Rothermere in 1925 in memory of his mother, Mary Geraldine Harmsworth, who often worshipped at Totteridge though she is buried in St Marylebone Cemetery, Finchley, beside another of her sons, Lord Northcliffe. In the churchyard, where a 19th century Lord Chancellor, the 1st earl of Cottenham, and Sir Lucas Pepys, physician to the unfortunate George III, lie buried, are great elm trees that flank the road, and a huge yew tree, 27 feet in girth. Just beyond the church, the pound for strayed animals is still standing.

The most famous person associated with Totteridge is Henry Edward Manning who was born there in 1808, the son of a West India merchant who was also a governor of the Bank of England. Educated at Harrow and Balliol, he entered the ministry of the Church of England and became first Rector of Woollavington in Sussex, where his wife died, and then Archdeacon of Chichester. Manning's heart gradually turned from the Church of England and he became a Roman Catholic. His promotion in that Church was rapid. After three years study in Rome, in intimate contact with the Pope, he returned to high office in London. On the death of Cardinal Wiseman he was made Archbishop of Westminster and 10 years later a Cardinal.

He was a man of severely ascetic temperament with rigid theo-logical views, yet he had a passionate sympathy with the poor and oppressed. He campaigned against drink and sat on the Royal Commissions for the housing of the poor and for education. He was a great preacher and a good writer and died in 1892 at the age of 73.

Eastwards of the London road are **East Barnet** and **Friern Barnet**; in both places the chief building of interest is the church. East Barnet is dedicated to Our Lady and is the mother church to which St John's at Chipping Barnet was once a chapel of ease. The nave walls and three small windows in the north wall are all that remains of the Norman church—the rest is late 19th century and the most remarkable thing about the church is its commanding position, for it looks out from the top of Church Hill across Pymmes Brook. A number of famous men are buried at East Barnet. Sir George Prevost was Governor General of Canada in 1812 during the last war between America and England. Of Swiss descent, he had opposed France on England's behalf in the West Indies and had been rewarded with governorships there, but his appointment in Canada did not go well, for he intervened in military operations and was summoned to London for court martial but died, broken with anxiety, before the trial could be held. His father, General George Prevost, is buried beside him.

Another father and son are here too—Daniel Beaufort who helped to found the Royal Irish Academy and who prepared a map of Ireland, and Admiral Sir Francis Beaufort, who drew up the table of winds still in use today and still known as the Beaufort Scale. Another benefactor of seamen lies here—John Hadley (1682–1744), son of a wealthy Londoner who was elected a Fellow of the Royal Society at the age of 35 and who produced the first reflecting telescope powerful enough to study the stars, and the reflecting quadrant which is still called by his name.

Near to the church in Park Road is the Abbey Arts Centre and Museum, where a collection of far eastern and primitive art is housed in a rebuilt 13th century tithe-barn which stands in an attractive garden with a well. The collection is open to the public on Saturday afternoons or by appointment. A visitor to the neighbourhood might well go on to admire Monkfrith Avenue Infants School, an outstandingly good example of modern architecture.

Although St James's Church at Friern Barnet is, with the exception of a 12th century doorway with zigzag carving, of the 19th century, the place has a long history and the fine trees along Friern Barnet Lane are witness to a rural past. The land once belonged to the Abbot of St Albans but all his territories in Barnet were summarily handed over by William the Conqueror to the Bishop of London who had supported the Norman's claim to the throne. The deprived abbot went to join Hereward the Wake and his rebels in the Isle of Ely, and about 1199 a later Bishop of London made this manor over to the Order of St John of Jerusalem. From this the name derives—the part of Barnet belonging to the Brotherhood. When the order was dissolved, Henry VIII gave the patronage to St Paul's Cathedral to whom the bestowal of the living still belongs, and his daughter, Elizabeth I, gave the land to Sir Walter Raleigh, who sold it to the Bacon family. In the churchyard lies Thomas Cavendish, the father

29

of Charles Cavendish, Cardinal Wolsey's faithful servant, and on the east wall of the south aisle (outside) is a Latin inscription to Edmund Duncon, a 17th century rector who attended George Herbert on his death-bed. All the virtues must have met in Sarah Rose who was only 27 when she died in May 1668, for her tablet reads:

> Stand back, I pray, Oh do not tread upon
> A tender bud cropped off before well blown.
> Religion, Beauty, Works, Peace, Prudence, those
> And all that's good, yea love e'en unto foes,
> Have flourished in this late sweet wife of Rose.

Facing the church is a fountain on the site of an old well from which Queen Elizabeth is said to have taken a cup of water when hunting in the neighbourhood. The story may well be true for she certainly visited Lord Chief Justice Popham who lived in the old manor house, on the site of which a 19th century house stands, now the Club House for the North Middlesex Golf Course.

Just beyond the church is Friary Park—22 acres pleasantly laid out with a huge figure of Peace standing on a rocky mound near the gate. Both park and statue were given by Sydney Simmons as a tribute to Edward VII. A fair for children is held here each Whit Monday.

The Great Northern Railway opened a station at New Southgate in 1851 and Friern Barnet began to expand so that a larger church was needed. The Rector of St James's, Prebendary F. Hall, chose J. L. Pearson, the architect of Truro Cathedral, to design St John's Church in 1886, with impressive results. The building is in North-amptonshire stone with a majestic nave and ribbed vaulting to the apse. The modern font has a pinnacled cover made of old oak from Exeter Cathedral.

On the other side of the parish at Colney Hatch stands the vast building now called Friern Hospital and formerly Middlesex county lunatic asylum. It was designed by S. W. Dawkes in 1851 with accommodation for 300 staff and 2000 patients who were kept "without shackle or even strait-waistcoat", as James Thorne observed in 1875.

The buildings on either side of the road between Whetstone and Finchley are changing all the time. A huge glass-fronted slab devoted to Ever Ready Batteries has replaced Woodside House at Whetstone, and the pleasantly solid early 19th century houses are being rebuilt as shops and flats. The site of Sellar's Hall has been built over with a close of comfortable little houses, and in Nether Street the ornate little gate house of Brent Lodge stands flanked by pebbledashed suburban dwellings.

Finchley itself has belonged, since time immemorial, to the Bishop of London. Two centuries ago, it was famous chiefly for its 2000 acres of open common across which it was dangerous to ride for fear of highwaymen. Troops have been drawn up there three times—by General Monk in 1660, against Charles Edward Stuart in 1745, and again in 1780 when the riots instigated by Lord George Gordon against freedom of worship by Roman Catholics threatened the peace and property of Londoners. The military turn-out of 1745 was satirised by Hogarth in his print *The March of the Guards to Finchley* as a drunken bawling rabble—the King, George II, was *not* pleased by it. An enclosure award was granted in 1816, railways were opened in 1867 and 1872, and the common shrank and disappeared. Today, the main building of historical interest is St Mary's Church. Saxon foundations were discovered in 1872; a 12th century church must have stood on the site for fragments of carved stone are built into the walls, but the tower and the greater part of the building are 15th century with the addition of two south aisles, one in the 19th and one in the 20th century, the latter having an elaborately carved roof which may be compared amicably with the old timber roof of the nave, flat-pitched with moulded tiebeams and curved braces. The font has a 13th century bowl on a modern base and there is a 17th century iron chest. The church was heavily damaged by bombs during the last war but has been well restored.

Inside there are several brasses and monuments of interest. The oldest of them is of an unknown lady of about 1480 in a pointed headdress. There is a tiny figure of Joan Prate in a horned headdress; she was the wife of Richard Prate who died in 1487 but his figure and those of their children are gone. There are three 17th century brasses, one of Simon Skudemore and his wife, another of Elizabeth Skudemore their daughter, wife of Nicholas Luke, with three daughters (she had three sons too, but their brass is lost and only the indent remains), and the third in memory of Thomas White, a grocer of London, kneeling with his three wives and their 13 children, some in swaddling clothes. There is a coloured monument, elaborate with Corinthian columns, cherubs and heraldry, to Alexander Kinge and his wife; he died in 1616 and the pair kneel at a prayer-desk. Two monuments of Charles II's day are to Sir Thomas Allen and Colonel John Searle, and there is a tablet to

William Seward, F.R.S. The only son of a brewer, he devoted his life to literature and to travel, and often visited Dr Johnson; it was he who suggested the epitaph for John Bacon's monument to the Doctor in St Paul's. Near the pulpit is a monument to John Oldham, who fell in the Charge of the Light Brigade at Balaclava, and to his brother William who fell in the Kaffir Wars.

Outside in the churchyard lies Major John Cartwright, who died in 1824. He was one of a remarkable group of brothers, of whom Edmund invented the power-loom, and he himself was famous for his tracts on parliamentary reform. He left the Navy because he would not fight Americans seeking their independence, and was removed from the militia for approving the taking of the Bastille. He advocated universal suffrage, annual parliaments, and the ballot as early as 1780, and was known as the Father of Reform. Four times he risked his life to save people from drowning, was tried and fined for sedition in 1819, and worked for Spanish and Greek independence. Near him lies Honest Tom Payne (1719–99) who had a popular bookshop near St Martin's-in-the-Fields. In 1740 he printed the first known list of books on sale, and continued to do so for the next 35 years.

Opposite the church is Christ's College, a school with a copper-roofed tower design by Anthony Salvin in 1857, and near to it a splendid red-brick Georgian house, Park House, now imaginatively converted into flats. Just beyond it is Hendon Avenue, leading down to the Mutton Brook which used to form the boundary between Finchley and Hendon. Hendon Avenue was laid out about the turn of the century—large prosperous mansions (too big to be called houses)—a 19th century version of the more graceful dwellings in Totteridge Lane. But today, in between the older houses, are one or two modern ones of exceptionally good design. A walk down Hendon Avenue and then along the path by the brook is both pleasant and interesting.

Returning to Hendon Lane at the top, Gravel Hill runs down to the main road and at its foot is the recently completed Catholic church of St Philip the Apostle, an imposing building in the Byzantine style. Up the East End Road opposite is Avenue House, an Italianate Victorian mansion which today houses borough council offices. The gardens have become an unusual and imaginative public park with an elaborate rockery on which children can climb and hide and some of the finest trees in London. It was given to the borough by its Member of Parliament, H. C. Stephens. Further up the hill is the Convent of St Marie Auxiliatrice which incorporates the former manor house. Just beyond, over the North Circular Road, is St Marylebone Cemetery, where the scientist Professor Huxley and the newspaper magnate Lord Northcliffe are buried, and where a monument, with a bronze bust and an angel pointing upwards and touching the shoulder of a man by his anvil, marks the resting place of Sir Peter Nicol Russell who founded and endowed the School of Engineering at Sydney. Not far away, on a little green triangle, where the North Circular Road crosses Regents Park Road stands a magnificent bronze statue of a woman poised on a sphere, her head thrown back and both arms stretched up exultantly, one hand holding a sword. Called *La Délivrance*, the statue is by Emile Guillaume and was given to Finchley in 1927 by Lord Rothermere to celebrate the victory of the Marne; she is known impiously to bus conductors as the Naked Lady. A couple of hundred yards farther along the road, is the Express Dairy Model Farm and Museum, where children can watch the cows being milked, visit the calves, and see the dairy equipment of past years.

Hendon. Between Hendon and Finchley the road sweeps over the Brent Cross Flyover and brings us to Hendon Central tube station. The extension of the line from Golders Green in 1923 raised the population of Hendon from 16,000 to 44,000 by 1931, and covered the fields, of which the majority were still farmland, with desirable four-bedroomed residences. The road, Watford Way, carries on up a hill to an ornamental lake which used to be a horse pond, and then sweeps on to join up with the M1, but if we turn aside to the right, we come to the Burroughs—first a group of 18th century houses, then early 19th century shops, then three large civic buildings—the former Hendon Town Hall (T. H. Watson, 1900) with large mullioned windows like a Tudor manor house, then the Public Library (T. M. Wilson, 1929) with a pillared portico which, besides the usual services, has a splendid local history collection and one of the best children's libraries in all England, and finally the Technical College (H. W. Burchett, 1937), soon to become a College of Advanced Technology.

Nearby at the top of Greyhound Hill is the parish church dedi-cated to St Mary. As at Harrow, this church on a hill is an ancient place of worship—land here was given to the monks of Westminster by Dunstan, Bishop of London, in 959—and standing under the yew trees in the churchyard, looking across to Hertfordshire and Buckinghamshire, one senses the antiquity of the place, conveyed in the name Hendon which in its Saxon form *Hean-dune* means "at the high down". The churchyard looks out across Sunny Hill Fields—an infinitely exciting place to a child for their extent is concealed by a series of hillocks up which one can scramble and valleys down which one can roll, and it is not till one climbs the last incline that one can see, away to the north, the traffic racing along the North Circular Road to join the M1, the cars as small as matchbox toys, and, beyond, the long ridge with Mill Hill village strung out on it, and farther away still a hill, which even today seems covered only in trees, from which the spire of Harrow Church suddenly projects.

Hendon parish church itself dates from the 13th century and is of flint with a strong, square, battlemented 15th century tower. There is a splendid carved Norman font—one of the finest in Middlesex. The original chancel and south arcade are 13th century, the north arcade 15th, and to them was added in 1915 a new nave, chancel, and south aisle designed by Temple Moore which really do blend in contentedly with the old. There are traces of 13th century paintings on the walls and a tiny brass to a child, John Downer, who died in 1515. Perhaps the most remarkable monument in the church is a black marble slab on the low tomb-chest of Sir Jeremy Whichcot who died in 1677 having lived at Hendon House, which used to stand at the junction of Brent Street and Bell Lane. The carving on the marble is very restrained—just a coat of arms and a border of leaves, with magnificently dignified lettering—one can return to admire the calligraphy of the inscription again and again. Edward Fowler, an 18th century bishop of Gloucester, has an elaborate monument with cherubs and heraldry. Sir Henry Rawlinson, Commissioner of the Great Seal in Queen Anne's day, reclines in his robes and wig on a monument sculpted by Rysbrack, while John Flaxman's panel to Charles Colmore has relief figures of Faith with a book and Hope with an anchor. A stone with his arms upon it covers Sir Stamford Raffles' grave; founder of modern Singapore and of the Zoological Society, he lived during the last months of his life on Highwood Hill and is buried here in Hendon.

Outside in the churchyard lies Abraham Raimbach who engraved the paintings of Sir David Wilkie and many others; there is a pelican on his tomb and a tablet to him in the church besides. Near him lie James Parsons, an 18th century physician and antiquarian; Joseph Ayloffe, another 18th century antiquarian; Thomas Woolner, whose low tomb has on it the mallet and modelling tools with which he shaped so many famous statues; Emily Patmore, the wife about whom her husband, Coventry Patmore, wrote his lovely poem *The Angel in the House* (a quaint little balustrade runs round her tomb);

and Nathaniel Hone, one of the original members of the Royal Academy.

Beside the church stands the Greyhound public house, where, in a previous building, the meetings of the parish council used to take place, and a little lower down the hill is the Church Farm House Museum. This is a particularly exciting place to visit. The house dates from the mid-17th century though there was probably an older building on the site which, from its proximity to the church, may well have been the demesne or manor farm. From 1688 till 1780, it belonged to a farming family called Kempe and thereafter to a succession of owners, till in 1944 it was bought by the Hendon Borough Council and in 1954 was restored and made into a museum. The ground floor is arranged as it would have been in the 18th or early 19th centuries—a parlour to receive guests, an oak-panelled dining-room with huge oak chests and a long table at which to entertain them, and a kitchen which, with its well-equipped range, its kettles and spits, and the baby's cradle, was the real centre of the farmhouse. Upstairs, the rooms are now used for a series of excellent temporary exhibitions, many of which are concerned with local history. The museum is open daily excepting Tuesday afternoons, and a visit to it is as instructive as it is enjoyable.

If we walk down Church End to Church Road, we pass a large open field on our right—once Hinge's Paddock—and then find ourselves facing Daniel's Almshouses, founded about 1737 with money left by Robert Daniel in 1681. Church Road leads to a crossroads, known as the Quadrant where the village pound used to stand. To the right runs Brent Street, passing first Hendon County School, built on the site of Hendon House, where Sir Jeremy Which-cot lived and before him the Middlesex antiquary, John Norden, and then comes Brent Green on which stand a newly built Christian Scientist church and the 19th century Alma White Bible College, till at last the road reaches the Brent Bridge, beside which Decoy Farm, demolished only in 1935, used to stand and where there is now a little public park beside the stream and its waterfall.

The opposite arm of the crossroads at the Quadrant is Parson Street which leads past Hendon Hall, now used as a hotel but formerly the manor house of Hendon. The lordship of the manor was bought in 1756 by David Garrick the actor who, though he lived chiefly at Hampton, built a fine house here with a magnificent portico which probably came from Canons, the Duke of Chandos's mansion at Stanmore (see p. 199). The portico is still in place but the obelisk which Garrick erected in his grounds as a memorial to

Shakespeare has disappeared within the last few years. Garrick's estate was built over in the 1920s and '30s, but the monument, adorned with statues of Shakespeare, Melpomene, Terpsichore and Thalia, all of them headless, stood stranded on a plot of land used as a builders' yard, in Manor Hall Avenue, an object of wonder and of mystery to the local children. At the end of Manor Hall Avenue runs Ashley Lane along which, 30 years ago, celandine, campion, sorrel, and moon-daisy used to flower, but which now leads the way to a cemetery.

Parson Street becomes the Holders Hill Road and runs on, past Hendon Golf Club, to Kelly's Corner where Frith Lane curves in a crescent to the east. This was once a separate sub-manor. The Lane doubles back to rejoin the main road at Mill Hill, having embraced Bittacy Hill whose summit is crowned with Mill Hill's barracks, called after Colonel Inglis, commander of the 57th (West Middlesex) foot regiment who was killed on May 16, 1811 at the dreadful battle of Albuera in the Peninsula. He fell, shouting with his last breath, "Fifty-seventh, die hard!" and his men memorably and bitterly earned their nickname, the Die-Hards.

Mill Hill can also be reached by the Watford Bypass which goes through Colindale where the British Museum Newspaper Library stands, an inexhaustible source of reference, and where the Metropolitan Police College has recently been rebuilt. A little farther on is Copthall Park, now municipal playing fields and a stadium; Copthall House (which should not be confused with Copped Hall in Totteridge Lane) used to stand in Bunn's Lane. It was built about 1624 by Randolf Nicoll, who also built almshouses in Mill Hill and was buried at Edgware; in modern times it was converted into flats but in 1959 was pulled down and the site is now being redeveloped. Opposite Copthall Park is Hendon Aerodrome, which is also about to be built over as Grahame Park Estate. The airfield was opened in 1910 by Claude Grahame-White as London Aerodrome and the first United Kingdom aerial postal delivery was made from it in 1911. It soon became a flying centre of first importance, and the annual air displays held there till 1939 were exciting and significant occasions. It saw hard service during the last war but its runways are too short to accommodate the aeroplanes in use today, and so it is about to disappear. An RAF museum is being built there and will open in 1972 with a large collection, including many early aeroplanes.

Along the bypass (Watford Way) is London University Observatory which is sometimes open to the public in the evening (it is advisable to write before visiting) and a little beyond is **Mill Hill**, the old village stretched out on a long spur of hill to the east of the road, the new to the west along Mill Hill Broadway. On the Broadway are three churches—the Roman Catholic dedicated to the Sacred Heart and Immaculate Conception and built in the Byzantine style with stone pilasters on brick walls and a west front with a wheel window and a pediment, the United Free church with a very friendly interior, the walls painted a soft lime colour with blue alcoves, and the parish church dedicated to St Michael and All Angels. This was conceived as a chapel of ease to St Paul's on the hilltop by the vicar there, the Rev. E. B. Hartley. The architect was Herbert Passmore and the work was begun in 1921 and was finally completed in 1957. The church is of stone in the late 15th century Perpendicular style; the chancel has a barrel roof and there is a very fine east window by A. E. Buss.

On the other side of the bypass, up Lawrence Street towards the old village of Mill Hill, is St Joseph's Roman Catholic College where students of every nationality are educated for the mission field. The building, designed by Messrs Goldie and Child in 1866–71, has a cloistered quadrangle and chapel with a campanile 100 feet high crowned with a huge statue in gilded bronze of St Joseph holding the Child. The college was founded by Cardinal Vaughan who died and was buried here in 1903. His funeral service was the only opening ceremony of Westminster Cathedral which his energy and enthusiasm had brought into being.

Lawrence Street ends on the Ridgeway which runs along the spine of the hill. To the left is Highwood Hill with the 17th century Rising Sun public house and beside it is Highwood House, the home of the explorer Sir Stamford Raffles from 1825–26. An earlier house on the site belonged to Lord William Russell, beheaded in 1683 for his part in the Rye House Conspiracy against the life of Charles II. His widow Lady Rachel lived here for many lonely years after his death. A well which she caused to be dug in 1681 and which she dedicated to her daughter is still there. A flight of steps leads down to the water and stonework encases both well and steps so that the whole structure is keyhole-shaped; it is all covered in ivy and there is a small tablet let into the stone which reads: *Mrs Rachell Russells gift, June y.10.1681*. Today Highwood House is a nursing home, the grounds have been divided up and the well is in the garden of another private house.

The village of Mill Hill stretches out along the Ridgeway with splendid views to the north across open meadows into Hertfordshire.

37

The first house when approaching from Lawrence Street is Holcombe House, today part of St Mary's Abbey School. It was built in 1775 by John Johnson for John William Anderson, a Danzig glove-merchant who became Lord Mayor of London in 1798. The drawing-room, today used as a library, has a particularly beautiful painted ceiling. In 1866, Cardinal Vaughan established his mission college there, while the present St Joseph's was being built, and when the theological students became too numerous for the little house and moved to larger premises, Holcombe House became a convent for Franciscan nuns who established a school there. The house is often open to the public on a Saturday afternoon and is well worth visiting, particularly for its elegant façade and well laid out grounds. On the opposite side of the Ridgeway is Belmont, built in 1765 for Sir Charles Flower, another Lord Mayor, probably to designs by Robert Adam; it is today Mill Hill Preparatory School. Beside it is St Paul's Church, a plain brick edifice erected in 1833 which caused a dispute between William Wilberforce, who lived at Hendon Park from 1826–31, and the Rev. Theodore Williams, who died aged 90 having been Rector of Hendon from 1812 till 1875.

Opposite the church is Mill Hill School, founded in 1807 for boys of Nonconformist families; the present buildings date from 1825 and were designed by William Tite, with a splendid portico and wings with cloistered walks. In front of the school, is the Gate of Honour, a war memorial to those who had been pupils at Mill Hill and who fell in the two World Wars. Among the school buildings is the scriptorium where J. A. H. Murray, a master there from 1870 to 1885, stored and sorted three tons of slips with quotations for his superb Oxford English Dictionary. The school is built on the site of Ridgeway House, the home of Peter Collinson the botanist (1694–1768), to whose wonderful gardens came scholars from all Europe, among them the great Linnaeus.

Beyond the school is the village green and pond and beside them are two groups of cottages, one of them almshouses founded in 1697 by Thomas Nicoll, and the other, Angel Cottages, built during the 1960s and winners of the Civic Trust annual award for an "outstandingly original" development. Nearby are Rosebank, a 17th century weatherboarded dwelling once used as a Quaker meeting house, and St Vincent's Convent and School. The convent was originally a 17th century house called Littleberries; it is said that Nell Gwynn lived there but there is scant documentary evidence for the statement. The house was much altered and enlarged when it became a convent in 1887. Farther along the Ridgeway are the splendid copper-roofed Medical Research Council Laboratories designed by M. Ayrton in 1950. Down the hill off Hammers Lane are the Linen and Woollen Drapers Cottage Homes, a pleasing spread of small buildings.

In Dean's Lane, between Mill Hill and Edgware, is John Keble Church designed by D. F. Martin-Smith and completed in 1936. It is a splendid, exciting and, for its day, an unorthodox building. It stands, four-square and of yellow brick, on a little hill, the ground terraced away below it. The congregation surround the choir on three sides and the altar is a table, 14 feet long. There is no division between nave and chancel and consequently priest and congregation are far more at one than is often the case. The church should be visited by any one who is interested in modern architecture. The interior is of white stone and the whole atmosphere one of peace and brightness; an old corn mortar serves as a font.

Nearby is the John Groom Crippleage, founded in 1866 in Clerkenwell and moved to its present modern building in 1931, where those who are disabled make artificial flowers, and a little way off is Scratchwood, a splendid open hillside, the venue of model aeroplane enthusiasts.

Edgware (the name probably means "Ecgi's weir") is a very old settlement. It is mentioned in a charter of 978 though it is not in Domesday Book, and in 1443 it was bought for All Souls' College, Oxford, who still own land there. But before any charter was written, the Romans were there—their earthenware has been found in quantities at Brockley Hill where there may well have been a pottery. Their village was called *Sullioniacae* and in the late 17th century William Sharpe, the Secretary to the Duke of Chandos, set up an obelisk, now in the grounds of the National Orthopaedic Hospital, to remind passers-by of those who had been there before them.

The village of Edgware was the first stage-coach stop on the road north along Watling Street. Until the first quarter of this century, it was little more than a crossroads, bordered with timbered cottages. St Margaret's Church and the inn opposite were the main buildings, and there were two groups of almshouses. On the pavement on the west side of the main street was an old forge which had once belonged to William Powell, whom legend has claimed as Handel's Harmonious Blacksmith. The story goes that the composer, who was in the service of the Duke of Chandos at Canons, a great house which lay at Whitchurch between Edgware and Stanmore (see p. 199), once sheltered from the rain in a smithy and afterwards was inspired

39

to write the little tune known as "The Harmonious Blacksmith" as his impression of the hammer and the anvil. Unfortunately the story is apocryphal, and did not appear till three-quarters of a century after Handel's death. For all that, some 88 years after Powell's death in 1780, a subscription was opened and a stone monument was raised over his grave at Whitchurch, with a hammer, an anvil, and a few notes of Handel's melody.

In 1924, the Northern Line tube was extended from Golders Green to Edgware, and the population figures tell the story of what happened to the village—1576 in 1921, 5352 in 1931, 17,523 in 1939, and 20,127 in 1961. Many of the timbered cottages have gone, and the public house has been rebuilt. St Margaret's Church still stands—a 15th century tower of Kentish ragstone with a nave and chancel built in 1845 and aisles added in 1928. There is a brass to little Anthony Childe showing him in swaddling clothes, for he was only three weeks old when he died in 1600, and a monument with arms, cherubs, and a skull to Randolf Nicoll who lived at Copthall House and who died in 1658. The blacksmith's forge has become a gift shop and the most noticeable building is the 14-storey high Green Shield House, used by the trading stamp company and partly let to the borough council.

The southern corner of the borough has become the Hampstead Garden Suburb, one of the most exciting housing adventures of the 20th century. It was begun in 1902, the brainchild of a remarkable woman, Dame Henrietta Barnett. She was the wife of the Rev. (later Canon) Samuel Barnett, the rector of St Jude's in Whitechapel and the founder of Toynbee Hall in the East End of London. The poverty and misery that she had seen there had inspired in her heart strong views on what a community should be like, so when she heard of the proposed extension of the Northern Line tube to Golders Green, she determined that at least a part of the inevitable housing development should be in accordance with her beliefs that all classes should live together in surroundings as beautiful and well-planned as possible, in tree-lined streets with woods and open spaces available to all. She formed the Hampstead Garden Suburb Trust in 1906, raised money, purchased 243 acres of land from the Eton College Trustees, and appointed her architects, Barry Parker and Raymond (later Sir Raymond) Unwin, who was to make his home in the Garden Suburb, at Wyldes in Hampstead Way. She could not have chosen better; the two young men, who were brothers-in-law, had just designed Letchworth Garden City; they now improved on their earlier experience.

The first sod was cut on May 2, 1907, and the foundation stones of the first two cottages, at 140 and 142 Hampstead Way, were laid on June 5. The overall plan, with its great variety in type and style of house and of street—wandering or straight, with many ingenious closes, and all of them tree-lined—was the work of Parker and Unwin, but the buildings on Central Square—two churches and an institute for adult education—were entrusted to the leading architect of the day, Sir Edwin Lutyens. In St Jude's (the dedication was the same as that of Canon Barnett's Whitechapel Church) Lutyens created one of England's finest early 20th century churches. It is a massive brick building with a spire and vast roof that begins very low to the ground. Inside there is a large central dome-vaulted space and tunnel-vaulted aisles. The walls are covered with frescoes by Walter P. Starmer of the life of Our Lord, of His parables, and from the Old Testament. On the wall of the Lady Chapel is a group of famous women from all periods and countries—Margaret Roper, Catherine Booth, Harriet Beecher Stowe, Florence Nightingale, Elizabeth Fry, Elsie Inglis, Edith Cavell, Agnes Weston, Mary Slessor, Mary Jones (of the Bible Society), Elizabeth Browning, Baroness Burdett-Coutts, Grace Darling, Christina Rossetti, Margaret Beaufort, Josephine Butler, Madame Guyon, Queen Victoria and Queen Alexandra, a Girl Guide and a Brownie. There is another small chapel in memory of Robert Harmsworth, Lord Northcliffe's young nephew, who died in 1921, and a tablet to the first vicar, Basil Graham Bourchier (d. 1934), who was so rare a preacher that the pews were filled and people thronged the aisles to hear him. The Free Church is similar in plan but with a dome instead of a spire. The Institute, which opened in 1909, fills the third side of the square, and on the fourth, which is otherwise open, there is a small memorial to Dame Henrietta.

To appreciate the architectural achievement of the Garden Suburb, one should walk the length of Hampstead Way along the edge of the Heath Extension, noting particularly Waterlow Court (designed by Baillie Scott), and then up Meadway to Heathgate and so to Central Square where Dame Henrietta's house, 1, South Square, where she lived from 1915 to 1936, can be seen. One should then go down Erskine Hill with its dignified grey brick houses, and explore Big Wood and Little Wood with its open-air theatre, and finally make one's way down Temple Fortune Hill to Temple Fortune. The walk is rewarding at any time of year, but is perhaps loveliest in spring when Heathgate and the other roads are warm with flowering cherry trees.

Golders Green (the name probably comes from the Goodyer family who used to farm there) is on the doorstep of the Garden Suburb but is a very different kind of development. It has however two really fine churches, St Albans (1932, Sir Giles Gilbert Scott) and St Michael's (1914–24, John T. Lee and Caroe and Passmore; tower, completed 1960, by J. Barrington Baker); and the Crematorium (1905, Sir Ernest George and Alfred Yeates) with its beautiful Garden of Remembrance. On the cloistered walls are tablets recording such names as Sir Isaac Pitman, Sir Henry Irving, Dr Barnardo, Sir John Tenniel and Sir W. S. Gilbert, Holman Hunt and G. F. Watts, Canon Barnett and Rudyard Kipling. Nearby is Golders Hill Park, one of the prettiest in London, with a children's menagerie which includes deer and peacocks, and an exceptionally fine flower garden. A little way along the road into London is Child's Hill, once famous for its brick kilns and hand-laundries which profited from the exceptional purity of the water there.

BRENT

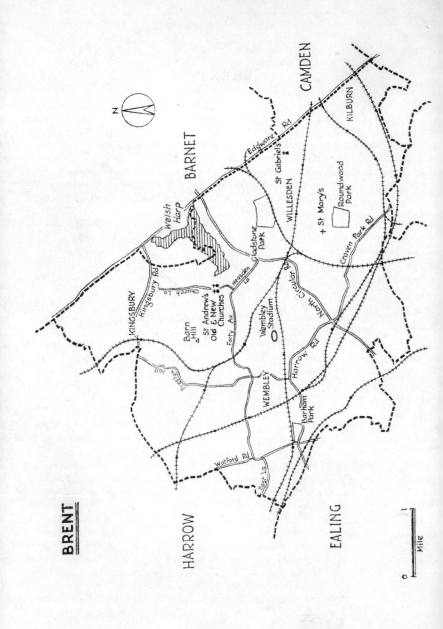

BRENT

The new borough of Brent lies to the north of the Greater London area and consists of the former boroughs of Willesden and Wembley. It takes its name from the tributary of the Thames, the Brent, which was once the boundary between the two. The river flows from the north-west to the south of the borough, and has been dammed to the north of its course to form the Brent or Welsh Harp Reservoir. The area is low-lying to the south with higher ground at Barn Hill, Sudbury Hill, and Preston Hill, to the north; and it is neighboured, reading clockwise, by Barnet, Camden, Westminster, Kensington, Hammersmith, Ealing, and Harrow. The borough covers nearly 11,000 acres, and had a population of 294,850 in 1965. It is a heavily built-up area and contains such important factories as Glacier Metals Ltd, and Messrs Heinz, McVitie, and Guinness.

Willesden itself was a village until little more than 100 years ago, but today it is a largely industrial area, covering some seven square miles and having engulfed the former villages of Kilburn, Harlesden, Brondesbury, Stonebridge, Dudden Hill, Dollis Hill, Oxgate, and Mapesbury. The name first appears as *Wellesdune* (the well on the hill?) in a charter of 940 whereby Athelstan, Alfred the Great's grandson, gave 10 manors in Willesden-cum-Neasden to the monks of St Erkenwald at St Paul's Cathedral. St Paul's held the land till the Reformation, but to this very day eight of the prebendal stalls in the cathedral bear the names of the manors—Willesden, Neasden, Oxgate, Twyford, Harlesden, Chamberleyne Wood, Brondesbury, and Mapesbury. Among the prebendaries of Oxgate were four famous men—William of Wykeham who became Bishop of Winchester and founded Winchester School and New College at Oxford. Then there was Polydore Vergil who came here from Urbino in Italy, was appointed to Oxgate in 1513, and wrote a history of England in most elegant Latin. In the 17th century, it was held by William Sancroft and John Tillotson, who both later became Archbishops of Canterbury. Sancroft was sent to the Tower by James II for daring to sign a petition against the Declaration of Indulgence but gave up his living at the accession of William III because he could not support James's supplanter. Tillotson was judged one of the greatest preachers of his age which was a time of splendid orators. The other prebends were held by less exciting people, excepting for one of the first prelates of Mapesbury, Walter Map, who was appointed in 1170 and served Henry II as an itinerant justice. He wrote a witty little book about the ironies of life at Court called *De nugis curialium* and an excellent drinking song *Mihi est propositum in taberna mori*—"I intend to end my days in an ale house."

Willesden was an important place for the religious life. There was a convent of 13 Benedictine nuns established in 1139 on the banks of the Kele-bourne stream (from which Kilburn takes its name), the ruins of which were still visible in the 18th century though it had of course been closed at the Reformation; its site is today covered by the junction of Hampstead Road with Oxford Road and Cambridge Avenue. The gardens of the Bell Inn are on another part of the site and they had a second heyday in the 18th century when the medicinal qualities of Kilburn Wells gave rise to a short-lived spa there.

Willesden's greatest antiquity is the parish church, dedicated to St Mary and the sole survivor of the former village. The south aisle is 13th century, the tower 14th with a sundial of 1732 on it. The grey walls are of ragstone rubble and flints and on the south-west and south-east are apparently unrestored. The font is Norman—one of the six in Middlesex of that period—with a square bowl and central pedestal with four slender side shafts. The chancel was restored about 1400 and the south door is of the same date, the south chapel a little later. There is a fine Elizabethan communion table and the long marble slab let into the nave floor may have been the mediaeval altar. A gallery was added at the west end and from it one has a view of the whole church, calm and grey and still.

St Mary's chief treasures are its six brasses; the oldest of them is to Bartholomew Willesden who died in 1492. He is a grave-looking man in a fur-trimmed robe with a purse hanging from his waistband; beside him stands one of his wives, Margaret, wearing a butterfly headdress and an elegant tight-waisted gown. The Roberts were the leading family in Willesden in the 16th and 17th centuries and there is a tiny brass, 18 inches high, to Margaret Roberts (d. 1505) which shows her wearing a kennel headdress and an elaborately embroidered belt, and another to Edmund Roberts (d. 1585) and his two wives, Frances and Faith. By Frances he had six children and another three by Faith, and they are all there, ranged behind their respective mothers. Edmund has a lovely epitaph:

> *Happy was he that lyeth heere*
> *In blood, in match and progenye.*
> *Whoo lyved three and threescore yeare*
> *And layde him down in peace to dye.*
> *Who long before the poore susteind*
> *In time of their great lack and neede*
> *His love was suche he thought all gaind*
> *To comfort them in worde and deed.*
>
> *And when his soule did seeke release*
> *From being bound with flesshy chayne*
> *In praising God he did not cease*
> *With happy fayth to live agayne.*
> *So like a lambe he went away*
> *And left good land unto his son*
> *Who long may live the poore do pray*
> *Good house to keep as he hath don.*

There is another brass to an unknown lady, perhaps also of the Roberts family, who died about 1550. She is shown kneeling, wearing a Mary Queen of Scots headdress, her six children, two boys and four girls, all on their knees behind her. Then there is Jane Barne, who died in 1609, and is shown with one of her two daughters. Both ladies wear farthingales open to show beautifully quilted petticoats; they have ruffs and pretty caps. Jane had been the wife of John Barne of Willesden for nearly 50 years when she died at the age of 64, so she could only have been 15 when she married. Finally there is Dr William Lichefield who was vicar of Willesden when he died in 1517, having been chancellor at St Paul's in 1504. He was a doctor of law so he wears a fur hat, and is attired in a cassock, a surplice, and a cope. There is one monument in the chancel to Richard Paine (d. 1616) and his wife. They kneel on red cushions. He had been a gentleman pensioner to five princes and is in armour; his wife is in black with a flat hat, and both have ruffs.

In the churchyard lies Charles Reade, writer and philanthropist. He was a fellow of Magdalen College, Oxford, but in 1852 wrote a play, *Masks and Faces*, which was produced with great success at the Haymarket. Thereafter he devoted himself to literature, but was often involved in court actions regarding his rights. He collected curious information of all kinds, which he entered in a great ledger—there is a description of his methods in his novel *A Terrible Temptation*. His best work was *The Cloister and the Hearth*, picturing mediaeval Europe. It is a vast romance, filled with historic and imaginary characters, each playing his part in palace, church, and inn or by the wayside. He used to say that he did not know whether anything of his would live but that this book deserved to do so, for he had put into it the reading of some 400 volumes. His friend, Laura Seymour, lies here too; he wrote her epitaph which tells us that her face was sunshine, her voice melody, and her heart sympathy.

Willesden remained rural till long after the coming of the railways in 1844. It was a green country place and the best descriptions of it are to be found in the novels of Harrison Ainsworth, notably in *Rookwood* and *Jack Sheppard*, for the writer lived at Kensal Green, where he was visited by Dickens, Thackeray, Marryat, and all the literary men of his day. The local water was peculiarly pure and soft, and laundering was the chief local occupation apart from agriculture. Then the railways came and multiplied, the tracks stretched across the fields, culminating in the opening of Willesden Junction—which is in fact in Hammersmith—in 1866, and the houses spread out on either side. A loop line was opened to Neasden in 1875 and the Metropolitan Railway came to Willesden Green in 1880. The villages were obliterated and the 20th century has dealt with the few remains that, even 10 years ago, could still be seen at Brondesbury, or at Oxgate Lane, or at the crossing of Neasden Lane and Tanfield Road. Yet the 19th century development has a peculiar individuality of its own. I know of no other area where there are so many ingenious variations in acanthus-leaf moulding on keystone and architrave, nor so many unexpected quirks at the sides and ends of houses and terraces.

The old parish church was joined by St Andrew's in the High Road at Willesden, built in 1886–87 by James Brooks; it is large and dull apart from its spectacular Flemish-style high altar. Then there is St Martin's at Kensal Rise, built as a memorial to Dr Charles John Vaughan, headmaster of Harrow, who also prepared candidates for the ministry. On the sanctuary wall is a bronze relief to this man who was "a wise teacher and a tender friend," and in a glass case at the west end are some books and notes he used in his work. The glass is a good example of its period, and the south window shows Caedmon, Oswald, King Alfred with a book and a sword and a ship above him, Florence Nightingale with her lamp and basket of medicines, George Herbert holding his book of sacred

Sir John Soane Museum, Lincoln's Inn Fields: the Dining Room

Gray's Inn: the gardens in spring

The Senate House, London University

The British Museum

poems *The Temple* (with Bemerton Church above him), St Crispin with shoes by his stool for he was a shoemaker, and General Gordon with a group of ragged boys. The streetlamp in this picture is a rare thing to find in a window and the artist must have made a mistake in giving it an incandescent burner, which was not known in Gordon's day. The war memorial has a figure of St Martin on his horse dividing his cloak with the beggar. And there is St Gabriel's Church in Cricklewood, built in 1897 by Philip Day, with a saddle-backed tower added some years later by the Rev. C. F. G. Turner, who had lectured at Louvain University but who left the Roman Catholic Church to join the Church of England and became rector of Coveny near Ely. For many years one of the parishioners was Gunby Hadath who died in 1954, writer of boys' stories and a close friend of Arthur Mee.

There is also St Augustine's, Kilburn, (now in Westminster since the realignment of borough boundaries) which is one of the most spectacular churches of the Catholic revival in the Church of England. It was consecrated in 1880 and completed in 1889. Built by J. L. Pearson, it has a spire 254 feet high. The nave is broad, the aisles narrow, and a processional ambulatory continues right round the building. The walls are exciting with patterns in the brickwork, and there is remarkable carving on the altar and rood-screen. The church is fortunate in possessing four fine Italian paintings, the gift of the 1st Lord Rothermere. They are the very beautiful *Blue Madonna* by Filippino Lippi, *The Holy Family* by Palmezzano, *Christ on the Cross* by Crivelli and *The Annunciation* by Titian.

Perhaps the most lovable 19th century relic in Willesden is Harlesden clock, erected to mark Queen Victoria's diamond jubilee; it is said to keep time erratically. There is another clock in Roundwood Park, this time a floral one given by Messrs Smith, freshly bedded out each year and in excellent working condition. The park is a pleasant one with a tree-topped hill and plenty of swings for children; it is here that the Brent Show of livestock, pets, and garden produce is held each September.

Not far away is Gladstone Park on Dollis Hill. The park was originally the grounds and gardens of Dollis Hill House, once the home of Lord and Lady Aberdeen where Gladstone was often a guest. The house, where one may have tea, is surprisingly small but has views across to Harrow. The walled garden is laid out with formal box-edged beds and crazy-pavements; it is shaded by old elms and in the centre is a sundial whose pedestal is an 18th century baluster from old Kew Bridge. The park is much as it must have

C

been in Mr Gladstone's day. There are fine trees, old and pleasant avenues of almond trees, and a small fir he planted just before the Home Rule Bill was rejected. In 1968 a statue by Fred Kormis was unveiled; it is a memorial to the spirit of those who suffered and died in or survived the prisoner of war camps.

On the hill, just outside the park, are the buildings of the Post Office Engineering Research Station, opened by Ramsay MacDonald when he was Prime Minister, and of St Andrew's Hospital. At its foot are the grand new buildings of Willesden College of Technology.

When we think of **Wembley**, a vehemently 20th century place comes to mind. The houses were mostly built in the 1920s and '30s, and the old brown trains that used to rattle through had *Live in Metroland* inscribed on their doorhandles. Metroland was anywhere along the Metropolitan Railway, but somehow Wembley was its epitome. This modernity all sprang from the buildings erected in 1924 to the designs of J. M. Simpson to house the British Empire Exhibition when, with the intention of encouraging trade, all the members of what was then the British Empire displayed their best, and the International Rodeo and Torchlight Tattoo were famous throughout the world. A year earlier the Empire Stadium had opened on April 28 and the Football Association Cup Final was played here for the first time between Bolton and West Ham, the former winning 2–0. When the Exhibition closed in 1925, the demolition of the subsidiary buildings and the management of the Stadium was undertaken by Arthur, later Sir Arthur, Elvin, and in 1934 the Empire Pool for swimming and under-cover sports was constructed. The Stadium and Pool were used for the XIV Olympic Games in 1948.

In addition to the Stadium, there are in Wembley two of London's best tube stations, Alperton and Sudbury, both designed by Charles Holden in the 1930s, and there is the massive Wembley Town Hall, now Brent Municipal Buildings, in Forty Lane.

And yet not everything about Wembley is modern. Its very name is ancient, appearing first as "Wemba's lea"—the farm or homestead of Wemba. It is given in a charter of 825 by which King Beornwulf gave 100 hides of land (about 12,000 acres) to Archbishop Wulfred at Hearge (Harrow), Herefrithingland, Wemba's lea, and Geddincggum (Yeading). In those days, England was divided into hundreds, and each hundred had its own court to decide local affairs. Wembley was in the Hundred of Gore and the Moot or meeting place of Gore Hundred was in a triangular field at Gore

Farm, now the site of Moot Court, a turning out of Fryant Way, near Kingsbury shopping parade.

For a good part of the middle ages, Wembley was a part of Harrow and was served by Harrow parish church. The Archbishop of Canterbury was lord of the manor, but after the Reformation two interesting families were living there, one prosperous and successful, the other tragically ill-fated. The well-to-do yeoman, John Lyøn, who in 1572 founded Harrow School (see p. 185) lived at Preston; his house survived until 1960 but the site is now regrettably covered with a number of small houses. The unfortunate family were the Bellamys, who were devout Catholics in Elizabeth I's day when this was not a good thing to be. When the conspiracy of poor foolish Anthony Babington to murder Elizabeth I and to put Mary Queen of Scots on the throne was discovered, the plotters took flight and lurked first in St John's Wood and then took refuge at Uxendon Manor on Uxendon Hill south of Preston where the Bellamys sheltered them and where they were discovered. Jerome Bellamy suffered horribly at Tyburn with the conspirators; his mother, Katherine, died in the Tower before she could be brought to trial, and her second son, Bartholomew, hanged himself there. A third brother, imprisoned for religion, also committed suicide in 1593, and the manor passed to the fourth son, Richard. He sheltered the Jesuit, Father Robert Southwell, was betrayed by his own daughter Anne, was imprisoned and at last after 10 years in gaol, was allowed to live abroad. The house passed to a family connection, the Pages, who remained there till the 19th century; the house was demolished in 1932–33 when the Bakerloo line was extended to Stanmore.

Since Harrow Church ministered to the inhabitants of Wembley, the parish church there is comparatively modern. It is St John's designed in 1846 by Sir George Gilbert Scott. There is also a remarkably fine new Roman Catholic church, All Saints, in Kenton. It has a steeply pitched roof and a separate bell-tower with an outdoor pulpit, which unfortunately can seldom be used because of the noise of traffic.

Northwick Park, which was formerly partly a golf-course, has now yielded a good acreage of that land to the new Harrow Hospital and Technical College, but the borough has received a new and most attractive open space—Barham Park at Sudbury. This was the house and grounds of Mr George Titus Barham, who was Mayor of Wembley in 1937—the year Wembley was accorded borough status. He died on the very day the charter of incorporation was signed, having been a great benefactor to the area, for he presented the site for Wembley Hospital and defrayed the whole cost of the charter celebrations from his own pocket. His house had previously been the home of the Misses Copeland who had also loved Wembley and who had contributed munificently towards the first village hospital, the Workmen's Hall, and the parish church of St John. The house has gone—the roughness of its foundations shows through the turf and the site is planted out with young silver birch trees—but the gardens remain, with rose-beds, a sundial high on a pillar, and a little lake spanned by a bridge. A subsidiary dwelling, Old Lodge, is used as a public library and there are regular displays of local history material. The park is a lovely and peaceful place, a good memorial to three people who loved their own corner of Middlesex. As neighbour they had Sir William Perkins, the research chemist who was also a philanthropist (see under Harrow, p. 190), and who lived at The Chestnuts, Sudbury.

Not far away is another park, named in memory of Edward VII, which runs down the slope of Preston Hill, and a very good game can be played, by those interested in such things, by walking along the Harrow Road which runs from Sudbury Circus, and dating the houses on either side and pondering how the land was developed. For there are old cottages, dating from 1800 or even earlier, left over from the farms which used to lie on either side of the road to Harrow. A few larger houses came about the middle of the century, and then another group in the 1880s and '90s, most of which today seem to house small businesses, including one which provides "superior scaffolds". Then there was a pause, and then pairs of semi-detached houses began to range the road in the 1920s and '30s. The war halted building, but afterwards older houses were pulled down and spaces filled up with small blocks of flats. This game can be played along any old road and can become very exciting, when one begins to observe that bricks are of different colours in different periods and how the whole shape and layout of houses changes over the generations. (For a variation to play in a heavily built up shopping area, see Hampstead, p. 93.)

In 1934, Kingsbury was divorced from Harrow and united with Wembley. In Kingsbury stands the oldest building in the whole borough, St Andrew's Church. The churchyard at Kingsbury is a fascinating place for in it stand two churches, both of them dedicated to the patron saint of Scotland. The older tiny church may have Saxon work in it; Roman tiles are certainly built into the walls and there are hypocaust flues in the chancel walls, while the north-east corner rests on a sarsen stone, brought by an Ice Age glacier, as a foundation. The fabric is chiefly 13th century with a 12th century south door, and scratch dials on the south doorway of the chancel and on the chancel window, and a 15th century roof. The interior is aisleless with a 13th century font and a brass to John Shepard (d. 1530) and his wives, Anne who had ten children, and Mawde who had eight. An inscription remains to Thomas Scudamore who for 47 years served Elizabeth I and James I. He would have known John Bul who died five years before him in 1621 and had charge of the King's falcons. The black oak lectern is an angel with wings supporting the desk, carved in the 17th century for a London church which has disappeared; Gladstone may have read the lessons from it for he often came to this church when staying at Dollis Hill House.

Beside the little church stands the great one, brought stone by stone from Wells Street, St Marylebone, in 1933. It was built in 1847 by Dawkes and Hamilton. It is perpendicular in style, with a superb spire and a spacious interior with tall generous arches and side aisles. It is an exciting church, a great monument to Early Victorian Anglo-Catholicism. In a niche in the wall is an effigy to James Murray (d. 1862), the first vicar; it is reminiscent of Rahere's tomb in St Bartholomew's, Smithfield, deliberately and successfully mediaeval. Murray was succeeded by Benjamin Webb, who was vicar from 1862 to 1885. He was a co-founder of the Cambridge Camden Society and the editor of *The Ecclesiologist*, and he was responsible for the exciting furnishings of the church. There is a wonderful metal chancel screen and pulpit designed by G. E. Street who also designed the fantastic carved wooden reredos which was carved by Redfern. The font cover was by Pearson and the litany desk was by Burges who also designed Murray's monument. The east window was done in Murray's time and was designed by Pugin himself; the painted wooden west gallery was by Alfred Bell. Anyone who is interested in this period of English architecture and design, or even simply in seeing a fine church should go to St Andrew's.

But St Andrew's did not come to Kingsbury till 1933 and by the late 19th century the old church was already too small so a new parish church was built in Kingsbury Road by Butterfield, and was dedicated to the Holy Innocents who were murdered by Herod. Kingsbury thus has three really interesting churches, for though Holy Innocents is not a major work of Butterfield's, it has his characteristic brick patterning in the nave and a most individual baptistry connected with the main church by a friendly and peaceful cloister.

When Lysons wrote at the end of the 18th century, there were only 52 houses in Kingsbury; now there are thousands. There is a most resourceful shopping centre built in the 1930s and near it is Moot Circle which marks the site of the Hundred Court. At the end of the shopping parade is Roe Green, a large open space visited in autumn by travelling circuses, which gives a country atmosphere to the whole urban area. Kingsbury Hill is open ground too.

To the east of Kingsbury is the large Brent Reservoir, created in 1838. It is used for boating and is a pretty sight at weekends with coloured sails bobbing to and fro. It is more popularly known as the Welsh Harp Reservoir taking its name from a public house, beside which Kingsbury Racecourse used to flourish in the last century. To the north-west is Barn Hill, now a recreation ground, topped with trees and grass and with a dew pond. Stand on the summit on an autumn evening when the dusk or a mist has obscured the buildings and one can sense how lovely and how friendly a county rural Middlesex once was.

CAMDEN

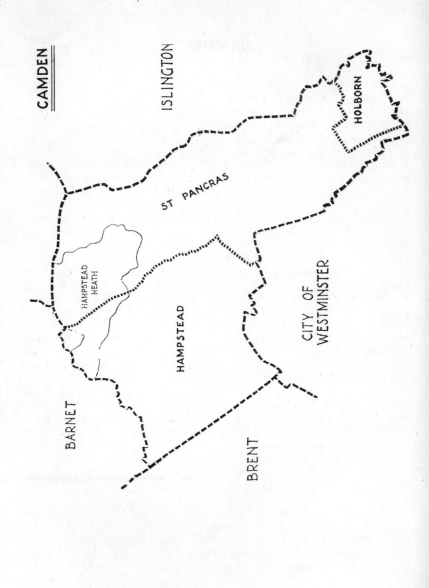

CAMDEN

ISLINGTON

HOLBORN

ST PANCRAS

HAMPSTEAD
HEATH

HAMPSTEAD

CITY OF
WESTMINSTER

BARNET

BRENT

CAMDEN

The London Borough of Camden, which combines the former boroughs of Holborn, St Pancras, and Hampstead, is shaped like an inverted L. The new name derives from the title of Charles Pratt, Marquis of Camden, who owned and developed land in St Pancras. The borough covers an area of 8½ square miles and has a population of almost 228,000 (1969). Its neighbours are the City and Westminster to the south and west, Brent, Barnet, and Haringey on the north-west and north, with Islington on the east. At the boundary between the City and Holborn, near to Holborn Viaduct, an iron griffin sits in the middle of the road, marking the site of Holborn Bar which straddled the road from early times till the 18th century, where tolls were collected and vagabonds and lepers turned away from the City. There is great variety and contrast, both geographically and physically, in Camden for its boundaries contain two of the main heights to the north of London—Hampstead and Highgate from which even today astonishing panoramas can be seen across the metropolis—and it falls away to the valley of the Fleet which rises at Kenwood and joins the Thames at Blackfriars Bridge. The contrasts in land usage are as diverse. The demurely laid out squares of Holborn, with the Inns of Court and the British Museum, grew up as one of the first expansions of the City and Westminster. The development of the Bedford Estate set the pattern of building throughout the 18th century and the streets and squares continue across into southern St Pancras, till the pattern is abruptly broken by the three great railway stations, Euston, King's Cross, and St Pancras. Behind them a more piecemeal development spread northwards till it reached the old village of Highgate. Westward lie the open spaces of Hampstead Heath with Hampstead Village on the neighbouring hill, while buildings cluster and throng again on the western and southern slopes to form West Hampstead and Swiss Cottage.

Holborn, previously the smallest of the former metropolitan boroughs, takes its name from that part of the River Fleet which ran between high banks just above Holborn Bridge and was literally "the burn in the hollow". The bridge connected High Holborn with the road into the City; the river is now entombed in a culvert but its line can be traced from Holborn Viaduct as one looks down to Farringdon Street below. Holborn is first mentioned in a 10th century charter of King Edgar's granting land there to Westminster Abbey. The grant included the old church of St Andrew's which today lies in the City outside Holborn's boundary. The village probably lay along the "wide army street" which the Romans had made running westwards from London along the roads which we now call High Holborn and Oxford Street. Domesday Book tells us that William the Chamberlain held a vineyard there for which he paid six shillings a year to the King's Sheriff.

Three great mediaeval institutions remain today in Holborn—the church of St Etheldreda's in Ely Place, Lincoln's Inn, and Gray's Inn. The church had its datable beginning in the chapel built onto his house after 1251 by John le Franceis, Treasurer of England, but it may well be that he was building on the site of a Romano–British church some five or six centuries older. When he died in 1268, the next tenant was John de Kirkby, Bishop of Ely, who completed the chapel and began the house which was thereafter to be the London palace of the Bishops of Ely. There is an undercroft or crypt and an upper church with some of the finest tracery to be found in London in the west window. The bishop's palace adjoining the church was often used for other important residents—Philippa of Hainault spent Christmas there in 1327 before her marriage with Edward III, and John of Gaunt, Duke of Lancaster, took up residence there after his palace of the Savoy was burnt by Wat Tyler's men in 1381. He died there in 1399 and it is here that Shakespeare places the scene in *Richard II* when the dying duke entreats his wayward nephew the king to cherish his realm, "this royal throne of kings".

The gardens around the house were famous for their roses and strawberries—once again Shakespeare takes up the point, making the future Richard III request some fruit of the bishop of Ely—and here Henry VIII and Catherine of Aragon were feasted by the sergeants-at-law with an entertainment which lasted for five days.

Ely Palace remained episcopal property after the Reformation but in 1576 Queen Elizabeth forced Bishop Cox to lease part of the house and grounds to Sir Christopher Hatton. In 1581, after the death of the bishop, Hatton acquired the whole estate which passed to his nephew William Newport when Sir Christopher died 10 years later. Newport changed his name to Hatton but only survived his uncle by six years; another relation inherited the bulk of the property but Lady Hatton, William's widow, retained the Holborn

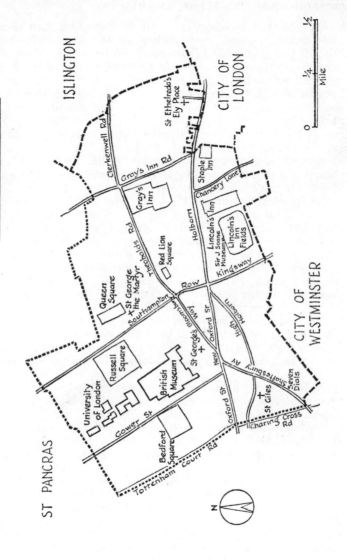

CAMDEN - (HOLBORN)

ST PANCRAS

ISLINGTON

CITY OF LONDON

CITY OF WESTMINSTER

University of London
Gower St
Russell Square
British Museum
Bedford Square
Tottenham Court Rd
St Georges
New Oxford St
Oxford St
Charing Cross Rd
St Giles
Shaftesbury Av
Seven Dials
Queen Square
St George the Martyr
Southampton Row
Theobalds Rd
Red Lion Square
Bloomsbury Way
High Holborn
Kingsway
Sir J Soane Museum
Lincoln's Inn Fields
Lincoln's Inn
Holborn
Gray's Inn
Gray's Inn Rd
Clerkenwell Rd
St Etheldreda's Ely Place
Chancery Lane
Staple Inn

N

0   ¼   ½
Mile

59

house. This gentlewoman can only be described as a termagant. She was wealthy and good-looking and the Attorney-General, Sir Edward Coke, married her as hastily as he could. He had plenty of leisure to repent, for she soon turned him out of the house and spent the rest of her long life quarrelling with him, with the rest of her family, with the Bishop of Ely who tried to regain possession of the house, and with the King when his favourite, the Duke of Buckingham, sought the hand of Lady Hatton's daughter, Frances, for his brother, Sir John Villiers. The marriage took place with great ceremony at Hampton Court but not till the bride had been kidnapped twice over by rival factions of her family; Lady Hatton refused to attend the wedding but entertained James I to a banquet afterwards just to show there was no hard feeling.

Her successor, another Christopher Hatton, pulled down part of the establishment and during the 1650s laid out Hatton Garden, Great Cross Street, and Kirby Street where the gardens had been. The Bishops of Ely were paid only £3,000 compensation in the late 17th century. The church remained in use—Wren's daughter, Ann, was married there—but was allowed to fall into disrepair until the Roman Catholic Fathers of Charity happily bought it in 1874 and since then, despite bombing in the last war, have restored it so that it now re-approaches its mediaeval splendour.

The houses on either side of Ely Place were built in the 1770s and still claim one of the rights of the Liberty of the See of Ely, namely freedom from the police; they are separated from the roadway by a pretty little lodge with iron railings and are a fascinating enclave to visit.

During the 14th and 15th centuries, the Inns of Court and Chancery grew up as necessary adjuncts of the King's Courts which dispensed justice from the Palace of Westminster. The Inns grew up as independent voluntary societies for the provision of legal advice and the training of young lawyers. Some, such as Thavies and Furnival Inns, have disappeared, and Staple Inn remains only as a building, but four exist unchanged—Gray's Inn, Lincoln's Inn, Middle Temple, and Inner Temple—and of these Gray's Inn and Lincoln's Inn are in Holborn. They were both established by the 14th century, the former in Lord Gray's old manor house of Portpool which site it still occupies today, and the latter first on the east side of Chancery Lane but removing to its present position on the west side in the early 15th century when it took over the Bishop of Chichester's house. It is uncertain whether the name is derived from the title of Hugh Lacy, Earl of Lincoln (d. 1311) or from

Thomas de Lincoln, the King's Sergeant. Both institutions are essentially collegiate in character, walled off from the surrounding metropolis even today. Each Inn has a Hall, where meals are taken in common, a chapel and a library.

At Lincoln's Inn, the Hall is approached through the gatehouse built in 1518, still with its original heavy oak doors. Inside are the Old Buildings erected between 1490 and 1520, of dark red brick with bluish diapering patterns, and opposite the gate is the Hall, built between 1490 and 1492, with a magnificent early 17th century screen across it. On the north wall is Hogarth's huge historical painting of *Paul before Felix*, a work less successful than his portraits or the genre paintings. The chapel stands just north of the Hall and was built in 1619. It is often ascribed to Inigo Jones though there is no documentary evidence that it was his work. It has an open undercroft, where John Thurloe, Cromwell's Secretary of State, is buried, intended as a place where students could "walk and talk and confer for their learnings". The chapel has a tunnel vault painted a rich warm red, and oak pews with carved ends and little doors. The east window is filled with coats of arms in stained glass and the early 18th century hexagonal pulpit is most elaborately carved. New Square was added in the 1690s by Henry Serle; the buildings are plain and elegant with one magnificent doorway leading out on to Carey Street and an iron screen at the north end, with two water pumps in front of it.

The severe Stone Buildings to the north of the chapel were designed by Sir Robert Taylor in 1774–80, and the New Hall and Library by Philip Hardwick in 1843. The latter are unashamedly and romantically neo-Tudor with a fine raised terrace from which the rest of the Inn can be admired. Along the north wall of the Hall runs G. F. Watts' fresco of *Justice* with 33 figures, including Moses, Confucius, Ina of Wessex, and Alfred the Great. Several of the faces are portraits of Watts' friends—Holman Hunt was the model for Ina. Lincoln's Inn has numbered the poet John Donne, as well as seven Prime Ministers—Walpole, the younger Pitt, Addington, poor murdered Spencer Percival (see p. 103), Canning, Melbourne, and Asquith—among her members, and she has trained such legal dignitaries as Sir Thomas More, Lord Erskine, and Lord Mansfield.

At Gray's Inn, much war damage was sustained. The Hall, where *The Comedy of Errors* was performed in 1594, the chapel and the library were all bombed, the library losing 30,000 books. The magnificent Hall Screen, said to have been presented by Elizabeth I, was happily saved; it is one of the most beautiful screens ever carved. It is of oak with five bays separated with decorated Ionic columns. In each bay is an arch, two of which serve as doors with windows in the tympanum or semi-circle of the arch; the other three tympana are filled with delicate flutings radiating from a rosette. The doors are ornamented with strap-work and above is a most elaborately carved musicians' gallery. The hammerbeam roof and central lantern have been restored. The chapel, library, and chambers of the Inn have been restored or rebuilt with equal success, but its greatest charm is still its gardens, originally laid out by Sir Francis Bacon, the Inn's most illustrious student, whose statue stands in one of the courtyards. The gardens are formal, with a fine avenue of trees, and a piquant arrangement on different levels. Three other great Elizabethans who were students there should at least be named—Elizabeth's Secretary, Lord Cecil, his son-in-law Sir Francis Walsingham who served both the Queen and James I, and the peerless Sir Philip Sidney.

We have already mentioned Staple Inn which stands in High Holborn and was originally the meeting place of wool merchants who dealt in England's staple export. By the 15th century it had become an Inn of Chancery. The beautiful hammerbeam hall was built by the Principal, Richard Champion in 1581, and the Holborn front was added five years later by another Principal, Vincent Engham. Eventually the chambers began to be used for purposes other than those of the law and Dr Johnson was living there in 1759 when he published *Rasselas*, written at great speed to pay the funeral expenses of his mother. In 1884 the Inn closed, the southern portion of the grounds was used to build an extension for the Patent Office, and the Hall and frontage on Holborn were bought by the Prudential Assurance Office who munificently restored them at great cost, rebuilding behind the original façade. The Hall was destroyed by bombs in 1944 but the façade remains, the most remarkable range of Tudor timbered domestic buildings in London. Almost opposite at No 22/23 High Holborn, Henekeys have a public house, the licence of which has run since 1695.

Until the Reformation, much of Holborn was church land. As well as Ely Place and the land belonging to Westminster Abbey beside St Andrew's Church, the manor of Blemundsbury passed in 1375 from the Blemund family, who had held it for two centuries and who are today commemorated in the modern name of Blooms-bury, into the possession of the London Charterhouse, while the Leper Hospital of St Giles, founded in 1117 by that beneficent and practical lady, Matilda, Henry I's queen, was endowed with lands which stretched from St Giles High Street to what is now Cambridge Circus; the curve of Shaftesbury Avenue roughly indicates the boundary of the old demesne. With the exception of the villages, all this was open country and as late as 1597 John Gerard the herbalist was able to grow oleanders and balsam from Peru in his garden in Fetter Lane, as well as musk and damask roses and all kinds of native plants and vegetables, such as the orchids which he found on Hampstead Heath.

With the Reformation, the church lands passed into the King's hands. St Giles' Church became the parish church, aptly known as St Giles-in-the-Fields; it was at its merciful door that poor souls on their way to death at Tyburn were given a last drink of ale. The manor of Bloomsbury (Blemundsbury) was granted to Thomas Wriothesley, Lord Chancellor and later Earl of Southampton. Later generations of the family added most of the old manor of St Giles as well as land fronting on High Holborn, where Southampton House stood at the north end of Chancery Lane, on the site now covered by Southampton Buildings. The 4th earl decided in 1640 to build a new Southampton House. A square, which was to become Bloomsbury Square, stood in front of it and John Evelyn noted in his diary that there was "a noble Square or Piazza, a little Towne; his owne [the earl's house] stands too low, some noble rooms, a pretty cedar chapell, a naked garden to the North, but good aire". The naked garden was soon to be adorned with a marvellous double avenue of lime trees which perfumed the air in spring with their blossom; Russell Square and Bedford Place run across the site. The earl died suddenly in 1667 and the estate was divided between his three daughters, his eldest, Lady Rachel, inheriting Bloomsbury, the manor of St Giles, and Fig's Mead, a substantial plot of land northwards of the main estate in what is now St Pancras. Lady Rachel married William Russell, second son of the Earl of Bedford and they resided in Southampton House which came to be called Bedford House. As neighbours they had Ralph Montagu who married Lady Elizabeth, Lady Rachel's younger sister, to whom the Russells sold some seven acres on which he built Montagu House, so that the two ladies were living next door to each other, and the Earl of Thanet who lived at Thanet House which survives, though completely refronted, as 100–102 Great Russell Street. It is with the Russells that the modern history of Bloomsbury begins.

While Lady Rachel's father had been building his fine new mansion, development had also been going on to the south of High Holborn. William Newton, a gentleman from Bedfordshire, had bought up the fields west of Lincoln's Inn and in 1638 obtained a licence to build 32 houses there, in spite of the protests raised by members of the Inn. The Fields had always been a place of terror and ill omen—Anthony Babington and his fellow conspirators who plotted against the life of Elizabeth I, had been executed there. The sentence in itself was reasonable but it was carried out with barbarity. Newton, however, determined to make the Fields an embellishment to London Town and the best architects of the day were employed. The south side lies in Westminster and has been largely rebuilt, but on the west and east Nos. 57–58 were built by Henry Joynes, Nos. 59–60, Lindsay House, are usually ascribed with good stylistic reason, to Inigo Jones, and on the north-west corner stands Newcastle House, designed in 1685 by Captain Winde, probably completed some 10 years later by Sir Christopher Wren, and well restored by Lutyens in the present century. Of the inhabitants of the houses we shall speak later, but it was in these fields on July 21, 1683, that another horrible execution took place, this time the execution of a man who was almost certainly innocent.

He was none other than Lord William Russell himself, who was accused of being involved in the Rye House Plot against the life of the Catholic heir to the throne, James, Duke of York. Despite his plea of Not Guilty, despite the agonised defence put up by his wife and friends, his head was lopped off, almost within sight of his own house which he had been able to glimpse, all hung in black, up Southampton Street as he went to the scaffold. His headless body was carried into Lindsay House to be laid in its coffin. On the accession of William and Mary, it was declared that he had been innocent and his father was created a duke by way of compensation. That however did not bring Lord William back to life and Lady Rachel lived out 40 years of widowhood in the great mansion that now became known as Bedford House. Her young son succeeded to the dukedom in 1700 but died of smallpox in 1711 and was followed in turn by his two younger brothers. It was not till after the death of John, the 4th duke, that the great development of the Bedford Estate was begun, the moving spirit being the widowed duchess who held the land in trust for her grandson, and the operative date being 1776.

Meanwhile a maze of courts and tenements between Great Russell Street and St Giles High Street had already engulfed the old monastic lands, to become The Rookeries, one of the most foully insanitary and cruelly criminal quarters of London throughout the 18th century. Nearby, in 1693, Sir Thomas Neale, a Master of the Mint, laid out to the south of St Giles High Street, that extra-ordinary radiating star of streets known as Seven Dials from the column that Neale set up in the middle, a sundial facing each street opening. It has since been moved to Weybridge Green where it stands now, surmounted by a ducal coronet, as a memorial to the Duchess of Northumberland. The original top of the column is now in Weybridge Museum. This too became one of the criminal areas of London, its horror being summed up in Hogarth's terrible indictment of society, his engraving *Gin Lane*, and epitomised in Dickens' *Bleak House* (chapters XVI and XLVI) as Tom-all-Alone's.

While Neale was laying out Seven Dials, a highly speculative, utterly unscrupulous builder was developing Red Lion Square in spite of the literally violent remonstrations of the gentlemen of Gray's Inn who fought pitched battles with the builders. The specu-lator was Nicholas Barbon, son of Praisegod Barebone, the common-wealth preacher. He was as thorough a rogue in his dealings as his father had been a Puritan, but his Square remained a desirable residential area and it was at No. 17 that William Morris and Edward Burne-Jones did much of their early creative work. Houses began to spread out to the east where William Lambe had charitably established a water conduit in Henry VIII's reign—the stone in-scription from it can still be seen, let into a wall in Long Yard, off Guilford Street—and a mansion was built for Lord Powis which later became the residence of the French ambassador.

By the middle of the 18th century, houses were built on either side of it to form Great Ormond Street, and Powis House itself was demolished before 1800. The doorways of Nos. 40 and 41 are especially elaborate and should be admired, while Richard Mead, the great and kindly doctor, lived at No. 49. His house has gone but the site is covered by the buildings of Great Ormond Street Hospital for Sick Children opened in 1852 and the good physician would want no other memorial to mark the spot where he spent many worthwhile years. Nearby Queen Square had been laid out in the early 18th century and was named for Queen Anne, though the regal statue which adorns it is in fact a figure of Queen Charlotte. Notable residents were Jonathan Richardson, the portrait painter, Edmond Hoyle, the expert on whist who published the first editions of *Hoyle's Book of Games*, and Dr William Stukeley, the antiquarian. Bedford Row and Harpur Street were laid out at the same time on land belonging to Peter Harpur, a gentleman from Bedford; they, and Great James Street, are comparatively unspoiled and give a wonderful impression of how dignified a well-to-do 18th century

London street must have been. At the bottom of Bedford Row stands an unusual pump with two spouts, erected in 1840; it must have been hard work to operate the handle. It is worth noting that even in a good residential area, a pump was still needed.

Inevitably, with all this development going on, more churches were needed. St George the Martyr in Queen Square was established in 1706 as a chapel of ease to St Andrew's, Holborn, and became a parish church in its own right in the 1720s; from 1747 to 1765 Dr Stukeley was the rector. The church was virtually rebuilt in 1869 and was restored again in 1952 after much bomb damage. By the early 18th century, the old parish church of St Giles was in a state of disrepair. As we have already said, the Leper Hospital was founded by Queen Matilda in 1101 and the church, which probably served the parishioners as well as the lepers, was part of the original buildings. It continued to be the parish church for a century after the Reformation but by 1630 had to be rebuilt at a cost of £2,016, much of which was provided by Alicia, daughter-in-law to Robert Dudley, Earl of Leicester, Elizabeth I's favourite, who was created a duchess in her own right by Charles I as a tribute to her good works. It was in this overcrowded parish that the terrible outbreak of plague in 1665 probably began; in that appalling time of suffering, the rector of St Giles, Henry Morse, supported and toiled with his suffering parishioners. The church itself had begun to decay by the end of the century, so much so that in 1715 a petition was presented to Parliament that it should be rebuilt. Now in 1711 an Act had been passed to provide for the building of 50 new churches to serve the needs of growing London. In the end, only a dozen were erected,* and to them the rebuilt St Giles was added by means of a special Bill and completed in 1733. The architect was Henry Flitcroft, son of William III's gardener, and a protégé of Lord Burlington. The church is plain and classical outside with a splendid tower, square in its first stages, octagonal above, and finally surmounted by a spire with a gilt ball and cross. Inside there is a noble barrel vault, galleries on either side for the charity school children, and four beautiful chandeliers. The pulpit comes from the 17th century church, as does Duchess Dudley's monument.

---

* By Nicholas Hawksmoor – St Alphege, Greenwich; St Anne's, Limehouse; Christchurch, Spitalfields; St George-in-the-East, Stepney; St George's, Bloomsbury; St Mary Woolnoth; the tower of St Michael's, Cornhill. By James Gibbs – St Mary-le-Strand; the steeple of St Clement Danes. By John James – St George's, Hanover Square; probably St Luke's, Old Street; possibly St John's, Horsleydown. By Thomas Archer – St John's, Smith Square; St Paul's, Deptford.

Andrew Marvell the poet was buried in the churchyard and there is an altar tomb, possibly designed by Inigo Jones, to George Chapman, whose translation of Homer so inspired John Keats.

St George's, Bloomsbury, is one of the most startlingly dramatic churches in London. The parish was carved from that of St Giles-in-the-Fields; the church was designed by Nicholas Hawksmoor under the 1711 Act. There is a splendid portico of Corinthian columns and these columns reappear as a baldachino or canopy over the altar; the interior might seem theatrical if it were not so assured and majestic. The one strange feature is the spire which rises from a tower set to the side of the church and is stepped upwards following Pliny's description of the Mausoleum of Halicarnassus. Right on the top is perched a statue of George I appearing as St George. The result is improbable and seems to have no relation to the dignity of the portico and interior. It is this spire that is to be seen in the background of Hogarth's *Gin Lane*.

While we are writing of churches in Holborn, there are two others of the 19th century which should be noted particularly: the Church of Christ the King, Gordon Square, and the Italian Church—the Roman Catholic church of St Peter's in the Clerkenwell Road.

Christ the King was built by Raphael Brandon in 1853 as the headquarters of the Catholic Apostolic Church, an interesting sect founded by Edward Irving in 1832. The church is now used by the students of London University. Its main features are an exciting entrance cloister and a wonderful carved screen behind the altar; the modern fittings and decorations, selected by the students, are among the most interesting and arresting in London.

St Peter's was built in 1863 by John Brydon. The front, with a two-bay loggia, is narrow, squeezed in between houses, but the inside is a surprisingly large basilica with some splendid statues. It is very much used by the Italian community in London and should be visited on a Sunday when the strong family feeling of the congregation can be sensed.

As we have already said, the real development of the Bedford Estate began after the death of the 4th duke when, in 1776, Bedford Square began to be laid out. It remains, of noble proportion, the one unaltered, unspoilt Georgian square left in London. The central houses on each side have a pediment and columns running from the first to the second floor windows; the houses are otherwise very plain, unadorned but most dignified and perfectly proportioned. The design was probably the joint responsibility of Robert Grews, William Scott, and Thomas Leverton. The estate was strict in its supervision of the quality of the work but generous with extensions of peppercorn rents during the building period. Inside, with the exception of No. 1, the prettiest house of all, the arrangement of the rooms is sacrificed to a grand staircase and an elegant first-floor drawing-room, but there is no doubt but that the houses were very desirable properties. By the end of the century, the duke had decided to leave Bedford House and to move to the more fashionable area of Arlington Street, St James's. Bedford House was demolished and the estate spread northward developing around seven squares of varying sizes and proportions—Russell Square, the largest of them, Tavistock Square, Torrington, Woburn and Gordon Squares, Bedford and Bloomsbury Squares already having been built. The gearter part of the work was carried out by that remarkable and steadfast builder, James Burton, who had come down from Scotland by 1786, changed his name from Haliburton and, undeterred by the shortage of capital and labour resulting from the Napoleonic wars, set about extending and expanding London. The city is lucky that so much of the work was carried out under the untiring supervision of such a meticulous sensitive man. The estate was virtually complete by the 1830s; the development of the northern part on Fig's Mead in St Pancras did not begin till after the coming of the railways. The site just to the north of where Bedford House had stood was left open as far as Keppel Street; great things were to happen there in the next century.

From the beginning of its early 17th century development, Holborn has always been a desirable place in which to live. Its proximity to London and its healthy open aspect towards Hampstead and Highgate have encouraged many famous men and women to make their homes here. In Great Queen Street, lived Judge Jeffreys who so brutally sentenced those who had supported the Duke of Monmouth's futile rebellion against his uncle James II, as well as pleasanter people, such as Gilbert Burnet, Bishop of Salisbury, an ardent supporter of Mary and William of Orange, who was married thrice, each time to highly intellectual women, and wrote a splendid and discursive *History of My Own Times*, and Richard Brinsley Sheridan, dramatist, theatrical manager, and witty politician, and Kitty Clive, the charming actress whom Horace Walpole befriended in her old age, as well as Sir Godfrey Kneller the painter, Dr Thomas Arne the composer, and James Boswell, Dr Johnson's biographer. Mrs Mary Anne Robinson the actress, better known as "Perdita" who was George IV's mistress, Thomas Barham, the author of the immortal *Ingoldsby Legends*, and the visionary poet and artist William Blake, all had lodgings there for a while. The main feature of the street now is the huge Masonic Temple built in 1933 on the site of older Masonic premises which had been in use since 1776.

Lincoln's Inn Fields was a distinguished address from the first. Sir William Blackstone, author of the *Commentaries on the Laws of England*, which was said to have brought him in £14,000 and which is still a standard text today, lived at what is now Nos. 55 and 56. Next door was Edward Montagu, the Earl of Sandwich, who died in the battle of Southwold Bay against the Dutch when his ship, the *Royal James*, was blown up, and what is today No. 42 was the home of Edward Sydney, the 2nd earl of Leicester, whose daughter Dorothy was the Sacharissa to whom young Edmund Waller, student at Lincoln's Inn, addressed so many and such sweet poems. Johann Zoffany the artist lived in rooms at No. 43 and was often in debt when there between 1765 and 1769. He left to work in Europe, was created a Baron of the Holy Roman Empire by Maria Theresa, made a fortune in India by his paintings there between 1783 and 1790 and died at Strand-on-the-Green in 1810. John Forster had rooms at No. 58 and there in 1844 Charles Dickens read *The Chimes* aloud to a group of his friends, but the two most famous residents of the Fields were Lord Mansfield and Sir John Soane.

William Murray, 1st earl of Mansfield (1705–1793) was trained at Lincoln's Inn and became Lord Chief Justice in 1756. He was believed to hold pro-Catholic sentiments and at the time of the terrible anti-Catholic riots of 1780, headed by the half-crazed, or at least eccentric, Lord George Gordon, his house in Bloomsbury Square was sacked and his library burned; he moved thereafter to Lincoln's Inn, though that quarter had suffered too, the chapel attached to the Sardinian Embassy having been burnt out. A well-documented and highly dramatic account of the riots can be read in Dickens' wonderful novel, *Barnaby Rudge*.

Nos. 12, 13, and 14 all belonged to Sir John Soane, who moved to the Square in 1792 and remained there until his death in 1837. He was a very great and utterly individual architect, a self-made man, a difficult and suspicious character, and a good friend. Time has not been kind to him—his greatest buildings, the Courts of Justice at Westminster and the Bank of England, have been destroyed by fire or by later and lesser developers—but one fitting memorial he has, his own house which he built to house his collection of classical and architectural specimens as well as works of art,

69

and which he left in trust as a museum for the nation. It is open, free of charge, daily excepting Mondays, and its greatest treasures are the two great series of paintings by Hogarth, eight of *The Rake's Progress* and four of *The Election*. This museum should be visited by everyone interested in London, in architecture, or in art, and visited not once but many times. The collection of paintings is so large that Sir John had to devise shutters which doubled back against the walls and so gave him extra hanging space; the shutters are worth admiring in themselves as remarkable pieces of engineering.

Henry Crabbe Robinson, the witty and sharp-tongued politician and diarist, lived at 30, Russell Square from 1839 to 1867, and Sir Samuel Romilly the barrister lived at No. 21, where he committed suicide in 1818, being utterly deranged by grief at the death of his wife. Sir Thomas Lawrence the painter was at No. 65 and there he painted the series of portraits of the princes and generals of the victorious allies at Waterloo; his house was guarded by Cossacks when General Platoff came for his sittings. Isaac D'Israeli, man of letters and father of the future Prime Minister, spent many years at 22 Theobalds Road and at 6 Bloomsbury Square, his son living with him the while, while at No. 11 was Henry Cavendish, the retiring and brilliant scientist in memory of whose great discoveries and experiments the laboratories at Cambridge were named. John Howard, the prison reformer, lived at 23 Great Ormond Street from 1777 to 1789, and Thomas Cook, the traveller and founder of the world-famous firm, lived at 59 Great Russell Street from 1863 to 1879. Sir Edward Lutyens the architect lived at 29 Bloomsbury Square from 1898 to 1914, and near him at No. 2 Gower Street from 1877 to 1922 was that brave woman, Millicent Fawcett, champion of feminine rights and wife to the blind MP, Henry Fawcett, one of the staunchest-hearted men who has ever lived.

Today, Holborn's most famous institution is the British Museum in Great Russell Street. It will be remembered that Ralph Montagu built a house here in the 1680s (see p. 63) but it was not used regularly by successive generations of the family. Nearby at 3 and 4 Bloomsbury Place lived Sir Hans Sloane the physician. His astonishing collection, relating chiefly to natural history, is described under Chelsea (see p. 318), where he moved towards the end of his life. When he died in 1753, he left the collection to the nation for £20,000, a fraction of what he felt it to be worth. The money was raised by a lottery, Montagu House was purchased and refurbished and became the home of Sir Hans' collection, and of the Harleian and Cottonian collections of manuscripts. It opened in January

1759 and Thomas Gray the poet, who was staying nearby, wrote of its "Manuscripts and rarities by the cart-load". From the first, admission was free though in the early years a letter of introduction was required. The addition of the Elgin and Townley marbles, as well as the Egyptian antiquities, such as the Rosetta stone, taken from Napoleon after the wars with France, soon filled its galleries, and when, at his accession, George IV presented his father's library, it was obvious that the museum was too small for the treasures it contained. Robert, later Sir Robert, Smirke was chosen as the architect for the new building which was begun in 1823 and took 30 years to complete. Its magnificent portico and the King's Library are architectural triumphs. Bedford House was demolished morsel by morsel as the work progressed.

But no sooner was the British Museum completed than it became painfully clear that it was still not large enough, especially since it was a copyright library and as the books increased in number, so did the hordes of scholars who came to consult them. Luckily, the Keeper of Printed Books was Anthony Panizzi, an Italian political refugee and scholar. He was a man of immense energy and determination and he had the central courtyard roofed in with an immense rotunda to form the Reading Room, which opened in 1857, the most harmonious and inspiring workplace in the world. He created the Catalogue and died as Sir Anthony in 1879. He made his ideals in the creation of the Reading Room perfectly clear:

I want a poor student to have the same means of indulging his learned curiosity, of following his rational pursuits, of consulting the same authorities, of fathoming the most intricate enquiry, as the richest man in the kingdom, as far as books go, and I contend that the Government is bound to give him the most liberal and unlimited assistance in this direction.

This expression of liberal scholarship has never been bettered and deserves to be cherished forever. In 1881 the Museum was expanded still further by the removal of the Natural History Collections to South Kensington and in 1914 the Edward VII Gallery was added with exhibits from many different departments. This is probably the best gallery to which to take a child on its first visit since it is sure to find something particularly exciting; boys also show a strong inclination for the Assyrian collection.

Today the British Museum houses departments of Printed Books and Manuscripts, Prints and Drawings, Coins and Medals, Western Asiatic Antiquities, Greek and Roman Antiquities, Oriental

Antiquities, Egyptology and Ethnography. There are collections of clocks and scientific instruments, and the student of London history will pay particular attention to the Department of British and Mediaeval Antiquities. The collection has recently been re-arranged and displayed to better advantage and includes such remarkable treasures as a bronze Celtic shield found in the Thames at Battersea, ornamented with a bold and intricate pattern, and the contents of the royal Anglo-Saxon burial ship excavated at Sutton Hoo, the most important grave of its period in all Europe. The future expansion of the Museum is at present under discussion.

Inevitably, the presence of the British Museum attracted other learned institutions to the area. In 1826, University College was founded by the efforts of Lord Brougham, the poet Thomas Campbell, and the philosopher Jeremy Bentham. A site was chosen off Gower Street (in fact in St Pancras) and the foundation stone was laid in 1827. The architect was William Wilkins and he produced a building with a splendid portico reached by a flight of steps, on which today's students sun themselves as they study, and above which rises a large dome. The internal arrangements are strangely cramped but there is still room to display the fine collection of paintings, both old and modern, which the College possesses, particularly the sketches and sculptural studies of John Flaxman. Wings were added and in that on the north is the Slade School of Art which, under directors such as Sir Henry Tonks and Sir William Coldsteam, has trained many good artists. The College has always been famous for its School of Anatomy which became particularly distinguished in the early years of this century under Sir George Dancer Thane; its association with University College Hospital on the other side of Gower Street has always been very close. After 1878 women were admitted and there has never been a School of Theology since from the first, University College has admitted all suitable students without regard to their religious views. It has its own tutelary deity—the body of Jeremy Bentham, whose skeleton is wired together and dressed in a suit of his own clothes. He resides, seated comfortably, in a large upright box and is still the heart of the College.

Inspired by the example of University College, Bedford College was opened for women students at 47 Bedford Square in 1849 by a redoubtable lady called Elizabeth Jesser Reid; the college now has premises in Regent's Park and has recently begun to accept men as students. Just before the First World War, many small mean buildings were cleared away around Keppel Street and to the north of the British Museum, and the site lay open for a quarter of a century till in 1927, after extraordinary vacillations on the part of the Government, the Chancellor of London University, Sir William Beveridge, visited the United States and returned with a munificent grant of £400,000 from the Rockefeller Foundation. With this and a grant of £125,000 from the British Government, the site was bought from the Duke of Bedford and on June 26, 1936, the foundation stone of the Senate House, the administrative centre of London University, was laid by King George V. The cost of the building was borne by the City Corporation and Companies; the architect was Charles Holden who created a skyscraper which, if less beautiful than University College, is a building that can only be dear to all Londoners. To it have been added accommodation for Birkbeck College, the School of Oriental and African Studies, the Institute of Historical Research and the School of Tropical Medicine. The University has two fine art collections which are freely open to the public. They are the Percival David Foundation of Chinese Art housed at 53 Gordon Square, where exquisite examples of Chinese porcelain can be admired, and the Courtauld Gallery in Woburn Square. This collection of pictures, sculptures, furniture, tapestries, and carpets was left to the University by Samuel Courtauld in 1958 in memory of his wife. It was originally housed in the Courtauld Institute in Portman Square, but after the war a new building was erected in Bloomsbury to accommodate both the Courtauld and the Warburg Institute, the latter a power-house of art-historical thought and philosophy which most happily moved to England from Germany in 1933, to the inestimable advantage of this country ever since.

It was only proper that Bloomsbury should have had a group of 20th century residents as distinguished as its learned institutions, and such inhabitants it had indeed in the Bloomsbury Group, as interesting an intellectual and artistic movement as the Pre-Raphaelites of the previous century (see pp. 411). In 1904, on the death of their father, Sir Leslie Stephen the man of letters and first editor of the *Dictionary of National Biography*, his children, Vanessa, Thoby, Virginia, and Adrian, moved to No. 46 Gordon Square. Vanessa married Clive Bell, Virginia married Leonard Woolf and became one of the finest of all English writers, and they were joined by Duncan Grant, John Maynard Keynes, the economist, E. M. Forster the novelist, and Roger Fry the art critic. Members of the group lived at various addresses, in Brunswick Square and at 52 Tavistock Square and the group continued to be one of the most vital forces in the artistic, literary, and intellectual life of London right up to the last war, while its influence is still felt today. Accounts of the group in Leonard Woolf's *Beginning Again* and David Garnett's autobiographical trilogy, *The Golden Echo*, make enthralling reading.

Three great road-development schemes were put through Holborn which altered the very face and orientation of London. They were New Oxford Street (1845–47), Shaftesbury Avenue (*c.* 1855), and Kingsway (1899–1906). New Oxford Street connected High Holborn with Oxford Street proper, cutting through and demolishing the slums around St Giles, Shaftesbury Avenue provided a useful connection with Piccadilly, and Kingsway abolished the slums around King Street and Aldwych. The Rookeries of St Giles were replaced by Parnall House, one of the first blocks of flats for the poor where the individual dwellings were connected with corridor balconies, while Shaftesbury Avenue sports the Saville Theatre, its façade adorned with a lively frieze by G. Baynes.

We have watched the country lanes gradually harden into thoroughfares while buildings aligned themselves across the fields. The prospect of Hampstead and Highgate hills is blotted out, Capper's farm has been replaced by Messrs Heal's excellent shop, and the weight of learning—eight million books in the British Museum and more still in the Senate House and University College with their attendant scholars—has obliterated Gerard's wild flowers. The skyscraper, Centre Point, rears its bulk upwards beside Flitcroft's graceful spire for St Giles. Bloomsbury remains, an academic centre to balance the intellectual nexus of South Kensington and, thanks to the humane and dignified development of the Bedford Estate and those who followed its style, one of London's most graceful and gracious quarters. It is to be prayed that future development undertaken by the University and the hospitals of the area will not be allowed to ruin a townscape which, when first built, was most perfectly proportioned.

St Pancras is a long thin strip of land, running four miles from New Oxford Street northwards to Highgate and never more than a mile wide at its broadest point. It originally consisted of four manors—Rugemere on the extreme west where Regent's Park now is, Tottenhall, the western half running from south to north with the eastern half divided between St Pancras to the south and Cantelowes to the north. The River Fleet runs through it, rising at Kenwood and being known as the Ken in its upper reaches—hence Kentish Town. Almost all this land belonged to St Paul's until the Reformation.

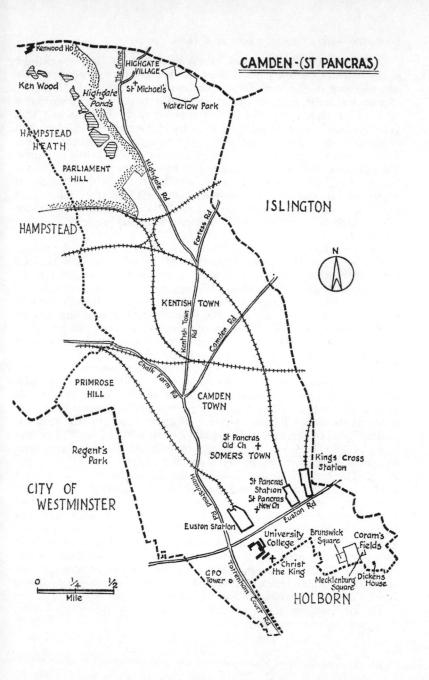

CAMDEN-(ST PANCRAS)

Kenwood Ho

Ken Wood

Highgate Ponds

HIGHGATE VILLAGE

St Michael's

Waterlow Park

HAMPSTEAD HEATH

PARLIAMENT HILL

The Grove

Highgate Rd

HAMPSTEAD

ISLINGTON

N

Fortress Rd

KENTISH TOWN

Kentish Town Rd

Camden Rd

Chalk Farm Rd

PRIMROSE HILL

CAMDEN TOWN

St Pancras Old Ch
SOMERS TOWN

Kings Cross Station

Regent's Park

Hampstead Rd

St Pancras Station
St Pancras New Ch

Euston Rd

CITY OF WESTMINSTER

Euston Station

University College

Brunswick Square

Coram's Fields

Christ the King

Mecklenburg Square

Dickens House

GPO Tower

Tottenham Court Rd

HOLBORN

0   ¼   ½
Mile

St Pancras Old Church lies, nearly forgotten, behind the sidings of the railway station named after it. According to tradition, this site was one of the very first near London on which a Christian church was built, and the dedication to the boy martyr, Pancratius or Pancras, does nothing to contradict an early foundation. The present church is a rebuilding of 1848 by H. Gough, in which a 13th century lancet window has been preserved in the chancel and a few morsels of early stonework in the north and south doorways. The piscina and sedilia remain but have been reworked in the last century. There is a monument to Philadelphia Woolaston (d. 1616) which shows her half-reclining, holding her baby, and another to Samuel Cooper, the wonderful 17th century miniature painter whose likenesses of Cromwell and his generals are so revealing.

The churchyard has been laid out as a garden, most of the tombstones being stacked around the base of an ash tree in a curious radiating pattern, while some more important memorials remain undisturbed among the grass. The rearrangement was completed in 1877 when the gardens were opened by that benefactress of London, Baroness Burdett-Coutts, who erected a large monument on the main path with the names of many of the more distinguished dead who lie here. It makes interesting reading though one cannot but wish that the Baroness had been as discriminating in her choice of design for the many memorials and fountains which she erected as she was generous in supporting worthwhile causes. Besides this memorial, there is another, designed by Sir John Soane, to his wife, and a massive altar-tomb inscribed with the names of several generations of the Rhodes family. William Godwin, the novelist and political writer, and his wife Mary were buried here. They had lived at The Polygon (see p. 81) in Somers Town where their daughter Mary was born. Her mother died two days after her birth. The little girl grew up to become the second wife of the poet Shelley and an author in her own right—she created the monster of Frankenstein. When she died, nearly 30 years after the poet had been drowned in 1822, she was buried in Bournemouth and her parents' bodies were removed to lie with her. In one corner of the garden is a meagrely equipped children's playground; surely, in such a crowded area, in the ground around a church dedicated to the patron saint of children, better facilities could be provided? The church is seldom open, its place having been taken, as we shall see, by St Pancras New Church built in 1822.

The counterpart of the mediaeval church was the manor house.

Little is known of the origins of Tottenhall Manor House, but in
1591 it was in the possession of Daniel Clark, chief cook to Elizabeth
I and to James I after her. It was demolished during the 18th
century and Tolmers Square now covers its site.

After the Reformation, the church lands in St Pancras were split
up among various landowners, among them the Fitzroy family,
the earls of Camden, Lord Somers, and the dukes of Bedford. The
development of the latter estate has already been described; that
part of the main section which lay within St Pancras included the
enchanting row of bow-fronted shops, Woburn Walk, which have
always been accessible only on foot. The duke's land reached almost
as far north as the New Road (today the Euston and Marylebone
Roads) which had been laid out in 1757 across the open fields as
London's first bypass, especially to facilitate the movement of cattle
from the country into Smithfield market. East of the duke's land,
on Bagnigge Wells Road (today King's Cross Road) was the tea
garden, Bagnigge Wells. One could drink or take a meal there,
stroll in the grounds, play cricket, listen to a concert, or watch an
entertainment. The garden closed about 1841, after the coming
of the railways.

A large part of Tottenham Manor was granted to Isabella,
Lord Arlington's daughter, who married Henry Fitzroy, Charles
II's son by Lady Castlemaine. At the time of the marriage in 1672,
the bridegroom was nine, the bride four years old. Henry became
Earl of Euston and Duke of Grafton, and by 1768 the estate had
passed to Charles Fitzroy, Earl of Southampton. It was at this time
that Charlotte Street (named in compliment to George III's Queen)
began to be developed. On the western side, near to Oxford Street,
stood Percy Chapel from 1785 till its demolition in 1867. The first
incumbent was the Reverend Anthony Stephen Matthew, who
encouraged the sculptor Flaxman throughout his boyhood and at
whose house in Rathbone Place the poet William Blake and the
artist Thomas Stothard were frequent visitors.

No. 76 in this street has particularly interesting memories, for
it was the home first of Joseph Farington, the first Secretary of the
Royal Academy, a competent artist and the keeper of a long
and enthralling diary, filled with the gossip of the art world of his
day, and later of John Constable, one of the greatest and most
inspired landscape-painters this country has ever produced. Constable died there in 1837 and for the last two years of his life he had
as neighbour Daniel Maclise, another artist, a close friend of Charles
Dickens, who spent nine years on the great historical frescoes which

adorn the walls of the House of Lords and who refused the Presidency of the Royal Academy.

The north end of Charlotte Street leads into Fitzroy Square, designed about 1790 by Robert and James Adam, though the north side was not completed till some years later. Sir Charles Eastlake, President of the Royal Academy, lived at No. 7 and died there in 1864, while No. 37 was the home of the painters Orchardson and Pettie from 1862 until 1865 and thereafter of Ford Madox Brown, during whose tenancy it was a meeting-place of the Pre-Raphaelites. The square is still elegant though later buildings and bombing have disrupted its Georgian equilibrium. Charlotte Street runs parallel with Tottenham Court Road in which stands the rebuilt Whitefield's Tabernacle. The original chapel was founded in 1756 by the Reverend George Whitefield largely for members of the Countess of Huntington's Connection and those whose views inclined to Methodism. John Bacon the sculptor was buried here. The old chapel was destroyed by bombs but a new one has been built and it flourishes. Near it in Howland Street is a wonder of 20th century engineering—the Post Office Tower. Standing 619 feet high, it is the London focus of the Post Office's microwave network. The public viewing platform at the top provides an unparalleled view of London on a fine day.

The most interesting of the St Pancras estates is the Foundling Estate. This consists of 56 acres of what had been Lamb's Conduit Fields, purchased in 1741 from the Earl of Salisbury. The land lies eastward of the Bedford Estate and its development, which did not begin till the end of the century, must be considered as an extension of that estate. The Foundling Hospital was the creation of Captain Thomas Coram (1668–1751). He was the son of a sea-captain, joined the merchant navy at the age of 11, trained as a shipwright and settled in Boston where he married Eunice Watt and prospered. The couple had no children. Coram returned to this country and was appalled to see babies abandoned in the streets, and small children fending for themselves, huddled in doorways, or dragged up unbefriended in workhouses. For two years he petitioned the King and on October 17, 1739, was granted a Royal Charter to found a home to care for abandoned children. As a stop-gap, he took a house in Hatton Garden and the first children were received there in March 1741. Within four years, the hospital had been built in the middle of open fields, the design being by Theodore Jacobsen. The arrangements were convenient and the frontage noble, with a wing for boys and another for girls, on opposite sides. Ten acres were reserved for playing fields. From the beginning, artistic

London supported the hospital. Handel gave an organ and the original score of *The Messiah*; Hogarth painted a wonderful portrait of the kindly founder, wearing an Indian red coat and smiling upon the children he had befriended. The same artist, assisted by Joseph Highmore, Richard Wilson, and Samuel Wale, painted the walls of the Court Room, and he supported the hospital still further for he persuaded Gainsborough, Highmore, Francis Hayman, Thomas Hudson, Allan Ramsay, Sir Joshua Reynolds, and Richard Wilson all to become governors and to exhibit their paintings there. These exhibitions were so successful that they led, in part, to the foundation of the Royal Academy. Hogarth's own paintings did not sell well in his lifetime and he decided to auction his *March of the Guards to Finchley*, a work strongly disapproved of by George III since it represented the troops assembling to face the Young Pretender as little better than a drunken rabble. The scene of the painting is outside the Adam and Eve public house in the Tottenham Court Road. Hogarth gave the 167 lottery tickets that remained unsold to the hospital, which most happily won the painting. All these treasures and many others, besides identification tokens tied round the necks or wrists of babies whose unhappy mothers hoped to reclaim them one day, can be seen on Mondays and Fridays at 40 Brunswick Square, the headquarters of the Foundation. It is an amazing collection and one which deserves to be far better known.

By the end of the century, the hospital decided to increase its income by developing half its estate. An excellent plan was devised by Samuel Pepys Cockerell and carried out for the greater part by James Burton. (Full accounts of the building of the estate can be found in the *Survey of London*, vol. XXIV, and in Donald Olsen's excellent book, *Town Planning in London*.) The charm of Cockerell's original scheme can only be appreciated today by studying a 19th century map such as John Britton's Map of the Parliamentary Borough of St Marylebone (1834, 2nd ed. 1838) which included St Pancras. The plan depended on a related group of squares, some of them left open on the fourth side and so affording each house an open aspect and a view of the hospital itself. Isabella Knightley, the elder sister of Jane Austen's heroine Emma, resided with her family in Brunswick Square and vowed she would never live in any other part of London for

"Our part of London is so very superior to most others . . . I should be unwilling to live in any other part of the town;—there is hardly any other that I could be satisfied to have my children in:—but we are so remarkably

79

airy!—Mr Wingfield [her doctor] thinks the vicinity of Brunswick Square decidedly the most favorable as to air."

Even today, a walk around Mecklenburgh and Brunswick Squares gives some indication of the former charm of the neighbourhood. In 1926, the governors decided to remove the hospital to Berkhamsted and the London site was sold, the preceeds going to finance the good work of the institution. Since 1954, a policy of foster homes has been adopted and the name has been changed to The Thomas Coram Foundation for Children. On the site of the hospital is a children's playground, one of the most imaginatively equipped in London, and the newly built Wolfson Foundation for the treatment of mentally handicapped children stands here—worthy uses for one of the most humanitarian corners of London. Behind the former gardens of the hospital are the old burial grounds of St George's, Bloomsbury, and St George the Martyr, and here lie Anna Gibson, sixth and favourite daughter of Richard Cromwell, the Protector's son, and the eight officers of the Manchester volunteer regiment which supported the Young Pretender and whose leaders were shot for their treason.

In the south-east corner of the estate Doughty Street was laid out, and here from March 1837 till December 1839 Charles Dickens lived at No. 48. When he and his wife moved in, their family consisted of their baby son, Dickens' young brother, and Mrs Dickens' young sister, Mary Hogarth. While they lived there, two daughters were born and Mary died, suddenly—a shock which was to prevent Dickens from writing for some two months and to mark him for the rest of his life. Here he wrote part of *Pickwick Papers*, *Oliver Twist*, *Nicholas Nickleby*, and began *Barnaby Rudge*. After two years, the house was too small for the family and they moved at the end of 1839 to No. 1 Devonshire Terrace, near Regent's Park. In 1925 the house was acquired by the Dickens Fellowship and has been turned into a museum devoted to the great novelist. It should be visited by all those who love literature and who love London, for there were few more devoted Londoners than Charles Dickens, and a more vivid picture emerges from his pages than from those of any other writer. Reference has often been made in this volume to his descriptions of the city, but apart from the great set-pieces of evocation, glimpses of a forgotten London are revealed time and again in chance sentences and phrases, and the 20th century citizen can only read them and respond to the man who could portray the city so well.

St Pancras Station

Kings Cross Station

Wharncliffe Viaduct, Hanwell

Hammersmith Flyover

A new parish church was built in 1819 designed by a father and son, William and Henry William Inwood. William had been born at Kenwood where his father had been bailiff to the 1st earl of Mansfield. The design of the church was inspired by Greek architecture—and was bitterly condemned by Pugin for that reason; he felt that Christian churches should have a Christian inspiration. The tower is modelled on the Tower of the Winds at Athens and the rest of the building follows the arrangement of the Erechtheum, a temple built in the 5th century before Christ, in honour of Erechtheus, a pagan king of Athens. Along the north and south façades are groups of caryatids, cast by John Charles Felix Rossi; they are quiet well-behaved maidens with plenty of draperies but not at all Christian. However the inhabitants of St Pancras and Holborn seem to have accepted them without a murmur and the sight of the fairylike ladies must have cheered Sunday services for many small churchgoers. The pulpit is made of wood from the Fairlop Oak, blown down in Hainault Forest in 1820 (see p. 17). The church cost £76,679 7s. 8d. to build—the most expensive since St Paul's Cathedral.

During the first two decades of the 19th century, the estates of Charles Pratt, Marquis of Camden, and of Lord Somers were laid out as pleasant, middle-class suburbs, and a grander development took place in Regent's Park, being virtually completed by the late 1820s. The eastern side of the park with the grandeur of Clarence and Cumberland Terraces and the fascinating market area which used to exist east of Albany Street lies within St Pancras, but their story belongs with that of the whole park which lies chiefly within St Marylebone and so is reserved for another volume, as is Primrose Hill which seems an integral part of the park area. Buildings spread northwards along the Hampstead Road, the church of St James (demolished in 1956) was built to serve the growing population and in its churchyard were buried the artist George Morland and his wife who died of grief, James Christie of the auction rooms and poor demented Lord George Gordon.

The architectural feature of the Southampton Estate was Mornington Crescent with a pretty garden in front of it, and on the Somers Estate was The Polygon, a curious circle of houses facing outwards with a garden in their centre. William and Mary Godwin (see p. 73) lived there. All this development shows clearly on the 1834 edition of Britton's map of the area, and a fascinating pictorial record exists in a series of detailed panoramas painted about the middle of the century by James Frederick King which show every

D

house and shop. They are preserved in the possession of Camden Public Library and are reproduced in full in vol. XIX of the *Survey of London*. By the 1838 edition, there is a startling and dramatic change—the railways had come. Before the end of Queen Victoria's reign, three wonderful railway stations had been built, facing on to the New Road.

It was a curiously fitting spot in London for such buildings to be erected for it was on the south side of the road, on part of the site now occupied by University College, that Richard Trevithick's steam locomotive, *Catch Me Who Can*, had given Londoners rides round a circular track at a shilling a head in 1804. The first station was Euston which opened on July 20, 1837—one month after Queen Victoria's accession. The line ran to Birmingham and was completed in the September of the following year, three months after the new queen's coronation. At first it was a simple two-platform arrangement, curiously unimpressive to judge from early prints, but from the first the humble station was fronted by Philip Hardwick's magnificent Doric Arch, proclaiming for all the world to see and realise that here was something new, something that was going to change the lives of everyone in England and indeed all over the world. The station was enlarged in 1846 and Hardwick added a great hall and a board room, while E. H. Baily added a statue of Robert Stephenson who planned the station, the worthy son of the man who had designed the first really practical steam locomotive and who had created the first real railway, from Stockton to Darlington. In 1947 the railways were nationalised and the decision was made to rebuild Euston Station. The new station designed by R. L. Moorcroft was opened in 1968. Now that its lines can be seen clearly, it is purposeful and dignified, a vast horizontal building all black and white with a huge passenger hall. It is a worthy successor to the original building but no lover of railways can cease to execrate the pointless and unnecessary destruction of Euston Arch which proclaimed the glory and achievement of the railway and which would have fitted as well with the new building as with the old.

Eastwards along the road is Kings Cross Station which takes its name from a statue of George IV which stood at the junction of Grays Inn Road, Euston Road and Pentonville Hill from 1830 till 1842. It served the Great Northern route to Yorkshire, Edinburgh and Aberdeen and that most poetic of all trains, *The Flying Scotsman*, still leaves punctually each morning at 10 a.m., though now the engine is diesel, not steam. The station building was designed by Lewis Cubitt, a member of the building and engineering family who even today still carry on James Burton's work in the building of London. The façade is beautifully and sincerely functional, the twin arches of the arrival and departure sheds, united by a clock tower is all that there is—there is no trimming, no elaboration, just a plain statement of what the railway meant—arrivals and departures. St Pancras Station was different. The station itself, designed by W. H. Barlow, the consulting engineer to the Midland Railway, is functional enough, and a triumph of engineering. It opened in 1867 and consists of one spectacular train shed, spanned with a single arch 240 feet wide without supporting pillars. It was made of glass and iron and the iron ribs, supplied by Butterley of Derby, rose from brick springers at platform level, the maker's name and the date of erection marked at the base of each where they can be seen to this day. But the front of the station was a hotel and that was another matter. It was designed by Sir Gilbert Scott and was completed in 1877. It was an utterly fantastic Gothic castle with 500 rooms and a grand main staircase, the whole approached by an impressive ramp. Today it is used as offices. Its greatest value is its adornment of London, for when its spires and pinnacles are seen against the setting sun from the top of Pentonville Hill, it seems an enchanted palace, as if the Industrial Revolution and all the romance of the middle ages have for one instant joined hands and been united, spiritually and physically.

Today, opposite Euston stand Friends' House, the headquarters and library of the Society of Friends, that noble and selfless religious body, and the Wellcome Research Institute, which in addition to scientific and medical research departments includes museums of the history of medicine and of medical science which can be visited on application.

The coming of the railways had done nothing to improve the neighbourhood to the north of the New Road. The immediate effect was of destruction; Dickens, who was an eye-witness, says in chapter VI of *Dombey and Son*:

The first shock of a great earthquake had, just at that period, rent the whole neighbourhood to its centre. Traces of its course were visible on every side. Houses were knocked down; streets broken through and stopped; deep pits and trenches dug in the ground; enormous heaps of earth and clay thrown up; buildings that were undermined and shaking, propped by great beams of wood . . . Hot springs and fiery eruptions, the usual attendants upon earthquakes, lent their contribution of confusion to the scene. Boiling water hissed and heaved within delapidated walls; whence also, the glare and roar of flames came issuing forth; and mounds of ashes blocked up rights of way, and wholly changed the law and custom of the neighbourhood.

The whole passage needs to be read carefully. Dickens had been at school at Wellington Academy, Granby Street and so knew the area before the railways; he was actually living in Doughty Street while the devastation was going on. The Bedford property at Fig's Mead was developed, not without a proper dignity of its own, as small working-class properties with such imaginative enclosures as Ampthill and Oakley Squares, and the streets and railway sidings closed in across the fields. The population increased from under 600 in 1776 to over 10,000 in 1831.

It was in these surroundings that the Old Bedford Music Hall flourished in Camden Town High Street and was visited by Richard Sickert and the artists who with him formed the Camden Town Group. They included such men as Spencer Frederick Gore, Harold Gilman, and Robert Bevan. They painted what they saw and besides the poverty and restrictions they recognised the vitality and colour of the area. The Old Bedford has closed and that epitome of 1930s architecture, the Carreras Factory, has been ruined by a 1960s face-lift, but Richard Cobden's statue still stands at the junction of Hampstead Road and Eversholt Street, gazing benignly on the traffic.

Northward beside Camden Town tube station, stands a public house, the Mother Red Cap, which has held a licence since the 17th century though the building is of the 19th. Here, the road divides into three, all travelling northwards. The westernmost runs to Hampstead, the easternmost to Holloway and Islington, and the central path leads on, past the beautiful 18th century Grove Terrace, past Gospel Oak where a Victorian working-class village is being redeveloped into flats, to the northern height of Highgate. The southern section of this road, Kentish Town Road, is one of the most rewarding stretches in London in which to play the house-dating game (see p. 52) but no detailed description can be attempted as it is changing too fast.

The village of **Highgate** grew up around the building which stood on the site now occupied by the Gatehouse Tavern. Tolls were collected here from very early times from those wishing to use the Bishop of London's road across his park at Hornsey which led to Finchley. This was the High Gate which gave its name to the hamlet. Opposite it, on the Hornsey side, was a chapel and hermi-

tage, the sites of which have been replaced by Sir Roger Cholmley's "Free Grammar School" which is today still flourishing as
Highgate School. Behind the Gatehouse, which soon sold refreshment as well as collecting tolls, were the village green and the pond,
filled in in 1864 by which time it had become stagnant and un-
healthy, and on the far side was Lord Arundel's house. The property
was first developed by Sir William Cornwallis, who probably
received Queen Elizabeth there on her visits to Highgate in 1589,
1593 and 1594. In 1610 he sold the house to Thomas Howard, 2nd
earl of Arundel who stayed there regularly and kept a permanent
staff on the premises till he sold it in 1632. The earl was a Privy
Councillor, travelled abroad widely and collected those statues
known as the Arundel Marbles which he presented to the
University of Oxford. It was at his house that Sir Francis Bacon,
one of the most intellectual men England has ever nurtured, who
was disgraced in office as Lord Chancellor for the taking of bribes,
died. Apparently Sir Francis decided to stuff a dead chicken
purchased from a poor woman in Swain's Lane, to see whether
refrigeration would delay the process of decay. He caught a chill
while doing so and feeling too ill to return to his own chambers in
the Temple, asked for a bed at Arundel House. The housekeeper
received him willingly and warmed a bed with the warming-pan,
but it was one that had not been slept in for a year and needed a
more thorough airing. Sir Francis caught pneumonia and died in
the arms of his relation, Sir Julius Caesar, on April 9, 1626. Just
before his death, he dictated a letter to Arundel, saying that the
housekeeper was "very careful and diligent" and that "your Lordship's house was happy to me". In 1632 Arundel sold the estate to
Thomas Gardner, a governor of Highgate School, who was to lose
both his sons in the king's service during the Civil War, and during
the 1670s the house was divided into two properties. In 1691 Sir
William Ashurst, later Lord Mayor of London, bought the western
portion, pulled it down and rebuilt it as the Old Hall which is still
standing, and still used as private residences, having been most
skilfully converted into six flats.

East of the Old Hall, on Highgate Hill, which drops away so
steeply that its summit affords an astonishing view over London, is
Lauderdale House, surrounded by Waterlow Park. There was a
building on the site of Lauderdale House by the end of the 16th
century when it was occupied by Sir William Bond and it was he
with whom in 1611 the unhappy Lady Arabella Stuart was lodged
on her way to Durham to be kept as a prisoner by the bishop there.

Her only crime was to be next in succession to James I in the case of his lacking an heir and to have married Sir William Seymour without the king's consent. She stayed four days at Highgate and then escaped from her guards at East Barnet and managed to take ship for France, her husband having successfully fled from the Tower. But her ship was intercepted and the poor lady died mad, imprisoned in the Tower, some four years later.

In 1644 the house was bought by John Maitland, Earl of Lauderdale, who then spent several years in the Tower too, for his support of Charles II at the Battle of Worcester. While he was there, John Ireton, brother of Cromwell's son-in-law, occupied the house but the earl had it again at the Restoration and probably rebuilt it. Pepys certainly visited the earl there, and there may even be truth in the traditions that Nell Gwynne stayed there and that Andrew Marvell the poet had a country cottage just to the north of the main house, though his name never appears on the court rolls for the period. The house passed from owner to owner till it was at last bought by Sir Sydney Waterlow and with its grounds was made into a park, opened to the public in 1889, "to be a garden for those who are gardenless". The house suffered from fire in 1963 but is being restored and may be used as a local museum, while the terrace, with its astrolabe and the steps which lead down past a good herbaceous border to the lawns, falling away to two ponds filled with eager gabbling ducks, makes it one of the pleasantest places in London.

Opposite the park, on the Hornsey side of Highgate Hill are Cromwell House and Ireton House. Their connection with the Lord Protector and his son-in-law extends no further than the names, but the former is a fine example of an early 17th century dwelling— it was built in 1614 for the Sprignell family, merchants of London— and demonstrates the Dutch style which wealthy burghers preferred to the new-fangled Italian elegancies brought in by Inigo Jones and the court circle.

Opposite the Old Hall is The Grove, a terrace of late 17th and early 18th century houses. In No. 3 the poet and philosopher Samuel Taylor Coleridge lived with his friends, Dr and Mrs Gilman from 1819 till his death in 1834. He was at school at Christ's Hospital with Charles Lamb and then went on to Cambridge but got so heavily into debt that he enlisted in the 15th Dragoons. He was discovered and bought out by his brothers. The rest of his long life he spent dependent on the goodness of first one and then another of his friends, his brother-in-law Southey and Thomas and Josiah Wedgwood among them. In 1796 he began to take laudanum and in 1804 turned to opium, thereby weakening his will-power and constitution. In spite of everything, he wrote many poems, such as *The Ancient Mariner*, *Kubla Khan*, and *Christabel* which have become part of English literature, and he was renowned for his unfailing powers of conversation. He is buried in St Michael's Church, which stands beside the Old Hall.

St Michael's Church was built in 1830 on part of the grounds of Arundel House. It is a narrow brick building designed by Vulliamy, but inside is the most wonderful east window of The Last Supper, designed and created by Evie Hone in 1954. It is one of the most exciting examples of modern English stained glass to be seen near London and deserves to be better known. Behind the church, the hill falls away and on the slopes is Highgate Cemetery where Karl Marx was buried in 1883; he spent the last 27 years of his life in St Pancras, first at 46 Grafton Terrace and then at 41 Maitland Park Road and now his tomb has become a place of pilgrimage for Soviet citizens. In the same cemetery lie buried Mary Ann Evans (better known as the novelist George Eliot) Christina Rossetti, Michael Faraday, perhaps the greatest scientific genius who has ever lived, and the witty diarist, Henry Crabbe Robinson.

Below the parish church, down West Hill, is an enchanting 18th century group of houses, Holly Terrace, and below it the eastern side of the slope has been developed as the Holly Lodge Estate. Holly Lodge was the home of Angela Burdett-Coutts, daughter of Sir Francis Burdett and granddaughter of Thomas Coutts, the banker. This wonderful woman lavished her great wealth and spent her life in the service of the people of London, and in 1871 Queen Victoria made her a baroness in her own right in recognition of her work. When she died in 1906, her body lay in state and one small boy was taken by his nanny to pass by the bier and could still remember as an old man how the respectful crowd seemed to be mourning a queen and a mother

To the extreme west of Highgate, between it and Hampstead, is Kenwood House, one of the most beautiful mansions, both in design and in situation, to be found near London. A house was first built here by John Bill, the King's Printer, soon after 1616. He died in 1630 but the house remained in the possession of his family till the end of the century after which it passed through various hands till Lord Bute sold it in 1754 to William Murray, the future 1st earl of Mansfield, who in that year had become Attorney-General, and who two years later, was to be Lord Chief Justice. He had been a close friend of Pope's in the poet's closing years and it was he who pronounced the judgment declaring that the Negro slave, James Somersett, was a free man once in England. He also dismissed a case brought by an informer against a man alleged to be a Roman Catholic and to have said Mass. This tolerance incensed popular feeling against him and when the Gordon Riots (see p. 69) broke out in 1780, his house in Bloomsbury was attacked and set on fire, he and his wife escaping only moments before the conflagration. Part of the mob then determined to march to Kenwood and burn Mansfield's other dwelling but the landlord of the Spaniards Inn near to Kenwood plied the rioters so liberally with drink that they were apprehended or scattered by troops before they could do any damage. Thereafter, Lord Mansfield took a house in Lincoln's Inn Fields but eventually settled at Kenwood which had already been remodelled for him by his fellow Scot, Robert Adam, in the years following 1764. Here he retired, two nieces, the daughters of Lord Stormont, keeping house for him after his wife's death in 1784, and here he was visited by his great-nephews—he was childless—whom he addressed, since they were pupils at Westminster as he had been, as "school-fellows". Here he died peacefully in 1793. He was succeeded by his nephew who had been ambassador at the court of Louis XVI and Marie Antoinette, and who added the north wings and service blocks according to the designs of an otherwise little-known architect, George Saunders. The house remained in the possession of the family until the 6th earl decided to sell the estate for development after the First World War. By an enormous effort on the part of the London County Council, and the northern boroughs of London and the generosity of the Earl of Iveagh, Edward Cecil Guinness, the house and its grounds were saved and opened for the enjoyment of all.

The house stands, virtually unchanged, and is entered from the north front. The main rooms are the domed hall, the wonderful library—one of the finest rooms Adam ever designed—with a curved ceiling painted by Antonio Zucchi and apsidal ends, the orangery which balances the library, and the music room which Saunders added. The main living-rooms all face south and overlook the grounds which fall away to a lake across which a white mock bridge arches, and beyond which are woods. Highgate Hill rises up to the east. The original furniture has gone, but Lord Iveagh left his own collection of paintings to the house which include the wonderful full-length portrait of Mary, Countess of Howe, by Gainsborough, a Vermeer, *The Girl with the Virginals*, and a Rembrandt self-portrait. Today concerts are given beside the lake in the summer and poetry readings are held in the house, while the gardens on the north front have recently been greatly improved and a new literary relic has been imported—Doctor Johnson's summerhouse in which he sat and wrote in the gardens of Mr Thrale's hospitable house at Streatham. It was discovered and recognised though almost derelict, and was resurrected here in 1968 to give delight and perhaps inspiration to all who come here.

The road from Kenwood to **Hampstead** leads past the Spaniards Inn which has a beautiful, panelled room on the first floor. The road is narrow here, for opposite the Inn is an old toll-house which strong local sentiment has preserved and caused to be rebuilt and which acts as an excellent impediment to rashly speeding traffic. It is uncertain whether the Inn takes its name from the nationality of a former owner or from a Spanish Ambassador taking refuge in this area in time of plague. The road which links it with Hampstead has the appearance of a causeway, standing above the Heath whose trees fall away on either side, the southern slope affording a view right across to St Paul's dome and to the heights of Blackheath beyond. But the road was not built up on marshy ground; its raised level is due to the sand, of which the tops of Hampstead and Highgate Hills exist, being excavated by a rapacious lord of the manor, Sir Thomas Maryon Wilson. The manor had been granted in the 10th century by a certain Mangoda to Westminster Abbey and their tenure was confirmed in Domesday Book. At the Reformation, Henry VIII granted Hampstead to Sir Thomas Wrothe and Belsize to Sir Armigel Wade, the Governor of the Tower of London. Sir Thomas sold it to Sir Baptist Hickes, later Viscount Campden, whose descendants, the earls of Gainsborough, sold it in 1707 and it passed eventually into the hands of the Maryon Wilson family. Now the great and particular beauty of Hampstead is its Heath, over 800 acres of open land, one of London's most effective lungs. It had always been regarded as common land, though various tiny hamlets, such as the Vale of Health, had grown up in corners of it and one or two great houses—Pitt House, Heath House, Bell Moor—had been built on it. Sir Thomas Maryon Wilson determined to lay it out systematically in the 1860s and for the purpose began to build a road and a causeway across the ponds on the eastern slopes—the causeway is still there, below the Vale of Health, and adds to the picturesqueness of the scene. The residents of Hampstead prepared to defend their Heath to the end, by physical force if need be and certainly by law. Action was brought against Sir Thomas which made builders unwilling to take up leases, and when he died in 1868 his brother sold the Heath to the Metropolitan Board of Works for £47,000, and some years later, Parliament Hill Fields were bought, largely due to the efforts of Dame Octavia Hill, the housing reformer and founder member of the National Trust, for £302,000.

The Heath divides itself into three main sections. On the south side of The Spaniards is a broad path along which a fair is held three times a year, at Easter, Whitsun, and at the August Bank Holiday. It is primarily an amusement fair and had begun by 1712 when, as we shall hear, Hampstead was for a while a spa. It still flourishes today, with roundabouts, coconut shies, hoop-la and bumper cars, and delights crowds who come from far and near. The astonishing thing about the Heath is the speed with which calm and mystery return after the noise and bustle of the fair ceases and the litter is cleared away. Below the fairground is the Vale of Health and the Heath then stretches out to Hampstead and Highgate Ponds.

Between the arms of the Spaniards Road and North End Road lie the Paddock and Wildwood. This open space was not secured till 1925. At the intersection of the roads is a restrained war memorial and Heath House, built in the 18th century. Behind them, off the North End Road, stood Pitt House, where the elder Chatham passed some months in 1767–68, suffering from extreme nervous exhaustion. The house was destroyed by bombs and all that remains is one archway, standing beside a chestnut tree, which can be discovered by anyone who cares to search for it. On the opposite side of the road is the Hill garden, being the grounds of Lord Leverhulme's house, now part of the Manor House Hospital, which were acquired as an open space by the London County Council as recently as 1963. The garden has a brick-work arcade which in summer is entwined with wisteria and roses. Below the site of Pitt House stands the Bull and Bush, one of London's best loved and most frequented public houses, immortalised in Florrie Forde's song, *Come, Come, Come and Make Eyes at Me down at the Old Bull and Bush.* Behind it is Wildwood, and Wyldes Farm, which lie in Barnet where John Linnell the artist used to stay for country holidays, to which Dickens retired after Mary Hogarth's death, and where Sir Raymond Unwin, the architect of the Hampstead Garden Suburb, made his home. On the other side of the road is Golders Hill Park, its lawns carpeted with crocuses in springtime, and backing on to it is Anna Pavlova's house, which she used as the base for all her tours from 1912 to 1931.

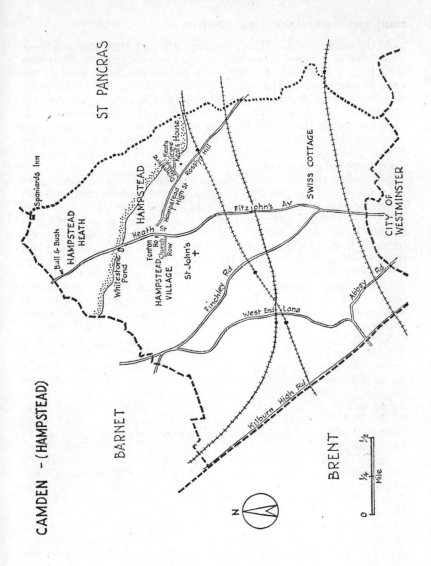

CAMDEN – (HAMPSTEAD)

ST PANCRAS

Spaniards Inn

Bull & Bush

HAMPSTEAD HEATH

Whitestone Pond

HAMPSTEAD HEATH

Keats House

Keats Grove

Rosslyn Hill

Hampstead High St.

Heath St.

Fenton Ho.

Church Row

HAMPSTEAD VILLAGE

St John's

Fitzjohn's Av

SWISS COTTAGE

CITY OF WESTMINSTER

Finchley Rd

West End Lane

Abbey Rd

BARNET

Kilburn High Rd

BRENT

N

0   ¼   ½
Mile

At the summit of the Heath is a flagstaff, 443 feet above sea level, and the White Stone Pond where early morning riders still water their horses, and children and their fathers sail boats later in the day. Donkey rides are to be had, and a Punch and Judy show plays most Sundays in fine weather. The old public house, Jack Straw's Castle, possibly named after one of Wat Tyler's followers who is said to have camped there with his men, has been given a new façade of what can only be described as Gothic weather-boarding, and behind the land falls away to West Heath, which varies from open tussocky grass to exciting woodland.

Just below the summit is Hampstead Grove, where George du Maurier lived from 1874 to 1895, and opposite it Fenton House, which belongs to the National Trust and is open daily excepting Tuesdays. It was built about 1693; the architect is unknown and the first owner whose name is recorded was a Mr Twysden. It took its name from a later owner, a merchant, Mr Fenton. It is a plain solid dignified William and Mary House, quite unromantic except for a pair of wrought-iron gates, so beautiful and so elaborate that they must have been worked by a pupil of Jean Tijou, if not by the master himself. The walled garden and orchard are delightful; the broad herbaceous border is invariably well-tended and stocked with great variety and some originality. Inside the house are two remarkable collections, the china and porcelain which, with some fine furniture, were presented by Lady Binning, and the keyboard musical instruments presented to the National Trust by the late Major George Henry Benton-Fletcher in 1937. There are harpsichords, clavichords, spinets and early pianos, all maintained in perfect order and practised upon by serious students. At any time of the day, one may be regaled with an impromptu concert at Fenton House, and formal entertainments are sometimes given in the evenings.

Beside Fenton House is a terrace where Joanna Baillie, the poetess and dramatist, passed happy and peaceful years from 1785 till her death in 1851, and opposite a white weather-boarded house where George Romney the artist lived at intervals. Near them is Admiral's House, where Admiral Mathew Barton resided till his death in 1795 and from the roof of which he used to fire a cannon at moments of suitable rejoicing. Constable painted it and in the 20th century, John Galsworthy the novelist and dramatist came to live in the house next door.

From the top of the Heath, narrow Heath Street leads down to the High Street which turns and runs down the southern slope of the hill until at last it reaches Chalk Farm and Camden Town. Heath Street is a curiously cosmopolitan area with some very smart dress shops and restaurants. Off it run little courts and alleyways—Money Yard, Golden Yard—too small to be shown on any but the largest scale of map but so picturesque that they are worth finding. They demonstrate that a hill top defies change—the same stability can be enjoyed on Highgate and Harrow Hills. The Mount, leading up to Mount Square, is the scene of Ford Madox Brown's great painting *Work*, now in the Manchester Art Gallery; the houses in the background are still there. Elm Row, Squire's Mount with a group of National Trust cottages, and Cannon Place with Cannon Lodge where a wonderful garden is often open to the public, are all worth discovering. Down Heath Street and the High Street, the game of trying to date each house and of looking above the shop front to see what was there before commerce overtook it, can be played with most satisfactory results.

At the end of Heath Street is Church Row, built in the late 17th and 18th centuries and when not blocked with cars, a remarkably peaceful and tree-lined place. Nos. 7 and 10 are particularly attractive. At the end is St John's Church, built in 1744–47, probably to the designs of John Sanderson. It is a strong, broad church with a sturdy tower and small spire. Below it is Frognal, where the houses range from the very early 18th century at the Old Mansion, through Norman Shaw's building for Kate Greenaway at No. 39 opposite University College School (1906–7), to No. 66, by Connell, Ward, and Lucas, which was the last word in advanced design in 1937, and to the comfortable modernity of No. 63 and a pretty little terrace, Nos. 27 to 29, designed by Dinerman in the 1950s, which demonstrates that an agreeable and commodious cottage can still be built.

Heath Street itself turns into Fitzjohn's Avenue—even Dame Octavia Hill was powerless to save this slope of the hill—which joins the Finchley Road at Swiss Cottage where in 1964 Sir Basil Spence built a new public library with a beautiful apsidal entrance. The whole site is being developed as a civic centre with a theatre. Camden is renowned for its libraries, for it possesses in Theobalds Road what is probably the most serviceably designed library in the whole country and another fine building has been opened on Euston Road. Just off Fitzjohn's Avenue is Maresfield Gardens, in which stands the new Roman Catholic church of St Thomas the Martyr. It is a circular church with seating arranged as in an amphitheatre.

At the start of Hampstead High Street is a turning, Flask Walk,

93

which ran down to a chalybeate spring. Its site is still marked by a stone drinking-fountain in Well Walk. At the beginning of the 18th century, this spring was almost as popular as that of Tunbridge Wells or even Bath and very much nearer to London. An assembly room was built, which has disappeared, and several fine houses, one of which, Burgh House, called after the musicologist and clergyman, Dr Allotson de Burgh, still stands and is agreeably used for meetings of local societies. The two public houses, the Flask Tavern and the Wells Hotel should be visited.

It was at No. 40 Well Walk that Constable took a country house, where he used to remove with his family and paint all summer, returning to town and Charlotte Street in winter. Lower down the High Street we pass the house where Clarkson Stanfield the artist lived, and the site of Sir Harry Vane's house. Vane was executed as a regicide in 1662, his house eventually became a school and was demolished in 1970. Lower down was Belsize House where Spencer Perceval the ill-fated Prime Minister, lived, and which later became a pleasure garden till it was built over in the late 19th century. Just above Chalk Farm a public house, the Sir Richard Steele, stands near the place where the essayist had a country cottage in which he took refuge when his creditors were too pressing, for not even the success of the periodicals *The Tatler* and *The Spectator*, which he edited in company with Addison, could keep him out of debt. It was in the latter periodical that the character Sir Roger de Coverley, created chiefly by Addison, appeared—"a gentleman of Worcestershire . . . very singular in his behaviour, but his singularities proceed from his good sense". At the foot of the hill is the Round House, built in the 1830s to designs by Stephenson and Robert Benson Dockray as an engine repair shed on the London to Birmingham line. It is a great piece of industrial architecture, a filigree of girders and arches all disciplined to serve a technological need as efficiently as possible.

One last house remains to be described in Hampstead—Keats House in Keats Grove off Downshire Hill. John Keats was born on October 31, 1795, probably at a livery stable in Finsbury, the Swan and Hoop, which belonged to his grandfather, John Jennings. He had two brothers, George and Tom, and a sister, Frances Mary. He went to the school of a Mr Clarke at Enfield whose son, Charles Cowden Clarke, was his lifelong friend. His father was killed by a fall from a horse and his mother died in 1810, whereupon John had to leave school and was apprenticed to a surgeon at Edmonton. In 1815 he became a student at the Medical School of Guy's and St

Thomas's Hospitals. He was attentive in his studies but had already begun to write poetry, some of which was seen by Leigh Hunt, who was then living in the Vale of Health. He encouraged the young man, who by this time had become a licensed apothecary, to devote himself to poetry and in April 1817 Keats and his brothers took lodgings in No. 1 Well Walk, in the cottage of Bentley the postman. The cottage has gone and the public house next door to it has been rebuilt, whilst the name has changed from the Green Man to the Wells Hotel. A month earlier Keats' first collection of poems had been published by Ollier Brothers but sold very poorly and received so much bad criticism that they regretted they had ever had anything to do with the author or his book. To a great extent, this criticism was due to the poet's association with Hunt, who had spent two years in prison when a younger man, for describing the Prince Regent as "a fat Adonis of fifty". Fortunately John Taylor of Taylor and Hessey recognised the young man's genius and wrote to his father: "I cannot think he will fail to become a great poet"; the firm agreed to become his publishers.

While he was living at Well Walk, Keats met Charles Wentworth Dilke and Charles Armitage Brown who had built themselves a pair of houses called Wentworth Place on a portion of what was then known as the Lower Heath quarter. In 1818 Brown and Keats set off on a walking tour of England and Scotland; after they had covered 642 miles, Keats' health broke down and he was advised to return home by a doctor. There is little doubt that the hardships of the march brought into life the consumption which was latent in his system and was already killing his brother Tom. Mrs Dilke welcomed him, fed him, and introduced him to a Mrs Brawne and her family to whom Brown had let the cottage while they were on the walking tour. Keats fell in love with the eldest daughter, Fanny, who was then 18. When Brown returned, the Brawnes took lodgings only a few minutes away on the corner of Downshire Hill and Rosslyn Hill. Keats returned to Well Walk where, on the night of December 1, 1818, poor Tom died. Brown, like a true friend, immediately begged him to leave his gloomy lodgings and to live with him, and Keats agreed, saying "I think it would be best". The following April, Dilke moved to Westminster and the Brawnes took his house, so that Keats and Fanny were living next door to each other and sharing a garden. That summer they became engaged to be married.

That year must have been the happiest in his life. During it he wrote five of his six great odes—*To a Nightingale* (actually written in the garden of Wentworth Place), *On a Grecian Urn*, *On Melancholy*, *To Psyche*, and *On Indolence* as well as *The Eve of St Agnes*, *La Belle Dame sans Merci*, *Lamia* and some sonnets. He prepared his final volume for the press but went into London in February 1820 and deceived by a thaw after cold weather, left off his heavy coat and was chilled returning home on the top of the coach. That night he had a slight haemorrhage. His medical training and the experience of nursing a consumptive brother left in him no doubt as to the malady; in Brown's words: "Before his head was on the pillow he slightly coughed and I heard him say 'That is blood from my mouth.' I went towards him; he was examining a single drop upon the sheet. 'Bring me a candle, Brown, and let me see this blood.' After regarding it steadfastly, he looked up into my face with a calmness of countenance I can never forget and said 'I know the colour of that blood—it is arterial blood—I cannot be deceived in that colour—that drop of blood is my death-warrant—I must die.' I ran for a surgeon; my friend was bled; and at five in the morning I left him after he had been for some time in a quiet sleep."

That spring, Brown went to Scotland again and Keats went to stay with Leigh Hunt, but his son Thornton Hunt opened a letter from Fanny by mistake and Keats went to stay with Mrs Brawne, once again in Wentworth Place. William Hone the antiquary saw him on a seat at the end of Well Walk "sitting and sobbing his dying breath into a handkerchief" and Coleridge, meeting the young man out walking, pressed his hand and remarked afterwards to his companion, "There is death in that hand." His doctors told him that he must winter in Italy and John Taylor, who had just published the third volume of Keats' poems, provided the money for the journey. His friend Joseph Severn accepted the task of accompanying him and Fanny Brawne prepared his clothes and lined his travelling cap with silk. He left Wentworth Place on September 13, 1820 and reached Naples after a hard voyage on October 21, from whence he wrote his last letter to Mrs Brawne ending it "Good bye Fanny! God bless you!" He died at Rome on February 23, 1821, brave to the end. His last words to Severn were "Severn—Severn—lift me up—I am dying—I shall die easy, don't be frightened—be firm and thank God it has come." And then "he gradually sank into a death so quiet that I thought he still slept". He was buried in Rome with an epitaph of his own choosing—"Here lies one whose name was writ in water."

In 1925 the houses in Wentworth Place were purchased as a Memorial to the poet who by this time was recognised as one of the greatest figures of English Literature and are open daily, free of charge, to the public. They had previously (1838–39) been converted into one house by the actress, Eliza Chester. In the collection are letters by the poet, portraits of himself and his friends, personal relics such as his notebook when a medical student, locks of his hair, books which he owned and first editions of his works. Fanny's engagement ring, an almandine set in gold, is here, as are her needlecase, scissors, the embroidery she was engaged upon when she died, her needle still in it, and a piece of silk which may be a fragment of the stuff with which she lined her sick fiancé's travelling cap. Fanny married a Mr Louis Lindon and was happy enough, but to the day of her death she wore the engagement ring Keats had given to her when they lived next door to each other in Wentworth Place.

EALING

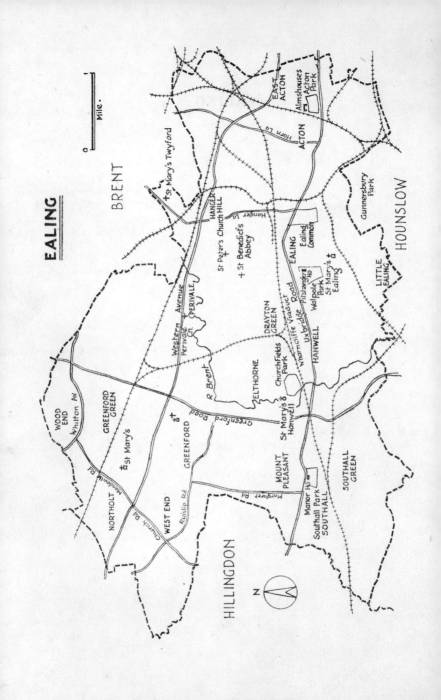

EALING

BRENT

HOUNSLOW

HILLINGDON

N

Mile.

Wood End
Whitton Av
Mandeville Rd
NORTHOLT
Church Rd
St Mary's
GREENFORD GREEN
WEST END
Ruislip Rd
GREENFORD
Greenford Road
Western Avenue
Perivale Ct. PERIVALE
R. Brent
ELTHORNE
St Mary's Twyford
HANGER
Hanger La
St Peter's Church Hill
✝ St Benedict's Abbey
DRAYTON GREEN
Churchfields Park
Wharncliffe Viaduct
Uxbridge Road
St Mary's Hanwell
HANWELL
MOUNT PLEASANT
Margaret Rd
Manor Ho
Southall Park
SOUTHALL
SOUTHALL GREEN
EALING
Ealing Common
Pitshanger Park
Walpole Ho
St Mary's Ealing
LITTLE EALING
ACTON
HORN LA
EAST ACTON
Almshouses Acton Park
Gunnersbury Park

EALING

The London Borough of Ealing lies to the north-west of the Greater London area. It consists of the former boroughs of Ealing (which latterly included the urban districts of Hanwell and Greenford and the parish of Northolt), Acton, and Southall, the whole covering nearly 20 square miles with, in 1965, a population of 303,660. There is high ground to the north at Horsenden Hill which slopes down to the River Brent at Greenford. Another ridge running from Castle Bar to Hanger Hill slopes southward to the Thames. The Brent runs through Perivale and Hanwell to join the Thames at Brentford. The borough's boundaries are Harrow and Brent on the north, Hammersmith to the east, Hounslow to the south and Hillingdon to the west.

Ealing, which has given its name to the whole modern borough, has been a favourite residential area near to London since the 18th century, when its proximity to the Court at Kew and the residences of Princess Amelia at Gunnersbury House and the Duke of Kent, Queen Victoria's father, at Castle Hill House, gave it great dignity. By 1900, it was so popular that it was known as the "Queen of the Suburbs", but its history, like that of its neighbour, Acton, is a long one, for its name probably comes from that of a 7th century tribe, the Gillings or "people of Gilla", who lived in the area. It gets no separate mention in Domesday Book, however, as it was then a part of the Bishop of London's huge manor of Fulham, though Hanwell, West Twyford, Greenford, and Northolt are all mentioned. Throughout the Middle Ages, the old custom of "Borough English" law persisted here, whereby the youngest rather than the eldest son inherited the main property, it being assumed that he was the least able to fend for himself.

Today, approaching by Hanger Lane, we come first to the expanse of Ealing Common which, even though crossed by busy roads still seems a silent piece of heathland. To the west of it is Ealing, its excellent main shopping street, the Broadway, strung out along the main road to Uxbridge. In the Broadway the eye is drawn to the pinnacled fantasy building of the Town Hall designed by Charles Jones, Borough Surveyor from 1863 to 1913—a notable local figure.

The older part of Ealing lies south of the Broadway stretching from The Green to St Mary's Road. The parish church, St Mary's, is at the far end. The mediaeval building was replaced in the 18th century by a neat little Georgian church, which was demolished in 1866 to make way for a heavy building with a clumsy tower, designed by S. S. Teulon. The interior has more dignity and an excellent set of parish rooms has been added in the last few years. One brass, a fine one to a merchant, Richard Amondesham (d. *c.* 1490) and his wife, survives from the old church, and there is a bronze tablet to John Horne Tooke, the clergyman who became a radical politician, and was buried in this churchyard "contented and grateful" as his tombstone says. Mrs Sarah Trimmer, who died in 1810, lies here too; she was an exceptionally well-educated woman who founded a Sunday school at Brentford where she lived, abridged the Old and New Testaments for the Society for Promoting Christian Knowledge, wrote instructive books for children, and usually carried a copy of Milton's poems in her pocket so that, when in the company of Doctor Johnson, she heard him arguing with a friend about some lines in *Paradise Lost*, she was able to settle the dispute and thus began a long friendship with the great man

Walking back towards The Broadway, we may notice two exceptionally pretty houses, formerly part of the workhouse, built sideways to the road opposite the parish church, and we then come to the new Technical College and to Ealing Studios where so many good films and especially comedies have been made. Beyond the Studios are several attractive Georgian houses and then we reach Pitshanger House. Today it houses the public library, but it was begun in 1770 by George Dance for his father-in-law, Thomas Gurnell, who lived there till his death in 1785. It was afterwards bought by the architect, Sir John Soane, who pulled it down excepting for the two best rooms in the south wing (now the Reference Library and Newspaper Room) and rebuilt it to his own design. He sold it again in 1810 and subsequent owners altered it considerably till in 1844 it was purchased for the unmarried daughters of the Right Honourable Spencer Perceval. The last lady died in 1900, the house became a library, and its grounds a park, one of the most delightful to be found in the London area, with a water garden and many old carved seats. Ealing is most fortunate in its parks, for in addition to Walpole Park where Pitshanger House stands—the Walpole and Perceval families were linked by marriage and were pillars of local society—there are Lammas Park, Ravenor Park, and Haven Green, all well laid out and stocked with flowers.

The connection of the Perceval family with Ealing lasted nearly a century. It began when Spencer Perceval, who later became Prime Minister, bought a house called Elm Grove or Hicks-on-the-Heath in 1808, and lived there with his wife and 12 children till he was shot in the lobby of the House of Commons on May 11, 1812 by a merchant called John Bellingham, who had gone bankrupt and felt aggrieved against the government. His family remained at Elm Grove and when his widow remarried, his daughters moved to Pitshanger House. This curious name come from *hangra*, a wooded slope, and *pyffel*, a kind of hawk.

Many famous people are connected with Ealing through Great Ealing School which flourished from the early 18th century till 1908, originally on a site now covered by Ranelagh Road. Mr Pierce was the first headmaster, followed by Dr Shury, and the school reached its peak of fame under the Rev. Dr George Nicholas and his sons, 1789–1858. Cardinal Newman and his brother, William Makepeace Thackeray and Frederick Marryat the writers, Richard Westmacott the sculptor, Sir George MacFarren the blind composer, the soldiers Sir Robert Sale and the brave brothers Lord Lawrence and Sir Henry Lawrence who fought and suffered in the Indian Mutiny, were all pupils there. On the staff at various times, were the exiled Louis-Philippe, King of France, who taught geography, and George Huxley who taught mathematics. He was the father of the wonderful scientist Thomas Huxley who also studied at the school as a boy and who went on to become President of the Royal Society. A rival school was kept by Doctor Samuel Goodenough, Bishop of Carlisle, who lived at Ealing. The flower Goodenia was named after him for he was a great lover of plants.

Another school flourished on the east side of Haven Green, under the Rev. Charles Wallington, and there Bulwer Lytton, the future novelist, was a pupil. Thomas Dibdin, the writer, author of that splendid song *Tom Bowling*, lived off Hanger Lane, and at Ealing Park, formerly Place House, the gardens were renowned when Sir William Lawrence, the surgeon, lived there. They were his wife's creation and were visited by Queen Victoria, probably in 1895. It is today a Roman Catholic girls' school, and another such school has occupied Rochester House, once the home of Thomas Pearce and his son Zachary (1690–1774) who became Bishop of Rochester and after whom the house is named. It was later the dwelling of Dumouriez, the French Revolutionary General who made his home in the country against which he had once fought. The residence in Ealing of Charles Blondin, the tightrope walker, is commemorated in the names of two streets, Blondin and Niagara Avenues.

Ealing's most important house, Castle Hill House, has gone, demolished in 1821. Mrs Fitzherbert had lived there and it had been the home of the Duke of Kent, Queen Victoria's father. On his marriage, he tried, unsuccessfully, to dispose of the house by public lottery. Kent House was built on the site by General Sir George Wetherall, whose father, Sir Frederick, had been the Duke's aide-de-camp. The site is now occupied by St David's Home for soldiers disabled in either world war.

There are several churches in Ealing well worth visiting either for their associations or their architectural qualities. In The Broadway stands Christ Church, built by Miss Lewis in memory of her father, William Thomas Lewis the actor, to designs by Sir George Gilbert Scott in 1852. The church has a fine spire and the nave walls are adorned with paintings of angels. The Church of the Ascension on the Hanger Hill Estate, by Lord Mottistone and Paul Paget, is a good piece of work, being very light and plain and bracing in its simplicity, and then in Mount Park Road there is St Peter's, designed by J. D. Sedding in 1893 and completed after his death by his pupil, H. Wilson. This is a most exciting church in which a traditional 14th century Gothic style is revitalised by Art Nouveau. There is a huge west window divided by buttresses and a very spacious interior with low wide arches carrying galleries. The plain rectory beside it is a delight to the eye, with St Peter's keys and fishes carved over the door, and the church is renowned for the quality of its children's services. Finally, there is St Benedict's in Charlbury Grove, the first Roman Catholic abbey to be founded in England since the Reformation. The building, by Frederick Walters, is beautiful, all of golden stone with a broad flight of steps leading to the entrance. The vast interior is golden too, and there is a spirited mosaic of the martyrdom of St Boniface.

Ealing's neighbour to the east is **Acton**, whose name means "the farm by the oak trees", and an oak is still the main symbol on the arms of the new borough. Although today Acton seems mainly a factory land, stretching from the grid-iron estate of Park Royal to Acton Vale where the saw-toothed workshop roofs of the C.A.V. diesel engine factory cut across the skyline, it is in fact an immensely old place, far older than its Saxon name, for in 1885 a whole Stone Age workshop was found where Creffield Road now is. Some 600 worked flints, now in the British Museum, were collected—spear heads, axes, drills and awls—so there is a long manufacturing tradition here! Besides the workshop, a Bronze Age crematorium was found in 1883 at Avenue Gardens in Mill Hill Park.

Acton is not mentioned in Domesday Book for, like Ealing, it was part of the manor of Fulham, but a part of it later belonged to St Paul's Cathedral who established a foundation, Berrymead Priory, here. St Paul's surrendered it to the Crown in 1544 and it was granted first to Lord Russell and then to the Earl of Worcester, and the priory was used as a secular dwelling house till the remains of it were, during this century, incorporated in the Constitutional Club in Salisbury Street. The building is now the Social Club of Neville's Bakery.

Acton really flourished from the 16th century onwards. It was a busy little village, on the road to Oxford and yet most conveniently near to London. When Charles I, whose headquarters were at the university, was advancing on London after the battle of Edgehill, his forces engaged the Parliamentarian troops at Brentford, took the town (see p. 260) and went on to fight another sharp engagement at Acton but were turned back by the solid resistance of the London trained bands at Turnham Green. When Cromwell defeated the king's son at Worcester on September 3, 1651, he came back to London by way of Acton and was met there by 300 triumphant coachloads of gentlemen—the Lord Mayor, the Aldermen, his Council of State, and Members of Parliament. His second-in-command, General Philip Skippon, made his home at Acton House in Horn Lane (now demolished), and his wife was buried in Acton Church. The learned and beloved vicar of Acton, Daniel Featley, was replaced by the Puritan Philip Nye, who was famous for his extreme religious views and for his broad bushy beard.

After the Civil War, Acton continued to be a popular place in which to live, and two of the most learned men in England made their homes there and became neighbours and friends. They were the non-conformist divine, Richard Baxter, of whom Dr Johnson said that all his writings were good, and Sir Matthew Hale, a judge and Lord Chief Baron of the Exchequer. When Baxter was in trouble for his religious views, Sir Matthew defended him, and when the judge died, the divine edited and published his writings post-humously. The Midland Bank in Acton High Street stands on the site of Baxter's House.

About 1750, it was realised that the wells in Acton had excellent mineral properties, and a little spa began to flourish. At Fordhook, where Fordhook Avenue now stands, one of our earliest and best novelists took a house. He was Henry Fielding, the author of *Tom Jones* and *Amelia*, the former being one of the liveliest works in our literature. Fielding was also a magistrate and with his half-brother, Sir John Fielding, the "Blind Beak", did much to stamp out robber-gangs in London. He suffered terribly from asthma and was advised to seek relief in the warmer climate of Portugal. He was bitterly loath to leave Fordhook and his children, but at length he and his wife obeyed the doctors and he made the voyage only to die two months later in Lisbon. Some years later, the house was occupied by Lady Byron after her divorce, and it was in the drawing-room that Ada, the only child of that unhappy marriage, was wedded to the Earl of Lovelace. Another fine house which remains and is today Twyford School, is The Elms, built by Sir Joseph Ayloffe, the antiquarian, in the early 18th century. It was subsequently occupied by Mr Wegg, a local benefactor, and by James Shoolbred, the founder of that splendidly elegant Edwardian dress house in the Tottenham Court Road.

The parish church of St Mary's is in the centre of the town. It is an unlovely building, designed in 1865 by Messrs Francis, though there has been a church on this site since the early 13th century. There is one brass, to Henry Cavell (d. 1544) transferred from the old church, and Elizabeth Barry the actress (d. 1713), Sir Robert Adair the surgeon, John Lindley the botanist (d. 1865) and the Rev. William Antrobus, rector at Acton for 55 years, are all buried here. The ancient altar stone was rediscovered a few years ago; it has now been repolished and rests in the church. The most exciting church in Acton is St Aidan's which is Roman Catholic; it was rebuilt in 1961 to a design by A. J. Newton and it should be a place of pilgrimage for all those who love art and believe that the works of the 20th century can hold their place beside the work of former generations. There is a Crucifixion by Graham Sutherland over the altar, perspex figures of the Evangelists and the Holy Spirit as well as the Stations of the Cross by Arthur Fleischmann, two superb triptychs by Roy de Maistre, and stained glass by Pierre Fourmaintraux (made at the Whitefriars Glass Works at Harrow) which all need to be seen and studied—seen to uplift the spirit and studied to trace the history of the Catholic Church in England.

A handsome establishment was set up at Derwentwater House by the young Earl of Derwentwater and his bride in 1714, but a year later he took part in the Old Pretender's Rebellion against George I, and in 1716 was beheaded for it. His widow raised an obelisk in his memory which today stands in Acton Park, a place remarkable for its herbaceous borders and for its collection of children's climbing frames, possibly the most varied and ingenious in London for they include a parabolic ladder and a tubular rocket. Beside the park stand the Goldsmiths' Company Almshouses, built in 1811. They are most picturesque buildings with two huge cedar trees in the gardens. They have now been fully modernised and beside them is Goldsmiths' Close, built in 1956, in conjunction with Acton Borough Council.

On the outskirts of Acton lies the finest of her remaining houses, Gunnersbury Park. The property takes its name from Canute's niece, Gunyld, who held it in the 11th century. It then passed to various owners but about 1375 it was bestowed by Edward III on his mistress, Alice Perrers. It is doubtful whether the lady ever lived there, and in the middle of the 17th century the estate was bought by Sergeant Maynard, "the ablest advocate and soundest lawyer of his time". He had prosecuted Laud and Strafford, been Protector's Sergeant to Cromwell, King's Sergeant to Charles II, and a Commissioner of the Great Seal to William III. So great a man of law was he that no government could do without him. He employed John Webb, Inigo Jones' nephew-in-law and pupil, to build him a house there and lived in it till he died, aged 90, in 1690.

In 1761, the property was purchased by Princess Amelia, George II's daughter, who entertained here till she died in 1786. Soon afterwards, the house was pulled down and two villas, Gunnersbury Park and Gunnersbury House, were built side by side for different owners but in 1835 the main estate was purchased by Nathan Rothschild and after 1889 the two houses belonged to one owner. The banker kept a fine establishment here and it was in the library that he promised financial support to Disraeli to purchase the lease of the Suez Canal. After his death, his son Lionel lived here till his death in 1917 and in 1925 the house and gardens were purchased by the local council. The house is today a museum where the Sadler Collection of prehistoric flint instruments can be seen, as well as a reconstruction of the Saxon manor house at Northolt (see p. 113) and there are historical costumes and carriages and much fascinating domestic equipment, including linen presses and goffering irons. The grounds, which fall away from the houses, are beautifully laid out and maintained with several old archways, erected for their picturesque effect, through which Princess Amelia must have walked, and a little lake, now used for children's boating, beside which is a temple, the last remains of the house that John Webb built for Sergeant Maynard.

Just north of Acton, on the very borders of the borough, is **Twyford**, for many years the smallest place in Middlesex but with a very fine church. In the 1861 census, only two houses and 18 inhabitants are reported as being there. The name comes from the two fords that cross the Brent nearby, and it is still the nearest place to London where there is need for the sign *Beware cattle crossing*. The church dates from the 16th century but stands on the site of older buildings, while in 1958 a new church was added to the old, making St Mary's Twyford a most arresting construction. The old church leads out of the new, and one modern east window, with the Virgin and Child, serves the two. The altar stands at the junction with an arch behind it so that the old church is visible. There are several interesting monuments in the old church. The earliest is to Adriana Gifford (d. 1601), granddaughter of that John Lyon who founded Harrow School and who held Twyford Manor in Elizabeth I's day; she is shown with her four sons and her four daughters. Then there are busts of Robert Moyle (d. 1639) and his son Walter (d. 1660). Robert is shown wearing a hat—unusual in church but a mark of his legal office because he was one of the Chief Clerks of the Court of Common Pleas. Walter died most pitifully of grief at the death of his "little sonne" who lies by the sacristry door that connects the old and new churches. Fabian Philips (d. 1690), who wrote a defence of Charles I, is buried here with his baby son, another Fabian, and an adult son, Andrew, whose wife described him on his monument as the "best of husbands".

The manor house, which stands just by the church, is called Twyford Abbey though there never has been an abbey here. It was built in 1808 by P. Atkinson for Thomas Willan, who had kept the largest farm in Middlesex, covering most of what is today Regent's Park and St John's Wood. When the park was about to be laid out, Willan moved to Twyford. The house today is the property of a Roman Catholic nursing order, the Alexian Brotherhood.

West of Ealing lies **Hanwell**, an attractive place beside the River Brent. In earlier times, it was a tiny village, famous for its watercresses; today, its most noticeable feature is the Wharncliffe Viaduct, designed by Brunel and constructed in 1838, which carries the Great Western Railway over the river. The viaduct is called after the company chairman, Lord Wharncliffe, and bears his arms on the southern side. The view from it is so fine that Queen Victoria always instructed her engine-driver to cross it slowly so that she might have time to savour the prospect. On the Hanwell side is St Mary's Church, built in 1841 by Sir George Gilbert Scott, its nave walls decorated by William Frederick Yeames who is more famous for his dramatic painting *And When Did You Last See Your Father?* Earlier churches stood on the site—Hanwell is mentioned in Domesday Book and it belonged to Westminster Abbey throughout the Middle Ages. An elegant monument has been retained; it is to Margaret Emma Orde (d. 1806) and is by P. M. van Gelder.

In the crypt is buried Jonas Hanway; we remember that he was the first man to carry an umbrella in England, though his wide philanthropy is forgotten. Born at Portsmouth, he became partner to a Russian merchant and travelled with a caravan of woollen goods to Persia. His caravan was plundered at Astrabad, though most of its value was restored to him through the intervention of the Shah. On the return journey, his ship was attacked by pirates, but he reached the Russian capital safely and, learning that money had been left to him, returned to England, published an account of his journeyings, and spent the rest of his life in working for good causes —the improvement of London's roads, the training of naval recruits, the protection of boy sweeps, and the establishment of Sunday Schools. He visited workhouses and poor districts to obtain facts about the high death rate among the children of the poor, and by his influence an Act was passed through Parliament providing that they should be brought up away from workhouses until they were six.

St Mary's stands on the edge of Churchfields, a lovely windswept open hillside which is preserved as a park. Two other parks adjoin it, Brent Lodge Park, where once stood the house of Dr Hume, Wellington's medical man who accompanied him on his campaigns, and which is laid out in a particularly pleasant and varied manner with a walled herbaceous garden; and Connolly Dell at the foot of the viaduct and full of rhododendrons. The park is named in memory of John Connolly, the second principal of Hanwell Asylum (now St Bernard's Hospital), who treated the insane with the same gentleness and humanity which his predecessor, the founder, Dr Ellis, had used.

Like Acton, Hanwell has prehistoric associations. In Elthorne Park, there is a three-ton polished boulder, found originally in Townholme Crescent near Boston Road, which was brought down from the north during the Ice Age, and indicates the southern limit of the glaciers. There was probably a primitive settlement near the site of the parish church, and in 1886, where Oaklands School now stands in Grove Avenue, seven Saxon warriors were found, their skeletons still wrapped in their cloaks which were fastened with brooches. They must have been killed in some affray, and the tradition must have been passed down, though the bodies lay there forgotten, for the place was always called Blood Field locally until it was built over.

On the edge of Elthorne Park in Boston Road is St Thomas's Church, designed by Edward Maufe, the architect of Guildford Cathedral. It is in concrete and contains sculpture by Eric Gill, as well as the reredos and organ from the demolished church of St Thomas in Portman Square. Two other local churches are St Melitus, dedicated to the first bishop of London, where there is a stained-glass window to a Boy Scout who died trying to save two people from drowning in the Brent, and Our Lady and St Joseph, a new Roman Catholic church with a high-pitched roof and a very spirited large sculpture which shows St Joseph as the kind and understanding man he must have been.

South-west of Hanwell are **Southall** and **Norwood**. The two have always been associated and the families which dwelt in Southall's manor house were buried, when their time came, in the church at Norwood. Both the manor house and the church still survive. The house dates basically from 1587—the date is over the door—when it was built by Richard Awsiter, but he in his turn may have only added to a building nearly a century older called Wrenns. The house was greatly enlarged in the 19th century, and is now being completely restored for civic functions. It is interesting to compare the brickwork of the central Elizabethan chimney with that of the four later ones on the corners. The gardens have become a park, and in the park is a fountain of the glazed stoneware pottery known as Martinware which was beautifully wrought by the four Martin brothers who worked in Havelock Road between 1877 and 1923.

Southall manor tended to be held for long periods by the same family. In 1339 it belonged to the Shoredyches who sold it about 1510 to the Chesemans and went to live at Ickenham where they were still flourishing in the late 19th century! Edward Cheseman was cofferer to Henry VII and Robert his son served Henry VIII and was painted by Holbein. The manor then passed to the Awsiters—an 18th century Dr John Awsiter discovered the health-giving properties of seawater, thus being responsible for the pros-

perity of Brighton. They retained the manor house but were replaced in importance locally by the Merricks. Members of all these
families lie in Norwood Church which retains its 13th century
chancel though it dates chiefly from Archbishop Chichele's rebuilding in the 15th. Edward Cheseman's helmet hangs over his
tomb, and there is a life-size figure of John Merrick reclining on a
sarcophagus besides brasses to Matthew Hunsley and Francis
Awsiter. There is a tablet to Antony Hinton who ministered here
for over 63 years and whose name is on the weather vane on the
gable. Norwood's greatest treasure is a window of 16th century
glass with Our Lady and the Child who holds a toy windmill.

Near the church is a good broad green with a fine Georgian house
on the east side. In 1790 there were only 40 houses in Norwood but
later it became a brick-making area and the bricks for Buckingham
Palace were made from the clay of these fields. Near the bridge
which crosses the railway are two pretty public houses, The Lamb
and The Wolf, which confront each other cautiously.

North-east, just off Western Avenue, is **Perivale,** though whether
its name is a corruption of the "pure vale" or whether it comes from
the perry that was made from the pears which once grew there, is
uncertain. Until Western Avenue swept through it in the 1920s, it
was a tiny hamlet with a church, a rectory, a manor house which
had belonged to Henry Colet, Dean Colet's father, and five good
farms. To the north rises Horsenden Hill, 273 feet high, today a
closely preserved open space, a splendid piece of unspoilt countryside, and near it is a wood which is the bird sanctuary of the Selborne
Society.

Today, the well-planned Hoover factory and other buildings of
the same kind have replaced the farms, the manor house has gone
and the rectory was demolished in 1958, but the church is still
there, tiny—about 60 feet long—and so old that its original dedication is uncertain, though it was probably to St Mary the Virgin and
is so called today. It is built of flint and rubble with a white weatherboarded 16th century tower—a most unusual and arresting feature.
The body of the church dates from the 13th and 15th centuries.
Inside there is a fine 15th century roof with kingposts, some stained
glass and a font of the same date. The font has an oaken cover with
a pinecone finial, which in 1665 was the gift of Simon Coston, a
local worthy whose ghost is still said to haunt the neighbourhood.
The east window is modern and the reredos is a war memorial.
There is a tiny brass to Henry Myllet (d. 1505) who lived in the

manor house, with his two wives and their 16 children, and a lovely memorial by Richard Westmacott to young Ellen Nicholas who died after three months of agonising illness in 1815. She was the grand-daughter of that Dr Nicholas who founded Great Ealing School, at which the sculptor had been a pupil.

A mile away is **Greenford** (Perivale was originally called Greenford Parva), another tiny ancient village which swelled up in the present century. It is first mentioned in a charter of 845 when Abbot Werhard exchanged lands with Weremberht of Hroces Seath (Roxeth near Harrow). In 1593 Norden described it as "a very fertile place of corn", but today the only reminder of its past agricultural prosperity is a 17th century weatherboarded barn at Greenford Green Farm. The 15th century church remains, however, and has been joined by a 20th century building which is fully worthy to stand beside its older sister. They are both dedicated to the Holy Cross. The old church is of flint and dressed stone and the chancel was rebuilt in the 17th century. There is some fine glass which came from the Provost's Lodge of King's College, Cambridge, and includes the arms of Henry VIII and Katharine of Aragon and a lovely little windmill. There is a superb candelabrum and three brasses—all to past rectors—Simon Hart (d. 1450), Thomas Symons (d. c. 1521), and William Henry Ogle-Skan who died only in 1915. The effigy of Michael Gardiner (d. 1630) kneels opposite a figure of his wife, and there is a monument to Simon Coston (d. 1637) in which his widow Bridget kneels, holding her baby son John, below her her daughters—Frances, Mary, Jane, Anne, and Philadelphia—and above her is her dead husband, his cheek on his hand, looking down on those he has left, as if from a window. Frances gave the church its lovely font with a carved cover.

The new church, designed by Sir Albert Richardson in 1939, is very exciting indeed. It has an enormous barnlike interior with a very steep open timber roof and wooden posts to separate the aisles from the nave. There is a good collection of modern embroidered banners.

In the middle of Greenford's modern shopping centre is a new Catholic church, designed by David Stokes in 1961 and dedicated to Our Lady of the Visitation. Inside it has parabolic arches and rainbow glass.

North-east of Greenford is **Northolt**, another tiny place that changed very little from its description in Domesday Book till the

Upminster: the smock windmill

Upminster: the tithe-barn

Rainham Hall, Rainham

Canonbury Tower, Islington

Syon House, Isleworth, from the south-east

Syon House: the Long Gallery

Kenwood House, Hampstead: an interior vista

Chiswick House: the White Hall

1930s. Domesday tells us that it had belonged to Ansgar, the Portreeve of London, who fought at Hastings, was carried wounded from the field, and recovered to negotiate the city's peace with the Conqueror. In 1354, the manor was held by Sir Thomas Holland, and it was his widow Joan, the Fair Maid of Kent, who married her cousin, Edward the Black Prince, whom she had loved since childhood, and became the mother of Richard II. By 1374, the manor was in the possession of Sir Nicholas Brembre, who stood beside Richard when he confronted Wat Tyler at Smithfield and who became Lord Mayor as the king's man in 1388 and lost his head for his support of his monarch. One wonders whether the local connection had any significance. The manor house itself lay just behind the church and has recently been excavated. It is an exceptionally interesting site, for there had been a house here since 1300, and earlier burials and remains showed that the place had been in use in Saxon times, as early as AD 700.

Northolt was built over with little houses in the 1920s and '30s, excepting for its small aerodrome (actually over the border in Hillingdon) used today for the arrival of important personages; as one passes by, the aeroplanes gleam silver against the grass. All that remains of the old village is its green and its church, St Mary's, which is built of flint and stone and rubble and dates from about 1300. The windows have carved foliage and there is a mediaeval bell-turret, a 15th century piscina and roof, and a Georgian gallery. The font was the gift of the unlucky Sir Nicholas; the Brembre arms are carved on it. There are brasses to Henry Rowdell (d. 1452), to the rector, Isaiah Burcs (d. 1560), and to Susan Gyfforde who had had 12 children before she died in childbed at the age of 30. Dr Demainbray, astronomer at the Royal Observatory at Kew for nearly 60 years in the 18th century, lies in the churchyard and there is a tablet, recently placed in the church, to Gronow Owen who was curate here for two years, but is famous as a Welsh master poet and prose writer who, in the 18th century, made plain the ancient beauty and dignity of his country's language. George Borrow called him the last of the great poets of Cambria. He was a tinker's son who, in spite of a drunken father, managed to get a schooling and made his way to Oxford. He became a curate and married at 24, but unhappily he suffered not only from ill health but from a craving for drink. To save him from this, he was sent to Virginia as a schoolmaster, but he lost his school after three years and was appointed minister of a church where he at last made good; he died in 1769. His poetry is still read and loved today.

E

Beside the church there are the open playing fields of Northolt school, and opposite, in front of it, is an unspoilt green with a nice public house, The Crown. There is a little fragrant garden of rest, where two old cottages have been preserved and serve as toolsheds, and nearby is a new Roman Catholic church, dedicated to St Bernard in 1965 and designed by Messrs Scott and Jaques.

ENFIELD

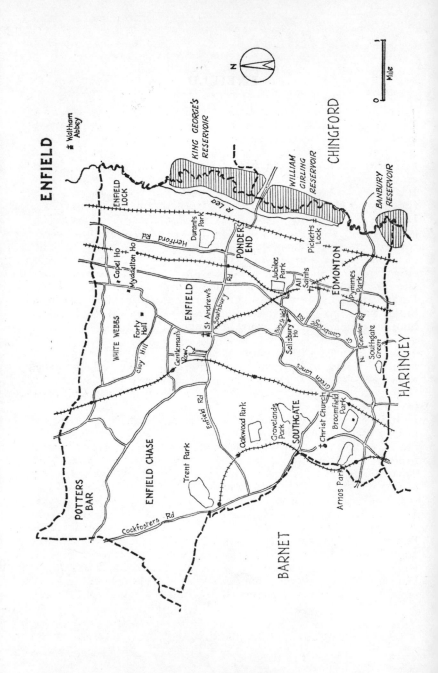

ENFIELD

The London Borough of Enfield unites the former boroughs of Enfield, Edmonton, and Southgate, though covering most of the land which used to comprise the old Hundred of Edmonton. It is the most northerly of all the new London boroughs and is bounded by Hertfordshire, Waltham Forest, Haringey, and Barnet. It covers an area of 20,060 acres, and has a population of 262,690 (1970). It is an area of great variety and still, in the north-western corner, so rural that it is a perpetual delight and astonishment to walk out of London so easily into green fields and farm lanes. On the low-lying ground along the River Lea, the eastern boundary, is much commercial development, as interesting to the industrial archaeologist as to the businessman; the undulating western area, now either agricultural land or residential quarters with an unusually large number of parks such as White Webbs, Forty Hill, or Trent Park, was once Enfield Chase, given over to hunting from Saxon to Stuart times, and, from the time of Henry IV, one of the Crown's hunting grounds near the court at London.

Enfield has given its name to the new London borough. Its origin is Saxon and probably means "Eana's clearing"—a space where trees had been felled in the vast Middlesex forest. The main body of the town lies squarely in the centre of the borough, away from Ermine Street, the Roman road to the North. This became the Hertford Road, along which many came in mediaeval times to nearby Waltham Abbey, a great place of pilgrimage, where Harold, last King of the English, lies buried. To the east of Enfield, divided from it by the modern bypass called the Cambridge Road, and contained between that road and the Lea, are the outlying districts of Freezywater, Enfield Lock, Enfield Wash, and Ponders End.

Enfield is an old place. Neolithic worked flints have been found by the Lea, and on Bush Hill are the remains of an Iron Age camp. A Roman coffin, now in Forty Hall Museum, was found in Bush Hill Park in 1893–94, while fragments of pottery, keys, a horse's bit and a spur head were found at Churchfields at Edmonton. The River Lea provided Alfred the Great and Guthrum, leader of the Danes, with one of the boundaries between Saxon and Danish territories in AD 885 and a channel, the Mardyke (Mark Ditch) was dug to define the boundary more clearly. Another stream here is locally believed to have its origin in King Alfred's hydraulic warfare of 895 when he diverted the river and stranded the longships which marauding Vikings had used to get as far up-stream as Bishop's Stortford. This is still the limit of navigation on the Stort, the Lea's chief tributary. The Lea continued to carry various traffic and it is likely that some of the Caen stone used in the fabric of the abbey at Waltham, just over Enfield's northern boundary, was brought by barge. The Lea was then much wider than it is now and would have been a formidable barrier to the passage of armies. Even today there is only one major bridge between those at Waltham Abbey and Edmonton and as recently as 1940 the river had some value as a military obstacle. Some of the emplacements and concrete blockhouses erected then are still to be seen scattered along the river banks.

William the Conqueror granted Enfield to Geoffrey de Mandeville and before the end of the 13th century it had been divided into eight sub-manors—Enfield, Elsynge, Durants, Suffolks, Honeylands, Goldbeaters, Worcesters, and Surlowes. By the late 14th century, the greater part of the land was in the hands of the de Bohun family, until Mary de Bohun married Henry Bolingbroke, eldest son of John of Gaunt, Duke of Lancaster. Richard II was deposed by this Henry, who then became King Henry IV in his cousin's place, and so vested the Duchy of Lancaster in the Crown. The Enfield estates became part of the Duchy's lands by inheritance through Henry's wife. By the reign of Henry VII, who came to the throne by overthrowing another King Richard, the manor of Worcesters belonged to Sir Thomas Lovell, friend of the king and minister both to him and to his son, Henry VIII, until his own death in 1524. He built or enlarged Elsynge Hall, which stood close to the present site of Forty Hall, and his successor, the Earl of Rutland, exchanged lands with Henry VIII, so that Elsynge Hall became royal property. Here Princess Elizabeth spent part of her childhood, her tutor, William Grindal, living in a cottage close by. It was at Elsynge Hall that she and her brother, the future Edward VI, heard of their father's death and wept in each other's arms, and it was in the arms of another Enfield landholder, Sir Thomas Wroth of Durants, that the poor sickly 16-year-old king died in 1553. Henry VIII had left Enfield and Worcesters to the Princess Elizabeth and a new manor house, Enfield Palace, was built on Enfield Green (near the present town centre) in 1552, but it is doubtful whether she ever stayed there when queen. Royal associations with Enfield became less in later reigns, though James I must often have passed through on his way to the nearby palace at Theobalds in Hertfordshire, where he resided when hunting in Enfield Chase.

The Chase, a plateau to the north and west of the town, is the remnant of the old forest of Middlesex, a dense woodland covering close on 2000 acres. When Cromwell appropriated the royal lands in 1649, his surveyors assessed the timber as worth £15,000 and, despite heavy felling, there were still 631,000 trees in 1700. Arthur Young, the zealous agricultural improver, thoroughly disapproved of the Chase: "Enfield-chase cannot be viewed by any lover of his country, or of husbandry, without so much regret; so large a tract of land, so near the capital, within the reach of London, as a market, and as a dunghill, is a real nuisance to the public." In 1777 it was dischased, roads were made across it, from 1803 onwards the land was gradually laid out, first for agricultural purposes and then, on the south-eastern slopes, for building. The hamlet of Botany Bay in the middle of the farmland area is thus of more recent date than the then remote antipodean penal colony from which it took its name. Around Crews Hill, where town and country meet, is the last stronghold of the tomato barons and the cucumber kings, whose greenhouse nurseries still cover acres of the Lea Valley in a sea of glass.

Today Enfield is still a market town, especially on a Saturday morning. It is not a mere suburb of London, but a town in its own right. At its centre are St Andrew's Church, the market house, and the grammar school. There was a church here in the 4th century, and the tower of the present building dates from the 12th; although extensive alterations and repairs have been made during the past 300 years there still remains a 13th century window and the 14th century ivory coloured pillars. Among a number of impressive monuments is the beautiful Tiptoft memorial which has a carved and painted stone canopy above a 15th century brass, nearly as fine as the magnificent one to Eleanor de Bohun, Duchess of Gloucester, in Westminster Abbey. The Enfield brass commemorates Jacosa, wife of Sir John Tiptoft, lord of the manor, who lived where Forty Hall now stands. Sir John was a good servant of Henry IV, both before and after he became king, and held various offices of state under him. He was a member of the council of regency set up in 1422 on the accession of the infant Henry VI. Lady Tiptoft died in 1446. Their son, John, was created Earl of Worcester whence his property at Enfield became known as the manor of Worcesters. A distinguished scholar, he spent some years in Italy, then the centre of European culture, and then became Constable of England. By his use of "Paduan" (i.e. Roman) law, he was able to ensure the speedy trial and execution of a number of Lancastrian leaders without the delays and publicity inseparable from trial by jury in the English way. From this, he gained a reputation for cruelty and ruthlessness. In 1462 he condemned to death the Earl of Oxford and his eldest son Aubrey de Vere. John de Vere, a younger son, became earl and in 1470 tried Tiptoft, who by a decline in Yorkist fortunes had fallen into his hands. Tiptoft's execution on Tower Hill had to be delayed a day on account of the populace of London which tried to lynch him when he was first brought out.

Another holder of these same lands, Sir Nicholas Raynton, builder of Forty Hall, has a monument of marble and alabaster in St Andrew's, depicting him in his robes as Lord Mayor of London, together with his wife and other members of their family. He reclines on his elbow, Lady Raynton on a cushion beneath, and their six children below them, kneeling, with a seventh baby who died in its cradle. Dr Abernethy, a medical man famous both for his work at St Bartholomew's Hospital and for his astringent tongue, who resided nearby in Baker Street before his death in 1831, and Joseph Whitaker (d. 1895) the creator of the famous Almanack, are also commemorated, and there are other fine monuments to Colonel Thomas Stringer (d. 1706), to Robert Deicrowe (d. 1586), and to Martha Palmere (d. 1617), the last by the great stonemason and architect Nicholas Stone, master-mason to James I and architect at Windsor Castle. The epitaph contains the beautiful lines:

Whose vertew did all ill so overswaye
That her whole life was a communion daye.

The patronage of the living was bestowed by Geoffrey de Mandeville on his newly founded monastery at Saffron Walden in 1136, and remained there until the Dissolution, after which it passed to Trinity College Cambridge, which has been the patron ever since. The churchyard contains several interesting monuments and epitaphs, including one to John White, surveyor to the New River Company, which begins:

Here lies John White, who, day by day,
On river works did use much clay,
Is now himself turning that way.

To the south of the church is the marketplace. Edward I granted to Humphrey de Bohun a licence to hold a weekly market in his manor in 1304, and a market has been held ever since. The present marketplace was acquired as a permanent site in 1532 and the stalls there on a Saturday are well patronised. For the rest of the week the cobbled square is a public car park. In the centre is the New Market House, an open building with a pitched roof supported on eight pillars, built in 1904 to replace an earlier structure and to commemorate the coronation of Edward VII. Beside the churchyard is Holly Walk which leads to the ancient grammar school, founded in 1548 and endowed with the revenues of a chantry in the parish church which was suppressed at the Reformation. Most of the school buildings date from this century but part of the old school survives from Tudor times.

Enfield Palace used to stand on the south side of the marketplace, and from 1660 onwards was used as a private boarding school. Dr Robert Uvedale (d. 1722) combined the headmastership of this school with that of the grammar school; he was a celebrated naturalist, developed the modern sweetpea, and raised a superb cedar of Lebanon in the palace grounds. The palace was of brick, elaborately and beautifully decorated inside, but it was partly demolished in 1792 and completely destroyed in 1928, though happily the best of the oak panelling, a stone fireplace, and a fine ceiling, were saved and re-erected in a wing specially built on to a house in Gentleman's Row by a benefactor of Enfield who could not bear to see so historic a building wiped out completely. The ceiling is an early example of the decoration that was to develop so exquisitely in the vicarage at Tottenham and at Boston Manor House (see p. 178 and p. 262). Gentleman's Row is some distance away, at the west end of the town's main shopping centre. It is one of the most intriguing streets possible. Being a cul-de-sac, it is cut off from the main stream of traffic and is curiously peaceful considering how busy Enfield is. Nos. 9 to 23 are all old, mostly built in the early 18th century, some weatherboarded cottages, others more substantial brick houses with fine doorways.

Charles Lamb the essayist came to stay at No. 17 (now Clarendon Cottage) in 1827 on his retirement from his clerkship with the East India Company. With him came his poor sister Mary who suffered from periodic attacks of insanity, in one of which she had seized a knife and killed her mother. Charles devoted the rest of his life to looking after her. He hoped to find peace for both of them in the green countryside but it was not to be. In the autumn of 1827 they rented a house, No. 87, in Chase Side, but Mary became so ill that Charles took lodgings for them with Mr and Mrs Westwood who lived next door. At first all went well, Charles completed his *Essays of Elia* there, but at last he began to find the Westwoods harsh, parsimonious, and grasping—they charged him extra after a visit from Wordsworth because the poet took so much sugar in his tea—and in 1834 he and Mary moved to a private asylum kept by a Mr and Mrs Walden in Church Street, Edmonton.

Just south of the centre of Enfield are the town park and golf course. The town's main railway station, the terminus of a branch line from Lower Edmonton, has a curious history. The original station building was in a house built in the 1670s by Edward Helder, a bricklayer who worked for Sir Christopher Wren. Isaac D'Israeli, the father of the Prime Minister, was born here in 1766. The house then became a school, kept by Cowden Clarke, and here John Keats, who was living with his grandmother, Mrs Jennings, in Edmonton, came as a pupil. He delighted in his studies and formed a firm and sustaining friendship with Charles Cowden Clarke, the headmaster's son, who became a distinguished author and Shakespearean critic in his own right. The house became a railway station in 1849 and was demolished in 1872; the façade of the central upper storey was preserved and is now in the Victoria and Albert Museum.

West of the town are Lavender Hill, called after the acres of that fragrant shrub once grown here, and Gordon Hill. The latter takes its name from Gordon House, demolished in 1860, which was the birthplace of Lord George Gordon, the strange fanatical young man who sparked off the anti-Catholic Gordon Riots in 1780 (see p. 69). Nearby is the Bycullah Estate, laid out in the 1880s on the grounds of Bycullah Park, the house of J. R. Riddell who had spent many years in India. The park took its name from Bycullah in Bombay, where the "gymkhana" was, and Mr Riddell organised steeplechases in the grounds of his house, the Great Northern line running special trains to Enfield Chase Station to accommodate his guests.

The old road through Enfield winds northwards, changing its name as it goes—Silver Street, Baker Street, Forty Hill, and Bulls Cross are all a continuation of the same thoroughfare. In Baker Street stood Holmwood where Mr Freeman kept a school attended by Frederick Marryat (later famous as Captain Marryat, the author), and Charles Babbage, the future mathematician and inventor of the calculating machine. Marryat was not a model pupil—he ran away so often that at last his father agreed to remove him and to send him to sea. On the western side of Forty Hill is Forty

Hall. The house was built between 1629 and 1636 by Sir Nicholas Raynton who demolished old Elsynge Hall to make room for the new mansion. The house is traditionally ascribed to Inigo Jones, but there is no compelling reason, either documentary or stylistic, for believing him to be the architect. Inside there are some fine plaster ceilings and a beautiful hall-screen. The house took its name from the owner of the estate, Sir Hugh Fortee, who had held it before Sir Nicholas; it was later the property of the Wolstenholme and Bowles families, and in 1951 was acquired by Enfield Borough Council. It is now open as a local archaeological and historical museum, and for the display of loan exhibitions. The grounds, with a lake and an avenue of lime trees, said to have been laid out by Le Notre, the great French gardener, are superb.

Near to the Hall are some other interesting houses, especially Worcester Lodge and Elsynge Cottage, said to stand on the site of William Grindal's dwelling—as we have mentioned, he was Queen Elizabeth's tutor. Beyond Maiden's Bridge at the edge of the estate, one of the many places where Sir Walter Raleigh, who had a house nearby, is alleged to have cast his cloak across a muddy puddle so that his Queen might cross dry-footed, the road runs north again, passing on the way the charming weatherboarded inn, the Pied Bull, a former hunting lodge, near Theobalds. Myddelton House built in 1814 and called after Sir Hugh Myddelton, the engineer of the New River, is on this road. Myddelton House is pleasant enough though not particularly distinguished, but it is set in an intriguing and beautiful garden created around it by its owner, E. A. Bowles, during the late 19th century and still well maintained. The house is now the headquarters of the Lee [sic] Valley Authority. It is hoped, as time and circumstances permit, to turn the whole of the Lea Valley, from Bromley-by-Bow to Ware, into one vast recreational area with parks, boating-lakes, facilities for athletics, museums, and other cultural activities.

Sir Hugh Myddelton did indeed live in Enfield during part of the time that his great enterprise was being carried out. He was a goldsmith by trade and, like many other 16th century goldsmiths, set up as a banker, but he was clearly a born engineer. He became a member of the House of Commons Committee considering London's drastic water shortage and he offered to undertake what became known as the New River Scheme to carry water from Amwell springs in Hertfordshire through Enfield to Islington (see p. 283), a distance of 38 miles. He began the excavation in 1609 and finally brought it to a triumphant conclusion, with the financial backing of

James I, on Michaelmas Day, 1613, when his brother, Sir Thomas Myddelton, Lord Mayor of London, presided at the opening ceremony. Throughout, he had to deal with opposition from local landowners who feared their property would be flooded, and with every sort of engineering problem, and the company never paid a dividend in its creator's lifetime. His most spectacular device was the "flume" or boarded trough which carried the river for some 660 feet at Bush Hill Park, Enfield, and needed no replacement till 1788 when a clay sluice was built. While the work was going on, he lived at Halliwick House on the top of Bush Hill. The old house has only recently been demolished owing to rotting timbers, and the site is today a hospital and school for physically disabled girls.

Bulls Cross runs north, almost to the border of the borough, and then turns west, becoming White Webbs Lane and passing what is perhaps the loveliest of the many parks in Enfield, White Webbs, covering nearly 300 acres and carpeted with daffodils in spring. White Webbs House, built in the 17th century, altered considerably in 1870, is now a home for the aged, but it was one of the meeting places of the Gunpowder Plot conspirators of 1605 when Guy Fawkes failed to blow up the Houses of Parliament. On the boundary of the park is the old King and Tinker Inn where James I is reputed to have knighted an outspoken tinker. Beyond White Webbs is the open farmland and countryside of Enfield Chase, astonishing to find within ten miles of the metropolis. One can drive 50 miles from London and still not find such good rough walking as there is to be had here. One part of it is enclosed, on the far north-west, namely Trent Park, granted to Sir Richard Jebb, physician to the Duke of Gloucester, and called after Trent in the Tyrol where the duke recuperated from an illness. The park was laid out, very beautifully, by Humphrey Repton, the terrace and grounds sloping away towards a lake from which the Salmon Brook runs. The house was refaced in 1926, for Sir Philip Sassoon, with brick from William Kent's Devonshire House in Piccadilly. In the grounds is an old earthwork, known as Camlet Moat, which Sir Walter Scott describes as the scene of the murder of Lord Dalgarno in *The Fortunes of Nigel*.

Returning to the east of the borough, we come to Capel Manor at the top of Bullsmoor Lane, beside Bulls Cross. The house was built in the late 18th century for a former Governor of Bombay, Rawson Hart Boddam. It has a broad, plain-fronted, dignified façade. The 30-acre estate was acquired by the borough in 1968 and the house has been opened as an agricultural college.

In the north-eastern corner of the borough is Freezywater, a flat area formerly subject to flooding from the marshes of the Lea. South of Freezywater is Enfield Wash, where the road was awash at the ford crossing the Maiden Brook, which comes down from Forty Hall. This stream, a tributary of the Lea, could here be a most attractive water-course, but is instead used by the local inhabitants as a convenient repository for old pram-wheels and bicycle-tyres. The ford has long been replaced by the Woolpack Bridge. The nearby Woolpack Inn ought to take its name from the use of wool-packs in bridge foundations—the saying "London Bridge was built on wool" refers as much to engineering practices as to fiscal measures.

Ordnance Road leads eastwards down to the Small Arms Factory. On its corner was once a cottage where, in 1753, the mysterious affair of Elizabeth Canning was located. She was a servant girl who disappeared for about four weeks and returned in a disturbed condition with a tale of having been kidnapped and imprisoned in the house of one Susannah Wells by a gipsy woman, Squires. The whole of fashionable society took sides on the truth or falsehood of her story. Some 36 pamphlets were published on the subject and the incident was investigated by Henry Fielding the novelist in his capacity as magistrate. Canning's charges were found to be fraudulent and she was sentenced to be transported, but the affair is not among those remembered in local folklore.

To the west, Turkey Street runs beside the Maiden Brook. There are a few large outbuildings and some weatherboarded cottages scattered along its length, and it contains the Turkey Inn but, despite the handsome fowl which appears on the inn-sign, the street derives its name from one John Tuckey, a merchant who held land nearby in the reign of Richard II.

In 1580, the Lea was dredged as far as Ware, despite active opposition from the "badgers" or road haulage men of Enfield, who were overruled on the grounds that the river would provide employment for watermen who would be available for the queen's service. Perhaps these "reservists" were among those mustered when the Armada threatened eight years later. In the 17th century it was peaceful enough, and achieved literary immortality in the pages of Isaac Walton's *Compleat Angler*. There is still good coarse fishing to be had in the Lea and its backwaters or in the reservoirs and derelict gravel pits along its banks, and anglers of all ages and degrees of competency come in due season. The present "Navigation" was made in 1767 at the beginning of the canal boom. £20,000 was spent on the construction of locks and weirs although, being a navigable river rather than a true canal, the waterway had no connection with the great systems of the North and the Midlands, and carried mainly bulk cargoes of grain from Hertfordshire and Essex. It also carried gunpowder from the powder-mills at Waltham Abbey, and weapons from the Small Arms Factory at Enfield Lock, for the river gave a smoother journey than the roadways for the less stable explosives of former times.

Enfield Lock on the river gives its name to the district round about. The Small Arms Factory was established here in 1804 by the Board of Ordnance. Walnut trees had been planted nearby to supply wood for gunstocks, and the manufacture of barrels for the "Brown Bess" musket was begun in 1816. The output remained at a few thousand muskets a year until 1854 when the high price demanded by Birmingham firms for the new rifles then coming into service, and the uncertainty of delivery caused by the high incidence of strikes among their labour force, led the Government to expand its own armament factories.

The new Enfield rifles reached the British Army in 1856 and the following year were issued by the East India Company to its troops. The drill required that the end of the paper cartridge containing the bullet and propellant be bitten off before loading. The story that these cartridges were greased with the fat of pigs and cows, the touch of which meant ritual pollution for the Muslims and Hindus respectively, was the spark that set fire to the Bengal Army, already smouldering with mutiny. The Indian Mutiny which followed the issue of the Enfield rifle led to the dissolution of the East India Company and the final transfer of its servants and dominions to the British Crown.

At the turn of the century some 2000 men were producing annually 60,000 rifles and 8000 swords and bayonets, for a weekly wage bill of about £3000. During the two world wars, output was increased, and Enfield became a household word in the mouths of a million soldiers, from the "Short Magazine Lee-Enfield" Rifle which, with its satellites, the bottle of oil and pull-through, lorded it over every British barrack-room. Another weapon, the Bren light machine-gun, took part of its name from *En*field, and part from the equally famous ordnance factory at *Br*no in Czechoslovakia. The factory remains a Ministry of Defence establishment, controlled from the Arsenal at Woolwich. The Ordnance Tavern stands at the gates, but nothing remains of its erstwhile rival, the Swan and Pike, except a road of that name. This runs through thickets of thorn and elderberry along the marshes to end at a neo-Georgian station of the Metropolitan Water Board, at the northern end of the great chain of reservoirs, constructed in the first half of this century, which runs southwards from here to Hackney.

A small terrace of Victorian cottages called Government Row still houses workers at the factory, and lines the river's eastern bank, apparently below the level of the waterway. On the west bank by the lock is a pleasant old house, now used by the British Waterways authorities, and the remains of a small wharf or jetty. Between the river, and the main-line railway to Cambridge, is now a wilderness of water-courses, marsh, and sewage works. In Saxon times, this was the site of Elsynge Manor, one of a chain of fortified strongholds strengthening the river obstacle. Ordnance Road is now a most unfashionable area but near Enfield Lock station are a number of Victorian villas of some dignity, some of which are still used, as they were originally, to house military and civil officers of the factory.

Below the Lock may be seen great barges carrying cargoes of iron to the Enfield rolling mills, and coal to the electricity generating station at Brimsdown. Although the western bank is given over entirely to the romance of industry, and is indeed a source of great interest to the industrial archaeologist, the sheets of water on the Essex side attract many rare birds and are a favourite haunt of the ornithologist.

A modern road runs between the reservoirs from Chingford to cross the Lea at Ponders End. A side road here leads to an attractive group of buildings, a mill-house and flour-mill, mainly early 19th century brick and weatherboarding, with a later addition to the upper part of the mill in dark-red corrugated iron. Prior to the construction of the bridge here early this century, Enfield had no road going into Essex. The next lowest bridge, carrying the North Circular Road at Cook's Ferry, is in Edmonton, and is indeed of more recent date since, as the name implies, this was formerly a ferry. The ferryman was notable for the large number of cats he owned and which insisted on sharing the ferry, often to the annoyance of passengers. These animals may still be seen, painted in the boat which appears on the signboard of the Cook's Ferry Inn nearby. On the Middlesex bank, opposite the inn, is a timberyard, one of many providing raw materials for the furniture industry which has several factories in Edmonton and Tottenham, ease of water transport being a major factor in their original location, and barges are still used to carry timber to the stacks.

In 1840 the Northern and Eastern Railway Company opened its line from London to Cambridge, taking advantage of the easy gradient to lay its tracks alongside the river from Stratford to Bishop's Stortford. This encouraged the growth of industry here, which in turn led to some increase in population, although the greatest rate of expansion, especially in Edmonton, was not to come till the 1870s, when the railway company, in compensation for the demolition of many small buildings in order to build its new terminus at Liverpool Street, began to run cheap workmen's train services along the line. The original company was absorbed in 1844 into the Eastern Counties Railway (later the Great Eastern). The 5-foot-gauge track was replaced by the standard 4 foot 8 inches, and in 1845 a branch line was opened from Angel Road station (near Cook's Ferry) to Enfield Town.

Just to the south of Enfield Lock, off the Hertford Road, is Durant's Park. The manor seems originally to have been one of the chain of Saxon frontier posts. About 1400 it came into the possession of the Wroth family—one of the few families to hold land in Middlesex over several centuries, and their name appears repeatedly as Knights of the Shire in mediaeval parliaments. Thomas Fuller, the historian of the Church in Great Britain and author of the *Worthies of England*, who was the incumbent of Waltham Abbey Church during the Commonwealth, wrote of Sir Thomas Wroth that he was a gentleman "of the Bedchamber and a favourite of King Edward the Sixth who (as I am informed) at his death passed out of the arms of him, his faithful servant, into the embraces of Christ, his dearest Saviour. Soon after Sir Thomas found a great change in the English court but no alteration, as did many (to their shame) in his own conscience, in the preservation of which he was fain to fly beyond the seas." He returned however on Elizabeth I's accession and sat in Parliament as a member for the county. His son, Sir Robert, was a courtier of James I, a juryman at the trial of Sir Walter Raleigh, and a commissioner at the investigation into Guy Fawkes and the Gunpowder Plot. His son, also Sir Robert, acquired Loughton Manor in Epping Forest which became the principal family seat. His wife, Lady Mary Wroth, the daughter of Robert Sidney, Earl of Leicester, entertained Ben Jonson, who dedicated *The Alchemist* to her and wrote a long poem to her husband.

Their son, Sir Henry Wroth, supported the Cavalier party during the Civil Wars, although most men in Middlesex and the surrounding counties held Parliamentary sympathies. He died, without a male heir, in 1671. His daughter Mary accompanied Princess

Mary, James II's Protestant daughter, to the Hague as maid of honour at her marriage to William of Orange, who was to become William III. There she married one of the future king's companions-in-arms, William Zuylenstein, who in due course was created Earl of Rochford, Viscount Tunbridge, and Baron Enfield, the latter title coming from his wife's estates. All these titles became extinct with the death of the 5th earl in 1830.

Before this, however, Durants passed to another local worthy, Sir Thomas Stringer. His eldest son, Sir William, married a daughter of the infamous Judge Jeffreys. The judge often visited his daughter and son-in-law at Durants and some fortifications, formerly to have been seen in an outbuilding, may have housed an escort for his protection. They were demolished in 1910 and the bricks were used as the foundations of the widened Southbury Road nearby which leads westwards to Enfield Town. Lady Stringer lived till 1727 and is buried in the churchyard at St Andrew's, Enfield parish church. Across the park are pleasant views of St James's Church at Green Street, a hitherto unremarkable church of the 1830s, but pleasantly restored and improved after a recent fire. Together with Durants Park it provides a green calm oasis in an area of busy commerce.

South of Durant's Park is the euphoniously named, but sadly built over, Ponders End, where Charles Lamb "had thought in a green old age (O green thought) to have retired to Ponder's End—emblematic name how beautiful" and south again, by this time in Edmonton, is Pickett's Lock, one of the most picturesque examples of industrial archaeology to be found anywhere. The Lock, apart from its hydraulic value, deserves notice as the first of the areas to be acquired by the Lee Valley Authority for landscaping and redevelopment.

Edmonton, in the south-eastern corner of the borough, appears as Delmetone or Adelmetone ("Eadhelm's farm") in Domesday. The manor can be traced back to Edward the Confessor's time, when it was held by Asgar the "Staller", or Master of the Horse. It was, with the rest of Asgar's lands at Enfield, given to Geoffrey de Mandeville after the Conquest, and later it formed part of the marriage settlements of two Stuart queens, Henrietta Maria, the proud, restless, intriguing, French wife of Charles I, and Catherine of Braganza, the Portuguese wife of Charles II, who in England was thought a neglected, passive, long-suffering, compliant creature, but who, on returning to Lisbon as a widow, played a remarkable and forceful part in her country's politics.

129

The general outline of Edmonton is very similar to the north-eastern districts of Enfield of which it now forms part. On the east are the slow waters of the River Lea, the great sheets of water formed by the Metropolitan Water Board's reservoirs, the railway laid in the early 19th century, and the resulting industrial development and housing estates associated with it. In the centre is the old road to the North, on which there have been settlements from mediaeval times, and which now has an abundance of houses, shops, and offices. To the west are the later suburban railways, a more modern bypass road, and housing, shops, and factories of more recent date. Unlike Enfield, however, Edmonton grew up on the main road rather than to the side of it, and therefore its oldest buildings, church, market, and municipal activities are closer to its commercial and industrial heart. Being nearer to London, it was built up a generation before Enfield, but in very recent years Edmonton's western districts still had orchards and smallholdings such as fringe Enfield's urban areas. The marsh levels, where Isaac Walton once fished, are now almost entirely covered by factories and power installations. The last salmon caught here was recorded in 1828, and the last otter five years later.

A stream called Salmon's Brook now flows through the ultra-modern Deepham Refuse Disposal Works, a wonder of the modern world, a centre of pilgrimage for civil engineers, which not only purifies and gives useful form to the waste products of an affluent industrial society but in the process produces enough power both to work its own machinery and sell another half-million pounds worth to the Electricity Generating Board.

Edmonton's two thriving annual Beggars' Bush Fairs were held under a charter granted by James I. They were originally hiring fairs for servants, but they ceased in the 1870s and all that is left of them is the name Fairfield Road (just north of the intersection of Fore Street, the main London Road) and Angel Road (which here forms part of the North Circular Road).

East of Fore Street, beside the Silver Street section of the North Circular Road again, are the 53 acres of Pymmes Park, now the property of the local authority but once belonging to Lord Burghley, Queen Elizabeth's minister, who built a house there in the 1590s. The house was twice rebuilt in the 18th century and was burnt down in 1940. The park has stately cedars, splendid lawns and a lake, and its old walled rose-garden is particularly attractive. Pymmes Brook, culverted for most of its modern length, drains down eastwards to the Lea. A pleasing group of cottages stands near the intersection of Fore Street and Angel Road, and the Angel and Bell public houses once stood here. Both claimed to stand on the site of the inn mentioned in Cowper's ballad of John Gilpin's ride, when his mount carried the City grocer so fast that he overshot his wedding anniversary celebrations, to the great distress of his spouse, who saw her husband galloping past, without hat or wig, clinging helplessly to his horse's mane, until it reached its own stables at Ware.

The centre of Edmonton is The Green—green, alas, no longer and its street market municipally tidied away. From it, Church Street leads westwards, taking its name from the church of All Saints, the parish church of Edmonton. Built about 1335, on the site of a church founded in 1136 by Geoffrey de Mandeville, it was heavily restored in 1772 and again in 1889, so that now the roof and pleasant buttressed west tower date from the 15th century, the north chancel aisle from the 16th century, the north aisle and chancel from the 18th century, and the south aisle from the 19th century. There are some interesting monuments in the church. A brass of Henry VII's time shows John Asplyn and Geoffrey Askew and the wife they both married; she wears a kennel headdress and both men have fur-edged gowns with wide sleeves. Two brasses of 1523 portray Nicholas Boone and his wife, and another of 1616 shows Edward Nowell and his wife and their four children, in their elaborate robes and ruffs. There is a handsome Tudor monument to John Kirton of about 1530 which has a cornice and cresting and has lost its brass. A 17th century monument commemorates George Huxley; it is adorned with fruit, painted shields, skulls and a figure of Father Time.

Charles Lamb and his sister Mary are buried in the churchyard. He died in 1834, she 13 years later, but their graves are marked with a single stone with a poem inscribed on it by Henry Cary, Lamb's friend and the translator of Dante. They both lived in Bay Cottage, Church Street, for the last year of Lamb's life. Peter Fabell, the hero of *The Merry Devil of Edmonton*, a drama written about 1608, is said to lie here too; he is reputed to have sold his soul to the Devil but to have outwitted Old Nick himself.

A row of almshouses flanks the churchyard; they were the gift of one Thomas Styles, intended for 12 poor parishioners, and the original houses were built in 1679 and then rebuilt in 1754. The present houses were erected in 1903. An unwashed Edwardian Gothic building faces the church; it is Lamb's Institute, built in 1907 and used as a parish hall. It has no connection with the essayist, save to commemorate his short association with Edmonton.

Near the intersection of Church Street and The Green stands Keats Parade, a row of small shops, built on the site of the house in which the poet lived with his grandmother from 1811 till 1815. During that time, when he was apprenticed to a local surgeon, Dr Hammond, he wrote most of the *Juvenile Poems* which were published in 1817. Also in Church Street, near The Green, is a charming statue of a small girl; she is wearing a long grey dress and cap and is holding a book; she stands above the entrance to what was once a charity school, founded in 1714; it was, the inscription tells us:

> *A structure of Hope*
> *Founded in Faith,*
> *On the basis of Charity.*

To the north of The Green, in the Hertford Road, stands what once must have been a fine crescent of 25 Regency or early Victorian houses. Despite their neglected appearance, their unity remains and the portico, although now off-centre, is still imposing.

Western Edmonton was the last part to be built up. Bury Street contains one of the most interesting buildings in the whole district, Salisbury House, now the home of the Edmonton Arts Centre, once a manor house built about 1600. It has a timbered front and plastered sides. The first floor projects beyond the ground floor and the gabled second storey overhangs all. A small park and garden beside the house is all that remains of the rural aspect which this area maintained till the 1920s and 1930s. The Stag and Hounds nearby was once a quiet country inn, surrounded by old brickfields from which the 19th century estates further eastwards were made, but which, abandoned and overgrown with bushes, were a natural "adventure playground", flanked by the higher reaches of Salmon's Brook, surrounded by farm cottages and rural outbuildings, until overwhelmed by the rising tide of modern housing. The most noteworthy modern building in Bury Street, near its junction with Ridge Avenue, is a public library, built in the 1950s, with high plate-glass walls and connected sloping roofs in butterfly style.

Bury Street serves as the southern link between Edmonton and Bush Hill Park. This area, entirely residential, lies between Edmonton, Southgate, and central Enfield, and is bisected diagonally by the branch line which, with one station at Bush Hill Park, ends at Enfield Town. The division is as much social as physical. The north-east part is less fashionable, and consists mainly of rows of small terraced cottages, although the streets are generally wide and tree-lined. South-west of the railway the houses are larger, the trees bushier, and the district is more affluent. St Stephen's Church, with a lychgate and a tower of interesting design, stands on the London road running south from Enfield Town and is much favoured for fashionable weddings in the locality. Enfield's cricket club ground has stood here for more than a century. Bush Hill Park formed part of Enfield Old Park estate, granted in 1660 to General Monk in recognition of his services in restoring Charles II to the throne. The name of Old Park Ridings, a pleasant area on the western edge of Bush Hill Park, between Enfield Town and Winchmore Hill, indicates the former extent of this estate. In 1902, building operations in the central part of Bush Hill Park disclosed a considerable number of Roman remains, including the lead coffin already mentioned, which can now be seen at Forty Hall.

Southgate in the west of the borough was once, as its name implies, the southern entrance to Enfield Chase. The old gate to the village now stands on a small green on the corner of Alderman's Hill and Cannon Hill, and the village itself is centred around the large green at the northern end of Cannon Hill. It has great charm with its ancient stocks and horse trough on the green; the roads are tree-lined and have some splendid old houses. Among the most notable are the early 18th century Essex House, Arnosside, and Old House, all in Waterfall Road.

Christ Church, also in Waterfall Road, was built in the 1860s on the site of a chapel built in 1615 by Sir John Weld, the merchant who owned Arnos House nearby. The present church was designed by Sir Gilbert Scott who built two other nearby churches, St Paul's in Church Hill and St Michael's in Palmerston Road. Christ Church has an attractive octagonal spire and splendid stained-glass windows; on the west of the south aisle is one designed by Rossetti, showing St James and St Jude, and in the north aisle one by Burne-Jones, showing the Christian virtues. The church stands beside the Minchenden Garden of Remembrance, a charming garden, opened in 1934, with flagged paths winding between lawns and flower beds. The famous Minchenden or Chandos Oak stands in the garden; it has a girth of over 27 feet and is reputed to be the biggest in the county. It may well be 800 years old, a last survivor of the Forest of Middlesex. The oak takes its name from Minchenden House, built about 1747 and demolished in 1853, the property of the 3rd duke of Chandos.

Facing the Olde Cherry Tree Inn at the junction of Cannon Hill and The Green is Northmet House, the headquarters of the Eastern Electricity Board. This was the site of Arnos House, Sir John Weld's mansion. His family removed to Dorset, the old house was bought and pulled down by James Colebrook in 1719 and a new one built by Sir Robert Taylor; Lord Newhaven made additions to it about 1776. In the central block is a staircase frescoe by Lanscroon, a pupil of Verrio, painted about 1723, and some late 18th century decoration. In the 19th century, the Walker family lived there; all seven brothers were fine cricketers and the nearby cricket ground in Waterfall Road is called after them. V. E. Walker was described in the 1859 issue of Lillywhite's *Guide to Cricket* as "undoubtedly the best all-round cricketer in the world". The Electricity Board added wings to the house in the 1920s and 1930s which somehow harmonise with the whole. Electrically illuminated globes on the gateposts, symbolising the terrestial sphere, advertise the business of the present occupants.

To the north of the High Street on the wall of Barclays Bank is a tablet recording that Benjamin Waugh lived in a house on that site. He was a Congregational minister who, together with the writer Hesba Stretton, founded the London Society for the Prevention of Cruelty to Children in 1884. Four years later it became the National Society for the Prevention of Cruelty to Children.

Leigh Hunt was born at Southgate, in Eagle House, a school kept by his father, in 1784. He wrote that it was "a pleasure to me to know that I was even born in so sweet a village as Southgate". He stammered so badly that he could not go to university, but he taught himself the classics and modern languages, though he never managed to learn even the most simple arithmetic. He became a journalist and founded a paper called *The Examiner*; he was prosecuted several times for his writings—for example, for describing George IV as "a corpulent Adonis of 50 without a single claim on the gratitude of his country", for which he was fined £500 and imprisoned for two years. He went on writing in prison. He encouraged Shelley and Keats, was never rich and frequently very poor, but always brave and philosophical. He is perhaps best remembered by the line in his poem, *Abou Ben Adhem*:

I pray thee then,
Write me as one who loves his fellow-men.

Arnos Grove Station, on the North Circular Road, was built in 1932 by Sir Charles Holden, as were the nearby Southgate and

Cockfosters stations. They are three of the best works of that always interesting architect.

There are parks all around Southgate. To the south is Arnos Park through which the Pymmes Brook flows and which is crossed by a viaduct bearing the Piccadilly Line. Tube trains flash and scud overhead to the great delight of all children playing there. Near it is Broomfield Park, one of the most charming and varied in all the London area. In it stands Broomfield Lodge, reputedly built as a hunting lodge for James I, and now an interesting local museum, which houses Dr Cresswell's fine collection of water-colours of Southgate as it was in the latter part of the 19th century, as well as stuffed birds and animals, bygones, and a fascinating glass-sided beehive with a glass exit tunnel to the park. The house itself is a rectangular brick building, spoilt in the 20th century by the addition of lavish half-timbering. The oldest parts of the exterior are 200 years old, though there are some older features inside, notably a fine oak staircase with carved balustrades of Charles II's period. In the hall are some attractive murals, depicting mythological scenes. They were attributed to Sir James Thornhill, Hogarth's father-in-law, but modern expert opinion credits them to Gerard Lanscroon, who did the paintings at nearby Arnos House (now Northmet House). The grounds are outstanding; there is a lake and a superb double avenue of elms leading to the village gate on Alderman's Hill. The conservatory and borders are beautiful, and the Garden for the Blind, full of scented flowers, is well worth a visit. The park has a quiet garden of remembrance and an aviary.

Southgate has another interesting park, Grovelands Park in Broad Walk, which became local authority property in 1913. The house was built by John Nash in 1798 and was first called Southgate House, then Woodlands, and now Grovelands. It houses a convalescent home and is railed off from the public park and lake, but the handsome garden front with its recessed loggia and four huge Ionic columns can be seen from the park. The striking iron gates at the entrance were presented by Lord Inverforth in 1925. Grovelands was the home of John Dinnithorne Taylor who hoped to check urban development and to keep Southgate as rural as it had always been. After his death in 1901, his 300-acre estate was put up for sale but a third of it was saved by the Council and the Middlesex VAD, and this at least is here in perpetuity, for all to enjoy. Nearby is Oakwood Park, with a large children's playground and a pond for model yachts, and both here and at Grovelands, avenues of oaks are being planted, one tree being added by each successive mayor of the borough.

The names of two literary men associated with Southgate should be remembered—Thomas Hood, the poet and social reformer, who lived in Rose Cottage, Vicarsmore Lane from 1829 to 1832, and the poet Gerard Massey who is buried in the cemetery in Church Lane. He was the son of a bargee, and one of a large and poor family. When he was eight he went to work in a mill, doing 11 hours a day for a wage of about 11d. a week. He was born near Tring in Hertfordshire and came to London where he was taken up by Charles Kingsley and Frederick Denison Maurice. Not surprisingly, he was a Radical and supported first the Chartists and then the Christian Socialists. He died in 1907, at the age of 80.

To the east of Southgate is Winchmore Hill, a pleasant and expensive residential district of large houses and tree-lined roads. The Friends' Meeting House is one of the oldest and most famous in the country, the original house on the site was built in 1688 and the present plain solid building in 1790. It was a popular meeting house in the days of religious persecution as it was close to London but was in a quiet enough village to escape notice. Meetings began here in 1662 and George Fox often preached at them. Beside it is the graveyard where many noble-hearted men and women lie.

On the green at the intersection of Fox Lane and Bourne Hill stands a cattle pound last used in 1904 for strays, but still preserved as a memento of Southgate's comparatively recent rural past.

HACKNEY

HACKNEY

HARINGEY

WALTHAM FOREST

STAMFORD HILL

Reservoirs

UPPER CLAPTON

STOKE NEWINGTON

Cissold Park

St Mary's Church

St Mary's Rd

Stoke Newington Rd

Lea Bridge Rd

River Lea

LEA BRIDGE

HACKNEY MARSHES

Clapton Rd

LOWER CLAPTON

Homerton High St

ISLINGTON

Dalston La

Sutton Ho.

HOMERTON

Eastway

HACKNEY WICK

Graham Rd

DALSTON

Albion Dr

Wick Rd

St John's

Victoria Park

Kingsland Rd

HOXTON

Hackney Rd

HAGGERSTON

SHOREDITCH

Geffrye Museum

TOWER HAMLETS

N

St Leonard's

CITY

0   Mile   1

HACKNEY

The London Borough of Hackney is composed of the former boroughs of Hackney, Shoreditch, and Stoke Newington. It covers an area of 4814 acres and has a population of 24,180 (in 1968). It lies to the north-east of the City of London, whose boundary Shoreditch touches, and is surrounded by Islington, Haringey, Waltham Forest, Newham, and Tower Hamlets. It was watered by the Hackney Brook to the north (now culverted), and the River Lea, Isaak Walton's "lovely river", bounds it on the extreme west; there is high ground at Stamford Hill, low-lying, open land at Hackney Marshes.

The names of the three areas which go to make up this new London borough all demonstrate their antiquity. Hackney is usually derived from "Hacon's eyot" or island (though it is sometimes ascribed to the Anglo-Saxon verb *haccan*, to kill, and *ey*, a river, and is thought to refer to a bloody struggle by a riverside). Shoreditch is probably a development of the soerdyke or town sewer, which lay outside London, and has, alas, nothing to do with Mistress Shore, Edward IV's mistress, while Stoke Newington comes from the Anglo-Saxon word *stoc*, meaning a wood, and thus refers to a cluster of new dwellings near a wood.

That human habitation went back even further than Anglo-Saxon times is born out by the display of flints in Mare Street Public Library. A Roman urn full of coins was found near Temple Mills and a marble sarcophagus (now in the crypt at Guildhall) in Brooksby's Walk, E.9., for the main Roman Road to Lincoln ran through the borough. In the Middle Ages, a Pilgrim's Way ran past the curative spring in Well Street, beside Hackney Churchyard, along Churchwell Path where there was another spring, and then by way of Lower and Upper Clapton Roads, to Waltham Abbey.

The three areas are most intriguingly different from each other. Shoreditch has always been comparatively urban, being so very near to the City. Hackney and Stoke Newington were both immensely pleasant country areas overtaken by the spread of the late 18th and 19th century London. Hackney was essentially a place where the wealthy had their country houses. Nowadays morsels of interesting architecture are hard to find—though worthwhile when once discovered—rather like raisins in a sparingly mixed rock bun. But all three areas have had an unusually large number of interesting people living in them.

Shoreditch is a tiny place with a large population. In 1861, at its most overcrowded, some 129,000 folk were crammed into a space no more than a mile and a half at its greatest extent. It is crossed from west to east by Old (once Ealde) Street, a former Roman road judging from the remains found below the surface during roadworks. Bishopsgate, beyond the south boundary, leads by way of Shoreditch High Street (a deviation from the original line of the old road) to Kingsland Road and Stamford Hill and follows the line of Ermine Street, the main Roman road to Lincoln which we have already mentioned.

Shoreditch is comprised of the two former villages of Hoxton and Haggerston, both mentioned in Domesday, and one of its boundaries is the City Road. Shoreditch can claim two nursery rhymes of its own, the first of them being:

> *Up and down the City Road,*
> *In and out the Eagle!*
> *That's the way the money goes.*
> *Pop goes the weasel!*

The old Eagle Public House where the money, obtained from the pop or pawn-shop, was spent, stood in the City Road. In the 1830s it became the Grecian Theatre under the management of Mr T. Rous and continued as such till 1882 when it became Salvation Army premises. A new Eagle now stands at the corner of City Road and Shepherdess Walk. This has been a pretty area and could be so again, though the Greater London Council development going on around Pitfield Street is not one of their most successful efforts. The original houses, many of which are still standing in streets whose names speak for themselves—Appleby Street, Pearson Street, Shepherdess Walk—were small, neat, and charming, and many of them still have their original front doors. It was near here that Mr Micawber, in *David Copperfield*, whose character Dickens modelled on that of his own father, lived: " 'My address,' said Mr Micawber, 'is Windsor Terrace, City Road. I—in short,' said Mr Micawber with the same genteel air, and in another burst of confidence—'I live there.' " (Windsor Terrace is now entirely rebuilt.)

Shoreditch's other nursery rhyme is a verse in that wonderful evocation of London's churches—"Oranges and Lemons",

> *When I grow rich,*
> *Say the bells of Shoreditch.*

The church to which the bells—all 13 of them—belong is St Leonard's in the High Street. The church was built by the elder George Dance between 1736 and 1740, and has a fine four-column portico and a wonderful steeple, tall—192 feet high—and slim, with an elongated stone cupola crowned with a lantern and on top of that a tiny thin elegant spire. Inside are giant Tuscan columns and one terrifying funeral monument by Francis Bird to Elizabeth Benson who died in 1710, a plaque on which two skeletons tug down two young oak trees, symbolising the Tree of Life. Outside the church are the stocks and whipping post, but it is the associations of the older buildings which stood on this site which bring us to it, for it was here, from the 13th century till 1736 when Dance commenced the rebuilding, that the Actors' Church stood, since it was Shoreditch which saw the birth of the English theatre. On the north wall of the church is a tablet set up by the London Shakespeare League in memory of some of those who lie buried here. Henry VIII's jester, Will Somers, lies here, as does that other clown, Richard Tarleton whom Stow called "the wonder of his age" and who danced a jig all the way from London to Norwich (see p. 208), also the actors Richard Cowley, William Sly, Nicholas Wilkinson, and that poor soul, Gabriel Spencer, whom Ben Jonson ran through with a sword and wounded fatally in a duel. Fortunatus Green lies here, whose father, Robert, called Shakespeare an Upstart Crow, and, chief of all, the three great Burbages, James the father and Richard and Cuthbert, his sons.

These men lie here because it was in the fields of Shoreditch that our English theatre was born. James Burbage lived in Holywell Street. He headed a troupe of wandering players, the Earl of Leicester's men, who travelled through the country, performing in inn yards, barns, or anywhere else that offered an opportunity. In 1576 he leased a plot of ground near his home for 21 years at £14 per annum from Giles Alleyne, and on it he built his playhouse, calling it with magnificent simplicity "The Theatre". A plaque on No. 90 Curtain Road, at the corner with New Inn Yard, today marks its approximate site. We have little idea of how the building looked—almost certainly of wood, probably round with a projecting stage—but it must have been a success, for a few months later another playhouse opened just south of The Theatre. It was called The Curtain, taking its name *not* from a theatrical curtain, but from the curtain wall of Holywell Priory which throughout the Middle Ages had stood where Hewett Street is today. It survived till at least 1627 but must have been demolished soon afterwards. The history of The Theatre was far more remarkable. Burbage had trouble with his ground-landlord and a year after his death in 1597, on December 28, 1598, when Alleyn was out of town, Cuthbert and Richard and the rest of the company pulled down the theatre, carried it away to Bankside, and there rebuilt it as The Globe. The brothers, with five others of the company, leased land there. One of the five was William Shakespeare, who had come to London in the late 1580s from Stratford-on-Avon in Warwickshire, and by 1592 was an established actor and writer. He began as any other member of the company might have done, by patching and altering old plays, but his genius soon became clear and it was for Richard Burbage that he wrote his greatest roles—Hamlet, Richard III (Burbage's triumph), Othello, Macbeth, and Lear. Shakespeare returned to Stratford, a well-to-do man, in 1611, though he continued to visit London and to keep in touch with his old friends. Richard died in 1619 and it was said that there was hardly a dry eye in London as he was laid to rest in old St Leonard's Church. Sir Philip Sidney's daughter, Elizabeth, his only child, lies here too. She was only three years old when he became immortal on the battlefield of Zutphen, and in his will it was found that he had left her a marriage portion of £4000. She was blessed with good fortune, for Queen Elizabeth was her godmother and she grew up to become Countess of Rutland, marrying Roger Manners, a traveller and soldier like her father. Ben Jonson thought much of her, and declared that she was "nothing inferior to her father in poesie". But her promising life was cut short, and she died while still young in January 1606 (St Leonard's Burial Register). We do not know why she should lie here in Shoreditch, except that she had kinsmen living at Brooke House nearby.

Shoreditch has other theatrical memories. The music hall, the Britannia, stood in Hoxton Street till it was destroyed by a bomb in 1941, and in the late 19th century McDonald's Music Hall ran it close for popularity in the same road. Near the Britannia was Pollock's Toy Theatre shop. Old Mr Pollock died in 1937 and he could remember being visited by Robert Louis Stevenson whose top hat was knocked off by one of the model stages hanging from the ceiling. Though the shop is no more, happily the toy theatres are still available.

Apart from St Leonard's, the churches of Shoreditch are interesting for their associations rather than their architectural qualities. St John's, Hoxton (consecrated 1826, architect Francis Edwards) has a fine site in the New North Road, and inside is the only surviving movable pulpit in London from which Dean Farrar, the famous Dean of Canterbury, used to preach when his son was vicar here. It was Dean Farrar who wrote *Eric, or Little by Little*, that Victorian children's classic which deserves to be reprinted.

Holy Trinity, Shepherdess Walk, designed by William Railton in 1848, had J. R. Green as one of its first vicars; he had a hard task and wrote to a friend in 1863, "Managing this parish is like walking on a wall adorned with broken bottles." It was in the vicarage here that he wrote the first chapter of his *Short History of the English People*, one of the most deservedly popular works of its kind ever to be produced. He left Hoxton for a Stepney parish, but had to give up the active ministry through poor health; he devoted himself, however, to history. The pulpit in the church came from St Mary's Somerset in the City; it was lodged first in St Mary's, Hoxton, but when that was bombed the pulpit was saved and placed in Holy Trinity.

Shoreditch should be noted for its excellent street market in Hoxton Street, and for its former Town Hall in Old Street (1866, by C. A. Long) with a jolly tower and a lovely statue of Progress; for the GLC Blue Plaque in Hoxton Square to James Parkinson, the physician who recognised the palsy which is called after him; for being the birthplace of Charles Bradlaugh, the Radical (1833–91), and of Edmund Halley the Astronomer Royal after whom the comet was named; and for its missions of which Hoxton Market Christian Mission is possibly the best known. It was begun in 1881 by two poor brothers, John and Lewis Burtt, who had a saddler's business. They invited wretched and hungry children into their shop which was at least warm and dry. They appealed for help to whomsoever they thought might be of assistance and at last a proper building was provided which, though bombed during the war, has been rebuilt and where noble work is carried on today.

In Haggerston, in the Kingsland Road, stands the Geffrye Museum. This was originally a group of almshouses built out in the fields beyond London in 1715. The money for them was provided under the will of Sir Robert Geffrye, Lord Mayor of London in 1685–86 and twice Master of the Ironmongers' Company, who had died in 1704. By 1918, the pleasant rural surroundings had disappeared and the Ironmongers' Company decided to rebuild the almshouses at Mottingham in Kent, so the old buildings were acquired by the London County Council. The statue of Sir Robert, which had stood over the door since the foundation, was taken to Mottingham and a replica put in its place, and in July 1912, the almshouses were opened to the public as a museum of furniture—the aptest choice possible, since Shoreditch has always been the centre of the London furniture trade. Inside there are London shop fronts which have been saved from demolition, including a wonderful reconstruction of a carpenter's shop taken from Narrow Street, Limehouse, an open-hearth kitchen (cf. Hendon Church House Museum, p. 35), and period rooms, ranging from the Elizabethan to the present day. The Stuart Room is particularly worth admiring; it comes from the Master's Parlour in the Pewterers' Hall and is in the style of Sir Christopher Wren; there is a fine plaster ceiling. The Geffrye Museum is directed particularly at children though it is a delight to visitors of all ages.

Not far away, in Pitfield Street, is the London College of Furniture which stands on the site of Aske's Almshouses, a very proper neighbour for the Geffrye Museum. Here it is possible to study furniture and textile design and production, as well as the technology of musical instruments.

Hackney has given its name to the whole borough. It is a large area, formerly part of the Bishop of London's Manor of Stepney, and consisted of several villages—Dalston, Hackney Wick (which takes its name from *wick*—a dairy farm), Clapton, and Kingsland. It was largely agricultural and London depended much on its bakers for the city's bread supplies. It was the site of a number of historic houses for, though completely and delightfully rural, it was but a short journey from the City and Westminster. Sir Thomas Vyner, the Master of the Goldsmiths' Company who so valiantly helped to rebuild London after the Fire, lived here awhile till he moved to a finer house at Swakeleys (see p. 234) and Brooke House, at the junction of Upper Clapton Road and Brooke Road, was standing till 1954 when, rendered derelict and desolate by bombing, it was reluctantly pulled down and has now been replaced by Brooke House School. It was a large, low house, built round an inner quadrangle and with an entrance courtyard; the west front was broken by seven ivy-clad chimney-stacks and the ceilings were of decorated plasterwork. It was the home of Henry Percy, the 6th

Strawberry Hill, Twickenham. Horace Walpole's house is the right-hand wing

Strawberry Hill: the Library

Osterley House, Isleworth: the east front

Osterley House: the Etruscan Room

duke of Northumberland, who arrested Wolsey and who lived here till his death in 1537 when he was buried in the old parish church of St Augustine's. Margaret, Lady Lennox, the mother of Lord Darnley and the grandmother of James I, lived there as did Fulke Greville, the first Lord Brooke who gave his name to the house. Edward de Vere, the Earl of Oxford, Shakespeare's patron, lived here too. Both Pepys and Evelyn visited the house; John Evelyn noted in his diary for May 8, 1654: "I went to Hackney to see my Lady Brooke's garden which is one of the neatest and most celebrated in England", and Pepys so coveted the oranges he saw growing there that he "pulled off a little one by stealth and eat it".

Another house, less fine perhaps, but just as interesting, is spared to us—it is St John's or Sutton House, Nos. 2–4 Homerton High Street. It was built in the first half of the 16th century on an H-shaped plan, in red brick with patterns of darker violet brickwork. Some of the rooms have fine linenfold panelling. It was the house of Thomas Sutton (b. 1531), who became Master of the Ordnance to Queen Elizabeth, who fought against the Armada in his own ship, the *Sutton*, and who had the good fortune to capture a Spanish galleon with a cargo worth £20,000. The tale goes that Queen Elizabeth I was so delighted with him that she permitted him to take the latticed glass from the galleon to use in his new house, and he was certainly known as the richest commoner in England in his day. He married the widow of John Dudley, the lord of the manor of Stoke Newington, retired from public life, purchased the Charterhouse from the Howard family and established there a school and a home for elderly men. His good work lives on today, and his house, which became the home of Sir Thomas Picton who fell at Waterloo and Dr Burnett the lexicologist, is now National Trust property and the offices of the Association of Scientific, Technical and Managerial Staffs.

Hackney has an interesting group of churches, particularly of the 19th century, and several fine parks and open spaces. There are two parish churches, though of the early one only the tower remains. In the 13th century the Knights Templar bought land in Hackney and built a church there, dedicated to their patron saint, St Augustine. A new church, St John's, was designed by James Spiller between 1792 and '97; it is in the shape of a Greek cross and it was feared that the new church would be unable to support the peal of bells, which accordingly remained in the old tower, the rest of the church of St Augustine being demolished. The bells are now in fact

F

in St John's, but the old church remains to delight all who see it. Part of the churchyard has been laid out as a rosegarden and is a joy to all those who visit it at any time of the year; a most imaginative use has been made of trellis-work in brick.

St John's Church is not especially interesting but contains several monuments brought from the old church which are well worth the visitor's attention. They are housed in little chapels on either side of the entrance and can easily be seen. There is a large early 16th century brass in poor condition to John Lymsey and his wife, and a fine one to Arthur Dericote (d. 1462) and his four wives. The rector, Christopher Urswyck (d. 1522), has an altar tomb which is also that great rarity in the London area—an Easter sepulchre (see Harlington, p. 240). Above him is a bust of David Doulven (d. 1633), Bishop of Bangor, and near him kneel Henry Banister (d. *c.* 1628) and his wife, Anne. They both wear fine ruffs; he was Lord Sheriff of London and Churchwarden of Hackney. On the other side of the entrance, railed off, is the grandest tomb of all, that of Lucye, Lady Latimer, whose effigy is life-sized, clad in a smart little French cap and a fur-lined gown with a jewelled clasp. Her four daughters all married well, having as husbands the Earls of Northumberland and Exeter, Sir William Cornwallis and Sir John Danvers. Above her tomb is a pretty and touching relief to Thomas and Susan Wood, their eight children kneeling behind them, one of whom, Thomas, became Bishop of Lichfield and founded a group of almshouses in the Clapton Road, which still flourish and were restored about 1900. In the chancel of the main church is a bronze memorial by Richard Goulden to the 800 men of Hackney who fell in the First World War, and in Wattisfield Road, adjacent to Millfields, is a group of homes for disabled men. In the churchyard is a tomb, that of a blind man, Fred George. In addition to the conventional inscription are three lines in Braille which read: *One thing I know: whereas I was blind, now I do see.*

There are several interesting Victorian churches in the borough. At Hackney Wick is the Mission of Our Lady of Eton. It stands in Eastway, once open country but now a wilderness of flats. It was built in 1880 by Bodley and Garner and is a rather fine red-brick edifice. The nave is broad with square pillars without capitals and a painted roof.

To the south of the borough, in Church Crescent, is St John of Jerusalem, a splendid Gothic Revival church with an entrance porch like a French cathedral, built by Hakewill between 1845 and 1848. St Matthew's, Clapton, was built by Francis Dollman in

1869 and has a fascinating series of tiled decorations round the walls and a modern stained-glass window wherein pop singers model as saints—Adam Faith appears as St George. St Thomas, Oldhill Street, Clapton Common, was a proprietary chapel, built in 1774. It was bombed completely, except for the apse at the east end. It has been rebuilt on the original plan and the apse has been gilded with a rich and noble effect. The huge church of St Mark's, which has been called the "cathedral of the East End", stands in Sandringham Road; its walls are adorned with dark Byzantine paintings. The Salvation Army Congress Hall stands in Clapton Road, and a mile from it, at No. 1 Rookwood Road, where General Booth and his family lived for a while, a blue plaque has been erected in memory of this great man who lies buried in Abney Park Cemetery, Stoke Newington. His family joined with him in his work; his redoubtable daughter, Evangeline, began by preaching from a soap box to a hostile crowd at the Triangle, Mare Street, at the age of 15.

In the extreme north of the borough in Castlewood Road stands the Cathedral Church of the Good Shepherd, the church of the Ancient Catholics. It was built in 1896 for the followers of John Hugh Smyth Pigott, the Agapemonites. The sect has ceased to exist but the church remains, designed by J. Morris, with a high tower and slender spire and four huge symbols of the Evangelists sculpted by Arthur George Walker. Inside is a fine stained-glass window by Walter Crane.

Even though the Hackney Marshes themselves are being built over by high-rise flats which completely limit the outlook, at least Lesney's factory is there, a highly imaginative design by Messrs Riley and Glanfield completed in 1965. It is here that those perfect scale-model *Matchbox* toys are made which so delight children all over the world. On the southern boundary of the borough is Victoria Park which is shared with Tower Hamlets (see p. 402). The money to purchase the land and to lay it out came from the Crown's sale of York (now Lancaster) House. In the centre of the borough, the rather bleak London Fields stand open, and Hackney Downs were saved after a great legal battle with the lord of the manor, Mr Tyssen Amherst, but at last the Metropolitan Board of Works won the day and the land remained, unbuilt upon. Near the church of St John of Jerusalem is pretty Well Street Common, the houses backing on to it having garden doors which give access to the open land, and nearby in Meynell Gardens are the enchanting Monger's Almshouses, built under the will of Henry Monger who died in 1669. To the north is Springfield Park where Springfield House still stands.

Though much of Hackney is crowded and some of the Greater London Council building is disappointing, there are still enchanting enclaves, such as the little group Albion Square, Albion Terrace and Albion Drive, with two fine public houses, the Duke of Wellington and the Brownlow Arms. No. 195 Mare Street dates from 1710; till 1913 it was the Elizabeth Fry Refuge for Penitent Females but is now the Lansdowne Club. All along Oldhill Street, facing Clapton Common, are fine doorways, worthy of refurbishing, and Cassland Road, especially the Terrace which runs from Nos. 20–54 is worth looking at with attentive admiration. Sutton Place, between the church and High Street, is elegant.

Hackney has its full share of famous and interesting residents. The greatest of all was Dr Joseph Priestley (1733–1804), the discoverer of oxygen and an eminent theologian. In 1792 he was the Minister of the Unitarian Church in Chatham Place, South Hackney. He was a friend of Dr Aitken whom we shall meet living in Stoke Newington. He was a man of powerful and original mind who maintained his opinions—usually right—in the face of all opposition; he eventually died in America.

De Beauvoir Square stands where once Balmes House stood. Originally a private dwelling, it was adapted as a lunatic asylum and it was to this house that Charles Lamb and his poor sister Mary would walk, the tears streaming down their faces, whenever she felt one of her attacks of insanity coming upon her; it was during such an attack that she had murdered their mother and Charles had devoted the rest of his life to the care of his afflicted sister (see also p. 121).

Major John Andre may have been born in or near Pond House, Clapton, in 1751. He joined the 7th Royal Fusiliers in Canada and was entrusted with negotiations with a certain Benedict Arnold who was planning to betray West Point, the American stronghold, to the British. Andre was captured and hanged as a spy. All the British Army went into mourning for him and in 1821 his body was returned to England and buried in Westminster Abbey where a cenotaph had been erected to him 40 years before. George Loddiges (1743–1826) was a famous horticulturalist and grower of shrubs—Loddigesia is named after him. He lived in Paragon Road and the house was surrounded by the nursery which was one of the show-places of London. Henry Fawcett who became Member of Parliament for Hackney in 1874, was the Postmaster-General under Gladstone's second administration, in spite of the fact that he was blind. The profitable use that he made of his life was an example to all who came in contact with him; he had always intended to enter public life but when he lost his eyesight as a young man through a shooting accident, it seemed as if his ambitions must fail, but his spirit was such that they did not. His wife was Millicent Garrett, the sister of Elizabeth Garrett-Anderson, the first woman to qualify as a doctor; she devoted herself as assiduously to helping her husband in his political and economic work as Elizabeth did to her own great achievements.

Before we leave Hackney, it might be as well to mention that the hackney carriage did not take its name from this part of London, but rather from the French verb, *hacquener*, to hire.

To the north of the borough lies **Stoke Newington**, still the most countrified of the three areas. Judging from Roque's map of the Environs of London of 1746, it must have been as pretty a place as one could wish for. In 1801, there were 208 houses with a total population of 1462; by 1891, there were 30,936 people there. The highest point is at Stamford Hill where James I was met by the Lord Mayor of London and his Aldermen and had his first glimpse of his new capital on May 7, 1603; an inn at the corner of Church Street was renamed the Three Crowns in honour of the occasion. Reliable tradition also records that Dick Turpin patrolled the lonely stretches of the road and robbed many travellers thereon.

Stoke Newington has two parish churches, which face each other across Church Street. Both are dedicated to St Mary. The new one, large and fine, was built in 1858 by Sir Gilbert Scott; its spire was added in 1890 by his son. The old church is essentially the sort of building one finds on a village green. Its foundation may date from the late Middle Ages, but was refurbished in 1563 by William Patten whose arms can be seen above the south porch. It has a brick tower with a timber spire of 1829, and is both quaint and appealing. The south aisles and arcade are of Tudor red brick—the only arcade of brick pillars and arches that we can remember in the London area. There is a fine monument to John Dudley and his wife Elizabeth (d. 1602); she married Thomas Sutton, "the richest commoner in England", after her first husband's death. Behind her kneels a meek little daughter and behind him is a carved helmet.

St Matthias's Church, one of Butterfield's most characteristic achievements, was damaged by bombing, but has been restored and

St Olave's, red brick and very solid, stands at the corner of Seven Sisters Road. St Faiths and All Saints were destroyed during the war and have not been rebuilt. Blomfield's imposing St Andrew's (1854) still stands on the corner of Bethune Road.

Behind the church is Clissold Park, in which old Clissold House still stands. It is as pleasant an open space as one can find and was saved for the borough by the devoted efforts of John Runtz and Joseph Beck, who were determined not to let it be built over. Beside it stands Park Crescent, which recently won a Civic Trust award for a successful re-adaptation of an old Victorian terrace to new living conditions. North of the park are the west and east reservoirs, now the end of Sir Hugh Myddelton's New River water supply to London (see p. 123) though the ghost of its passage can still be traced in certain narrow parks and playgrounds as far as Islington. Nearby, in a room in the public library, is the Chalmers Bequest, presented to the borough in 1927; it is an agreeable collection of 18th century English paintings, portraits and landscapes, bequeathed by Alexander Henry Chalmers.

Stoke Newington's other park has been turned into a cemetery; it was originally the grounds of Abney House and the iron gates of the mansion still stand in Church Street. General Booth and his wife Catherine lie here, and near him are the Rev. Andrew Reed, founder of the London Orphan Asylum, Samuel Morley, MP and noted philanthropist, and Mr Braidwood, the gallant Chief of the London Fire Brigade who perished during the great Tooley Street Fire of 1861.

Church Street, Stoke Newington, is a fascinating mixture of dates and styles. The manor house stood on the site now occupied by Stoke Newington Town Hall, and here Elizabeth Dudley lived with her first husband John and her second, Thomas; he did not move to Sutton House till after her death. In the early 17th century Sir Henry Mildmay lived at Stoke Newington; he was one of Charles I's judges and his brother had the responsibility for the dead monarch's burial. The Manor House was demolished in 1695 and in its place Church Row was built, a pretty group of houses which were pulled down to make way for the Town Hall, now council offices.

Stoke Newington's greatest resident was undoubtedly Daniel Defoe (1661?–1731) who was sent to school at the Reverend Charles Morton's Academy at Newington Green, since both Defoe's father and that minister were Dissenters. Dr Morton was an unusual preceptor for his day for, instead of stressing the importance of Latin, he emphasised the use of pure and forceful English and gave all his lessons in that language. His pupil certainly profited from his instruction. A fellow pupil, Timothy Cruso, lent his name to Defoe's most famous novel, *Robinson Crusoe*, which he wrote when living in Stoke Newington Church Street; a blue plaque marks the site of his house at the corner with Defoe Road.

John Howard, who was born in Hackney in 1727, also lived in Church Street, and married Sarah Lardeau, a lady some twice his age who had nursed him through a long illness. His attention was drawn to the shocking condition of prisons in this country and throughout Europe, and he devoted all his strength and courage to improving matters and promoting the welfare of those within. His many books were edited by his friend, Dr Aitken, who came to live in Stoke Newington too, and with him his sister, Mrs Anna Barbauld, the poetess and author of *Hymns in Prose for Children*. She was a brave woman who supported her husband—he was a clergyman—through a long madness till his death, and still found the strength to write many beautiful poems. She died in 1824 and lies in the churchyard at old St Mary's. Perhaps her best-known lines are the concluding verse of her poem on *Life*:

> *Then steal away, give little warning;*
> *Choose thy own time;*
> *Say not Good-night, but in some brighter clime*
> *Bid me Good-morning.*

Among her friends were numbered Robert Southey, Sir Walter Scott, Charles Lamb, and William Wordsworth. Another Stoke Newington author was Thomas Day who was born in Limehouse where his father was Customs Officer, but who moved with his widowed mother to live on the higher ground when he was a small boy. He wrote an excellent book for children, *Sandford and Merton*, which, like Dean Farrar's *Eric*, can still be reread with pleasure today.

There was a strong Quaker community in Stoke Newington, such as the anti-slavery campaigners, Samuel Hoare and his son Jonathan. Another family were the Hanburys, whose son, Cornelius, married Mary Allen and founded the pharmaceutical firm.

Even today, Stoke Newington is a pleasant place. There is exciting development going on at Woodberry Down where a great GLC estate has been built which includes a really fine comprehensive school designed by Professor Robert Matthew and where the curriculum includes Chinese. In Church Street still stands one of the prettiest private houses in London, Sisters' Place, built in 1714, and still as fresh and as beautiful as the day on which it was completed; it is called after the four Bridge sisters, Mary, Isabella, Frances, and Naomi, who inherited it in 1813. Beside it is a dentist's surgery, built at the same time, with the most delightful bow windows that we have seen in London.

HAMMERSMITH

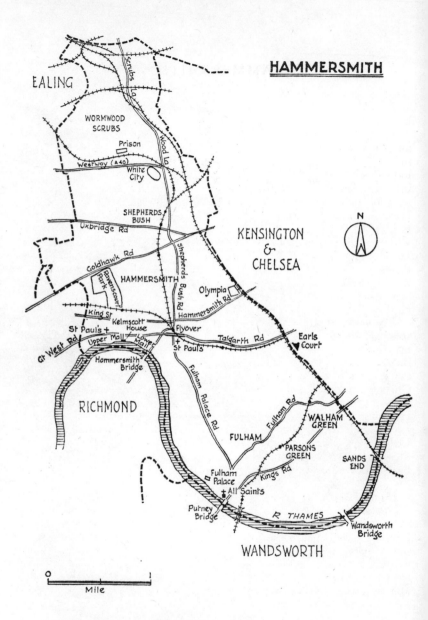

HAMMERSMITH

EALING

Scrubs La.

WORMWOOD SCRUBS

Prison

Wood La.

Westway (A40)

White City

SHEPHERDS BUSH

Uxbridge Rd

KENSINGTON & CHELSEA

Goldhawk Rd

Ravenscourt Park

HAMMERSMITH

Shepherds Bush Rd

Olympia

King St

Kelmscott House

St Pauls +

Upper Mall

Lower Mall

Flyover

Hammersmith Rd

+ St Pauls

Talgarth Rd

Earls Court

Gt West Rd

Hommersmith Bridge

RICHMOND

Fulham Palace Rd

Fulham Rd

WALHAM GREEN

FULHAM

PARSONS GREEN

SANDS END

Kings Rd

Fulham Palace

+ All Saints

Putney Bridge

R THAMES

Wandsworth Bridge

WANDSWORTH

N

0 — Mile — 1

HAMMERSMITH

The London Borough of Hammersmith combines the former boroughs of Hammersmith and Fulham. The association is an old one, for both were part of the Bishop of London's manor of Fulham, and they only became separate parishes in 1834. Hammersmith lies to the west of London, a long thin tongue of land cradled by a loop of the River Thames on the south and west, and bounded inland by Hounslow, Ealing, Brent, and Kensington. It covers an area of 3995 acres with a population of 187,980 (1970). Scrubs Lane, Wood Lane, Shepherd's Bush Road, and Fulham Palace Road link up to produce a spine running roughly from north to south, which is crossed by a zigzag of roads running from east to west for Hammersmith is on the direct route from London to Oxford or to the West of England. Across Fulham ran the New King's Road, leading from Kensington Palace to Hampton Court, by way of the ferry where Putney Bridge now stands.

The popular view of Hammersmith is that of the motorist who sees it from the Flyover, built in 1961. Suddenly one's vehicle rises up from the West Cromwell and Talgarth Roads, leaps over the Broadway, and skims away, level with the tower of St Paul's Church, and then descends as suddenly to join the Great West Road through Chiswick and Hounslow to London Airport, or onwards, towards the west. At ground level, the superficial visitor might well feel that Hammersmith was nothing but a maelstrom of traffic, with Shepherd's Bush and Hammersmith Broadway, and the hustle along the Uxbridge, Goldhawk, and Hammersmith Roads, but between these thoroughfares lie pockets of building, most of it interesting, some of it beautiful, and altogether of an astonishing variety.

Hammersmith, which now gives its name to the new borough, was originally the less important half of the bishop of London's huge manor of Fulham. The old village grew up on the riverside, around a little harbour which is today marked by the remains of Hammersmith Creek. The creek was spanned by the High Bridge, now vanished, and northwards was joined by the Stamford Brook. A notice on the wall tells us that until 1921, boats of some 200 tons were able to unload there. Today, lighter craft moor at the floating jetty, and the embellishment of the river front is something of which Hammersmith can be very proud. The Upper and Lower Malls run from Hammersmith Bridge to Chiswick; the low tower and tiny steeple of Chiswick church gives focus to one of the loveliest views along London's river, just as this is one of the pleasantest and most civilised walks along its banks. The suspension bridge, a robust, swaggering, gilded pepperpot-turreted creation of Sir Joseph Bazalgette's, built in 1887, replaces an earlier structure built in 1827 by W. Tierney Clark. This was London's first suspension bridge, and can be seen on its designer's memorial slab in St Paul's parish church.

Upstream from the bridge, the first building of interest is Westcott Lodge, built in the first half of the 18th century, used for a while as the vicarage, and now the property of the borough council, which allows it to be used for society and committee meetings. It stands solitary in the well-laid-out Furnivall Gardens, which lie between the river and the traffic of the Great West Road. The gardens are called after Dr F. J. Furnivall (1825–1910), a distinguished scholar and editor of Chaucer and Shakespeare, who founded the Hammersmith Sculling Club (today rechristened with his own name) for young women and men who would otherwise have had small opportunity for sport.

Beyond the gardens is Sussex House, built about 1726 and replacing another house some 100 years older. It is fronted with warm-coloured brick, five windows wide, and has a beautiful doorway with fluted pilasters and a curved entablature. It probably takes its name from the association of Augustus Frederick, the Duke of Sussex, Queen Victoria's uncle, with the neighbourhood; in 1825 he laid the foundation of Hammersmith Bridge and frequently presented petitions on behalf of the Vestry. It was here that Sir Emery Walker did his engraving work. Between Sussex House and the river are The Seasons and the Dove or Doves Inn, built as a single house about 1750 but enlarged separately. The master binder and printer, J. T. Cobden-Sanderson, lived at The Seasons and in 1900 founded, with Sir Emery Walker, the Doves Press and Bindery. Their elegant, restrained work is still cherished. The Dove Inn has been a hostelry since 1790 at least and is well worth visiting, as are its neighbours along the Mall, the Old Ship and the Black Lion.

Here the Mall opens out on to the river and at No. 26 is Kelmscott House, the home of William Morris from 1878 till his death in 1896 (for his story see pp. 410–11). He installed a tapestry loom in his bedroom, held meetings in the stables, and started to print books for the

Kelmscott Press in part of Sussex House. It is a study in change of style to compare his works with those of the Doves Press; both are wonderful, but so very different. Morris rejoiced to think that the same river flowed past his house in London and his beloved home at Kelmscott in Oxfordshire. This house was also the home—as plaques testify—of Sir Francis Ronald, who invented the electric telegraph in 1816, and George MacDonald, that rather eerie, utterly individual writer whose books for children are at last beginning to enjoy a well-deserved revival.

Beyond Kelmscott House is Rivercourt, built in 1808 and today a part of the Latymer Upper School, established in the borough by Edward Latymer in 1624. Rivercourt is built partly on the site of a house occupied by Catherine of Braganza, Charles II's queen, during her widowhood before she returned to Portugal; she was often visited here by her brother-in-law, James II. Beyond it is Linden House where the London Corinthian Yacht Club occupies superb early 18th century premises. Here the river walk has been laid out and paved by the local authorities, to great advantage. Beyond, it narrows to a passage through the buildings of the Vitamins factory and reaches the Old Ship Inn and the West Middlesex Water Works, which were laid out in 1810 by W. Tierney Clark, their clerk of works. Then a passage leads to the Black Lion Inn where a magnificent climbing frame shaped like a helicopter, provides entertainment for the children of clients, and then come the 16 houses of Hammersmith Terrace, fronting on to the river and built about 1755. The artist Philippe de Loutherbourg occupied 7 and 8; he provided the scenery at Drury Lane where he was employed by Garrick and Sheridan. A blue plaque marks Sir Emery Walker's residence at No. 7, and in 1970 Sir A. P. Herbert, the wittiest of poets and yachtsmen, lived at No. 12.

Opposite the Mall, but separated from it by the Great West Road, is St Peter's Church, built in 1827–29 by Edward Lapidge. It is a rectangle of brick with an Ionic portico and a west tower topped with a tiny plastered cupola. Within, a gallery runs round three sides with a pretty little organ at the west end, and some attractive murals on either side of the altar. Outside on the roadway, is an impressive statue by Dr Karel Vogel of a reclining woman, her folded arms intriguingly askew to the road; it was unveiled in 1959. St Peter's is a blunt, lumbering, utterly lovable building and it stands in the pleasantest quarter of Hammersmith—apart from the Mall—namely, Black Lion Lane and St Peter's Square. In the Lane, the houses are small, pretty and unpretentious; the Square is grander, ringed round with groups of four houses, three-storeyed and adorned with eagles and pineapples. It was built about 1825–30 and is still delightful.

The modern centre of Hammersmith has shifted from the Creek and Mall to the Broadway. Our landmark is St Paul's Church, whose tower is seen so arrestingly from the Flyover. A church was first built here in 1631 as a chapel-of-ease to Fulham parish church, All Saints, which lay a full mile and a half to the south-east. Laud was bishop of London when permission was sought to build it and he took an interest in the little chapel. It was rebuilt in 1883 by J. P. Seddon and Hugh Roumier Gough in pale brick and stone, with a tall, rather forbidding nave and the pinnacled tower which we have already noticed. The marble font, from the old church, is late 17th century, the octagonal pulpit, beautifully carved, is from Wren's church, All Hallows, Thames Street. The eight bells are from the old church and are said to be one of the sweetest-toned rings in England. The third is dated 1657, the fourth, fifth, and seventh were given by Sir Nicholas Crisp in 1639, and the sixth, the "Town Bell", is of the same date. There are three particularly interesting monuments, one of which, to W. Tierney Clark, the designer of the first suspension bridge, we have already mentioned. In the chancel is a large black and white marble memorial to James Smith (d. 1667), Alderman of London, and his wife Sarah (d. 1680); the upper part is a sarcophagus surmounted by a coat of arms which supports a bust of the Alderman. On the west wall beside the north door is a marble pillar, bearing a bronze bust of Charles I; below it is an urn in which rests the heart of Charles's devoted supporter, Sir Nicholas Crisp. His body lies outside in the churchyard, having been brought here from St Mildred's, Bread Street; for a century after his death it was the annual custom to take out his heart and refresh it with a glass of wine.

Just east of the church, off the Broadway in Queen Caroline Street, is the frontage of Bradmore House rebuilt and re-sited about 1900, now concealing a London Transport bus garage. It was built during the 1730s as a new addition to Butterwick House (demolished 1836), a Tudor mansion which may have been the residence of Thomas Sheffield, Earl of Mulgrave, who commanded the *White Bear* against the Spanish Armada, and who was buried in Hammersmith Chapel (now St Paul's). Officers of the Parliamentary forces were probably quartered here during the Civil War. The London County Council and London Transport are to be congratulated on a brave and imaginative attempt to preserve this façade.

Westwards again is Ravenscourt Park running from King Street to Goldhawk Road. This delightful park marks the site of the manor of Palyngswick, one of the properties held in trust for Alice Perrers, wife to Sir William de Windsor and mistress to Edward III. She also held the manor of Gunnersbury. After her death in 1401—she was buried at Upminster in Essex, now on the extremity of the Greater London area—the manor was held for a century by the Frowyk family, noted citizens and merchants of London; Henry, who died in 1460, was Lord Mayor twice and MP for the City five times. A new house was built early in the 18th century and was given a new name—Ravenscourt. The grounds were laid out by Humphrey Repton soon after 1812, when the property was acquired by George Scott, and it is this inspired planning which gives an unusual charm to the park of today. The house, which had been used as a public library, was destroyed by bombs in 1941; the stables remain and today tea is served in them. There are some attractive 18th century gates at the entrance to the Old English Garden.

North of the Hammersmith Road is Brook Green, a long curving strip of grass and trees. On one side is St Paul's Girls' School, built in 1904, a sister establishment to St Paul's Boys' School which had moved in 1884 to the Hammersmith Road from its site in the City where it had been since its foundation in 1510. (St Paul's Boys' School moved across the river to new premises at Barnes in 1968.) Beyond the Green, on the edge of the borough, is Olympia, an enormous exhibition and entertainment centre, which opened on Boxing Day, 1886, with the Paris Hippodrome Circus. Since then, it has housed Barnum's and Bertram Mills' Circuses; in the 1890s spectacles of Venice, Constantinople, and the Orient were staged here by Imre Kiralfy; the Motor Show, beginning in 1905, was held here, and the Daily Mail Ideal Home Exhibition, beginning in 1920, still is. In addition to the original Grand Hall, starkly refronted in 1930 by Joseph Emberson, there are the National Hall (1923) and the Empire Hall (1929)—altogether 500,000 square feet of exhibition space which draws millions of visitors anually to Hammersmith.

All the area we have been describing—indeed, the whole borough, both Hammersmith and Fulham alike—was, from the early 17th century at least until the mid-19th century—an area of market-gardens, supplying the metropolis with their produce. Potatoes, green vegetables, strawberries, raspberries, currants, and goose-berries were all sent up to London. There were 13 market-gardens in Hammersmith in 1845, varying in size from a few acres to the 40–50 acres worked by the Wills family around Brook Green. The most famous garden of all, the Vineyard Nursery, belonging to Lee and Kennedy. was founded about 1745 and is today covered by Olympia. It flourished under successive generations of the two families till 1894, supplied Napoleon's Empress, Josephine, with £2300 worth of plants in 1803 for her garden at Malmaison, and produced quantities of young trees for the original landscaping of Regent's Park, as well as cultivating roses, gladioli, chrysanthemums, and many other flowers. The only industry of the neighbourhood was brick-making.

The coming of the railways changed all this. Whereas, until the 19th century, Hammersmith's main communications with the outside world had been to supply London with fruit and vegetables, and to provide post-horses along the Uxbridge and Great West Roads, everything changed when the Metropolitan Line was extended southwards to Hammersmith Broadway in 1864, to be followed ten years later by the District Line from the east. In 1881, a branch line reached southwards to Putney Bridge. Immediately houses, sensible respectable family houses, to be rented at about £30 a year, began to spring up from the Hammersmith Road to the Goldhawk Road, around the Green at Shepherd's Bush (where today a new pedestrian shopping precinct is being built), and to fill the land between the Goldhawk and Uxbridge Roads. An attentive walk along these two broad streets, examining the older buildings set back behind ground-floor shop-frontages, is most rewarding; 19th century villas and terraces stand alone or lurk under heavy disguises, but rebuilding is going on so fast that any detailed description would only be misleading. To entertain the newcomers, the Lyric Theatre was opened in 1888; its heyday was from 1918 till 1933 under Sir Nigel Playfair, when *The Beggar's Opera* ran for 1463 performances, when Edith Evans scored her first great success in *The Way of the World*, and when Sir Alan P. Herbert's revues and light operas were acclaimed. It has now been closed.

North of the Uxbridge Road the houses begin to thin out. There is a welcome rectangle of green at Wormholt Park, and an interesting garden suburb development by the council on the western edge of the borough, where the streets all have delicious names, such as Bryony Road, Hemlock Road, Yew Tree Road, Lilac Avenue, and The Curve. This last shelters a remarkably pretty little public library, built like a tiny Temple of Learning. Wood Lane runs northwards, with the British Broadcasting Corporation's Television Centre and White City Stadium on its western side. The White City was built by the brothers Kiralfy; it covered 200 acres, 100 of which were gardens with half a mile of artificial waterways. All sorts of spectacular amusements were to be found there, among them a great wheel and a water chute. Today, the BBC Television Centre stands on the site of the Court of Honour, and all that remains is the Stadium, built to house the 1908 Olympic Games, when Pietro Dorandi ran his historic marathon race from Windsor to Hammersmith and lost the title because a track official tried to help him up when he fell just before the finishing post. Queen Alexandra sent him a special medal.

From Du Cane Road to the northern extremity of the borough is Wormwood Scrubs. The name describes its early history—the Wormeholte or Snake Wood; it is now a bleak, open space, breathtaking under snow, a little gentler in summer, with Hammersmith Hospital and Wormwood Scrubs Prison on its southern edge. The prison was built by convicts to the designs of Sir Edmund Du Cane, the penal reformer, in 1874; it is one of the most staggering Victorian castles—no less—in existence. Today much excellent book-binding is produced by the inmates, of whom there are about 1000. On the south side of Du Cane Road stands the church of St Catherine Coleman. There is some industrial development here, a network of railway lines at Willesden Junction, and the still useful Grand Union Canal. There is access to the pleasant walk along the towpath where Scrubs Lane crosses the canal. In the Roman Catholic portion of Kensal Green Cemetery were buried Cardinal Wiseman (he now lies at Westminster), Antony Panizzi who fled from Austrian rule in Italy and became principal librarian of the British Museum and creator of its present cataloguing system (see p. 71), and Francis Babington Tussaud, grandson of Madame Tussaud, the originator of the Waxworks.

Fulham occupies the southern half of the borough. Even today, it is a collection of units rather than a unity for it grew up from four hamlets, Fulham Town, Parsons Green, Walham Green, and North End. The whole area belonged to the see of London from the early 8th century when Tyrhtilus, Bishop of Hereford, granted it to Waldhere, Bishop of London. We do not know when the bishop first built a palace here but the present building, which is the most important monument in the borough and one of the most interesting in London, was begun by Richard Fitzjames, who was bishop from 1506 to 1522. It consists of two quadrangles, of which the western, built of red brick with darker diaper work, is the older. Bishop Fitzjames' arms are on the south face of the south block and on the east side is a small bell-turret with a weather-vane and clock. Entering under the clock tower, the Great Hall is on the left. It was here that Bishop Bonner held Thomas Tomkins' hand in a candle flame to warn him of the heat of the fire in which heretics died, but Tomkins would not change his Protestant views and died in the flames at Smithfield on February 9, 1555/6. The Hall was later used as a chapel but when the new chapel was built by Butterfield in 1866–67, it was restored to its former usage. The eastern quadrangle was rebuilt by Bishop Terrick who held the see from 1764–77, and a new east front was added under Bishop Howley between 1814 and 1815. The work was by S. P. Cockerell and the front is elegant and plain, like the nicest sort of country vicarage. Bishop Porteus, who held the see from 1787 till his death in 1809, gave it his library which is kept in the palace and a collection of portraits, to which his successors have added, of previous bishops of London, dating from the Reformation.

Since the Palace is the Bishop's private residence, it is not open to the public, but several times each year the gardens are opened and they should be visited without fail. They were first laid out by Grindal (he held the see from 1559 to 1570) and it was he who originally laid the emphasis on trees, for which the grounds are famous, by planting a tamarisk and a vine. Bishop Compton who was tutor to James II's daughters, the future queens Mary and Anne, added tulip trees, ilex, cork, Virginian oak, and black American walnut. Bishops Howley and Blomfield were ardent gardeners too, and the tradition of care and of studied planting is carried on to this day. Around the grounds was a moat, only filled in in 1924, which is believed to have been dug by the Danes about 880 to 881 when they encamped at Fulham for the winter. On it large white water-lilies, known as Bishop's Wigs, used to float.

Perhaps the noblest person ever to have held the see was Nicholas Ridley who was Bishop of London from 1550 to 1553. He succeeded Bonner who was imprisoned for omitting to say in a sermon at Paul's Cross that Edward VI's authority was as great in his childhood as it would be when he became a man. Ridley never failed to invite Bonner's old mother to a seat of honour at his table where he addressed her as "My Mother Bonner". Bonner was restored to the see under Mary and Ridley perished in the flames at Oxford on October 5, 1555, in company with Hugh Latimer, the Bishop of Worcester, the two scholars encouraging each other till the end.

A part of the palace grounds was opened to the public in 1893 as the Bishop's Park. A row of fine plane trees leans over the main path and more grow along the river embankment, which affords a splendid view of the Thames and its southern bank, where the blue-painted plasterwork of the Duke's Head (in Putney) is a distinctive landmark. Just outside the palace grounds is Putney Bridge, originally built as a wooden toll-bridge in 1729 when it replaced an ancient ferry service. It was the first bridge to be constructed up-stream from London and there was considerable opposition from the City merchants. The present granite bridge was designed by Sir Joseph Bazalgette and was opened on May 29, 1886. It was widened in 1933 and today is as graceful a sight as ever it was with the square embattled towers—each with a supernumerary turret—of Putney and Fulham parish churches rising up at either end of its arc.

Fulham parish church is dedicated to All Saints. The four-storeyed west tower was completed in 1440; the rest was rebuilt in 1881 by Sir Arthur Blomfield. It contains an unusual number of interesting memorials. There is a brass to Margaret Hornbolt (d. c. 1529) with a half-figure in a shroud supported by angels, and a touching monument to Margaret Legh, wife to Sir Peter Legh, who died in 1605. Her effigy sits bolt upright in a niche, wearing a widow's cap, a swaddled baby in her right arm, her left hand at her breast, and another tiny swaddled figure beside her. Sir William Butts who was Henry VIII's physician and who died in 1545 has a little tablet in the north aisle. William Payne (d. 1626) and his wife kneel opposite each other, and Katherine Hart (d. 1605) kneels too, her four children around her. John Mordaunt, Viscount Mordaunt of Avalon, a staunch and fiery cavalier, who died in 1675, is sculpted by John Bushnel as a swaggering figure in semi-classical draperies, a baton grasped in his right hand. He lived and died at Peterborough House near Parsons Green, where he cultivated a wonderful garden which John Evelyn admired. The churchyard is exceptionally well-tended with avenues of holly and yew.

Behind the church lie the Powell Almshouses, founded on another site by Sir William Powell in 1680 for 12 poor women. The houses were rebuilt here in 1869 rather quaintly, and beyond them is Church Gate, in which Egmont Lodge and its neighbour are all that remain of the late 17th and early 18th century houses that used to approach the church, but the ground behind them has been re-developed as Steeple Close, a cluster of modern, deliberately Georgian, wholly successful three-storey houses. They are composed and at peace with their surroundings.

A little farther inland from the approach to the bridge, at the junction of the New King's Road and Burlington Road, stood the

Fulham Pottery founded about 1671 by John Dwight, who had been Registrar to the diocese of Chester. He produced all sorts of jugs, jars, and domestic utensils, as well as a fine portrait bust of Prince Rupert, now in the British Museum, and a very lovely half-effigy of his little daughter, Lydia, modelled after her death; her small hands clutch a posy of flowers. The firm continued under Dwight's descendants and their connections by marriage, the Whites, till 1859. It was then taken over by C. J. C. Bailey and from 1873 to 1877 the four Martin brothers used to fire their pottery here till they established a works of their own at Southall (see p. 110). The firm has only recently closed.

The river winds sharply here and upstream from Fulham Bridge is the starting point of the Oxford and Cambridge Boat Race, which was first rowed over the $4\frac{1}{2}$-mile course to Mortlake in 1845. North of the Bishop's Park are the grounds of Fulham Football Club, founded in 1889, with a clubhouse on the site of Craven Cottage, where Lord Lytton wrote his dramatic novel, *The Last of the Barons*. Still farther upstream is the site of what was once Brandenburgh House and its grounds. The house was built in the second quarter of the 16th century by Sir Nicholas Crisp, possibly on earlier foundations. He had been born in 1599, the eldest son of Ellis Crisp, a prosperous merchant who was Sheriff of London at his death in 1625. Nicholas traded with West Africa, dealing in ivory, gold, and slaves, and with the East Indies for spices and indigo. He became associated with the Court and helped to supply Charles I with money, becoming one of the most important tax-farmers of the day, so that the king called him "his little old faithful farmer". In 1641 he was knighted and continued to serve the king with money, good advice, and his sword. He was heavily fined by Parliament but was allowed to live quietly at Fulham till Charles II was restored. In 1665 he was made a baronet but died the following year. As we have told, his heart was embalmed and placed in Hammersmith Chapel (now St Paul's) which he had helped to establish. His grandson sold the house to Prince Rupert, for his mistress, the lovely actress Margaret or Peg Hughes, who lived there for many years.

From 1792 till 1819, the house was occupied by the Margrave and Margravine of Brandenburg. The Margravine had been Lady Craven but after her husband's death she remarried, the Margrave sold his principality to his cousin, the King of Prussia, and they came to live in Fulham. The Margravine was an enthusiastic amateur actress and entertained many visitors, often playing the lead in theatrical performances. From July 1820 till her death a year later, the house was the refuge of the unhappy Queen Caroline. The princess from Brunswick had been married to George, Prince of Wales, in 1795. They had never met, and he took an instant dislike to her; he had only married so that Parliament should pay his debts and he infinitely preferred Mrs Fitzherbert to whom he was already married in secret. After the birth of a child, Princess Charlotte, they separated and Caroline went first to live at Blackheath and then to travel on the Continent with a strange and somewhat unruly retinue. On the death of George III she determined to return to England and arrived on June 6, 1820. Her principal supporter was Alderman Matthew Wood, a former Lord Mayor of London, and to his house in South Audley Street she went, but the mob which supported her made such a tumult outside that quieter premises seemed desirable, and Keppel Craven, her vice-chamberlain, suggested his mother's house, where on July 29, the inhabitants of Hammersmith offered her a Loyal Address. The House of Lords was ordered to hold an enquiry into the queen's conduct but was unable to establish impropriety though it was clear that she had been indiscreet in the company she kept. Popular feeling was all on Caroline's side. However foolishly she might have behaved when deserted by her husband, his reputation was such that he had few supporters. Deputations of sailors, of brass founders, and of the watermen and lightermen of the Thames in decorated barges, all came to Brandenburgh House to express their sympathy. Caroline attempted to attend the coronation of George IV, but was barred from the Abbey. She returned to Brandenburgh House where she died on August 7, 1821. She wished to be buried in Brunswick, and the funeral cortège set out on August 14. It was intended to carry the coffin round to the north of London but the crowd was determined that it should pass through the City. Fighting broke out at Tyburn and the troops fired on the crowd, killing Richard Honey and George Francis, both of Hammersmith. The mob resolutely barricaded every street entrance and at last the coffin was led through the City by the Lord Mayor himself, and was embarked at Harwich on August 16. Honey and Francis were buried in Hammersmith churchyard by public subscription. The whole affair was sordid and pitiful to the last degree. A year later, Brandenburgh House was pulled down.

East of Putney bridge stands Hurlingham House. Built about 1760 for Dr William Cadogan, it was enlarged in 1797 and became a pigeon-shooting club in 1869. By 1905, it was famous for the polo played there, though this ceased in 1939. In 1952, the polo grounds were acquired by the LCC and made into a park, and a well-designed estate, Sulivan Court, was built on yet more of the grounds by Fulham Council but the Hurlingham Club still flourishes with about 5000 members and much tennis and croquet are played.

From this point onwards the river frontage—all the fields that were once the Town Mead—are now occupied by Fulham Generating Station, Watson House Research Centre, the walls of which are adorned with abstract murals by John Piper, and various factories. Inland is South Park, which had been a nursery garden, Southfield Farm, from 1711 till it was acquired by the borough council in 1903. Near it in Peterborough Road is Hurlingham Secondary School, designed in 1956 by Richard Sheppard, built low round a double courtyard, its entrance gaily faced with bands of yellow, orange, and black tiles. An equally interesting building is Watson House Outstation in Waterford Road; it has been added to a much older gas works and the whole makes a most picturesque and impressive industrial group. Among the works is Sandford Manor House, dating from the mid-17th century as can be seen from within, though the façade was altered in the 19th century.

Inland again, on the New King's Road which was used by the court from Stuart times as the quickest route from London to Hampton Court is Parson's Green and beyond it Eel Brook Common. Today the Green's main adornments are Elm House and Belfield House, once the property of the Child banking family, now the premises of Lady Margaret School, founded in 1917 under the headmistress-ship of Enid Moberley Bell, undoubtedly one of the greatest educators of all time. Near the Green was Peterborough House, the seat of the Mordaunt family. Viscount Mordaunt is buried in All Saints' Church, his son, who became the Earl of Peterborough, was Commander-in-Chief of the British forces in the Iberian Peninsula during the war of the Spanish Succession. Owing to political complications, he was not very successful, but he was a brilliant soldier and a man of incredible courage.

Three churches in the borough should be mentioned—St Dionis's, St Thomas's, and St Etheldreda's. St Dionis's stands at Parson's Green. It was designed in 1886 by Ewan Christian who is said to have restored 350 churches and to have built at least as many as well as the National Portrait Gallery. Inside are the font and pulpit from Wren's St Dionis Backchurch. St Thomas's Roman Catholic church stands in Pylston Road. It was designed in 1847–49 by Augustus Pugin, Sir Charles Barry's collaborator in designing the Houses of Parliament. It has a good purposeful spire and is restrainedly mediaeval within. Warrington Taylor, William Morris's devoted business manager who died very young in 1870 from consumption, is buried here and so is Joseph Hansom, the designer of the "Patent Safety Cab". St Etheldreda's stands in Fulham Palace Road. It was first built in 1897 but was severely bombed in 1940 and so was rebuilt in 1958 in brick and concrete to designs by Guy Biscoe. The most striking features are the bell-tower and semi-circular baptistry with vivid stained glass by Carter Shapland, depicting episodes from the life of Christ. Near it are the Lygon almshouses and beyond them, northwards up Fulham Palace Road, is Fulham Hospital which is at present being rebuilt in conjunction with Charing Cross Hospital.

Two houses, which once stood in Fulham, should not be forgotten. They were The Grange at North End, which was only pulled down in 1958 amidst a storm of protest, and Fulham House in the High Street. The Grange was the home of two admirable men, Samuel Richardson and Sir Edward Burne-Jones. It was built as twin houses about 1714 and half was let to the Countess of Ranelagh. In 1740, Samuel Richardson, a prosperous master printer, leased part of it and here he spent his weekends till 1754, when he moved to Parson's Green, and here he wrote his novels, *Pamela, Clarissa*, and *Sir Charles Grandison*. He delighted to escape from London to the open countryside and to welcome his friends when they joined him, as they frequently did. In November 1867, Sir Edward Burne-Jones the pre-Raphaelite painter came to The Grange. His wife wrote of the bed of lilies-of-the-valley, 20 feet long, and the peaches, plums and apricots that grew along the walls. Their little nephew, Rudyard Kipling, thought the place a paradise. William Morris would walk over from Kelmscott House on Hammersmith Mall to see them, and Ruskin visited them here. While they still lived here, the railways came, houses replaced the walnut and elm trees at the end of their garden, and North End was called by the new name of West Kensington—a change at which Burne-Jones continued to protest. He died in his sleep there peacefully in 1898 at the age of 62; a housing estate covers the land where his house and garden, with its lily-bed, stood.

Fulham House stood in Fulham High Street and was the home of the Sharp family. William Sharp was a surgeon practising at Guy's Hospital. On retirement he settled at Fulham in 1780 and lived there till his death 30 years later. He delighted in music—all his family were accomplished performers—and they used to give concerts on board their yacht. Zoffany painted such a music party with Fulham

167

Church in the background; the painting is perhaps his masterpiece and still in the possession of the family. George III and Queen Charlotte used to drink tea with Mr Sharp and his wife on board and to listen to the playing. William Sharp's younger brother was the philanthropist, Granville Sharp. He held a position in the Ordnance Department but resigned it during the American War of Independence sooner than help to send armaments against a people with whose cause he sympathised. In 1765 he chanced to meet a Negro called Jonathan Strong who, being ill, had been turned adrift by his master. Granville cared for him, found him employment and, when his master claimed him two years later, fought the case from court to court till the ruling, that no man can be held a slave in this country, in December 1771, in the similar case of James Somersett (see p. 88), freed Strong too. He was one of the originators of the Association for the Abolition of Negro Slavery, and was one of the kindest of men. He died at Fulham House July 6, 1813, in his 79th year, cared for by his widowed sister-in-law, who died too the following February. The house was demolished in 1842 but the memory and work of that kindly, stout-hearted family lives on in the struggle to promote equality among all races.

HARINGEY

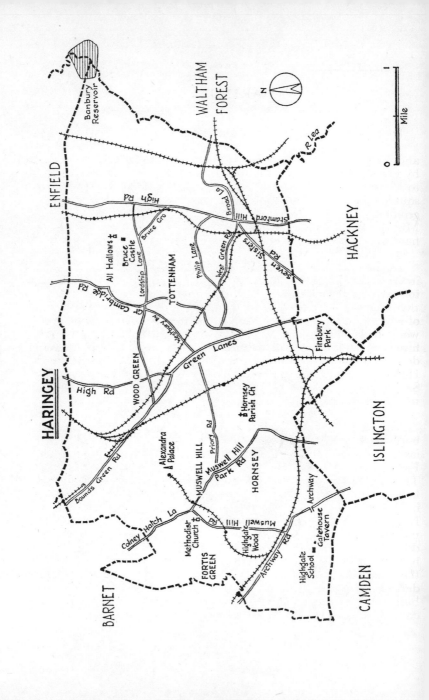

HARINGEY

The borough of Haringey lies to the north of the Greater London area and consists of the former boroughs of Hornsey, Wood Green, and Tottenham. It is bordered to the west by Barnet, to the north by Enfield, to the east by Waltham Forest (formerly in Essex), and to the south by Hackney, Islington, and Camden. It covers 11·7 square miles and has a population of 245,270 (1970). There is high ground to the west, especially at Highgate, Alexandra Park, and Muswell Hill, falling away eastwards to a plain and then to Tottenham Marshes and the River Lea.

The new borough of Haringey has chosen for itself one of the most interesting of all the fresh names though it is really a very old name indeed. Its meaning has been much debated. Lysons suggested that it meant "the hare's meadow" and as a result, when the Mayor of Hornsey needed a new chain of office in 1903, some of the links were made in the form of little hares. However, that excellent historian, Dr Madge, after listing 160 variant forms of the name, decided that it derived from *Heringeshege*, meaning "the enclosure of Hering". A war-leader named Hering is mentioned in the Anglo-Saxon Chronicle for AD 603, and though he may not have been our man, the name is certainly Saxon.

Another form of the name is **Hornsey** (Harnyssey). The former borough covered a large area of land in which there were, until this last century, a number of villages—Crouch (Crux or Cross) End, Fortis Green, Muswell Hill, Stroud Green, and a part of Highgate. The land belonged to the Bishop of London who had a hunting lodge at Lodge Hill. There is some very good modern architecture in Hornsey and one interesting relic of the past—the old tower of old Hornsey parish church. Its lower part dates from about 1500 and may be made of bricks from the bishop's house which was pulled down at about that time; the upper part is modern. Other St. Mary's have stood beside the tower, the last built as recently as 1927, but the foundations shifted so that it became unsafe and had to be demolished. A new church, designed by Mr Cecil Brown, is being built at this moment and is to be connected with the old tower by a covered walk. In it a place will be found for the memorials from the old church which include a chrisom brass of a child in swaddling clothes who must have died about 1520, and a marble memorial to Francis Musters who died in 1680 at the age of 16. The boy kneels with clasped hands, a book and a skull in front of him, while two cherubs put a crown on his head. There is also a superb incised floor slab showing George Rey and his two wives, their hands at prayer and all wearing big ruffs. George has a fur mantle and his wives' gowns are finely embroidered. By the feet of the first wife kneels her son, another George.

In the churchyard lies Samuel Rogers, who at the age of 30 inherited a share in the family bank which carried an income of £5000 a year. Rogers was a competent poet—when Wordsworth died, he was offered, but refused, the Laureateship—but his delight was in hospitality and friendship. It was said of him that if you borrowed £500 from him, he would not say a word against you till you attempted to return it. He gave splendid breakfasts at his house in St James's Street, where all the literary and artistic talent of London foregathered. He brought quarrelling friends together, Byron and Moore among them. He comforted Charles James Fox in his last illness and supported the dying Sheridan. A robbery at his bank lost him £40,000 but he bore it calmly and said he would have been ashamed of himself had he not been able to sustain such a shock. His joy was in his friends, his books, and his art collections—the latter producing £50,000 at the sale after his death.

In its Town Hall Hornsey has one of the best civic buildings in London. It was designed in 1935 by R. H. Uren and won the RIBA bronze medal. It is built round two sides of a little square with a tower rising from between the wings. The square is planted with lime trees which smell sweet in spring and early summer. The Harringay hare appears again on the ironwork which adorns the doors. Nearby is the Clock Tower, an important local landmark, erected in memory of Henry Reader Williams, JP. Behind the Town Hall is the new central library opened in 1965 by Princess Alexandra; it is equally well designed by F. Ley and G. Jarvis. Adjoining the west wall is a bronze sculpture by T. E. Huxley-Jones, set in a pool with a curtain of water jets, and there is a staircase window, over-looking a courtyard garden, with engraved glass by F. J. Mitchell representing Hornsey past and present.

Haringey is fortunate in both the quantity and variety of its open spaces. They stretch right across the borough—Coldfall Woods in the north, Highgate and Queen's Woods and Priory Park (where

H. R. Williams used to live) in the middle, and Finsbury Park in the south-east corner, besides a generous supply of playing fields. Excavations have been going on in Highgate Woods where a Roman kiln and pottery have been discovered. The wood itself is the property of the City of London. In addition to the woods and parks, since 1945 it was the policy of the Hornsey borough council, which has been maintained under the new regime, to establish small municipal gardens on bombed sites and other convenient corners throughout the area. Two of the pleasantest are at Muswell Hill and Shepherd's Hill, but there are 71 in all and more than another 50 attached to municipal housing schemes.

Village centres such as Fortis Green and Stroud Green have virtually disappeared, though there are several interesting late 18th and early 19th century houses to be seen along Fortis Green Road, but one area, Muswell Hill, deserves special mention. 150 years ago, Tom Moore, the poet and musician, had a country cottage there. The cottage has gone and so has the countryside, but there are several interesting churches to be visited. At the top of the hill, in the middle of an excellent shopping centre, is the parish church of St James, with a spire which makes the most of its position. On the northern slope is the Methodist church with a most interesting set of stained-glass windows, designed and executed by Nora Yoxall and Elsie Whitford and presented by Harold Guylee Chester in 1937. They demonstrate the relevance of Christianity to modern life and so groups of students and boy scouts and girl guides and doctors and a father helping his son with a toy train, all appear beside scenes from the life of Christ. The top light in each window is a portrait of some person whose life has been an example to all—Christ, Susanna Wesley, Abraham Lincoln, Albert Schweitzer, Robert Raikes, Baden-Powell, John Wesley, and Wilfrid Grenfell. These windows are worth seeing as an artistic achievement, as a carefully planned scheme of church decoration, and as a record of domestic scenes a generation ago. Descending Muswell Hill to the south, we pass a pleasant old house, The Grove, in the grounds of which the Greater London Council gives entertainments in summer, and then at the foot, in Priory Road, is a church of the Moravian Brotherhood. This sect came to England from Czechoslovakia by way of America about 1750. The brotherhood observes great simplicity of worship and the church is one of the friendliest and most peaceful little buildings one could find. Nearby in a rather fine late 18th century house is the Moravian Library. A few streets away, in Cranley Gardens, is St George's Church, designed by Ronald Morris in 1959. An older

173

church of that dedication was bombed; the new church has some interesting modern embroidery.

There is one spectacular piece of engineering in Hornsey—Archway Road. The road is built to avoid the long steep drag up Highgate Hill from the City to the Great North Road. The hill was badly surfaced and, as it was illegal to use a team of more than five horses, some loads failed to reach the top and there were often breakdowns and accidents. In 1810 a company was formed, money was raised, John Nash and John Rennie gave advice, and a tunnel about 250 feet long was begun through the hill itself. In 1812 it fell in with a crash that could be heard at Kentish Town. More money was raised and a road in a cutting was completed though, till Telford redesigned the drainage in 1829, it was far from satisfactory. A viaduct was built across the road to carry Hornsey Lane but so many people threw themselves from it to commit suicide that in 1885 iron railings seven feet high were put up which did not improve its appearance. The view from it is still as spectacular as it was when Hans Christian Andersen, who was in England visiting Charles Dickens, crossed it by night and "saw the great world metropolis mapped out in fire below him".

On the Archway Road where a new traffic development is being undertaken, is the church of St Augustine, designed in 1855 by that interesting architect J. D. Sedding. At the top of the hill, to the west, lies Highgate village, a part of which is within Hornsey (see also under Camden, p. 84). Here is Highgate School, founded in 1565 by Sir Roger Cholmley and still an excellent school today. The school chapel served as a chapel-of-ease for the neighbourhood till St Michaels was built (see p. 87). In the High Street there are plenty of pretty shop-fronts, whose upper storeys retain their 18th century brickwork while their ground floor windows display 20th century goods most alluringly. A little down the hill stands one of the finest 17th century houses left in London, Cromwell House. Next door to it is Ireton House, built some while later. Their connection with the Lord Protector and his son-in-law is only legendary, for Cromwell House was built for the Springell family with fine panelling and a superb carved staircase. At the top of the hill is the Gate House public house, a modern building replacing a very old inn beside the turnpike to the Great North Road. Here the curious ceremony of "swearing on the horns" would take place, when any gentleman so minded might take an oath to the innkeeper that he would always drink strong ale rather than weak and would always kiss a pretty woman were she willing. The oath-taker then bought drinks for all the company, so it would seem to have been a profitable device for the innkeeper. The ceremony is observed today at The Wrestlers, North Road.

On the North Hill, as it runs down to the Great North Road, is the Bull public house, famous in coaching days, some nice 18th century houses, and Highpoint 1 and 2, two blocks of flats built in 1936 and 1938 by Tecton and Lubetkin. Both are interesting and Highpoint 1 is really successful—one of the best pieces of 1930s architecture to be found in London.

Moving eastwards across the borough, we come to **Wood Green**. There is very little that is old here, but the new Civic Centre buildings, designed by Sir John Brown and Henson in 1958, are here and are very successful. Behind the Civic Centre is St Michael's Church (1865–74 by H. Curzon) with a pleasant interior, and beside it are the Fishmongers' and the Printers' Almshouses. The high ground is usurped by the huge sluggish building of Alexandra Palace standing in a blowsy litter-ridden park, part of which is now used as a car auction meeting place. The park was laid out in 1863, with a race-course, as a pleasure garden; it was to have been the North London counterpart of the Crystal Palace at Sydenham. The palace opened in 1873 and was burnt down a month later. It was rebuilt to J. Johnson's designs in 1875 and had a huge organ built by Willis in the main hall. In 1936 it became the first Television Centre in England. Television had been invented 11 years earlier by J. L. Baird, who was working in a garret in a back street in Soho. When at last he was able to make a picture of a wooden doll come through, he ran downstairs in his slippers to find a human being. On the floor below he found a crippled boy, William Taynton, and borrowed him. The boy sat like a graven image and was the first human being to be seen on a television screen.

Farther eastwards still and on much lower ground, lies **Tottenham** with its three claims to fame—a cross, a church, and a castle. Its broad High Road follows the line of Ermine Street, the Roman road from London to Lincoln. Beyond it lie the marshes of the River Lea and Pymmes Brook where Izaak Walton used to fish and where the whitewashed walls of the Ferry Boat Inn are now the pleasantest things to be seen. The High Road is an excellent shopping centre with plenty of vegetable stalls; at Page Green it is joined by Seven Sisters Road, so called from a group of elms that used to stand on the Green. They were replanted several times and in 1955 a group of poplars replaced them. Half-way along it stands Tottenham High Cross, originally a wooden mediaeval wayside cross (*not* one erected to the memory of Edward I's Queen Eleanor). It was replaced about 1600 by one of brick which in its turn was covered over with stucco and embellished in 1809 and so remains today.

The castle has had an exciting history. The manor of Tottenham (Tota's *ham* or settlement) belonged in the days of Edward the Confessor to Waltheof, the Earl of Northumberland, who married Judith, the Conqueror's niece, but plotted against William and lost his head in 1075. Their daughter married a Scottish prince and the manor at last descended to Robert de Bruis in 1254. A house was built but the property was sequestered by Edward I in 1306 when Robert Bruce asserted his claim to the throne of Scotland. In 1514, Sir William Compton acquired it and probably rebuilt it. It was at his house that Henry VIII met his sister Margaret, Queen of Scotland, in 1516; and when the house passed to Compton's grandson, Henry, Queen Elizabeth I stayed there in 1578. It was probably at this time that the curious brick tower that stands in the grounds was built; its purpose is uncertain. The house was enlarged by Lord Coleraine in 1684, and again by the Townsend family in the 18th century. It stands today, a broad-fronted, three-storey building, with an elaborate 17th century porch and octagonal towers on either side. The clock tower rises from the second storey of the porch and inside is a fine staircase.

Early last century, the house became a school, run by the Hill family. The school had its own importance, but one of the Hill brothers, who taught there, found a surer way to fame, for it was his introduction of the Penny Post that made the name of Sir Rowland Hill a household word. Today, the house is known as Bruce Castle and contains a most interesting museum. It has three sections—local history material, exceptionally elegantly displayed, a postal museum, and a collection of material connected with the Middlesex Regiment. There are several representations and relics of the battle of Albuera, where the regiment won its nickname of the Die-Hards (see also p. 36). The postal collection is superb and exclusive. In addition to prettily framed prints of the Royal Mail in coaching days, there is a vast number of stamps and franked envelopes. Stamp collectors of all ages should visit it.

Bruce Castle stands in a park of 20 acres and just beyond it is the parish church of All Hallows. Its story is said to go back to its foundation by David I of Scotland, born in the days of the

Harrow School

Houses at Strand-on-the-Green

Boston Manor, Brentford: the main room on the first floor

Crosby Hall, Chelsea: the roof

Conqueror. A copy of a document in which he gave the church to the canons of Holy Trinity, London, is kept here with a copy of another document by which the Earl of Angus gave all his hay growing in Tottenham's fields to these same canons. On the south wall of the church is an old mass dial which used to tell the time for the service.

The tower was begun over 600 years ago but its top is 18th century. One of its bells is stamped with the date 1663, but was brought here at the beginning of the last century. It is a famous bell, for there was a night in September 1759 when its ringing might have changed history. It is claimed it was the alarm bell of the garrison of Quebec which was rung so strenuously when it was discovered that General Wolfe had managed to scale the Heights of Abraham and was threatening the city.

The 14th century chancel and nave were thrown into one in the last century and while the arcades are 14th and the south aisle 15th century, the north aisle and chapel, the chancel and the vestry, all date from the extensive 1875 restoration by William Butterfield. A clerestory was added and the roof raised, thereby enlarging and dignifying the interior of the church but rendering it far less friendly than it once had been. The rector at the time was the Reverend Alexander Wilson, a very impressive character, so much so that Butterfield, Thackeray, and Macaulay would all drive out from London to hear him preach.

The window at the west end of the north aisle is of late 16th century French glass, showing David, Isaiah, and Jeremiah; the glass of the canopy in the middle light is still earlier. There are a number of interesting brasses and monuments. Elizabeth Burrough who died in 1616 is shown with her husband and three children, and another brass shows Margaret Irby (d. 1640) with her three daughters kneeling behind her. Her kinsman Sir Robert Barkham and his wife appear as busts on a black-and-white marble monument and below them are their 12 children, seven of the eight daughters in a very quaint stepped row with their arms linked. A small son and daughter are lying on skulls, for they died before their parents. Two husbands and their wives kneel on the opposite wall; they are Richard Kandeler and his wife Elizabeth, their daughter Anne and her husband Sir Ferdinando Heybourne. Another husband and wife, Sir John and Lady Melton, are also at prayer. As a war memorial, there is a copy of Perugino's *Madonna and Child* the original of which is in the National Gallery, and in the north chapel is a Jacobean altar-table.

One vicar of Tottenham was of particular significance; his name was William Bedwell and he was one of that remarkable group of men who were responsible for the translation of the Bible which was made at James I's command, which we know as the Authorised Version, and which is the glory of our English literature. He also wrote, in 1631, one of the first studies in English local history, an account of his own parish of Tottenham. He was buried in the church and in the churchyard lies Margaret Lydia Samuel, daughter of James Hogg, the poet who was known as the Ettrick Shepherd.

The charming old house in the grounds by the church, known as the Priory, is now the vicarage. It was built about 1620 by Joseph Fenton, whose initials appear on plaster ceilings and on the over-mantels of some of the old fireplaces. Some of the rooms have also their original panelling, though the house was much rebuilt in the 18th century. The beautiful iron gateway into the garden is also 18th century and was brought here from the old vicarage.

There are several nice late 17th and 18th century houses in the High Road, two good 18th century dwellings in White Hart Lane near the station, some pretty houses in Bruce Grove and Prospect Place, and one farm, Asplins, dating from the 17th and 18th centuries but now surrounded by factories. Other buildings have vanished, among them the almshouses built in 1596 by Balthasar Sanchez who came to England with Philip of Spain, Mary Tudor's husband, as his confectioner, but unlike his royal master, settled down here contentedly and became a Protestant, dying at last in 1602.

Sir Abraham Reynardson's house, which stood on the north side of Tottenham Green, has gone too. Reynardson was a rich Turkey Company merchant who was Lord Mayor in 1649 but was deposed when he refused to proclaim the Act abolishing royal power and rule in England, for which he was fined £2000 and imprisoned. He died at his house in Tottenham on October 4, 1661, and his body lay in state in the Merchant Taylors' hall. The house later became a boarding school from 1752 to 1810, run by the Forster family; when it was pulled down and the site redeveloped, its place was taken by the Grove School which flourished from 1828 till 1879, where Lord Lister, the author J. H. Shorthouse, and the architect A. Waterhouse were all educated.

Until the 18th century there was a well east of the High Cross which in the Middle Ages had been dedicated to St Loy or Eloy and which was famous for its purity, but it has now vanished. Then there was the Black House, east of the High Road opposite White

Hart Lane, which belonged to George Hynningham, gentleman of Henry VIII's household, and much later to Sir Hugh Smithson, an ancestor of the present Duke of Northumberland, who was beloved for his charity to the poor.

Modern Tottenham is a busy bustling place and is perhaps best known for its first-class football team, Tottenham Hotspur. There is a well-planned GLC estate at White Hart Lane with small friendly houses, and a number of factories, such as Gestetner's in Fawley Road, are models of their kind.

HARROW

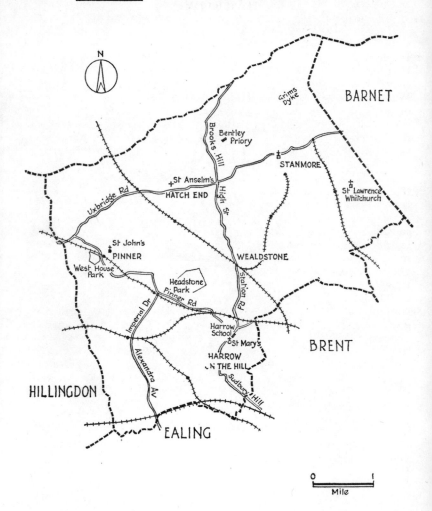

HARROW

N

BARNET

Crims Dyke

Brooks Hill

Bentley Priory

STANMORE

St Lawrence Whitchurch

Uxbridge Rd

St Anselm's
HATCH END

High St

WEALDSTONE

St John's
PINNER

West House Park

Headstone Park

Pinner Rd

Station Rd

Imperial Dr

Harrow School
St Mary's

BRENT

HARROW
ON THE HILL

Sudbury Hill

Alexandra Av

HILLINGDON

EALING

0   1
Mile

HARROW

Harrow is the only borough whose boundaries have remained virtually unchanged under the new Greater London arrangements. It lies to the north-west of London, and is bounded on the north by Hertfordshire, on the west by the hills of Ruislip and Northwood, on the south by Ealing, and on the east by the Edgware Road, ancient Watling Street, and by Hendon. These boundaries enclose an area of 20 square miles and house a population of about 210,000. There is high ground at Harrow Hill itself, at Pinner and at Stanmore, and the borough is watered by the Yeading Brook, the River Pinn, and the River Brent.

Daniel Defoe, in his *Tour through England and Wales* (1724–26), tells the tale that when Charles II heard his divines disputing about the meaning of "the church visible", he declared that the phrase always suggested Harrow Church on its tree-covered hill, its spire soaring heavenwards. The hill—406 feet high—and the church have changed remarkably little in 300 years and the spire is still a landmark as it was in Charles II's day, but the association with worship goes back long before the arguing bishops, possibly back to heathen times, for the very name **Harrow** comes from the Saxon word *hearg* meaning a pagan shrine. The name first appears in a 12th century copy of a charter drawn up in AD 767 when Offa, King of Mercia, gave to Abbot Stidberht 30 hides of land between the *hearg* of the Gumeninga and the river Lidding. The Gumeninga were presumably the clan who inhabited the area; the River Lidding is usually identified with the Wealdstone or Kenton Brook. All traces of the temple have vanished though the word *hearg* remained embalmed till recently in the Herga Lawn Tennis Club. How many of the players realised the antiquity of the name? The club has now gone.

The land granted by Offa was acquired by Wilfred, Archbishop of Canterbury, but he was deprived of it by Cenulf, one of Offa's successors, though Cwoenthryth, the king's daughter and herself an abbess, restored it in AD 825. Thereafter, until the Reformation, Harrow was usually considered to be the property of the see of Canterbury, though the descent of the manor is sometimes obscure. We do know, however, that Archbishop Lanfranc founded a church there—possibly on the site of an earlier church which may have replaced the heathen temple—which was consecrated by his successor

Anselm in 1094. Two of the greatest men ever to hold the see of Canterbury are thus associated with the church, though the building has disappeared.

The earliest remaining stonework, in the base of the tower, dates from between 1130 and 1140; the south wall of the chancel with its lancet windows are late 12th century, the nave and aisles are early, the transepts late, 13th century. Between 1437 and 1467, when John Byrkhede was rector, the roof of the nave was removed, a clerestory inserted, above which a fine new carved timber roof was installed, and the south porch was added. The marks of the beams of the original roof can still be seen in the plaster above the arches. By the 19th century the church was in need of repair and was heavily restored by Sir Gilbert Scott in 1847 who reconstructed all but the south wall of the chancel, added battlemented parapets and encased the exterior of the church, with the exception of the tower, in flint.

Inside the church, the marble font and the oak chest by the south door were both made in the 13th century. The north door, originally an outer door of the church, is 800 years old; the pulpit, presented in 1708 by Tanner Arnold Esq., is a fine piece of late 17th century wood-carving. The church has 13 brasses, some of them very fine. The earliest is Sir Edmund Flambard's, *c.* 1370, closely followed by Sir John Flambard's, about 20 years later. There is one for John Byrkhede, the rector who built the new roof, and a splendid one to George Aynsworth (d. 1488) who is shown with his three wives and 14 children. Most interesting of all, on a column on the north side of the nave, is that of John Lyon, founder of Harrow School, of whom we shall have much to say later. He died in 1592 and is shown with his wife Joan. He wears a doublet with a short cloak and ruff; she has a broad felt hat and her skirt is a little torn away, for when the brass was taken up from the floor during the last century her dress was damaged and the figure of Zachary, their little son who died, was lost. Left childless themselves, the Lyons founded the famous boys' school, leaving it lands in Preston to provide for the maintenance of the Harrow Road, which charge the school still partly carries today. Besides the brasses, there is a 17th century monument to William Gerard who kneels at a desk with his wife, and another by Richard Westmacott the younger to Joseph Drury who was headmaster when Byron was at Harrow and who was so successful that the number of pupils rose from 139 to 345. The 19th century also added a little memorial to John Lyon, carved by John Flaxman, showing a teacher with three boys before him, studying intently.

It has already been said that Harrow was usually the property of the Archbishop of Canterbury. It was to Harrow that Thomas Becket came in December 1170. He had been Henry II's most trusted friend and Lord Chancellor but when, against his will, the king had forced the archbishopric upon him, Becket had upheld the privilege of benefit of clergy which protected clergy against the ordinary penalties for criminal actions, and he had quarrelled bitterly with his monarch. After seven years in exile, he returned to England and tried to see the king at Woodstock. He stopped at Harrow; his manor house there was cold and unvictualled, but his friend Abbot Simon of St Albans sent plenty of food and drink and came himself, and the two clerics embraced each other. Abbot Simon went to see Prince Henry, but came back to report the king would not see the archbishop.

We do not know where Becket's manor house was in Harrow, but by the 14th century a fine new one had been built at Headstone, which is still there today. One wing of the original building remains, with 15th, 16th, and 17th century additions including a chapel, and the whole makes an extremely attractive dwelling. It is surrounded by a moat, and on the other side of the water is a huge barn, built about 1600 and still in use. When the Reformation came, Cranmer surrendered the manor of Harrow to the king, who sold it to Lord North. Thus the archiepiscopal country house became a farm until it was taken over by the borough council in 1928 when the farmlands were transformed into an exceptionally agreeable park, the house, in a good state of repair, into a home for the chief groundsman and his family, and the barn a storage place for the equipment needed to keep the park in order.

From the Hill, if we look out over the churchyard wall, we can on a fine day see 13 counties—their directions indicated by an engraved bronze plate on a stone pedestal. The huge white NO painted on the surviving South Harrow gasholder, is not an understandable protest, but shows aircraft flying low over the Hill where Northolt aerodrome, now belonging to the RAF but once an important civil airport, lies beyond.

Leaving the churchyard by the lychgate, we look out on the buildings of Harrow School. One of the best known of all our public schools, it was founded in 1572 by John Lyon, yeoman of Preston, whose brass in the church tells us that he "hath provided a free grammer schoole in this parish to have continuance for ever". It was a revival of a church school which had languished at the Reformation, and after the deaths of Lyon in 1592 and his wife in 1608 their bequest was made good and a red-brick schoolhouse was built on the windswept top of the Hill in 1615. Inside was one classroom, today called the Fourth Form Room, 100 feet long and 20 wide, with low narrow forms arranged so that the boys would sit facing the desks of half-a-dozen masters sitting by the walls. It was the only classroom for more than 100 years and had no desks for writing, the boys resting their books on their knees. Two hundred boys repeating their lessons at the same time must have made plenty of noise! On each side of the narrow doorway (the only one in the room) are low screens to keep out the draught; they are at least as old as 1660, for that is the date one of the pupils carved on them. On the outside of the door itself is carved W. R. James, 1663, and the forms and the desks for the masters are 17th century too.

Running round the wall to a height of seven feet is panelling with a cornice which rises into a shapely curve at the north window in front of which the headmaster sat. The panelling is carved with names and we may think of one of them as the name of a hero, for he dared to begin this remarkable series of names by carving his own, T. Basil, in 1701. Harrow has nurtured seven Prime Ministers; four of them have cut their names here—H. Temple for Lord Palmerston, Haddo for Lord Aberdeen, in huge letters R. Peel, and in very small ones Winston Churchill. There is a great 17th century oak chest with iron straps and ornamental escutcheon plates, and the cupboard where the headmaster kept the birch is still there.

An exactly matching west wing was added to the old Schoolhouse in 1819–20 and outside is the yard where the boys assemble for Bill or roll-call on half-holidays. Besides the four we have already named, Spencer Percival, Lord Baldwin and Viscount Goderich also became Prime Ministers, and among her pupils, Harrow can number soldiers such as Lord Gort and Lord Alexander, poets and writers such as Byron, Sheridan, Trollope, Galsworthy and Trevelyan, churchmen like Cardinal Manning and Archbishop Davidson, and philanthropists like Sydney Herbert and the 7th earl of Shaftesbury. Indeed it was at Harrow that the young Anthony Ashley Cooper saw the sight that made him dedicate his life to the service of his fellow men. An inscription on the wall of Speech Room tells how he stood one day in Crown Street and watched a drunken bawling mob staggering upwards to the church carrying the rough coffin of a pauper. As they passed him, the bearers fell and the coffin crashed to the street. This awful sight roused in the boy a determination to do something to help those too degraded and down-trodden to help themselves; he fulfilled that resolution nobly.

Byron's schooldays were an equally formative time in his life though he was not a particularly easy pupil. He would slip away to the churchyard where, on the flat tombstone of John Peachey who died in 1780, he would write poetry or brood to himself. Today the tombstone is railed round and a school song reminds us how

> *Byron lay, lazily lay,*
> *Hid from lesson and game away,*
> *Dreaming poetry all alone*
> *Up-a-top of the Peachey Stone.*

An elm tree used to shade the boy as he lay there but it was burnt down by a bonfire lit in it one November 5 during the First World War; the stump is preserved at the school and a young tree has been planted in its place. When Byron left the school and went out into the world, he remembered Harrow with affection, and when his little daughter Allegra, born to him out of wedlock by poor pretty headstrong Clare Clairmont, died at the age of five in Italy, he had her body embalmed and sent back to Harrow where she was buried under the church porch in September 1822. Allegra was a naughty, pretty little creature and her father loved her dearly though he found her very difficult to manage; he asked his old friend and headmaster, Joseph Drury, to read the funeral service and instructed that a tablet with the words from the Second Book of Samuel, XII, 23—"I shall go to her but she shall not return to me"—should be made; it lies in the grave with her.

The school buildings and the Houses—Druries, Moretons, The Grove, The Park, Bradby's, Elmfield, Newlands, Headmasters, The Knoll, West Acre, and Rendals—into which the boys are divided (an essential part of Harrow's tradition)—have spread out along the top of the hill. Below the School House is the semi-circular Speech Room, modelled on an ancient Greek theatre by William Burges in 1872. On the wall, facing downhill, is a statue of Queen Elizabeth I, who gave the school its original charter; it was given by the Harrow members of Lord Claude Hamilton's family in memory of him. Inside the hall hang the flags of the regiments of Harrow's 19 winners of the Victoria Cross and every chair has the name of an Old Boy carved on it. It was to Speech Room that Sir Winston Churchill would return, whenever he could as he grew older, for the annual Songs, for he cherished the memory of his school days, and Harrow has a finer collection of songs than any other school. Those who were present will always remember the enthusiasm with which the boys greeted Sir Winston and the old man's joy in responding to their welcome. Harrow has had a series of outstanding directors of music, and one of them, John Farmer, wrote the music of the best known song of all; the words were by another master, Edward Bowen.

> *Forty years on, when, afar and asunder,*
> *Parted are those who are singing today,*
> *When you look back and forgetfully wonder*
> *What you were like in your work and your play,*
> *Then it may be there will often come o'er you*
> *Glimpses of notes like the catch of a song,*
> *Visions of boyhood shall float them before you,*
> *Echoes of dreamland shall bear them along.*

Adjoining Speech Room is the War Memorial Building designed by Sir Herbert Baker and completed in 1926. The ground floor is a hall with a shallow vaulted roof and an apse in which there is an altar tomb with a bronze sword resting on it. In the hall are busts of famous pupils, including one of Sir Winston Churchill by Clare Sheridan, and up the oak staircase hang water-colours by J. M. W. Turner, David Cox, Copley Fielding, Thomas Girtin, John Varley, and De Wint, for the school has a good collection.

Upstairs are three fine rooms, the largest of which is used for special meetings and seminars for the senior boys. One of them, built and furnished in memory of Alexander Fitch, who was only 19 when he fell at Jeancourt in 1918, has walls covered with panelling from Brooke House at Hackney, and the floor is made from the timbers of the *St Vincent*, one of the ships of George III's navy.

Opposite the War Memorial Building are the Chapel and the Vaughan Library, designed by Sir George Gilbert Scott in 1854–57 and 1861–63. The library houses a good collection of books and portraits, a number of relics relating to Byron, such as a letter from his mother saying that he refused to return to school as he was "so distractedly in love with Miss Chaworth". There is a letter from Nelson, an autograph of John Lyon, and a suit worn in about 1776 by Henry Read of Brookland, Kent, for archery, for in 1684 Sir Gilbert Talbot founded an archery contest for a prize of a silver arrow (the arrow appears held by a lion on the school crest). It took place in August, at the top of Roxeth Hill, and the competitors used to wear special costumes of satin. The day concluded with a ball given by the victor, but the competition was suppressed in 1771 because it had become too disorderly, and Speech Days were instituted instead. Today a rifle competition bears the old name.

Another Harrow tradition has continued unchanged, the *Contio Latina*. This is the annual delivery of an oration in Latin before the governors by the head of the school; it began in 1674. The formal dress of the Upper School is another link with the past, for a tail-coat is still worn on Sundays with top-hats for the monitors. Since the First World War, a blue flannel blazer has been accepted for every-day wear, but all boys still wear the straw hat with its shallow crown and very wide brim—one of the best possible objects for throwing! But the school lives with its past, not in it. The Science is larger than the Classical Sixth—new laboratories have just been built—and when the school celebrated its fourth centenary in 1971, it was seen how much it looks to the future. There is a splendid continuity between the tiny school founded by the local yeoman and the 700-strong establishment entering its fourth century—a continuity of scholarship and service and the courage to hold fast to those qualities which are worth preserving in a changing world, for as a 20th century headmaster, Dr Cyril Norwood, wrote in another school song:

> *On Lyon's road is always Spring*
> *For souls that go a-journeying.*

The ridge of the hill is worth exploring for its own sake, apart from the church and school. It runs in a long spur three-quarters of a mile from Church Hill and Grove Hill in the north to Julian Hill in the south. At either end there is a memory of a monarch. On the wall of the Art School, at the top of Church Hill, is a tablet reminding us that Charles I paused here in 1646 as he fled from Oxford to surrender himself to the Scottish Army at Nottingham. He had only two companions with him and one of the horses had lost a shoe and had to be taken to the blacksmith. The king must have waited here, hoping that he would not be recognised as he looked out towards his dear London, which he was only to enter again three years later on his way to his trial and execution.

At the farther end of the High Street stands the King's Head Hotel, parts of which are said to date from 1535 though the façade is much later. All along the High Street are pleasant 18th and 19th century houses, and on the eastern slope lay Julians where the Trollope family lived and which was the model for Orley Farm in the novel of that name. On the opposite slope, in West Street, is the old Pie-Powder House where the magistrates met to regulate and control the annual fair, Matthew Arnold came to live at Byron House at the junction of Middle Road and Crown Street in 1867, and on the southern slope of the hill is a preparatory school which has taken the name of Orley Farm. It is architectually most satisfying, having been designed for its purpose in 1901 by Arnold Mitchell.

But there has always been a great deal more to Harrow than the Hill. When Domesday Book was made, the manor was assessed at 100 hides—the largest in Middlesex (not the richest—that honour fell to Isleworth)—and today there is a large town all around the foot of the Hill kept at bay by the school playing fields—cricket to the east, football to the west. The Midland Railway reached Wealdstone in 1837, and the Metropolitan Harrow-on-the-Hill in 1880, and from that time onwards, South, North, and West Harrow, Harrow Weald, Greenhill, Roxeth, Pinner, Hatch End, Rayner's Lane, Headstone, and the two Stanmores began to be covered with a spread of buildings. This resulted in the creation of a number of new parishes and in the building of new churches, some of which are well worth visiting. Near to Harrow-on-the-Hill station is St John's, Greenhill, built in a traditional 14th century style around the turn of this century by Messrs Thompson to designs by J. S. Alder. The woodwork in the sanctuary roof and in the chancel screen and stalls is richly carved and there is a painting over the sanctuary arch of Our Lord in glory, seated on a rainbow with the Madonna and St John on either side of Him. The streets around the church are soon to be redeveloped with a shopping precinct. A new hospital and a large technical college are almost completed on what used to be the golf-course at Northwick Park.

Three other interesting churches are St George's, Headstone, St Alban's, North Harrow, and Christ Church, South Harrow. St George's, designed in 1910 by J. S. Alder has some fine 20th century glass, including a *Te Deum* east window. It is in a traditional style but St Alban's (A. W. Kenyon, 1936) is starkly modern and wholly successful with distinctive aisle arches. Christ Church is less exciting as a building but it is in the churchyard here that Sir William Henry Perkin lies. A brilliant chemist, his discoveries founded the coal-tar dye industry. He had been set to seek quinine from coal-tar products and in making his experiments he produced from aniline black a beautiful mauve which he called magenta because the day was the anniversary of the Battle of Magenta. He set up a factory at Greenford Green in 1857 but retired when still a young man in 1874 and devoted the last 33 years of his life to pure scientific research and to taking an active part in the religious life of Sudbury where he lived at The Chestnuts, now Chestnut Court flats in the Harrow Road.

Some two miles north-west of Harrow is **Pinner**, a former urban district which has always somehow remained at heart a village. It has one of the prettiest High Streets in Middlesex, dominated by the 14th century church which is dedicated to St John. The body of the church dates from 1321 though the plan and lower nave walls may be older still. The tower is 15th century and is crowned by a huge wooden cross covered in lead and erected in 1637. Inside, the chancel is longer than the nave, and there is a fine 15th century east window with five lights. The font dates from the same period and the altar-rails are some 300 years old. There is one brass and several interesting monuments. The brass, which is kept in the vestry, is to little Anne Bedingfield who died in 1581 when still a baby and is shown in her swaddling clothes; it is cut from an older Flemish brass for the words *Hier licht* appear on the back. There are three 17th century memorials, to Thomas Hutchinson and his wife of Pinner Park, to Christopher Clitherow, the grandson of a Lord Mayor of London, and to John Day, a clergyman. Two plain tablets commemorate Henry James Pye, Poet Laureate from 1790 to 1813, and the wife of John Zephaniah Holwell, the governor of Bengal. Pye was a most unsuccessful poet and owed his laurels to his political support of Pitt; Byron, who was a schoolboy at Harrow when Pye was living at Pinner, wrote of him disdainfully, "Better to err with Pope than shine with Pye".

Holwell, who is buried with his wife, lived a more dramatic life. He was a surgeon who went out to Calcutta and rose to a position of importance with the East India Company and became zemindar of the court of justice. In 1756, the Nawab of Bengal attacked the white settlement at Calcutta, the governor fled and Holwell was asked to take charge of the defences and the remaining civilians. For two days he led the fighting till ammunition gave out and they were forced to surrender. The Nawab promised honourable treatment but the little company of 146 men and women were forced into a tiny room and left there without water through the stifling heat of the Indian night. Next morning only 23 were left alive, Holwell among them. He was carried out and his life saved by the intercession of the Nawab's grandmother who reminded the prince of his captive's justice and mercy in the courts. The survivors were eventually saved by Clive, and when that brilliant soldier left India, Holwell was for a time governor of Bengal, but his health was broken by his experiences and he returned to England and settled at Pinner Place (demolished 1954). He set up a monument in memory of the victims of the Black Hole of Calcutta which was placed over the common grave in which their bodies were laid.

There is a curious monument in Pinner churchyard, an obelisk with what appears to be a stone coffin projecting on either side. It is not a coffin, in fact, but simply a memorial which marks the resting place of the parents of the wonderful gardener, John Claudius Loudun. Nearby, in Pinner cemetery in Paine's Lane, lies Horatia Nelson Ward, the daughter of Lord Nelson and Lady Hamilton. She was born in January 1801 at the Hamiltons' home in Piccadilly and was at first brought up by a nurse in Little Titchfield Street, Marylebone, and then, after Sir William Hamilton's death, by her mother in the house Nelson took for her at Merton. It was from this house that Nelson left to join the *Victory* for his last battle at Trafalgar. His letters to Lady Hamilton abound with loving references to the four-year-old Horatia; his last letter to her, as the *Victory* was bearing down upon the enemy, ends: "I love you before any woman in this world, and next to you our dear Horatia." After his death and that of Lady Hamilton, Horatia was brought up very kindly by her Nelson relations; she married the Reverend Philip Ward, vicar of Tenterden, and they had eight children. They lived at Beaufort Villa, Woodridings, Pinner, and her husband, one son, and one daughter lie in the grave with her, the daughter having been knocked down and killed by a horse that bolted from the stableyard of the Queen's Head in the High Street at Pinner.

The High Street itself is well worth a visit. Many of the shops are whitewashed, with magpie timbering, the shop now the Victory public house bears the date 1580 and the Queen's Head on the opposite side nearer to the church dates from the 17th century. There are some fine early 18th century brick houses on the right-hand side as one faces the church, beside which is the Cocoa Tree, an 18th century house to which in 1878 a tile-hung coffee tavern was added which became a popular rendezvous for Sunday School outings. In the 1930s, it was the headquarters of Pinner Conservative Association and now is being renovated to serve as offices. Once a year, on the Wednesday after Whitsun, the High Street is put to resoundingly good use, for in 1336 Edward III granted the right to hold an annual fair on St John's Day (Pinner Church is dedicated to St John the Baptist) which has continued to this very year, and long may it go on! In the 14th century it was a cattle and general trading fair; in 1969 there were 14 roundabouts and two big wheels and more coconut shies and hoop-la stalls than could be conveniently counted in the High Street and perhaps twice as many along Bridge Street.

The Metropolitan Railway reached Pinner in 1886 and a number of good substantial houses were built between then and 1914. Further development went on in the 1920s and early 1930s until the Slump, of well-built, individually designed houses—Highview contains good examples from both periods—but all the building, by chance or by design, spared the heart of Pinner so that, even today, there are a surprising number of 16th, 17th, and early 18th century houses and cottages. Particularly worthy of notice are East End Farm in Moss Lane (the cottage attached to it is thought to be 14th century and Pinner's oldest dwelling), East End House, the home of Henry James Pye, Moss Cottage in Paines Lane, Waxwell Farm, Bee Cottage, and Orchard Cottage, all in Waxwell Lane and all 16th century, Pinner House (1721) in Church Lane, and Church Farm, 17th and 18th century, opposite the church. One splendid landmark has gone—Woodhall Towers, otherwise known as Tooke's Folly, a mass of towers and spires erected by Mr A. W. Tooke in the 1860s. It was his son who paid for the whole of the restoration of Pinner Church in the 1880s which was carried out most successfully. Tooke's Folly was demolished in 1965 but another tower which he built in Pinner Hill Road still stands. On the whole, modern building in and around Pinner has been of an impressively high standard, as some of the houses in Moss Lane demonstrate. St Luke's Catholic Church in Love Lane is also much to be admired; designed by F. X. Velarde and completed in 1957, it has a gloriously open chancel and nave, and three splendid pieces of sculpture by David John. Pinner has a vigorous local residents' association, so the village is likely to remain unspoiled.

The Pinner Association was responsible for the preservation of the gardens of West House, to which the Harrow council added the land known as Bennett's Park, the whole now forming an exceptionally pleasant open space with a small water-garden, an aviary, and fine well-established trees. Part of West House has been restored as an adult education centre. A little way north are the open fields of Pinner Park and to the west is Cuckoo Hill where there are several weatherboarded houses, a cricket field, and a public house, The Case is Altered. The River Pinn runs past here and its banks are being reclaimed from their wartime use as allotments and, freshly grassed over, are being preserved as an open space, as are the fields on either side of the Yeading Brook.

193

On the outskirts of Pinner lies **Hatch End**, developed as a suburb around the turn of the century, and here are two buildings of particular interest—the school for daughters of commercial travellers, built in 1853, and the church, dedicated to St Anselm and designed by F. E. Jones in 1895–1905. It is worth visiting for its superbly carved rood-screen, which gave rise to a dispute of ritual when it was installed, and for its windows, designed by Louis Davis. In summer the church is surrounded by roses. Nearby at No. 2 Chandos Villas, lived Mrs Beeton, the compiler of that admirable work on cookery and household management which, a century after publication, is still the English housewife's most reliable adviser.

Due north of Harrow Hill lie Harrow Weald Common and Harrow Weald. **Wealdstone** was agricultural land till the London–Birmingham railway was, owing to local protests, deflected from the foot of Harrow Hill and made to pass through the Weald. It is today a built-up area but the word *weald* means a forest and indicates that once all the land here was covered by the heavy Middlesex woodlands, while its landmark, the Wealdstone, is very old indeed—as old perhaps as the trees that have vanished. The Stone, some three feet tall and two thick, lies embedded in concrete outside the Red Lion Hotel. Geologically, it is not of local origin but we do not know whether it drifted here in glacial times or whether the very early inhabitants of the Weald brought it here for religious purposes. The first written reference to it is in 1508 when it served as a boundary mark. Another antiquity in Wealdstone is Grim's Dyke, a huge earthwork which can still be traced for some four miles westward from Cuckoo Hill at Pinner across to Harrow Weald. It consists of a ditch and a bank and, like the Stone, its origin is unknown. Its name indicates that it was considered by the Saxons to be the work of the Devil. It is too long to have been a practical-line of defence and is more likely to have been a boundary of some sort, possibly thrown up in the 5th and 6th centuries to mark the limits of authority of sub-Roman London during what used to be called the Dark Ages. But a prehistoric origin is also possible and we must hope that one day excavations will produce fuller information.

The earthwork ends in the gardens of a house that bears its name —Grim's Dyke. The mansion, for it is huge, has an awe-inspiring façade. It was designed in 1870 by Norman Shaw for the painter Frederick Goodall, RA and it afterwards became the home of Sir William Schwenk Gilbert who lived there from 1890 till his death in 1911. He had always wished to die in his garden on a summer's day and the wish was granted, for a guest fell into the lake, her host leapt in to save her, succeeded in doing so but collapsed with a heart attack. He is buried in Stanmore churchyard.

He was born in 1836 at the London house of his grandfather, a doctor who had known Dr Johnson and Sir Joshua Reynolds. As a boy he was captured by brigands in Italy and ransomed for £25. Called to the Bar he made £70 in four years and supplemented his poor income as a comic poet, reviewer, and dramatic critic. His early work, illustrated by his own drawings, included the *Bab Ballads* which contain the germs of practically all the operas and other plays. It is on these operas, written in collaboration with the composer Arthur Sullivan, that his fame rests, but they did not meet till Gilbert was over 40. He was already famous for such plays as *Pygmalion and Galatea* (which brought him £40,000), *The Wicked World*, *Sweethearts*, and *Broken Hearts*; for 24 years, from the age of 24, he always had at least one play running in London. The combination of his talents with those of Sullivan was inimitable. Gilbert did not know a note of music and could not hum a line but he had an exquisite sense of rhythm; Sullivan was a brilliant and witty composer. Success followed success at the Savoy theatre and the pair produced an incomparable body of opera, full of humour, satire, merriment, and invention. Gilbert used his librettos to mock pretence and folly but he himself was a most humane man, who hated cruelty and injustice. The 100 acres of his estate were a sanctuary for bird and beast and he was active in protecting Harrow Weald from being used as building land. His house and its grounds are now the property of Harrow borough council.

Nearby in Tudor Road is the Whitefriars Glass factory. It was founded in 1680 in London on the site of a Carmelite (White Friars) monastery off Fleet Street. Until the middle of the 19th century, it produced ordinary domestic glass but from the 1840s onwards the factory began to make stained-glass windows; one of its most famous modern achievements are the windows for Liverpool Cathedral. Whitefriars Glass moved to its present factory in 1923.

Stanmore lies to the extreme north of the borough with Stanmore hill rising to a height of 504 feet and beyond it Stanmore Common and Bushey Heath. The name is derived from the stony mere or pool at the top of the hill which is popularly claimed to have been dug to provide water for a Roman encampment. There does not seem to be much evidence to confirm the story, but there was a Roman–British village at Brockley Hill, two miles to the east with a posting-house and pottery, so the possibility should not be dismissed too lightly. Offa of Mercia who gave Harrow to the Abbot Stidberht, gave the manor of Stanmore to St Albans' Abbey in 793, and the abbey continued to hold it, with interruptions, until 1300 when it was leased to the priory of St Bartholomew, Smithfield. After the Dissolution, it passed from hand to hand and its owners included Sir Peter Gambo, a Spaniard who was murdered by a Fleming near St Sepulchre's Church, Newgate, in 1550. In 1714 it was bought in trust for the Earl of Carnarvon, later the Duke of Chandos, and then it became the property of Lord Temple.

A church was first built during the Middle Ages about half a mile south-south-west of the present one. It stood near the now-disused railway station, in the garden of a house called Haslemere in Old Church Lane. A tombstone to Baptist Willoughby, incumbent from 1563 to 1610, can still be seen. A new church, built at the expense of Sir John Wolstenholme, was consecrated by Archbishop Laud in 1632; it was of red brick with a magnificent tower and a south porch possibly carved by the king's stonemason, Nicholas Stone. About 1845, this church was thought to be in a dangerous condition, the roof was removed and it was left to become a picturesque ivy-covered ruin. A new, less interesting church was built by Henry Clutton in 1850; it is, however, worth visiting for the monuments it houses, many of which were removed from the old church. The oldest is to John (d. 1605) and Barbara Burnell (d. 1612) who owned the manor during the early 17th century; Dame Barbara gave the land on which the old church was built. The couple in their stiff ruffs kneel on either side of a desk and below them are tiny figures of four sons and four daughters, three of them holding skulls to show they died young. The monument is kept in immaculate repair by the Clothworkers' Company of which John was a member.

There are two fine monuments to members of the Wolstenholme family which had come from Lancashire about 1540. The first John Wolstenholme settled at Stanmore and became a close friend of the rector, Baptist Willoughby; the two friends were buried in the same grave. His second son, another John, made a fortune as a merchant and helped to finance the expeditions of Henry Hudson in 1610 in search of the North-West Passage, and of William Baffin in 1615. Cape Wolstenholme at the entrance to Hudson Bay and Wolstenholme Sound in North Greenland off Baffin Bay are both named after him. He was knighted in 1617 and it was he who paid for the building of the 17th century brick church. He died in 1639 and a life-sized effigy was carved by Nicholas Stone. His inscription tells us that he was "most honourable in all the offices of life, of simple probity . . . He denied himself more than he ever denied others." His tomb was opened in 1870 and his body being uncorrupted, a death-mask was made; the likeness of it to the statue by Stone is impressive, demonstrating the excellence of the sculptor's work.

His son, the second Sir John, lost his fortune and estates in the Civil War though he was created a baronet and recouped his losses to some extent at the Restoration. He died in 1670, a year after he had lost his eldest son who would have become a third Sir John. An elaborate monument—so large that there is no place for it in the church and it has to be kept in the Tower Room—was raised to the young man, showing him lying on a great four-poster bed, his widow Dorothy beside him about to wipe his forehead with a stone hand-kerchief.

There is another large monument in the south aisle to George Gordon, 4th earl of Aberdeen. His wife was Catherine Hamilton, second daughter of the Marquess of Abercorn who, as we shall hear shortly, lived at Bentley Priory, Stanmore. She died young leaving him with four children, one of whom became rector of Stanmore. Lord Aberdeen was Prime Minister at the outbreak of the Crimean War; his government resigned in 1855 and he retired into private life.

Two of the windows are particularly worthy of notice. The large east window by Thomas Willement was the gift of Queen Adelaide who rented Bentley Priory after the death of William IV. The widowed queen also gave the font near the south door, so Stanmore has two fonts, for the one from the old church, carved by Nicholas Stone with the Wolstenholme arms and with a superb wooden cover possibly by Grinling Gibbons, stands in St George's chapel near Sir John's tomb. A second beautiful window on the south wall is ascribed to Burne-Jones. It is to the memory of Robert Hollond (d. 1877) and his widow Ellen Julia (d. 1881), who lie with their family in an elaborate mausoleum in the ruin of the old church. In 1836, Hollond, accompanied by Mr Green and Mr Mason, ascended in a balloon from Vauxhall Gardens, crossed the Channel and landed in Nassau the next day—Dean Barham described the event in *The Ingoldsby Legends*. The next year, Hollond became MP for Hastings. His wife, who lived at Stanmore Hall, was an author and a philanthropist. She had a salon in Paris and established the first crèche in London in 1854; her portrait is in the National Portrait Gallery.

There is one more interesting monument—an exceptionally graceful monument by the sculptor John Bacon to the memory of John

Dalton. The composition—a life-sized female figure by an urn—is not original in itself but the execution is exquisite. On the base, two cherubs carved in low relief float towards each other. In the church-yard, in an unmarked grave, lies William Hart (d. 1683), the eldest son of Shakespeare's sister Joan. A child-angel marks the grave of five-year-old Betty, Admiral Jellicoe's little daughter, and Mrs Eliza Brightwen (d. 1906), a naturalist and botanist who lived at The Grove on Stanmore Common, is also buried here.

The great house in Stanmore is Bentley Priory. The original Bentley Priory was founded about 1170 by Ranulf Glanville; its history was uneventful enough except that in 1248, as Matthew Paris records, the prior was suffocated by a badly built hayrick falling on him, and that it was suppressed, with the other monasteries, at the Reformation. All traces of the original buildings have disappeared. In 1766, the estate was acquired by James Duberly, an army contractor, who built a house there which, in 1790, was bought by the Marquess of Abercorn and enlarged for him to the designs of Sir John Soane. The Rotunda, a fine circular room with a domed ceiling, was added, and the gardens, with a magnificent view across to Harrow church, were laid out in terraces. The Marquess was a keen sportsman and had a bowling green laid out on the Common; today it is kept up as a cricket ground. His son-in-law, Lord Aberdeen, succeeded to the property and for a time, as we have said, it was let to Queen Adelaide who died there in 1849. On the ground floor is a particularly pretty little room, its walls and ceiling painted with posies of flowers; as she grew frailer, the queen spent much time there. In 1854 the priory became the home of Sir James Kelk, the contractor for the Albert Memorial. But it was in this century that the old house was put to its noblest use for it became the headquarters of RAF Fighter Command during the Battle of Britain in 1940. Today, as the headquarters of 11th Fighter Group, the walls are hung with drawings and photographs of the young airmen who took part in that struggle. In the hall hang the flags of all the allied nations and in the mess is a Nottinghamshire lace panel, stretching from ceiling to floor, depicting the Battle of Britain; 12 such panels were made, one for each nation concerned. The whole large house is full of memories, very proud and very poignant. Today, the Rotunda and drawing-rooms are used as club rooms for RAF officers; the building and its grounds are, very properly, closed to the public.

Whitchurch or **Little Stanmore** lies slightly to the east of Great Stanmore. It was once the residence of a most magnificent nobleman, James Brydges, Duke of Chandos. Having made a fortune as paymaster-general during Marlborough's wars, he spent between £200,000 and £300,000 of it on a house. It was called Canons, the manor having once belonged to the Augustinian Canons of St Bartholomew's. Building began in 1715 and Chandos employed and quarrelled with several architects—John James, William Talman, James Gibbs, John Price, and Edward Shepherd among them. The result, though not in fact huge, was pompous and uncomfortable, if we are to believe Pope who, though he denied the charge, was probably quite fairly accused of having lampooned the duke and his mansion in his *Epistle to Burlington*. He wrote:

> *At Timon's Villa let us pass a day,*
> *Where all cry out, "What sums are thrown away!"*
> *So proud, so grand, of that stupendous air,*
> *Soft and agreeable come never there . . .*
> *To compass this, his building is a Town,*
> *His pond an Ocean, his parterre a Down:*
> *Who but must laugh, the Master when he sees,*
> *A puny insect, shiv'ring at a breeze!*
> *Lo, what huge heaps of littleness around!*
> *The whole, a labour'd Quarry above ground.*

Daniel Defoe, however, thought the house was "As beautiful as it was Magnificent" and engravings of the period confirm his testimony. But the duke's fortunes declined and three years after his death in 1744, his son found it impossible to maintain the house or to sell it. It was sold by lots at auction for its demolition value and realised £11,000 having cost about a quarter of a million. Parts of it are scattered all over England: the great staircase went to Chesterfield House which William Kent was building in Mayfair and when that mansion was demolished in 1934 it was moved to Harewood House in Yorkshire; the iron gates to Hampstead Parish Church; the portico to Wanstead House and then to Hendon Hall which is now a hotel; the pulpit, altar, font, and pews, to Fawley Church, Buckinghamshire. The estate was bought by a cabinet-maker, Hallett, who built a modest house from the remains which later became the home of Captain Dennis O'Kelly (d. 1786), owner of the racehorse Eclipse, perhaps the finest animal ever to run on English turf. In 1930, the house was taken over by the North London Collegiate School for Girls and such of the grounds as had not been built over were bought by Harrow urban district council. Of the three avenues of trees which led to Edgware, Stanmore, and Whitchurch, only the last remains and from that many trees have been felled and the grass is rough and long; it must have been magnificent when complete. The garden walls remain, however, and inside them the council has laid out a beautiful garden with a pool in memory of George V. Chandos's own domain can hardly have been lovelier than this, especially in high summer when the herbaceous borders are at their most exciting and the catalpa trees are in blossom, and in a wilder part beyond are two small summerhouses, back to back, one dating from Brydges' day, the other probably more recent.

All that remains of the duke's magnificence is the parish church of St Lawrence, Whitchurch, which he rebuilt, with the exception of the 16th century tower, in 1715. The outside is plain enough; the inside quite astonishing. The walls are covered with frescoes, in colour and grisaille, probably by Laguerre and there are high box-pews, but the family pew is a little gallery up at the west end, with a painted ceiling and cushions like a box in a theatre. Behind the altar is an organ on which Handel, who was in charge of the duke's music for a while, may well have played, though the chapel for which he was responsible was the private one at Canons, of which Pope wrote:

> *Light quirks of Musick, broken and uneven,*
> *Make the soul dance upon a Jig to Heaven.*
> *On painted Ceilings you devoutly stare,*
> *Where sprawl the Saints of Verrio and Laguerre,*
> *On gilded clouds in fair expansion lie,*
> *And bring all Paradise before your eye.*
> *To rest, the Cushion and soft Dean invite,*
> *Who never mentions Hell to ears polite.*

The dean's soothing sermon has gone forever, but the painted walls and ceiling by Bellucci are at Great Witley, Worcestershire. Returning to St Lawrence's, on the north side of the church is the Brydges' family mausoleum on which the figures of the duke himself and his two wives are by Grinling Gibbons, one of his comparatively rare works in stone. Outside in the churchyard is the grave of William Powell, whom legend has claimed as Handel's harmonious black-smith (see p. 39).

HAVERING

HAVERING

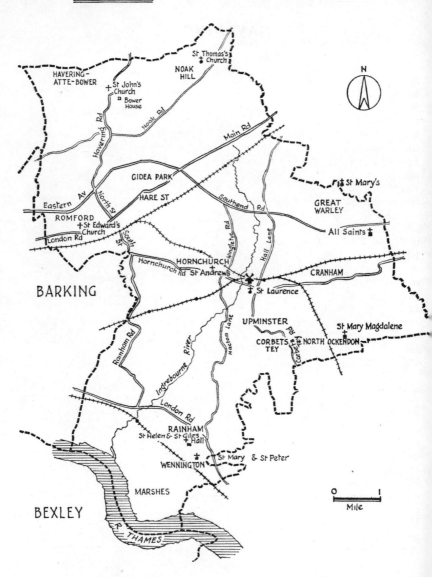

HAVERING

Havering lies to the extreme north-east of the Greater London area and is the second largest of the new boroughs in area, Bromley being the biggest. Havering consists of the former borough of Romford and the former urban district of Hornchurch, both of them previously in Essex. It covers 46 square miles and in 1965 had a population of 250,430. It is an exciting area with sudden unexpected stretches of open countryside, hilly to the north at Havering itself but a flatter land at Hornchurch and Rainham marshes where the River Beam, whose upper reaches are called the Rom, and Rainham Creek at the mouth of the Ingrebourne River, flow into the Thames.

The amalgamation of Hornchurch and Romford into one borough is a matter of history repeating itself, for from 1465 till 1892 they had been united in the Royal Liberty of Havering. A Liberty was an area which enjoyed special rights granted by the king himself. It managed its own jurisdiction and had special privileges in matters of trade, commerce, and freedom from tolls. The village of **Havering-atte-Bower** itself has a long royal tradition. Edward the Confessor built a hunting lodge and improbable legends are told of his sojourns there. It is said that he prayed that the nightingales should cease to sing since they disturbed his meditations and that they immediately were silent in the park but sang beyond its pale.

The hunting lodge soon became a small palace or bower, probably rather like Eltham in Kent which we shall describe in another volume, and the plane was known as Havering-atte-Bower. It was here that Edward III invested his grandson, the future Richard II, as his successor and it was here that Richard's child-widow, Isabella of France, waited for her husband to return to her in vain, for he had been murdered at Pontefract castle. For many years it was the home of Joan of Navarre, Henry IV's widow. She had been Duchess of Brittany and when her husband died, she became regent for the eldest of her eight children. In 1403, she married Henry IV, was crowned at Westminster and voted a dowry of 10,000 marks a year. When the king died, Henry V seems to have continued to be on good terms with his stepmother, though at Agincourt her son Arthur fought against him and was brought captive to her door.

Four years later, however, the queen was accused of plotting Henry's death by witchcraft, was deprived of her possessions without trial and imprisoned at Pevensey in Sussex. The charge now appears to have been a gross piece of injustice and corruption, trumped up so that the Exchequer, drained by the wars with France, might receive the benefit of her dowry. Henry V said as much on his death bed and the queen, who had been very well treated in captivity, was set free and the remains of her dowry returned. She was treated with honour for the remaining 15 years of her life and, dying at Havering, was buried at Canterbury; from the portrait on her tomb, she must have been very beautiful.

It was to Havering that Charles I came in 1636 to meet and greet his mother-in-law, Marie de Medici, when she visited her daughter, Henrietta Maria, Charles's wife. The lady hoped to settle in England but Parliament persuaded her to return to Europe with a generous leaving present of £10,000, for she was known for her difficult temper. During the Commonwealth period, the old palace fell into decay and its stones were used to erect the present Bower House which was built in 1729 for John Baynes, sergeant-at-law, from the designs of Henry Flitcroft. The grounds were planned by Charles Bridgman and the staircase was decorated by Sir James Thornhill with paintings of *The Judgement of Paris*, *The Drunkenness of Silenus*, and *Vulcan at his Anvil*. The house produced by these three artists is utterly delightful, on a smaller, more manageable scale than might have been expected, with marvellous views across to Bedford and Pyrgo Parks which are still open countryside. In 1959 the house was bought by the Ford Motor Company and is used as a residential management training centre.

Bedford and Pyrgo Park lie to the north- and south-east of the Bower House and were once part of the manor of Havering. Another small palace stood in Pyrgo Park, where the queen consort usually stayed when the king was using the main dwelling.

Less than quarter of a mile north of the Bower House is the parish church of St John, and the village green. In the adjacent fields, mares still graze with their foals. The church is an old foundation—its existence is first recorded in an Exchequer Roll for 1202 when 50 shillings was paid to Andrew the chaplain for taking services there. The old fabric was restored in 1836 but 40 years later it was found to be too small for the growing population of the parish so it was pulled down and a rather impressive new flint church was built by Basil Champneys and was consecrated in 1878. The font is Norman and may have come from the old church. The oldest grave is to Thomas Cheek, Lieutenant of the Tower of London who died in 1688, the year of the Glorious Revolution and William III's accession to the throne. The stocks which used to stand beside it have gone too, to be replaced by a modern pair! As far as we know, they are for ornament only. Nearby is a pretty little schoolhouse, built with the bequest of Dame Anne Tipping in 1724; the present school is a rebuilding of 1837.

North-east of Havering, **Noak Hill** rises up and on its summit in a tranquil churchyard is the little church of St Thomas, built by Blore in 1841–82. Inside is a carved wooden panel of Christ carrying the Cross which is said to have come from a Florentine monastery, and some fine 16th century continental glass. Southward lie the pleasant residential areas of Harold Hill and Harold Wood where the manor house of Dagnams once stood. It was to Dagnams that Samuel Pepys came frequently in July 1665 to help arrange a marriage between Philip, later Sir Philip, Carteret, and Jemima, the Earl of Sandwich's daughter. The young man was charmed by his bride but unversed in courtship and Pepys had to give him much good advice. The marriage went well and the couple had three sons, but their happiness did not last long as Sir Philip was blown up with his father-in-law in his flag-ship, the *Royal James*, in the battle of Solebay, against the Dutch on May 28, 1672.

Eastwards again, across the open land of Tyler's Common, and on the very edge of Essex, is **Great Warley**. Here one really feels that one has escaped from the buildings of London. We passed a smithy where a horse was being shod and came to a most hospitable 17th century inn, the Thatcher's Arms. There are several interesting houses nearby—as that great historian of Essex, Philip Morant, wrote in 1768: "It abound with Villa's [sic], where the rich and industrious Citizens retire, at this convenient distance, from the thick Air and Hurry of London." There is Wallets, which dates from the later Middle Ages; the Jacobean Franks' Farmhouse; Boyles Court built in 1776 by Thomas Leverton; and the late Victorian Heseltine Manor, with its fine grounds, which is now a hotel; but the great glory of the place is the parish church, dedicated to St Mary. It was built in 1904, replacing Christ Church which stood some little distance from the site of the present church and which has now been demolished. St Mary's was built by Evelyn Heseltine as a memorial to his brother Arthur; his architect was Harrison Townsend who was also responsible for the pews and choir-stalls, and his designer was Sir William Reynolds-Stephens. The church is beautiful—its style is pure Art Nouveau without ever being stilted or mannered. Reynolds-Stephens was a sculptor, perhaps best known for his work in the Tate Gallery representing Elizabeth playing chess with Philip of Spain; St Mary's Church is his masterpiece. Marbles, metals, and coloured woods are all used to express the symbolism of the life of faith. The three-stemmed font supports two bronze angels. Six ribs encircle the nave roof, lilies decorate walnut panels on the walls, while the rose of Sharon on a green ground fills the springing arches; both lilies and roses are in aluminium. The front of the pulpit is in the shape of a cross; trees support its arms, and the whole is of oxydised bronze and copper. Of copper also is the lectern, flowering branches upholding a bronze book-rest. Behind the pulpit and the lectern is a screen, the most interesting thing in the church. Expressing the idea of the text: "The fruit of the Spirit is Love, Joy, Peace, Long-suffering, Gentleness, Goodness, Faith, Meekness, Temperance," the screen is formed from flowering fruit-trees in brass, which spring from a marble base, each bearing an angel representing one of these virtues. In front of the organ is a little angel, and on its case are metal reliefs illustrating *Benedicite*. Crowns of thorn encircling roses of Sharon form part of the altar-rail and in the apse a great vine springs up behind the altar, tendrils and grapes showing in relief against aluminium. In the centre of the reredos Christ stands with hand upraised in blessing, trampling a serpent underfoot, while panels on each side show the Nativity and the Entombment, and on the wall round is carved a choir of angels.

On leaving the church, we pass under an inscription, Evelyn Heseltine's own epitaph:

His Life an Inspiration—His Memory a Benediction

and we go out into an immaculately kept churchyard, which is laid out so that it is as pleasant for the living as it is peaceful for the dead to rest there. On top of the spire is a dove with an olive branch in its beak and we leave by a lychgate with another inscription, one of reassurance: *Yea, I will strengthen thee; yea, I will help thee.* The church is remarkable both as an artistic achievement and as a memorial of brotherly love.

South-west from Great Warley is **Romford**. It grew up at the crossing of the London to Colchester road with the road leading from the royal palace at Havering to the priory at Hornchurch. In 1859 a coach bearing 28 passengers, 16 outside and 12 in, ran twice daily from the White Hart to the Goose and Gridiron in St Paul's church-yard in just under two hours for one shilling (or 1s 6d inside). It is difficult to do it faster, impossible to do it more cheaply, today. It is an old town with Roman and Saxon associations and has had its own market ever since Edward I granted it one in 1247. The broad marketplace has a continental atmosphere, as if some northern French town had been transplanted across the Channel. There was a chapel in Romford in 1177, probably near Old Church Road, but a new one, dedicated to St Edward, was built in the market place, on the town's main crossroads, in 1406. The 15th century building was replaced by another designed by John Johnson in 1849–50 which now dominates the marketplace, its 162-foot spire being a landmark for miles around. The monuments from the older building are still safely there, and include a magnificent one to Sir Anthony Cooke whose family was dominant in Romford for 200 years. He kneels in Tudor armour facing his wife in a ruff and cloak. Behind him kneel two of his sons and behind his wife are the four daughters who are believed to have composed his long Latin epitaph and to have been the cleverest women of their day. They certainly belonged to a remarkable family.

Sir Anthony was the great-grandson of Sir Thomas, a wealthy Lord Mayor of London who began to build himself a great house in Gidea Park near Romford, but made the mistake of backing the losing side in the Wars of the Roses and barely escaped the scaffold. Still, he died rich and his descendants flourished, so much so that Sir Anthony completed Gidea Hall and as Steward of the Liberty of Havering-atte-Bower entertained Queen Elizabeth I there. Sir Anthony Cooke was a student, in love with country life, and a believer in education as the most broadening influence. He acted as tutor to his five sons and four daughters and their accomplishments were so much admired that he was chosen tutor to the young King Edward VI who knighted him at his coronation. The four daughters on the monument all married well. Mildred married the great Lord Burghley, Elizabeth I's trusted adviser; Ann became the mother of Sir Francis Bacon; Elizabeth's husband was Lord Russell, of the famous Bedford family; Katherine married Sir Henry Killigrew, one of the busiest of Elizabeth I's ambassadors. Gidea Hall is gone and its grounds are now a public park, the family is extinct, but the alabaster group, passed on from the old church to the new, preserves an enduring household.

Another servant of Queen Elizabeth I is on his monument in the church porch. He is Sir George Hervey with his wife, five sons and six daughters. He was the Lieutenant of the Tower. On the opposite wall is Anne Carew's monument, showing her life-sized, leaning on her elbow; it was erected by her son, the Earl of Totnes. Beside the church is an interesting 15th century building, originally a home for a chantry priest. Then it became the Cock and Bell Inn, now it is once more a Church House. Timbered and plastered, it has old beams and 17th century panelling. While the Cookes and the Herveys and Carews were living in Romford the town witnessed a nine days' wonder, for that was how William Kemp, the comic actor, described his journey from London to Norwich in 1599, since he danced the morris all the way. He rested at Romford at the end of his first day's journey. It was for Kemp that Shakespeare wrote the parts of Dogberry in *Much Ado About Nothing* and the Grave-digger in *Hamlet*.

At the west end of the marketplace and well able to serve those trading there are two public-houses, the Lamb, a pretty 19th century building with dormer windows like raised eye-brows, which still advertises "Delicious hot dishes as eaten by the gentry", and the Golden Lion at the corner of North Street and the High Street, which is early Victorian with a 16th century back wing. Everywhere is a genial smell of brewing for Ind Coope have their headquarters at Romford. Overlooking the north-east end of the marketplace are the new ring road roundabout, the Town Hall, and Central Library which won a Civic Trust award. None of them is very exciting individually, in the way that Haringey Town Hall is, but seen together they are a sensible achievement in civic architecture and worth attention. At the other end of the market is a little round Salvation Army tabernacle all of stained glass, one of the most fascinating modern churches to be found near London. The inhabitants of Romford are well served by Raphael Park with its fine iron gates, part of the ground where Gidea Hall once stood, and by Lodge Park Farm, both agreeable places in which to wander.

Another link with Romford's past is a modern group of almshouses in Church Lane, a little way from where the River Rom winds its way through the town to become the Beam River and so reach the Thames. Their history goes back to 1482 when Roger Reede's will bequeathed his new-built house of Hoocrofts "to be a dwelling place for five poor men, not blasphemers of the name of Almighty God, not common beggars, but such as have been of good governance and fallen into poverty; the saddest and wisest to be

St John of Jerusalem,
Clerkenwell: the crypt

St John of Jerusalem,
Clerkenwell: the
gatehouse

The Tower of the Charterhouse, Clerkenwell

Kensington Palace, with the statue of William III

Holland House, Kensington

The Royal Hospital, Chelsea:
the south side of the courtyard

Carlyle's house in Cheyne Row
Chelsea

ruler". In Brentwood Road, Gidea Park, stands what was once Hare Hall, a fine Palladian house, built in 1769 by James Paine, and now housing the Royal Liberty School. Romford provides good school buildings; in Bennett Road at Chadwell Heath is the Furze Infants' School by H. Conolly, a most distinguished design, as is his Gobions School at Havering.

In the manor house at Romford a child was born in 1592 who was for a time perhaps the most popular serious English poet. Few people now read Francis Quarles but he was once a prevailing fashion—Horace Walpole complained that "Milton was forced to wait till the world had done admiring Quarles". The poet's family had associations with the Stuart court and Francis was an ardent pamphleteer defender of Charles I; at the same time he was a Puritan in spirit. His style has similarly contradictory qualities—he followed the fashion of elaborate conceits, yet no one could write more smoothly and plainly as we see in this verse:

> *My soul, sit thou a patient looker-on,*
> *Judge not the play before the play is done.*
> *Her plot hath many changes; every day*
> *Speaks a new scene: the last act crowns the play.*

South-east from Romford is **Hornchurch**, where there is a wonderful church and near to which lay one of the airfields on which England depended in 1940 during the Battle of Britain. The church is dedicated to St Andrew and according to local tradition dates from Saxon times. The tradition cannot be proved or disproved but at all events the church was the mother or parish church for the whole Liberty of Havering—that is, for Havering-atte-Bower, Noak Hill, and Hornchurch itself. Its recorded history begins in August 1158 when Henry II gave to the Brethren of St Bernard and St Nicholas at Montjoux in Savoy land worth £25 a year in Havering. The monastery was a hospice and the king's motive may well have been gratitude for hospitality and aid given to English travellers as well as a desire to gain the political support of the Count of Savoy against Louis VII of France. Monks came over from Montjoux and settled in Hornchurch, building a priory there which flourished for nearly two and a half centuries. Many of them, including one of their canons, Boniface de Hart of Aosta, lie buried here. In 1390, Richard II took over the lands of alien priories such as Hornchurch and in the following year, William of Wykeham bought it for 4000 English gold nobles and 500 French francs to endow his foundation

H   209 at New College, Oxford. The vicar thereafter was known as the chaplain, and to this day New College appoints to the living, though in 1902 the Bishop of St Albans took over other responsibilities for Hornchurch.

Nothing survives of the monks' first church but the present building includes all the later stages of its history. Parts of the chancel—the triple sedilia, the restored piscina, the squint in the wall behind the west arch—besides the nave arcade, are 13th century and were built by the brethren. In the 15th century, under William of Wykeham, much rebuilding was carried out in the chancel, aisles, and nave. The north and south chapels were added and so were the north porch and the tower. The spire was added after 1476 under a bequest from Thomas Scargill. There are traces of wall-paintings and the wooden roof of the nave is ornamented with bosses carved like heads and painted. Between 1404 and 1408, 167 feet of stained glass were ordered for the three chancel windows but only fragments remain, now in the east window of the north chapel; they include a headless crucifix, to which some restorer has added the head of the Virgin Mary and a king, possibly Edward the Confessor. Perhaps the greatest peculiarity of the church is the bull's head and horns affixed to the east end. No one knows why it is there, though there it has been since at least 1610, and there is a reference to *monasterium cornutum* (literally "horned church or monastery") in 1222. It could be a reference to a seal of the monastery of Montjoux though no such seal has been found earlier than 1384–85, 160 years after the appearance of the name, or it could be a reference to the tanning industry which flourished in the area.

The church contains a fine collection of tombs and monuments, including a superb table tomb to William Ayloffe (d. 1517) which stands between the north chapel and the chancel. The family lived at Bretons, a fine mansion just outside Hornchurch, and William's grandson, Sir Thomas, married Maria Guicciardini, a member of the family which produced many bankers and the best historian of Florence; one wonders how the young lady from Italy settled down in England—let us hope that she was happy here. High on the chancel wall is a delicately carved group by Flaxman to Richard Spencer and his wife, and kneeling under marble curtains are Richard Bealestone and his wife, buried here on the eve of the Civil War. Humphrey Pye, letter-writer to James I is here, carved in alabaster, and another group shows the 16th century family of Francis Rame, his wife and their 10 children. There are portraits in brass of the two wives of William Drywood wearing fine

Elizabethan hats, and another of their kinsman Thomas Drywood and his wife. Two brass tablets nearer to our own times awaken deep memories, for one is to Joseph Fry whose mother reformed English prisons (see p. 19) and the other is to the 769 members of the Sportsman's Battalion who were trained at Hornchurch and lost their lives in the First World War.

One memorial is particularly interesting; it is to Thomas Witherings who started the Post Office, and he is commemorated with a black tablet with a tiny carving of a skeleton. In 1633 he was granted a patent as postmaster for foreign letters. There were already regulations for the carriage of government mail, but postal matters generally were in hopeless confusion. Witherings was a far-sighted organiser; he so speeded up the mail between London and the Continent that he was able to point out to the king that his subjects could receive a quicker and surer reply to a letter from Madrid than from Scotland. He drew up a new scheme for the post in England and thereafter a letter to Edinburgh took three days instead of a month. Witherings made it a rule that the speed of a letter should be seven miles an hour in summer and five in winter, and he also introduced registration and postmarks; in his own words, "Every postmaster is to keep a faire paper book to enter the packets in, and shall write upon the labell fastened to every or any of the packets the time of receit thereof." Even with royal support there was much hostility to his reforms and in 1640 he was accused of misdemeanours and his office was given to a London merchant. A long wrangle ensued in Parliament and the courts, during which the mails were often seized and the postal revenue fell to £5000 in 1643. Witherings was worried almost to death and he actually died on his way to Sunday service in Hornchurch church. There we can still read what his friends thought of him, the "Chief Postmaster of Greate Britaine and foreign marts, second to none for unfathomed policy, unparalleled, sagacious, and divining genius: witness his great correspondence to all parts of the Christian World."

Hornchurch can boast of an excellent civic theatre, the Queen's Theatre, and of a beautiful park, formerly the garden and grounds of Langtons, a pretty 18th century house now used as council offices. On the south side of the High Street is Harrow Lodge Park with a boating lake fed by the River Ravensbourne.

To the south of the town lay Hornchurch airfield. It was established during the First World War to combat the menace of Zeppelin raids on London, and covered the site of Suttons Farm, a part of the manor of Suttons which William of Wykeham presented to New

College. In 1916, the first three Zeppelins to be destroyed were brought down by Hornchurch pilots—the first of them, Capt. William Leefe Robinson, being awarded the Victoria Cross. When the Second World War came, Germany prepared to invade Britain and, as part of the preparations, an all-out attempt was made to destroy airfields and RAF stations. Three heavy attacks were made on Hornchurch in August 1940 but the station continued to operate without any break and during that year, for a loss of 132 planes and 73 pilots, 3351/2 enemy aircraft were certainly and 1871/2 were probably destroyed. The RAF gave up Hornchurch in 1962; a painting, *Wings over Hornchurch*, by Bryan G. Moore, which had hung in the Officers' Mess, is now in the possession of the Havering council. The site, in spite of bitter resentment by the local community, was sold for building land and developed with roads which bear the names of the men who were stationed there—Bader Way, Broadhurst Walk, Tuck Road, Tempest Way, Kingaby Gardens, Malan Square, and Finucane Gardens.

West of Hornchurch lies **Upminster** with the oldest building in the borough, the mediaeval tithe-barn in Hall Lane. Perhaps it is not as noble as the barns at Harmondsworth or Uxbridge, but it is still very fine and of a quite individual design. Indeed, the history of Upminster goes back a long way, for its name was originally Chafford, a corruption of St Chad's Ford, and tradition says that the missionary brothers, St Chad and St Cedd, used it as one of their preaching centres when they brought Christianity to Essex about AD 670.

There may have been a Saxon church here, of which nothing remains, but the present church, St Laurence's, is remarkable enough for its tower, the base of which is 12th and the upper part 13th century. It has a distinctive broached and shingled spire, a fine tower arch, and the nave arcade dates from the 13th century too. The body of the church was much altered in 1771 by Sir James Esdaile, and again in 1862, when much of it was rebuilt. There are several interesting brasses, six of them having portraits of Tudor and Stuart times. An unknown man in civilian dress is of Henry VIII's day, and Elizabeth Dencourt has a horned headdress and mantle of the century before. Nicholas Wayte and his wife Ellen are on a palimpsest mediaeval brass which has an abbot on the back, and there is another of a lady of 1560 with a book in her hand. Dressed in elaborate armour is Gerard d'Ewes, and Grace Latham, who died in 1626, is wearing a beautiful dress with a wide collar.

The church possesses a fine chalice made in 1608—the only Jacobean piece in the diocese. The original font has gone but a 15th century one was brought from the manor house when it was demolished in 1777. There are three bells, the largest of them inscribed *God save our nobel Queene Elizabeth 1602. R.H.* The next one tells us *Robert Mot made mee 1583* and the oldest and smallest bell is mediaeval and bears the words *Sancte Gabriele ora pro nobis.* In the north aisle is a window of about 1630 containing some much earlier glass; among the fragments is a partridge, butterflies, a family walking in a garden, a swaddled baby and two men each armed with an arquebus, the earliest form of hand gun.

Upminster has had one particularly distinguished rector, Dr William Derham, who held the living from 1689 to 1735. He was chaplain to the Prince of Wales and a learned member of the Royal Society. He was an astronomer and used the church tower as his observatory; from it he also observed the gun flashes from Woolwich Arsenal and was able to calculate the speed of sound accurately. He was skilled in medicine and it was said that while he was rector, his parishioners needed no other physician.

Upminster as a place is all one long street. In 1920, the District Line was brought here from Barking and all at once the one street became a dormitory suburb. Farms with lovely names like Bretons and Gerpins became sewage works and refuse tips, yet Upminster has still retained its windmill, a four-sailed smock mill of the late 18th century with a rare first-floor sack-loading device and magnificent views from the top. Upminster Station is modern and successfully so, but the golf club is housed in the Elizabethan Upminster Hall, and Clock House Gardens are as agreeable a park as one can find with its lake and swans. North of the town in Bird Lane is one of the most charming 15th century houses in Essex, Great Tomkyns, with lovely windows and projecting wings and a hall open to the roof. By it is a 17th century thatched barn with three bays. South of Upminster in Corbets Tey are Harwood Hall, built in 1790 by Sir James Esdaile, and the High House, built about 1700, a strange, beautiful, elongated building with a dreamlike quality.

Close to Upminster is **Cranham**, a tiny village till very recently, with a white manor house, Cranham Hall, and a church, All Saints, rebuilt in the last century, though there are some Tudor bricks re-used from a much older building, and a fine spire. There are three bells from the old church, one of which was made by Henry Jordan, the London bellfounder who made a peal of bells for King's

College, Cambridge, in 1460. But though the church is not of great architectural significance, it is the burial place of General James Edward Oglethorpe (1696–1785), the founder of the State of Georgia and an exceptionally courageous and interesting man. After serving in the Austro-Turkish war under Prince Eugene, he entered Parliament for Haslemere and, coming in contact with the horrors of our prison system, brought the matter before Parliament in 1729. Three years later he organised a scheme for the colonisation of Georgia with the double purpose of relieving poor debtors and checking Spanish aggression. He sailed with 35 families in 1732, explored the Savannah River, chose the site for the first settlement, made friends with the Creek Indians and concluded a treaty with them. He forbade slavery, the drinking of spirits and the exploitation of the native Indians. On a second expedition he took with him John and Charles Wesley, and when Charles came home appointed George Whitefield in his stead. When war broke out between England and Spain in 1739 (the War of Jenkins' Ear) Georgia, being the southern-most colony, was threatened and Oglethorpe was put in command of the British troops. When the Spanish invaded, he defeated and repulsed them at the Battle of the Bloody Marsh. He returned to England in 1743 and married Elizabeth Wright, the heiress of Cranham Hall, but two years later was called to march against Prince Charles Edward Stuart with the troops he was raising for Georgia. He was accused of excessive sympathy with the enemy and was court martialled; although he was acquitted, he retired into private life and spent his remaining 31 years in farming his wife's estate and enjoying the company of the literary men of the day. Dr Johnson wrote of him, "I know no man whose life would be more interesting; if I were furnished with material, I would be glad to write it." That chance was missed and Boswell, to whom Oglethorpe did give some details for the purpose, neglected it too, and the general, who had commanded a colony and a British force, died quietly at his country home and was buried in the family vault in the church. In 1925, there was a suggestion that his remains should be re-interred in Georgia but the request was refused; the church has greatly benefited however from American interest and the altar-rails and choir-stalls were given by the National Society of Colonial Dames.

Once again, at **North Ockendon**, the church, St Mary Magdalene, is the main centre of interest. It is approached up a long avenue of beeches and entered by a Norman doorway. The chancel and the main body of the church date from about 1170, the north aisle was added about 1240, the north chapel and arcade in 1300, and in 1500 the tower was added and the chancel arch rebuilt. Each pier of the nave is different and the pillar between the chancel and chapel is lovely with 700-year-old carving of oak and vine leaves, all as fresh as if the sculptor had just left it. The nave roof is very fine and in the east window of the north chapel is a 15th century St Mary Magdalene with long hair holding a pot of ointment, a 13th century St Helen, and fragments of 14th century glass. The monuments are chiefly to the Poyntz family who lived in the manor house, and most unusual they are. On a huge table tomb lie Sir Gabriel Poyntz (d. 1607) and his wife Audrey (d. 1594). The effigies are fully life-sized and Lady Poyntz' embroidered skirt and the gold chains about her neck are magnificently rendered, as is her husband's armour and ruff. Sir Gabriel also erected eight small wall monuments to himself, his son, and their six direct ancestors going back to Pointz FitzPoyntz of Edward III's day. They are quite fascinating and most unusual as a staunch attempt has been made to render the ancestors' costume historically correct. There is another good wall monument to Sir James (d. 1623) and his son Richard (d. 1643), who kneel, both in armour, and a bust of Sir Thomas Poyntz who lived into Queen Anne's day and has four cherubs lamenting him.

The manor house, North Ockendon Hall, has gone, destroyed during the Second World War, but the Tudor post office remains and a Roman burial ground of 16 acres has been discovered here. Another interesting house, Stubbers, has gone too and its grounds are used as an outdoor pursuits centre by young people, but it was once the home of William Coys, a famous Stuart botanist, in whose garden the yucca tree and the ivy-leaved toadflax first grew in England. The Hampshire botanist, John Goodyer, visited the garden and helped Coys to make the first complete English garden list with all the plants scientifically described. Botanists went on pilgrimage to the garden 300 years ago, and though everything has now changed it is good that the grounds are used for camping and other healthy activities and not built over with little cramped houses.

Nearby is **Wennington**. The church still stands alone but building is going on all over the nearby fields. The church of St Mary and St Peter has a 12th century doorway, and the chancel, nave, and south aisle, now demolished, were built in the 13th century. The north aisle was added early and the west tower late, in the 14th century. There is a good 14th century kingpost roof, and the 17th century furnishings—the pulpit, the carved font cover, and iron hourglass stand for timing the sermons—are all interesting and unusual. There is a fine 13th century chest for documents and other valuables, and in the north aisle a monument to Henry Bust, who died in 1624, to be followed a year later by his son. It was raised to them by the widowed mother.

We come to **Rainham** in the southern corner of the borough and at first glance it seems a flat marsh land, filled with factories, their car-parks shimmering in the sun, and patrolled by pylons, but there are two fine churches here, one old and one new, and a splendid manor house. It was in Rainham that two Saxon glass drinking-horns were discovered in the 1930s. This find is unique in Britain. The drinking horns are now in the British Museum.

Rainham church, dedicated to St Helen and St Giles, is that rarity, a virtually complete late Norman church, built chiefly about 1170. It is small and dark and utterly peaceful and friendly. The chancel, nave, aisles, and tower are all of the same early date. The chancel arch which may, long ago, have been widened, is slightly asymetrical and has chevron ornamentation; in front of it is a late 15th or early 16th century screen, rather plain and very lovely. There are some small brasses, a nice piscina and on the wall of the rood-loft staircase, a scratched drawing of a ship with two masts. There are traces of wall-paintings in both nave and chancel.

Charles Churchill, poet and satirist, became curate here in 1756, and of his own preaching he wrote that "Sleep at my bidding crept from pew to pew". But the people of Rainham did not suffer in this way long for after two years he succeeded his father at St John's, Westminster. He loved the theatre and in 1761 leapt into fame with a masterly satire on the actors of the day. He joined Wilkes' party, wrote many satires, and led a wild life till he died at 34 of fever while visiting Wilkes at Boulogne. Cowper called him "Great Churchill, with a certain rude and earth-born vigour", and Garrick said of him "Such talents, with prudence, had commanded the nation." But there was little in him to outlast the popular whim of his age and today his verse is almost forgotten.

Next to the church is Rainham Hall, a small sumptuous house of about 1729. It is of red brick and has a superb and elaborate door-way adorned with flowers and a porch with Corinthian columns. Inside is a handsome hall and staircase. The house is now National

Trust property but is open to the public by arrangement with the tenant at certain times of the year.

A little way off, in Rainham Road, is the new Roman Catholic church of Our Lady of La Salette, planned by Messrs Burles, Newton, and Partners. Inside are exquisite aumbries, designed by Hurst Franklin. The unusual dedication refers to a vision of the Blessed Virgin to two children at La Salette near Grenoble in France in 1846. A dried-up spring began to flow again after this apparition and has since been responsible for many cures. In an architecturally bleak area, this church seems rather like a spring of water itself and is a worthy companion to the lovely parish church.

HILLINGDON

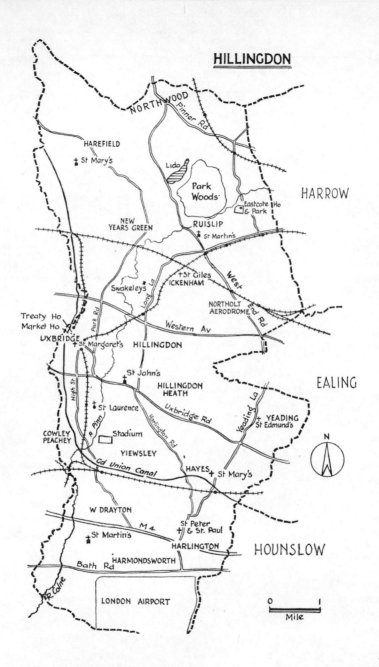

HILLINGDON

NORTHWOOD

Pinner Rd

HARROW

HAREFIELD

† St Mary's

Lido

Park Woods

Eastcote Ho & Park

NEW YEARS GREEN

RUISLIP
† St Martin's

† St Giles
ICKENHAM

Swakeleys

Long La

West End Rd

NORTHOLT AERODROME

Treaty Ho
Market Ho
UXBRIDGE

Park Rd

Western Av

† St Margaret's

HILLINGDON

EALING

† St John's

HILLINGDON HEATH

Yeading La

High St

Uxbridge Rd

† YEADING
St Edmund's

R. Pinn

† St Laurence

Harlington Rd

COWLEY PEACHEY

Stadium

YIEWSLEY

Gd Union Canal

HAYES † St Mary's

N

W DRAYTON

M 4

St Peter
† & St. Paul

HOUNSLOW

† St Martin's

HARLINGTON

Bath Rd

HARMONDSWORTH

R. Colne

LONDON AIRPORT

0   1
Mile

HILLINGDON

The borough of Hillingdon lies to the extreme north-west of the Greater London area. It consists of the former borough of Uxbridge, and the three urban districts of Hayes and Harlington, Ruislip and Northwood, and Yiewsley and West Drayton. These include the former villages of Hillingdon, Harefield, Eastcote, Ickenham, Cowley and Harmondsworth. Hillingdon is the third largest borough in the London area, covering 27,258 acres with a population of 233,030. It is bounded to the north, west, and south by Hertfordshire, Buckinghamshire and Staines, which is no longer a part of Middlesex having been transferred to Surrey; on the east are Harrow, Ealing, and Hounslow. There is high ground at Hillingdon and Harefield, and a plain to the extreme south of the borough, where London Airport lies.

Hillingdon, the hamlet that has given its name to the modern borough, is still a village on top of the hill above Uxbridge. It was mentioned in Domesday Book, though today the Uxbridge Road is a six-lane highway that almost completely divides the manor from the church.

The church is dedicated to John the Baptist, and its commanding tower holds the eye for a great distance along the main road. It contains work dating from the 13th to the 19th centuries and yet its appearance has a great unity. The chancel arch is 13th century with capitals of stiff leaves resting on corbels carved with a grimacing face whose tongue protrudes, and with two small monsters—perhaps the finest of its date in the London area; the nave and aisles are 14th century, the tower dates from 1629, and the eastern half of the church—the chancel, transepts, and chapels—was rebuilt by Sir George Gilbert Scott in 1848. The flint-covered church is especially worth visiting for its brasses and monuments. There is a huge brass—the most magnificent in Middlesex—to Lord L'Estrange (d. 1509) and to his wife Janet; she was the sister of Elizabeth Woodville, Edward IV's queen, and was thus the aunt of the two little princes who were murdered in the Tower. Between the L'Estranges is a tiny portrait of their daughter. The other brasses are 16th century and commemorate a merchant, Drew Saunders (d. 1579), with his wife and his merchant's mark, and John Attlee who died in 1599.

The remains of another brass shows six little girls and three little boys, but their names are unknown.

The earliest and most charming monument is to Sir Edward Carr (c. 1657), his wife and daughters. The parents kneel, he in armour and she with exquisitely carved curls and a deep lace collar; the middle of the 17th century is late for such a formal grouping. Above them, on a pinnacled canopy, sit two allegorical figures, but in front of them, stepping out of the monument, are their daughters, Philadelphia and Jane, holding hands, the little one clutching a posy and her elder sister a book. Nearby is a most accomplished monument to Henry Paget, Earl of Uxbridge (d. 1743); he is in Roman dress, his head and arms splendidly carved. In the nave there is a graceful allegorical figure, sculpted by John Bacon; she holds a medallion portrait of the man commemorated, Thomas Lane, who died in 1795 "having acquired a fortune by constant application". In the north aisle there is a handsome monument to John Mist who flourished during the reigns of George I and George II. He died at Hillingdon worth £50,000 having enjoyed the following positions: "Paviour to the Royal Palaces, Paviour to the Office of Works, Slater, caretaker, thatcher, scavenger, foundation digger, etc. He was a great undertaker and a slave to business. He finished the great drain in Pall Mall and since the new road in Hyde Park." The modern glass in the window is worth careful attention, that in the east window having won a special award in 1955 for its excellence.

In the churchyard lies John Rich, to whom we owe a world of laughter, for he introduced pantomime into England. It was he who produced John Gay's *Beggar's Opera*, which was so successful that the wits said it had made Rich gay and Gay rich. There are considerable fragments of an earthwork near the churchyard, but little is known of their origin or purpose. To the west of the church is the Red Lion Inn, where Charles I rested for a few hours on the morning of April 27, 1646. He had left Oxford with only two companions for the city was besieged by Cromwell, and was making his way north to surrender to the Scottish army. At two o'clock he engaged a villager to guide him through Harrow, where his horse lost a shoe, to Barnet.

To the north of the church, on the far side of the busy main road, is Cedar House. It was built in Queen Elizabeth I's day and was remodelled in the 18th century. For many years, it was the home of Major-General John Russell, Oliver Cromwell's grandson, who was buried in Hillingdon churchyard in 1735. Before him the house

Brass to
Lord and
Lady
L'Estrange,
St John's,
Hillingdon.

had belonged to Samuel Reynardson, the botanist who in 1683 planted the magnificent cedar, now one of the oldest in England, from which the house takes its name. He presented the church with the font and parochial library, which was destroyed during the 1940s. Today the house provides offices for a commercial school, and there is another nearby called Bishopshalt which commemorates the fact that from 1281 onwards, successive Bishops of Worcester would break their journeys to and from London at Hillingdon.

Nearby is Hillingdon Court, once the home of the Barons Hillingdon, and now a Roman Catholic convent and girls' school, and Hillingdon House, built about 1840 for the Cox family, bankers and army agents, and today the property of the RAF. In the grounds is the war-time centre for the Battle of Britain, an underground operations room. The house stands on the site of an older building which was once the property of the Duke of Schomberg, William III's Dutch commander who was killed in Ireland at the Battle of the Boyne. So fiery-tempered a man was he that it was said that in one campaign he quarrelled with everyone except the enemy.

Although **Uxbridge** is today far larger than Hillingdon, it was once dependent upon the village on the hill and its church was a chapel of St John's. It is an old place—its name probably came from that of the 7th century tribe of Wixan. By 1170, it was important enough to be granted a charter to hold a weekly market which came to deal primarily in corn, for during the 18th and 19th centuries milling was the main occupation of the area. Even today, the immensely elegant Market House, built in 1788, is an excitingly busy place selling all sorts of fruit, vegetables, and other wares. Lying as it does on the main London–Oxford road, Uxbridge became an important coaching centre, and in 1798 when the Grand Junction Canal was opened, its links with the capital and the Midlands improved still further. The Great Western Railway reached Uxbridge in 1856 and the Metropolitan in 1904; from these two dates, the growth of the town accelerated. Today, the canal is busy with pleasure boats rather than with barges.

Uxbridge has now become a suburban sprawl but parts of the centre of the town are still compact and attractive. Some of the shops in Windsor Street look like illustrations from one of Beatrix Potter's stories, and the public house, The Metropolitan, has a superb sign showing a tube train. The station in the High Street, which is about to become a traffic-free precinct, has a large and chilling façade but good ticket halls and behind it, a little up the hill in Belmont Street, is the Friends' Meeting House. Vine Street commemorates the vineyard that Domesday Book tells us once flourished here.

The church, dedicated to St Margaret, is chiefly 15th century, with a Tudor south chapel and a 14th century tower rebuilt in 1820. The font with leopards and roses in quatrefoils is 15th century as are the roofs, the finest of which has nine bays and hammerbeams springing from brackets carved with heads of kings and queens and humbler folk. Two carved armchairs and a chest are 17th century. The chancel screen, with a cornice of trailing vine, is in memory of the Uxbridge men who did not come back from the First World War. The church's most interesting monument is the tomb of Dame Leonora Bennet who died in 1638; a life-sized effigy, most resplendently dressed, reclines on a tomb chest into which a grating has been inserted and behind it is a grisly carving of a charnel house with skulls grinning through the bars. The lady lived in the mansion now known as the Treaty House with her third husband, Sir John Bennet, Chancellor to the queen of James I, and a man of most unpleasant reputation. When impeached as a judge for taking bribes, he pleaded the possession of a wife, 10 children and 40 grandchildren, all of whom would be disgraced should sentence of imprisonment be carried out; he escaped with a fine and died in 1627.

There have been two particularly dramatic moments in the history of Uxbridge. One was a tragic day in August 1555 when John Denley, Patrick Packingham, and Robert Smith were brought from other parts of the country and were burnt at the stake on Bishop Bonner's orders for their Protestant beliefs. Denley was singing a hymn among the flames when John Story, more brutal than his master the Bishop, threw a burning faggot in his face. Glorifying his deed in Parliament, he said: "I threw a faggot in the face of an earwig at the stake at Uxbridge and set a bushel of thorns at his feet and see nothing to be ashamed of or sorry for." Sixteen years later this pitiless fanatic suffered an equally terrible fate at Tyburn.

For 20 days in January 1646, the fate of England was debated at the Treaty House, then the home of Sir Edward Carr whose monument is in the church, and now the Crown and Treaty House Inn. In this "good house at the end of the town" as Clarendon called it, a conference was arranged by the Parliamentarians in an effort to compromise with the Royalists about the Church, the militia and Ireland. The historian has described the scene when "the fair room in the middle of the house was handsomely dressed up for the Commissioners, who never went through each other's quarters nor met but in the great room". The conference ended in stalemate and the Commissioners returned, the Royalists to Oxford, the Parliamentarians to London, to report their failure. The struggle dragged out its bitter course. The house has been much altered but two of the rooms used at the conference remain; the panelling from them was stripped out, sent to America in 1929, and installed in the Empire State Building, New York, but it was returned as a coronation gift to our Queen Elizabeth in 1955, and has now been restored to its proper place. Besides the Treaty House, there are two other interesting public houses, the Three Tuns which was built in Tudor days and is still an inn, and the King's Arms which has 15th and 16th century remains but which has now become a gardening shop with a modern façade.

The surroundings of Uxbridge are very pleasant with the rivers Colne and Frays nearby, and fine views from the top of Uxbridge Common across to Harrow on its hilltop. On the common is held "London's premier country show"—the Hillingdon, formerly the Uxbridge, Show.

Four miles north of Uxbridge is **Harefield** with one of the most picturesque parish churches in England. Dedicated to St Mary, it lies half a mile from the main village at the bottom of a little dell and in February the churchyard is white with snowdrops. It is of flint and brick and stone, and all three meet in the massive low tower, standing at the west side of the north aisle, which has fine chequer work. Like the tower, this aisle and the north chapel are 16th century. The south aisle is 14th century, with clustered pillars on modern bases, and the heads of a bishop and a woman with a jewelled band on one of the capitals. There is a gallery of heads by the south aisle windows. The masonry of the side walls of the chancel is 13th century, but the east is new and the chancel arch is 18th century. The thick walling at the west end of the nave is probably 12th century. Scratched on the south wall is an ancient mass dial.

The interior has low white ceilings, a three-decker pulpit, a wide gallery over the north aisle, high pews with fleur-de-lys poppyheads, and box-pews through which the north chapel is entered. The traceried screen enclosing the chapel is from about 1600, with some modern work; the font cover, a chest, and the table in the vestry are Jacobean. The superb pierced carving of the altar-rails and the reredos was the work of Flemish craftsmen late in the 17th century. Both have foliage and scrollwork, with heads of a monk, a nun, and

226

cherubs on the rails, and on the reredos two kneeling angels holding the Commandments written on glass. A new east window has been made in the north chapel but it is filled with 16th century glass.

Harefield Church is exceptionally rich in all kinds of funeral monuments. There are more than 50 portraits engraved on brass, 19 of them on a table tomb in the south aisle which shows John Newdigate who acquired the manor in Henry VIII's day. His family have held it ever since with one gap of 90 years. He is shown with his wife, her gown fastened with roses, and their 17 children. One of the sons, John Newdigate who died in 1545, appears again on a brass in the chancel, this time with his wife and 13 children, fine groups in rich dress. The oldest of the brasses is Editha New-digate (d. 1444) wearing a horned headdress and a high-waisted gown with full sleeves. There are three palimpsest brasses, one of which is hung in chains so that we may see on the one side the inscription to John and Barbara Crugge (d. 1533) and on the other a skeleton in a shroud. The other brasses are of the Asshebys, an important local family. George (d. 1514), Clerk of the Signet to Henry VII, is with his wife and seven children. William (d. 1637) and Jane are with a row of seven daughters facing a lonely son. The two fathers are in armour. The reverse side of these brasses cannot be seen as they are fixed to the floor, but casts taken from them, show-ing figures in shrouds, and a priest, are displayed on the wall.

There are other, later Ashby monuments, one to Sir Robert of 1717 and another to Sir Francis (d. 1623) and his wife, who are shown kneeling at a desk, five sons, one in armour, kneeling below them. On a pillar of the north arcade is the bust of William Ashby, who in 1744 set up a tablet to his gamekeeper on an outside wall of the church. It reads:

> *In frost and snow through Hail and rain*
> *He scour'd the woods and trudg'd the plain,*
> *The steady pointer heads the way*
> *Stands at the scent and springs the prey.*
> *The timorous birds from stubble rise*
> *With pinions stretch'd divide the skys.*
> *The scatter'd lead pursues their flight.*
> *And death in Thunder stops their flight.*
> *His spaniel of true English kind*
> *Who's gratitude inflam'd his mind,*
> *This servant in an honest way*
> *In all his actions copy'd Tray.*

The Ashbys lived at Breakspear, an old farmhouse which they enlarged. It had formerly been the property of the Breakspears, and it is possible that the only English pope, Nicholas Breakspear, Pope Adrian IV (d. 1159), may have come from this family. The house was largely rebuilt in the 17th century and has now been modernised to become an old people's home. There is a fine 17th century dovecote in the grounds.

Returning to the Newdigate monuments in the church, there is a charming one of 1610 in the south aisle, splendid with colour and gold, where Sir John kneels in armour, facing his wife who wears a French headdress and a farthingale, a desk and a winged skull between them. Below them kneel two sons and three daughters. A poem tells us of the knight's virtues; it ends:

> *Weepe, then, whoe'er this stone doth see*
> *Unless more hard than stone thou bee.*

In the aisle are two tablets to John Newdigate of Charles I's day and to Sir Richard, sergeant-at-law, who died in 1678. Then beside the altar is a huge canopied tomb by Grinling Gibbons to Mary (d. 1692), wife of Sir Richard Newdigate, on which the lady, clad in loose classical draperies, reclines comfortably against a sarcophagus. On the north wall of the chancel is an urn, also by Grinling Gibbons, to Sarah Newdigate (d. 1695), a cherub on either side of it, and on the south wall are three recesses, each of them with a Newdigate urn. The centre one is to Elizabeth (d. 1765), the mother of the Sir Roger who founded the Newdigate Prize for poetry at Oxford, that on the left is to Sophia, his first wife, and that on the right to Hester, his second. The urns are so still and white and elegant that they make a strange contrast with the more robust 17th century monuments around them.

But rich as it is in funeral pomps, the chief glory of the church is the painted tomb of Alice, Countess of Derby (d. 1636). She lies under a domed and curtained canopy supported on Corinthian columns, wearing a red dress and ermine cloak, her golden hair spread out over the two pillows that support her head. Beneath her kneel her three pretty daughters in ermine cloaks and ruffs; they all married earls. The countess was widowed and married as her second husband Sir Thomas Egerton, Queen Elizabeth I's Chancellor, himself a widower with children. They lived in a great house beside the church and here in 1602, Sir Thomas and his lady entertained the queen herself for three days and it is said that the

Lord Chamberlain's Men acted *Othello* before her with Shakespeare in the company. Their house was demolished in the early 19th century but the avenue of elms leading to it remains and is still called the Queen's Walk. Lady Egerton, who was always known as the Countess, became a formidable local figure; she founded the almshouses near the church (they have recently been restored), and fought a long and brisk battle with the townsfolk of Uxbridge over the payment of market tolls. In 1634, the countess had become a grandmother but was not too old to enjoy another theatrical performance, a masque called *Arcades* by young John Milton, a friend of her protégé, the musician Henry Lawes. The old lady, who had entertained Queen Elizabeth I and had probably spoken to Shakespeare, sat in a chair of state and watched torches coming towards her up the avenue in the dusk of a summer evening. The verses were spoken by her grandchildren who were doubly dear to her, being the offspring of her second daughter, Frances, and her stepson, John Egerton, who became the Earl of Bridgewater. When it was all over, it was declared such a success that Milton was asked to write something else to be performed at a family gathering at Ludlow Castle that autumn where John Egerton was the Keeper; he wrote the masque called *Comus*. Two years later Dame Alice died and they buried her in the little church beside her great house. But the life-sized figure on her tomb shows, not the old lady who was laid to rest, but the magnificent long-haired beauty who had welcomed England's queen.

The Newdigates were the grandchildren of Lord Chancellor Egerton and the house where they all lived has gone, but where it stood are the graves of 110 Australian soldiers who died at Harefield Hospital; each year, a memorial service is held on Anzac Day (April 25) in Harefield Church and each year there are those who travel from Australia and New Zealand to be present. Nearby is a white marble cross with a big bronze replica of the Victoria Cross set in it; it marks the resting place of Major Gerald Goodlake who won the Victoria Cross in the Crimean War for his courage when commanding a little band of volunteer sharpshooters.

Harefield village, about half a mile from the church, is centred on a broad green, with the King's Arms, a half-timbered 17th century inn, on one side, and Harefield House, built in the early 19th century, a little to the south. Going down the hill to the church are the almshouses which we have already mentioned, and at the foot of the hill there stood, until 1961, a 13th century chapel, the remains of Moor Hall which, in the Middle Ages, had belonged to the order of St John of Jerusalem. It was destroyed to make room for more factory buildings.

Two miles to the north east of Harefield, almost on the Hertfordshire border, is **Northwood**, which even today is a pleasantly wooded area. Holy Trinity, the parish church, was designed in 1854 by S. S. Teulon; it has a flint and stone exterior and a short spire. The interior is spacious with some good glass, including a fine memorial window to the Grosvenor family by Burne-Jones, and some interesting modern carving on the clergy stalls. The high altar was presented in 1962 in memory of Michael Robert Redman Harper, a young flying officer who was killed in an air accident.

Two fathers and two sons are buried together in this churchyard. Victor Morier died in 1892, at the age of 25, and was followed by his father, Sir Robert, a year later. Sir Robert had been a most popular ambassador to Russia and the Tsar sent a massive cross of Siberian marble to mark his tomb. In the same year died another diplomat who had also seen service in Russia, Lord Robert Grosvenor, later Baron Ebury, who was a champion of Protestantism. He joined Lord Shaftesbury in demanding the reduction of factory hours, and presided at a banquet to Garibaldi. It was he who paid the greater part of the cost of building this church. Near to him lies his third son, Norman Grosvenor, who died in 1898, his grave marked by a fine bronze panel showing an angel with a drawn sword standing at a door.

Sheltering in trees near the church is Northwood Grange, rebuilt as flats but keeping a 15th century block and a long range of Elizabeth I's day. To the north of the village (actually in Hertfordshire), are the buildings of Merchant Taylors' School, with green lawns and playing-fields bordered on one side by magnificent trees. In a rose garden is a statue of Sir Thomas White, sculptured in marble, wearing a long fur-lined cloak and a narrow-brimmed hat and holding his gloves. Born in 1492, he was apprenticed to a member of the Merchant Taylors' Company and lived to be one of the founders of the school in 1561. He was Lord Mayor of London and founded St John's College at Oxford. The school left its old premises in 1933 and moved to Sandy Lodge, Northwood.

In the cemetery at Chestnut Avenue is the journalist who suggested the Two Minutes Silence, the nation's homage to the fallen of the Great War on Armistice Day and later in Remembrance

Sunday. He was an Australian reporter, and the idea came to him in a Fleet Street tea-shop. He wrote an article explaining his idea, which was read by Sir Percy Fitzpatrick of the South African government, who put the idea into operation in South Africa and placed it before King George V. The king invited the journalist, Edward Honey, to a rehearsal at Buckingham Palace, and he lived to see the idea carried out, but died just before the second Armistice Day.

Ruislip is one of the most interesting places in the borough. The name is a combination of "rush" and "leap", and first appears in Domesday Book. The manor farm, built about 1500 with 18th century additions, which is today used by the borough council, marks the site of a cell or daughter house of Ogbourne Priory in Wiltshire, which itself belonged to the Abbey of Bec in Normandy. In the manor grounds are the remains of an earthwork, once perhaps the motte and bailey castle of Ernulf de Hesdin who gave the manor to Bec in 1096, before he went to the Crusades and died outside Antioch. He had been implicated in a conspiracy against William Rufus and, though nothing could be proved against him, he thought it wiser to leave the country.

The river Pinn runs just north of the manor farm and on the far bank are 234 acres of Park Wood; beyond lie Mad Bess Wood, apparently called after a poor crazy old woman who made her home among the trees, and Copse Wood. Between the woods is an expanse of water known as Ruislip Lido which was originally a feeder of the Grand Union Canal. Today it is used for swimming and water-skiing and on the banks is a model railway on which children can ride through the woods.

During the wars with France, the manor of Ruislip was confiscated by the Crown and the priory was closed in 1414. The land was granted first to the Earl of Bedford and then to King's College, Cambridge, who owned it outright till the 1930s and still hold the lordship of the manor. The Metropolitan Railway reached Ruislip in 1904 but the inevitable development was controlled and planned from the start with the result that Ruislip is still a very pleasant and pretty place in which to live. The heart of the village has scarcely changed since the Middle Ages and is always a surprise from whatever direction one may approach it. The manor barns, the finest in Middlesex excepting for Harmondsworth, are intact, one still used for general agricultural purposes, and the other converted into one of the most exciting public libraries that the writer has ever seen. Outside is a well-patronised bowling green and it is a splendid sight in summer to watch the white-clad players on the green turf outside the old red brick and timbering of the barns.

The church, dedicated to St Martin, is on the opposite side of the High Street, screened from the road by two groups of 16th and 17th century cottages and almshouses. Deep peace fills the secluded churchyard. The church was begun about the middle of the 13th century, and the chancel arch and nave still remain. The south aisle and chancel were rebuilt during the 15th century and the north aisle at the end of it. A sturdy tower was added and the walls were painted. We can still distinguish a crowned madonna, St Lawrence, St Michael, and the Seven Deadly Sins issuing from the mouths of seven dragons. The church was rather successfully restored in the 1870s.

The church's oldest possession is a 12th century font, its square marble bowl carved with leaves. Two piscinas and a stoup are 15th century; the roofs are 15th and 16th; and there are Tudor doorways to the rood-loft, two Tudor chests, and a patch of 14th century tiles in front of the altar. One of several old doors is in the north wall of the chancel, still keeping its original locks and handle. The carved pulpit is 17th century, and a copy of Bishop Jewel's *Apology* (1611) is in a case. There is a charming Jacobean bread cupboard on the wall, the bequest of Jeremiah Bright; it has his shield and carvings of ears of wheat, even the edges of the four shelves being decorated with leaves and flowers.

There are several brasses and monuments of interest, many of them to the Hawtrey family who lived at Eastcote House. They include one to Ralph Hawtrey and his wife, their six sons and six daughters; this was sold by auction in the last century but was returned to the church in our own. There is another to John Hawtrey (d. 1593) and his wife Bregget, and in the chancel there is a marble monument to a later Ralph and his wife, carved by John and Matthias Christmas, who were Master Carvers to Charles I and adorned his ship, the *Sovereign of the Seas*. On the opposite wall is a memorial to Ralph Hawtrey's daughter, Mary, who as Lady Bankes twice defended Corfe Castle for the king during the Civil War. In 1643, she beat off the attackers, but in 1645 she and her little garrison were forced to surrender through starvation.

The wide High Street is very pleasant, with an old post office near the church with a 16th century chimney stack, and three rebuilt 16th and 17th century inns, the George, the Swan, and the Bell, though the Bell is no longer a public house. There is the Plough Inn in Bury Street and at the corner of Bury Street, the High Street, and the Eastcote Road, the old village pump still stands.

Eastcote, a hamlet on the edge of Ruislip, has an unusually large quantity of fine, well-preserved 16th, 17th, and 18th century houses and farm buildings. Lack of space forbids a description of each individual building, but a walk along Eastcote High Road, Field End Road, and Catlins Lane is extremely rewarding. Haydon Hall in Joel Street has just been demolished but it was built about 1700 and had panelling removed from an older house; it was once the home of the early 19th century theologian, Dr Adam Clarke. Field End Lodge and Field End Farm are exceptionally attractive and the latter has a fine barn. Eastcote House, once a large, gabled, weatherboarded, 16th century mansion, was demolished in 1964. Only an outhouse remains, but the gardens and grounds have been turned into a park by Hillingdon borough council. The walled garden is so sheltered that flowers bloom there even in the bitterest weather, and in spring and summer it glows with blossoms.

To the south is **Ickenham** which possesses one of the finest houses and one of the most pathetic funeral monuments to be found in northern London. The monument is in St Giles' Church and is to Robert, the infant son of Sir Robert Clayton and his wife Martha, who died on August 16, 1665 within a few hours of his birth. It is a figure of a swaddled, shrouded baby—possibly the finest to be found in England—but as one looks at the small round face and down-turned mouth, all one can think of is the anguish of his parents. They had no other children and the estates passed to a nephew.

St Giles' Church itself is a pleasant modest building set in a pretty churchyard. It was built in the 14th century and enlarged with a north aisle almost as large as the rest of the church in the 16th. The bell-turret with a shingled spire was added in the 15th century. The chancel and nave roofs are mediaeval, that over the west aisle Elizabethan. The timber-framed south porch is very pretty, and there is a bust of the Earl of Essex, the Parliamentary general, in a niche in the wall. Off the north aisle is a mortuary chapel, built in the mid-17th century by the Harington family who lived at Swakeleys, the manor house. There are niches in the walls which were filled with coffins. Today, the coffins have been removed and the chapel is dedicated to St John. There are three good Elizabethan

233

brasses to the Say and Shoreditch families, and a fine relief of a seated youth reading, by Thomas Banks, in memory of John George Clarke, a young barrister who ruptured an artery and died at the age of 25. His family owned Swakeleys in their day. The church is also notable for its modern oak woodwork by Clifford Robert Davie, who worked on it from 1926 to 1928, and for the altar-kneeler and hassocks which are being embroidered by the parishioners; they are of an exceptionally high standard.

Half a mile from the church stands Swakeleys, a splendid red-brick, H-shaped 17th century mansion, now the property of the London Postal Region Sports Club. It has Dutch gables and clustered chimneys and over the two-storeyed west porch is the bust of a man in classical drapery. The house is much as it was built by Sir Edmund Wright, a Lord Mayor of London in Stuart days. Across the hall is an oak screen with three bays, adorned with cherubs and shields, Doric columns and pilasters, and a bust of Charles I framed by a pediment on which lions are crouching. On the other side of the screen is a bust of Fairfax, a companion to the one of Essex that is in the church. In 1665 the house was sold to Sir Robert Vyner, the goldsmith who lent much money to Charles II and saw small return.

Sir Robert was the City Sheriff who gallantly strove to check the Fire of London and his own place being destroyed, was allowed to store his money, jewels, and plate in Windsor Castle. He lived here like the merchant prince he was. Pepys wrote of a visit to Swakeleys in his own candid fashion: "By and by to dinner, where his lady I find yet handsome, but hath been a very handsome woman: now is old but hath brought him nearly one hundred thousand pounds, and now he lives, no man in England in greater plenty, and commands both King and Council with his credit he gives them." But the thing that interested Pepys most was this: "He showed me a black boy that he had, that had died of consumption, and, the boy being dead, he caused him to be dried in an oven, and he lies there entire in a box."

The walls and ceiling of the staircase are painted, probably during Sir Robert's day, and possibly by the artist Robert Streater; they show the death of Dido, and the founding of Lavinium by Aeneas, and a landscape, and (on the ceiling) Juno and Iris in the sky. The staircase has been renewed but some of the posts and panelling are original. The magnificent drawing-room on the first floor has a coved ceiling with exquisite plaster work. Around the house there are many fine trees and to the north is a brick dovecote with pyramid roof and lantern, and small oval openings in its walls; it is a good 300 years old.

On the way to Hayes, we pass through **Yeading**, where St Edmund's Church stands, designed by Antony Lewis and consecrated in 1961. It is rectangular with no real separation between chancel and nave, and is worth visiting for its exceptionally fine furnishings and for the Crucifix, the figure of St Edmund, and the altar, all carved by Robin Dawson.

Today, **Hayes** is a large built-up place with many factories, but it is very old. It is mentioned in Domesday Book, where the name is given as "hesa", probably meaning a hedge or undergrowth. The name is Anglo-Saxon, but Hayes is older still, for, when digging for the foundations of the EMI factory was going on, an Egyptian statue was found of a priest carrying in his hand the shrine of a god. It is now in the British Museum. No one knows how it came to be there, but perhaps a Roman soldier who had served in Egypt came to Britain bringing this religious symbol with him.

The manor of Hayes was bequeathed to the Archbishopric of Canterbury in AD 830 by a priest called Warderhus, and it remained the property of the Archbishopric till the Reformation, when it was sold to Lord North. Subsequently, it belonged to the Earl of Jersey and to Charles Henry Mills, who became Lord Hillingdon in 1886. It remained with the Hillingdons till it was sold piecemeal in the 1930s.

Despite the factories and suburban houses that surround it, the heart of the old village has remained comparatively undisturbed. The parish church, St Mary's, faces the manor house, a fine 16th and 18th century building which is today used as council offices, and in the grounds of Hayes Court nearby was an 18th century dovecote.

St Mary's Church is approached through a 17th century lychgate and is of flint and stone with a low 15th century tower. Inside there is a good deal that is worth noticing. The chancel is 13th century and still has its sedilia and piscina; the windows are decorated with carvings of leaves and heads. The north arcade of the aisle, with big overhanging capitals, is 13th century too; the south arcade is of the 16th as is the charming porch with open timbering on the low walls, a tiled roof, and bargeboard with pierced carving. The first impression of the imposing interior is of stout leaning arcades and great stretches of oak roofs—15th century in the chancel and north aisle, 16th in the nave and south aisle. Stone corbels carved with heads, angels, and foliage support the north aisle roof. The nave has panelling all awry and flat bosses carved with Passion emblems, flowers, and Tudor badges. The long waggon roof of the chancel has flat rafters, like the inside of a wooden ship. Where it overlaps the north arcade, this roof is supported on three wall arches resting on corbels carved with a man holding a book, an angel with a shield, and a man with his hands on his knees. There is no chancel arch to hide the awkward meeting of the nave and chancel roofs. The font is Norman and in the north aisle is a 15th century wall-painting of St Christopher with a huge stick and a flying cloak, wading across a stream with the Child astride his shoulders; a hermit is in the background, and a little boy in red sits fishing by the stream in which there are crabs, eels, and a little mermaid looking in her mirror.

In the chancel is the oldest brass in the county, a half-figure of a priest, Robert Lance, and there are two other brasses, to Walter Green (d. 1456) in armour and to Sir Thomas Higate (d. 1576) with his wife and nine children. Nearby are two elaborate monuments. Sir Edward Fenner, a judge who died in 1612, reclines, dressed in his red legal robes and black cap, under a canopy upheld by Corinthian columns and on the opposite chancel wall is another memorial to a man in armour, who is believed to be Edward Fenner who died in 1615.

A number of interesting men have held the living of Hayes. Among them were Henry Gold who opposed Henry VIII's marriage to Anne Boleyn and was hanged at Tyburn in 1534 for being an accomplice of Elizabeth Barton, "the Holy Maid of Kent"; Robert Wright who became rector in 1610 and was later Bishop of Bristol; and Patrick Young, librarian to James I and Charles I and one of the most eminent Greek scholars of his day. Another resident was Dr Thomas Triplett, who taught there and was buried in Westminster Abbey when he died in 1670. He left money for the apprenticing of children in the parish and is today commemorated by a school which bears his name.

Nearby there are two fine new Roman Catholic churches, St Jude's and the Immaculate Heart of Mary. Both are exceptionally beautiful and worth entering whether to admire or to pray.

West Drayton, some 2½ miles west of Hayes, has a splendid village green and an unusually picturesque setting for St Martin's, the parish church. Beside the churchyard is a superb red-brick

Tudor gatehouse, with octagonal towers and massive doors, the entrance to the now vanished manor house of the Paget family. Throughout the Middle Ages, the manor belonged to St Paul's Cathedral but at the Reformation Henry gave it to Sir William Paget, his Secretary of State. Paget was a friend to Protestor Somerset, and when he fell, Paget lost his office too, was fined and imprisoned in the Tower. He recovered some of his fortune in Mary's day but did not again hold office, and dying in 1563, was buried in West Drayton churchyard. Others of his family lie there too. One was a grandson, William, who was with Essex at Cadiz, and another was a great-grandson who raised a regiment for Charles I, fought for his king at Edgehill, and lost his fortune in the royal cause.

The manor passed to the Fysh Coppinger (later de Burgh) family who, since the old house had been pulled down, built a new one, Drayton Hall, some little way away from the church, which is today used as council offices. The gatehouse now serves as a home for the proprietor of the local market garden.

Apart from its lovely setting, St Martin's Church is an interesting place. It is built of flint and stone and dates chiefly from the 15th century, though if the piscina with its richly moulded arches is in its original place, then the chancel is 13th century. The fine tower has three diminishing stages, and its massive arch, opening on to the nave and aisles which make up a square, create an impressive interior. The high timber roofs rest on stone pillars with carved corbels, and those in the nave are strange and grotesque, some with grinning, crouching beasts and some with bearded men with open mouths.

The 15th century font is the most elaborate in Middlesex. Carved on the eight panels of the bowl are angels and three scenes—a Pietà, a Crucifixion, and a hooded man looking like a sculptor at work. Under the bowl are hooded men like jesters, and round the base are four horrible creatures, some with animal, some with human faces. A fine ironbound chest is 300 years old and the works of the clock in the tower are said to be older still. There are several brasses, one to James Good (d. 1581). He was a physician and is shown with his wife and 11 children. The small portrait of a nameless civilian is from about 1520, and a shield remains of the brass of Richard Roos of 1406. There is a beautiful portrait of Margaret Burnell (d. 1529) showing her in a fine kennel headdress and a girdle with a flower clasp; her son and daughter are beside her. There are three 18th century monuments to the de Burgh family carved by the elder and younger John Bacon, and a splendid one of 1720, sculpted by an unknown hand, to a sea-captain, Rupert Billingsley, showing his three-masted ship, the *Royal George*. The north window to Mrs Mercer is by Burne-Jones, and the south window was painted in our own day. It shows St Martin on a black horse sharing his red cloak with a beggar sitting on the castle steps, two page boys in red and green and gold standing by. St Martin is on the cobbled way by the river, across which is Tours Cathedral, and on the bridge are women, a horseman, and boys landing fish.

The village green is a little distance from the church and is picturesque with houses ranging from The Old House and Southlands of the early 18th century to the rather sweet Daisy Villas of 1896. The first trial run for the Great Western Railway, opened between London and Maidenhead in 1838, was made with the engine *Vulcan* on December 28, 1837, between West Drayton and Langley. Isambard Kingdom Brunel, England's greatest engineer, stood, smoking a cigar and wearing his huge top hat, and watched his achievement prove its workability. The great technological university, Brunel University, was founded at Acton in 1957 as a College of Technology, and by 1966 had received a Royal Charter. In 1968, it moved to a 170-acre site just outside Uxbridge, where in 1970 some 1800 students studied the sciences and engineering. Brunel University specialises in "sandwich courses" linking academic study closely with industry. Its buildings, which are still growing, have been designed chiefly by Richard Sheppard and partners.

East of West Drayton lies **Cowley Peachey**, with the smallest parish church in Middlesex. The name first appears as Cofenlea in a charter of 959—the land of a man called Cofa. The Peachey was added when Bartholomew Pecche bought land here in 1252. The church, dedicated to St Laurence, is a very small 12th century building of flint rubble, with a 13th century chancel and a timber bellcote added in 1780 with a leaded spire. There is a fine group of three 13th century lancet windows in the chancel, and a priest's doorway. Poppyheads from old pews and fragments of old tracery are in the screen; a west gallery, added much later, has made use of some Elizabethan panelling.

There is one brass, to Walter Pope who died in 1505 and is shown with his wife in the north chancel. He wears a fur-trimmed gown and has a curious questioning look in his eyes; his wife has a butterfly headdress and fur cuffs. In the churchyard lie Barton Booth, an 18th century actor famous for his playing of the Ghost in *Hamlet*, and his wife, the actress Hester Santlow. Edward

Hampton, who was born in 1632 and died in 1738, lies here too, as does the botanist John Lightfoot, one of the original members of the Linnean Society, who wrote a great study of Scottish plants. And William Dodd, the king's chaplain who was hanged for forgery, is buried at Cowley for his brother was rector here and was determined to give the poor corpse a decent grave.

William Dodd was born in 1729, the son of the vicar of Bourne in Lincolnshire. He was a brilliantly clever youth who was given every educational advantage. Before he was ordained, he wrote a highly successful novel and a volume on Shakespeare; afterwards, his preaching drew the most aristocratic congregations in London, and he was chosen as tutor for the 5th earl of Chesterfield. His fall can be traced to a successful lottery ticket. Having won one gamble, he tried another, seeking to obtain the rectorship of the fashionable St George's, Hanover Square, by bribing the Lord Chancellor's wife. He was at once disgraced, struck off the list of court chaplains, lampooned in the press, reviled on the stage, and made bankrupt; in his desperation he forged the name of his old pupil, the Earl of Chesterfield, on a bond for £4200. He was discovered, arrested, and condemned to be hanged, though the earl was ready to redeem the bond. Dr Johnson, eager to support him, wrote him a speech asking for mitigation of his sentence and, when that was refused, a *Convict's Address to his Unhappy Brethren*. These Dodd delivered as his own and suffered at Tyburn on June 27, 1777.

In Cowley, there is a reminder of the time when the canal was one of the most efficient means of transport. The Bridgewater Canal was constructed in 1759–61 by a descendant of that John Egerton who married his stepsister, Lady Frances Stanley (see p. 229) and became the 1st earl of Bridgewater. The Grand Junction Canal linking Birmingham with London was begun in 1793 and opened in the Hillingdon area in 1798; branches were dug between Norwood and Paddington, and Cowley Peachey and Slough. These canals carried to the new London suburbs the vast quantities of bricks manufactured in the brick-clay areas of Hayes, Yeading, West Drayton, and Yiewsley with the result that some areas now lie several feet lower than they did 200 years ago. The canals are little used today but at Cowley the Paddington Packet Boat Inn still flourishes and is worth visiting.

The two remaining places to be described in Hillingdon, Harmondsworth and Harlington, are both famous for the superb Norman doorways to their churches. **Harlington**, where the parish has been cleft in half by the new M4 highway, was once one of the prettiest villages in Middlesex. The name comes from *Hygereding tun*—"Hygered's farm". Until the First World War it was chiefly an agricultural area and was famous for its cherry orchards. The main local industry was brick-making and in 1866, a local gazetteer tells us, there were only 234 houses. Now the church, dedicated to St Peter and St Paul, stands among houses 100 yards from the motorway, and of Dawley House, where Henry St John, Viscount Bolingbroke, had his country retreat, all that remains is one brick wall.

The church, built of flint rubble and ironstone, stands in the churchyard with the stump of a gigantic yew tree, said to be over 1000 years old, beside it. Before it fell in 1959, the trunk had a girth of 34 feet; the stump is still growing vigorously. The church has a 12th century nave and doorway, a 14th century chancel, an early 16th century porch, a late 16th century tower, and a north arcade and aisle of 1880. There are two particularly interesting features— the superb Norman doorway, the best in the county, and the only Easter sepulchre in Middlesex. The doorway has two little pillars, carved with chevrons, on either side, and four deep bands of carving above the arch. The first is a simple chevron pattern, but the second is an arc of 25 watchful cats, their paws drawn up, their eyes seeming to examine all those who enter the church. Above them is a zigzag pattern and then a band of elegant little rosettes. It is worth journeying a long way to look at that doorway. The 14th century Easter sepulchre is on the north side of the chancel. Throughout the Middle Ages, a shrouded crucifix was laid in the little recess on Good Friday and the opening was covered up. On Easter Day the crucifix was back in its place above the altar and the sepulchre was seen to be empty so that all the congregation could rejoice and believe.

There is a 12th century font and two interesting brasses, one to the rector, John Monmouth, who died in 1419, and the other to Gregory Lovell (d. 1545) and his wife. There is a memorial to Joseph Trapp (d. 1747), once rector here, who was first Professor of Poetry at Oxford though he was a poor poet himself. Vainly does the epitaph on his marble tablet implore: *Hear me, at least, oh hear me from my grave!* for fewer read him now than when Dr Johnson unkindly said that his translation of the *Aeneid* would live as long as schoolboys could use it as a crib. In the nave is a monument to Sir John Bennet, Secretary of State to Charles II, who became Earl of Arlington, for he took his title from Harlington. There

Tottenham High Cross

East Ham Church, from
the south

Georgian houses in The
Butts, Brentford

Cottages in Horseshoe Lane,
Enfield, facing the New River

is a fine bust of him, and two equally well-carved portraits of his two wives.

The manor passed from him to Lord Bolingbroke and then was sold to the de Salis family, several of whom are commemorated in the church. In niches by the altar lie marble statues of Count Jerome Fane de Salis (d. 1836) and his wife Henrietta (d. 1856) carved by R. C. Lucas, and there is a bust of General Rodolph Leslie de Salis who led the 8th Hussars in the Charge of the Light Brigade at Balaclava in 1854. He survived, served through the Indian Mutiny, and died in 1880.

There is some agreeable modern glass, especially a memorial window to Robert Goodacre Long, churchwarden here, who died in 1953; it shows the Adoration of the Shepherds. There are great plans for the redevelopment of the rectory and its grounds, and a new church, Christ Church, has been built to serve the needs of the population on the far side of the motorway. There is no memorial to William Byrd, the composer, "the father of the English madrigal", who lived at Harlington from 1577 till 1592 but perhaps he needs none, for he is still remembered by all those who love English music.

Harmondsworth is a strange place. Within the parish boundary lies London Airport with all its noisy busy usefulness and its modern buildings, yet Harmondsworth village is tranquil and undisturbed, having changed very little in the last three centuries.

The village sits around a little square with two fine houses—the Grange of 1675 and Harmondsworth Hall, a red-brick, 18th century mansion—several pretty ones—Sun House and The Lodge—and two agreeable public houses—The Crown and The Five Bells. Its glories are the mediaeval church and the barn. St Mary's is of flint, with a large tower, which has brick upper courses and a little cupola. The doorway and south aisle date from the 12th century, and the doorway is very nearly as fine as that at Harlington. It has three orders, the inner one with rosettes and knotted patterns which are continued from the arch down the sides of the doorway to the ground. The next band is of strange primitive beaked heads which spring from two little plain pillars, and the outer band is a zigzag which runs uninterrupted from the floor to the arch. Inside there is a solid plain Purbeck marble font of about 1200, and the 13th century south arcade with round pillars and scalloped capitals. The north arcade was built later in the 13th century and the piers are more widely spaced. The chancel was rebuilt in the 15th century, its arches being made continuous with those of the nave, and an odd

I

effect is given by the meeting of the two, forming a bay with half a big arch rising from a low pillar, and half a smaller arch set on a high pillar. The tower was added about 1500 and the north chapel towards the end of the sixteenth century. This chapel has its original steep hammerbeam roof while the nave and aisles have 15th century roofs with modern kingposts in the nave. The dignified and substantial oak pews with buttressed ends are over 400 years old, and the sedilia and piscina are 15th century. There is a window with beautifully coloured stained glass in memory of Louis Hugo Kellner, who died in 1967.

In the churchyard there are some very early earthworks, and under a yew tree is the grave of Richard Cox, a farmer at Colnbrook, who in the 1850s developed the Orange Pippin apple that has immortalised his name.

Beside the church stands the huge tithe-barn, the best in Middlesex and one of the finest in all England. It is 190 feet long, 36 feet wide, and 36 feet high. It is divided into three aisles like a church, by two rows of massive posts in stone bases. The splendid roof, with kingpins and tiebeams, continues over the side alleys. It is still part of a farm and very much in use to store agricultural machinery whereas once it would have held corn. It was probably built about 1391 when Harmondsworth was bought by William of Wykeham who settled it on Winchester College. The tenure of the manor is a microcosm of English mediaeval history. Before the Norman Conquest, it was held by Earl Harold, but afterwards William settled it on the abbey of Rouen. The Benedictine monks established a cell in Harmondsworth, the successive priors of which were in constant—and sometimes violent—conflict with their villagers. When England was at war with France in 1340, the manor was confiscated to the crown and was subsequently given to William of Wykeham. After the Reformation, Henry VIII bestowed it on Sir William Paget who already held the adjoining manor of West Drayton.

The name Harmondsworth first appears in Domesday Book as *Hermodesworde*—"Heremode's farm"—and indeed the farms are still there, market-gardening going on at Sipson's Farm right up to the edge of the airport. As we drove along Sipson's Lane between Harmondsworth and Harlington, a cock pheasant flew up out of the hedge and almost stunned himself on the windscreen.

London Airport (Heathrow) was created during the 1939–45 war and was opened for civil use in 1946. It has wiped out the farms of Heath Row and Perry Oak and the main runway has obliterated the foundations of a colonnaded Iron Age temple built about 300 BC—the only one of its kind recorded in Britain.

Within the lifetime of many local residents, Heathrow was an area of market-gardens. In 1929 the Fairey Aviation Company built the Great West Aerodrome, a small grass airfield, there and used it mainly for experimental flying: many famous pre-war aircraft made their first flights from it. In 1944, it was reconstructed and became Heathrow RAF Station, but the war ended before it was used. The Ministry of Civil Aviation took it over, and began to build London's principal airport; it opened as such in 1946, and some of the original, prefabricated offices dating from the forties can be seen along the Bath Road. In 1966, the control of the airport passed to the British Airports Authority, who are responsible for an area of 2718 acres, where over 43,000 people are employed—in fact, a town called Heathrow, used by over 50 airlines and over 13,000,000 passengers a year.

The Central Area of the airport is approached from the north by a four-lane tunnel, 2080 feet long, running under two of the airport's five runways. Looking around the Central Area, one sees a vast complex of multi-storey car-parks and huge buildings, the most dominating of which is the red-brick Control Tower, started in 1950. The top floor of the 127-foot tower has a balcony and distinctive windows, behind which is the nerve-centre of the airport—the Approach Control Room. Every aircraft approaching or leaving the airport is watched by radar and is in radio communication with the Control Room: the incoming aircraft are "stacked up" over certain areas of outer London to await clearance for landing, at which point the Aerodrome Control (housed in the Cupola on the top of the Control Tower) takes over.

There are three passenger terminals at the airport: Terminal 1, opened in April 1969, which is used for passengers on domestic routes, Terminal 2, the first to be built, which is used for middle-distance flights, and Terminal 3, with its distinctive Stefan Knapp murals, opened in 1961, and used for long-haul traffic. All three terminals have similar plate-glass and concrete exteriors, and all have interiors designed to soothe the fears that most people experience when flying. Terminal 1, which is by far the most interesting building, has a gallery all round the interior, overlooking the airlines' desks and a row of shops, each of which has a plastic dome in front of it, displaying some of its wares. These vary from chocolates to a boutique, from lacy underwear to embroidery equipment—perhaps the latter is another attempt to soothe the passengers. The building has a long frontage, which allows a number of vehicles to set passengers down at the same time, and all its double glass doors are electronically operated to open automatically at the approach of a passenger. The Terminal cost some £11,000,000 to build and equip, and the architects, who designed all the airport's main buildings, were Frederick Gibberd and Partners.

A new terminal is now being built by Terminal 3, to deal with passengers from the jumbo jets, each of which can carry 500 people. The terminal will have moving walkways, and enclosed telescopic jetties to link the planes to the terminal.

Queen's Building, which was opened by the Queen in 1955, has a roof garden, which also extends over Terminal 2, and which is open to the general public. It has restaurant and buffet facilities and provides an excellent view of the aprons and a number of the runways, which are arranged in a pattern resembling the Star of David: this pattern was developed to utilise the original triangular system of runways built during the war, while allowing further runways to be built to a pattern that would allow any aircraft to take off or land in any possible wind direction, with a four miles per hour cross-wind, and with at least 1500 yards between each pair of runways, to allow simultaneous use. The longest runway is 12,000 feet.

A recent addition to the airport is St George's Chapel, a small, interdenominational chapel built underground like a catacomb which precaution unfortunately does not protect it from the screams of jets. High walls surround the cobbled courtyard and wooden cross, and steps lead down to the very severe but charming vaulted interior, which must be unique. It has three circular apses, each of which accommodates an altar and communion table: they were originally intended to be used by the Anglican, Roman Catholic, and Free Churches, but in practice all the denominations use the same altar.

The airport is highly commercial, but it does have two sentimental memorials: a statue of Sir John Alcock and Sir Arthur Whitten Brown, the first men to make a non-stop trans-Atlantic flight, in June 1919, and a model of the R.34 airship, commemorating the first two-way crossing of the Atlantic in July 1919. It may soon have another memorial: the cannon used to mark the end of the first Ordnance Survey base line, surveyed by General Roy in 1784, which extended from Hampton to the airport. The cannon was discovered during excavation for the airport.

Near the northern perimeter of the airport is the RSPCA Hostel, which deals with nearly 100,000 animals, birds and fish, most of which are in transit.

To the south is the 160-acre Cargo Terminal which can be approached by a 2905-foot-long tunnel from the Central Area. Heathrow is the third largest port in the United Kingdom, second only to the London and Liverpool docks in terms of the value of cargo transported.

On the south-eastern perimeter of the airport are the maintenance areas, and any traveller on the A30 notices particularly the huge BEA and BOAC complexes of hangars and offices. It is here that all BEA and BOAC planes are stripped down and reassembled after a certain number of flying hours.

HOUNSLOW

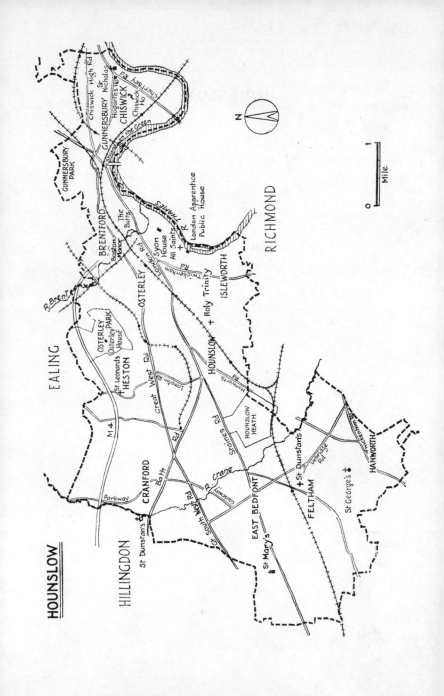

HOUNSLOW

The London Borough of Hounslow lies to the west of the Greater London area and consists of the former boroughs of Brentford and Chiswick, Heston and Isleworth, and the urban district of Feltham. It includes the sometime villages of Heston, Cranford, East Bedfont, and Hanworth. It is a flat area covering 23 square miles and is almost entirely built up, with a population of nearly 206,000.

The name of the borough comes from *Honeslaun* meaning "the hill of Hund"; in this context Hund was probably a personal name instead of meaning a dog, as it usually does.

Hounslow has been noted for its cavalry barracks, its eminence as a coaching town, and for its Heath which was the haunt of high-waymen and footpads. Its only claims to fame nowadays are its position as the administrative centre of the borough and its large cosmopolitan shopping area which has an extraordinary number of shoe shops. Hounslow has been a shopping centre since the end of the 13th century when its market was established. Although the barracks (which lie between the Bath and Staines roads) are now the headquarters of Southern Command, Hounslow does not have its former military associations which are borne out by the number of public houses with military names such as The Light Horse, The Hussar, The Duke of Wellington, or The Rifleman. The barracks were built in 1793 but most of the surrounding buildings date from 1860 or later. They are of red-yellow brick and are formed up around a grassy square; a considerable amount of white paint has been used on and around them.

Hounslow was the first coaching stage on the road from London to Bath and in its heyday some 2000 horses were stabled there, mostly at the George, the Red Lion, and the Rose and Crown. In 1833 over 200 coaches passed through Hounslow each day but by 1845 there were only 300 coach horses left in its stables and the High Street ceased to be the main route to the west when the Great West Road was built in the 1920s. The High Street had been part of the Roman road, Thamesis Street, leading to the south-west. Similarly the Heath, which covered 4293 acres in the 16th century, is now only 216 and is a barren area of scrubland and gravel pits, most of which are unused. The Heath was Crown property, part of the

Forest of Staines, so in the 12th century the Forest Laws applied to it; those found guilty of poaching the king's game were mutilated. The Heath became common land some time after Magna Carta but a number of monarchs still hunted there; Henry VIII in particular liked the Heath. It was not enclosed until the 18th and 19th centuries and was never an attractive area; Thomas Baird, reporting to the Board of Agriculture in 1793, wrote that "almost the whole of the Heath is sacrificed to a few farmers who live on the borders of it, and put on it immense quantities of greyhoundlike sheep that hunt about for their food, and devour with avidity every pile of grass they can meet with".

The Heath cannot have been made any more attractive by the row of gibbets that lined the route across it, each one of which held the rotting body of a highwayman. The gibbets ceased to be used in about 1801 but were not removed until 1809. The thick bushes which covered the Heath made it easy for a thief to lose his pursuers, and its proximity to London meant that loot could be disposed of easily to a fence. It was a safe place for no one, though the botanist, Sir Joseph Banks, suffered more from law officers than highwaymen for he was arrested while collecting specimens on the Heath and was not released till he had been brought before the local magistrate who recognised him as a neighbour.

The Heath was often the site of military camps; the Earl of Gloucester established an army of Londoners there in 1267 in opposition to Henry III and both Roundhead and Cavalier forces used it during the Civil War. Charles II assembled his troops there in 1678 and James II had an army of over 13,000 men there from 1685 to 1688 in an attempt to overawe the people of London, but instead a visit to the camp became a popular day out for the citizens and the camp was finally disbanded when the soldiers showed that they too were against their king when they cheered the acquittal of the Seven Bishops. It is said James heard the shouts as he rode away from the camp and asked what the tumult was. "Only the soldiers cheering, Sire," he was told. "Only that?" he replied. "It is the sound of a throne falling." George II too had a military camp on the Heath in 1740.

There are a number of factories on what was once Hounslow Heath but traditionally it was associated with the manufacture of swords and gunpowder. The sword industry was probably established by the end of the 16th century as a part of the iron-forging work in the area; it was well established by 1630 when Benjamin Stone opened a blade factory there, the earliest sword-blade factory known in the country. Richard Hopkin set up another in 1655. The industry flourished, for Sir William Waller, the Roundhead General, wrote to Westminster asking Parliament to supply him with 200 Hounslow blades.

Edward III employed William of Staines to make gunpowder for the Battle of Crecy in 1346; it was certainly made on the Heath by the time Henry VIII died and James I granted the factory a royal charter. There were a number of powder mills by the 18th century but they had all gone by 1930. There were inevitably numerous explosions, the worst being in 1796 when a mill caught fire and both it and a barge containing 30 barrels of powder exploded and nothing was left of either. Horace Walpole wrote to a friend: "In short, nine thousand powder mills broke loose yesterday on Hounslow Heath . . . All the north side of Twickenham and Brentford are shattered. At London it was proclaimed an earthquake and half the inhabitants ran into the streets."

The Heath was the site of the base line of the first triangle for General William Roy's survey of 1784, the first ordnance survey of the United Kingdom. The base line was five and a half miles long and ran from Heathrow to Hampton Hill. The survey was begun at the suggestion of the French government who were surveying France. General Roy died before the work was completed but so accurate were the measurements taken by him and his successors that when the last line of the triangles was measured on Romney Marsh, it proved to be only 28 inches different from the calculations based on the first line on the Heath. Roy marked the ends of his base line with wooden markers but they decayed so he had two cannons sunk into the ground with only their muzzles showing to mark the spots. One of the cannons was removed when a runway for Heathrow Airport was built over the spot but the other is still visible on the Heath, marked with a plaque. George III was very interested in Roy's work and he personally defrayed the cost of the special surveying instruments that had to be made.

Hounslow's most interesting building is Holy Trinity Church in the High Street. It was built in 1963, on the site of the priory that the Friars of the Holy Trinity built in England, when they first arrived from France at the beginning of the 13th century. These friars collected money to ransom Christians captured by the Moors and sold into slavery, and their order was called the Brethren for the Redemption of Captives or the Maturines. In 1296 Edward I granted them the right to hold a weekly market and an annual fair as a part of their fund-raising. The priory was dissolved in 1539 though the chapel continued to be used as the parish church till 1828. A new chapel was built in its place but was destroyed in 1943 by two small boys who set fire to both Hounslow and Isleworth churches.

The new church was built in 1963, by local people as far as possible. The architect, Lt. Colonel W. E. Cross, was a member of a Hounslow firm, and the builder, sculptor, and most of the craftsmen were from the neighbourhood too. They have produced an exceptionally striking modern church. It has narrow windows running from top to bottom of the building interspersed with concrete. The tower, which is approached across a tree-edged courtyard, forms the entrance to the church; it is 95 feet high and has a fibre-glass sculpture by Wilfred Dudeney of two angels. Set into the wall of the tower is a memorial from the old church, thought to be part of the 16th century tomb of Lord Windsor, and in the grass to the right of the tower is the clock face from the previous building.

The interior is open and very light, with a great feeling of space. The roof is high and the walls are simple with columnlike windows and ribs of concrete. Most of the windows are plain—they appear blue from the outside but are colourless from within. There are two stained-glass windows, however; one is a war memorial with a modern glass figure of Christ and regimental crests in older glass at the foot. Under the gallery are three panels of stained glass; two were saved from the old church and the third is a memorial to the architect. Another fibre-glass sculpture by Wilfred Dudeney, this time of Christ, dominates the interior.

The communion rail has crosses on it, a link with the Trinitarian Friars who wore a cross on their habits, but there are other links with the earlier churches. The most interesting are the two painted figures in the crypt which were probably made in the 1540s; they show a knight and his lady, kneeling facing each other, and they are early examples of this type of funeral memorial. In the vestry is another to Margaret Trevelyan who was buried in the chapel in 1646. She had travelled from Somerset in an ox-cart to ransom her husband who had been in the king's army during the Civil War and had been imprisoned in the Tower by Parliament. Tragically, as they were on their way home, Margaret caught smallpox and died at Hounslow.

On the stairs leading down to the crypt is a handsome monument with a bust of William Bulstrode, a member of the noted Hounslow family who died in 1724. He was a lawyer and published a number of controversial tracts and essays; he bought Hounslow Manor in

1705 and restored the chapel when it was damaged by fire in 1710.

Beneath the church is the chapel of St Mary Magdalene which has three unusual engraved glass panels by Anna Zinkeisen showing scenes from the saint's life.

St Michael and St Martin, a Roman Catholic church built in 1929, stands in the Bath Road and farther along to the west is St Paul's with its pleasant spire, built in 1877 by Habershon and Pite. Farther west on the Great West Road, the small brick church of the Good Shepherd stands on a housing estate. It was built by Richard Farey in 1958 and is designed to serve as a church hall as well as a church; a sliding screen can be used to cut off the altar area. South of the High Street in St Stephen's Road is the large red-brick church of St Stephen; its body was built in the Early English style by E. Christian in 1875 and its huge square tower was added in 1935.

The Town Hall stands in Treaty Road just off the High Street. It is an awesome red-brick building with statues of Wisdom and Justice and a colonnaded porch of puce tiles. It was built in 1904 together with Nowell Parr's more restrained Public Library and Baths which face it. The buildings are an interesting attempt at a civic centre.

An interesting quadrangle of houses stands in the Staines Road near the Bell. They were built by the Butchers' Charitable Institution in 1928 for the relief of those of the butchers' trade who fell into need. In the central block is a chapel and clock tower with a bull on the weather vane.

Hounslow's nearest neighbour is **Isleworth**. The manor of Isleworth was granted by William the Conqueror to Walter de St Valéry and it stayed with that family for many years.

The centre of Old Isleworth is on the banks of the Thames and is best seen from the opposite bank of the river. Beside the docks stands the London Apprentice on one of the oldest public house sites by the river. Lady Jane Grey and Charles II both visited this inn, though the building was reconstructed in 1905. Beside it, facing the river, is a charming terrace of houses in Church Street; numbers 59 and 61 (the Vicarage) are Georgian and Richard Reynolds House was built in 1700. It was on this site that Reynolds lived; he was chaplain to the nuns at Syon and was executed in 1535 because he refused to accept the Crown's supremacy over the church.

All Saints' Church dominates the other end of the short river front. The church was burnt down in 1943 by the same two small boys who accounted for Hounslow Church, and only the shell and the 15th century tower remained. A new church by Michael Blee is now being built and the old tower is to be incorporated into the new building.

The church had six brasses and five of them were saved; two particularly fine ones show a 15th century knight in armour and an Elizabethan gentleman—the pair are unidentified. Two monuments escaped the fire quite undamaged; one is an elaborate memorial to Sir Orlando Gee who is shown wearing a long curly wig and holding a document. He was Registrar to the Admiralty and left £500 for the rebuilding of the nave of the church, when he died in 1705. The other monument is a bust of a very old lady, Ann Tolson.

Her brother-in-law died on the same day as, but slightly before, his wife (Ann's sister) so that all his estate passed, by his wife's will, to Ann Tolson who was 80 and blind. She promptly married a man much her junior and died six years later with only £6000 left of the £40,000 she had inherited. She left a bequest for almshouses to be built which her husband unsuccessfully contested.

Nearby is Mill Platt, a traffic-free alley containing a group of charming little one-storey almshouses founded by Sir Thomas Ingham in 1664.

The famous painter of miniatures, Isaac Oliver, lived in Isleworth and died 10 years before the almshouses were built. Charles I owned many of his miniatures but many of them were sold to raise money during the Civil War. The story is told by G. E. Bate in his fascinating history of the area *And so Build a City Here* that Charles II visited Oliver's widow at her home in Isleworth to purchase some of her husband's pictures for which he offered her £1000 or an annuity of £300 a year for life. She accepted the latter and it was paid for some years but when Mrs Oliver heard that the king had given most of the miniatures to his mistresses, she said that had she known that they would be given to strumpets and bastards she would not have parted with them. The only result of her outspoken comments was that the annuity was stopped.

The river bank to the south of the church, bordering Richmond Road, was once the site of a number of fine houses. Richard Brinsley Sheridan, playwright, politician, and wit, lived in Lacy House which has now gone. Nazareth House, at the northern end of Richmond Road, was built by E. Blore in 1832, and was called Isleworth House. It is now occupied by a Roman Catholic institution.

At the end of the path to Rails Head Ferry is the early Victorian

Gordon House with its mass of Italianate turrets. It now houses the Maria Grey College of Education. The original Gordon House was bought by William IV for his daughter by Mrs Jordan but the 2nd earl of Kilmorey pulled it down and built the present house in 1867. Rails Head Ferry itself is reputed to be the site of Turner's *The Watercress Gatherers*.

Twickenham Road had similar large houses; Dickens mentions it in *Oliver Twist* when he says that Oliver and Bill Sykes walked along it past "many large gardens and gentlemen's houses on both sides". Van Gogh taught Bible History at a school in number 158 for a short while; it is now industrial premises. George I's mistress, the Duchess of Kendal, lived in Twickenham Road. Gumley House, now a convent school, was built in 1700 though only the central part is of that period. The side wings were added in the 19th century. Opposite is the Roman Catholic church of St Bridget.

Syon House has pleasant lodges by Adam; that on the London Road is now an antique dealer's premises and the grounds are crowded with a multiplicity of goods for sale ranging from garden statues to Adam fireplaces. Nearby is the gateway to Syon with its wrought-iron screen that Horace Walpole so disliked; he called it "all lace and embroidery". A lion stands on top of the gate with its outstretched tail pointing to Windsor and a similar lion stands above the arcade on the east front of the house. They were brought from Northumberland House in the Strand when it was demolished in 1874. Syon House itself is set in open parkland and has an extensive and unspoilt river front; the best view of the square battlemented house is from the opposite, Kew, bank of the river. The arcade on the river front of the house is traditionally attributed to Inigo Jones. Syon is built around an open quadrangle and has turrets at the corners thus retaining its original Tudor shape.

The house belongs to the Duke of Northumberland and is open to the public on certain days; it is well worth visiting for the glory of its suite of rooms designed by Robert Adam. The rooms are linked in design and are of startling colour. The entrance hall is black and white with marble paving and copies of the Apollo Belvedere statue and the Dying Gladiator. The anteroom is gold and green with an excellent mantelpiece, and the withdrawing room has red silk wall hangings and a painted ceiling by Angelica Kauffmann. The 16th century gallery is 136 feet long and Adam tried to break up its length by sub-dividing its walls and ornamenting them. He wanted to turn the open central courtyard into a circular saloon but had to abandon the plan.

In 1969 the Duke of Northumberland, in conjunction with Imperial Chemical Industries, opened a 55-acre Gardening Centre at Syon. It has laid-out flower beds, a huge rose garden, and a supermarket selling plants and equipment as well as the beautiful gardens and walks planned by Capability Brown and the lovely glass house designed by Charles Fowler in 1827. Paxton's source of inspiration for the Crystal Palace which housed the Great Exhibition in 1851.

There is a public right of way across the park along the route taken by Henry VIII's funeral cortège as it bore his body from London to Windsor for burial. Syon was one of two religious foundations established by Henry V, who wished to absolve his father's soul from its guilt in the murder of Richard II. The convent was founded at Twickenham in 1415 but was moved to Syon about 1431. The nuns went to Europe at the Dissolution but the order returned to this country in 1861 and now occupy a convent in Devon. The convent was pulled down in Edward VI's reign by the Duke of Somerset who built Syon House in its stead with the old materials.

Many men and women of importance in England's history have lived there; two of the most tragic were Catherine Howard, Henry VIII's fifth wife, who was confined there for several months before she was beheaded, and Lady Jane Grey who married the son of Syon's owner, the Duke of Northumberland, and lived there with her husband until her father-in-law persuaded her to press her claim to the crown, a claim which led to her death on the scaffold. A later owner, Henry Percy, the 9th earl of Northumberland, spent 15 years in the Tower because he was said to have been privy to the Gunpowder Plot and it was from Syon House that Elizabeth and Henry, the children of Charles I, were taken to bid farewell to their father before his execution. That Duke of Somerset who had built the house was the first of this tragic succession for he was beheaded.

During the Civil War an unusual encounter took place at Syon. A group of Cavaliers occupied the house after their victory at the Battle of Brentford in November 1642. They included a body of musketeers and had some cannon and when they saw 14 armed barges sailing downstream past Syon they opened fire on them. There were some 600 Roundheads on the barges and they had 13 cannon with them so a sharp duel broke out at a range of about 500 yards and four or five of the barges were sunk and the rest captured. It was most unusual, at that period, for guns to fire at a moving target.

Nearby is Syon Park House where Shelley went to school for a time but his biographer, Medwin, wrote that the school was for

Shelley "a perfect hell". Robert Louis Stevenson went to school further to the north of Isleworth, in Witham Road. His school, at which he was not particularly happy either, was in the building now occupied by the Order of St Vincent de Paul. Close by, in Borough Road, is a vast building with a central section in Gothic style, which now houses the Borough Road College of Education. The main block was built in 1867 by Norton and Massey, for the International College. The intention was to have a number of colleges, each in a different country, but all working to the same syllabus so that pupils could transfer from one to another and the only difference they would find would be in the language used for teaching. There was a college in Bonn, another in Chatou near Paris, and there were plans for one in Italy. The course took seven or eight years during which time the pupil spent two or three years at one of the colleges outside his homeland. The Prince of Wales opened the Isleworth college in 1867 but the scheme failed some years later and in 1890 the British and Foreign Bible Society moved its training college to the building. Richard Cobden, better known for his Anti-Corn Law League activities, was one of the founders of the International College and the composer Delius was one of its most famous pupils.

The Church of St Francis stands on the Great West Road to the west of Syon Lane. It is a large red-brick church, built in 1933–35 by E. C. Shearman and is unusual in that its altar is at the north end. Farther west, in Osterley Road, is St Mary's, a church built by J. Taylor in 1856. He used a new method, which he had invented himself, of putting a stone facing over brick. The church was part of a complex of gentlemen's houses put up in the 1850s around Spring Grove by a speculative builder, H. D. Davis, but his attempt to make it a fashionable area failed.

The Great West Road at Isleworth has several miles of factories along its length, of various styles. Gillette's factory with its very high clock tower, is notable. Traditionally, Isleworth is associated with several industries; there have been breweries since the reign of Elizabeth I, its pottery is famous though the factory closed in the mid-19th century, and Pears' Transparent Soap originated here. Its inventor was a Cornishman, Andrew Pears, who came to London to make his fortune. He set up as a barber and found all the soaps then in use so unpleasant that he invented his own. He began to market his transparent soap in 1739 and it was so successful that there were soon a number of imitations for sale, so Andrew Pears signed the wrappers. The firm was one of the pioneers of advertising in the 1860s. Francis, Andrew's grandson, bought land near the factory on the London Road, and built a mansion there in 1886 on the site of the house which the botanist Sir Joseph Banks had owned. Pears' house is to be demolished after years of service as a school and polytechnic, to make way for a new building for Isleworth Polytechnic.

Osterley House, at the northern end of Isleworth, has become National Trust property, having belonged to the Earl of Jersey. Sir Thomas Gresham started to build a palace there in the 1560s, though all that is left of his house are the four corner towers of the present building, the stable block, and some of the west wing. The cupola and clock tower on the stables were added later. Queen Elizabeth I visited Sir Thomas at Osterley in 1578 and suggested that the courtyard would look better with a dividing wall across it, so he had one built overnight while she slept. He could well afford to do so for he was one of the richest merchants in England and the founder of the Royal Exchange.

The house has had a number of owners, including Sir Edward Coke, the Lord Chief Justice of England. He was one of the judges who upheld the independence of the law courts against the king and ruled that James I had no right to issue proclamations creating new offences. He was also one of the authors of the Petition of Right. Sir William Waller, the Roundhead general, was another owner: he died at Osterley House in 1668. He was a member of the Long Parliament in 1640, and as he was also a zealous Puritan, it was inevitable that he took up arms at the beginning of the war. He soon earned himself the nickname "William the Conqueror". He gave up his commission after the Self Denying Ordinance (when Parliament decided that no member could hold a commission in its army) and he became a political figure. After the war, he was accused of plotting with Henrietta Maria, Charles I's widow, and he was arrested in 1648 and imprisoned, untried, for three years. He certainly had a part in the plan to bring Charles II back, but he received no financial aid after the Restoration, and was unusual in that he asked for none, though he had little money: his estates had suffered in the war, and the £2500 that Parliament had voted him was never given to him.

Sir Francis Child, who bought the house in 1711, was a goldsmith who amassed a fortune and started a bank, and it was his grandson, another Francis, who commissioned first Sir William Chambers and then Adam to alter the house. The reconstruction took 19 years, and Francis Child did not live to see it completed. It became the property of his brother, Robert, whose daughter Sarah Anne eloped with the Earl of Westmoreland. The couple were married at Gretna Green but her father never forgave her and died prematurely, some said from grief, leaving a will that bequeathed his property to her second child. That child was a daughter and so Osterley House passed by marriage to the Jersey family.

When Adam started to remodel Osterley, it was an Elizabethan mansion built in a square with towers at the corners and an open courtyard. Adam raised the principal apartments from the ground to the first floor, refaced the towers, raised the courtyard and built a magnificent colonnade and steps across the entrance so that visitors approached the house up the steps and across the uncovered courtyard. His alterations to the interior were just as drastic. The impressive entrance hall is similar to Syon's with its marble floor, classical sculpture, and apses. The library is a dignified room with inset paintings by Antonio Zucchi whose work can also be seen in the eating room set amidst beautiful plaster work. The gallery is 130 feet long and though Adam did not decorate it, he designed its furniture. It has some noteworthy tapestries. A contemporary visitor, Horace Walpole, said that the drawing-room was "worthy of Eve before the Fall"; it is plainer than most of the other rooms and has a very beautiful plaster and painted ceiling, the motif of which is echoed in the carpet.

Adam tried several experiments at Osterley; one is the tapestry room where a set of beautiful rose coloured tapestries line the walls and cover the furniture. Walpole thought this room "one of the most superb and beautiful that can be imagined". He did not like the Etruscan Room, where the walls and furniture are painted with classical figures and decorations, which he called "black and yellow small grotesques". Much of the furniture Adam designed for the house is still there, from the domed bed which Walpole found "too theatrical" to the beautiful mirror and chairs.

The extensive grounds of the Park include lakes, a wooded walk, and fields; the nearby Jersey Rock Gardens, on the Great West Road, are well worth a visit. Wyke House, standing nearby in Syon Lane, was originally part of the Osterley Estate. It was built some time after 1635 and Adam made some additions to it in 1778. In 1827 it became a school and is now a private mental hospital.

North-west of Isleworth lies **Brentford**, formerly the county town of Middlesex, though after the county council was formed in 1888, it always sat in Westminster. Brentford has been more important in the past than it is now though the borough's redevelopment plans, which include opening up the river frontage, altering the town centre and building a relief road, and would return it to something of its former significance.

Its ford across the Thames was the first above London that was always usable and it was probably at Brentford that Julius Caesar and his invading army crossed the river in 54 BC. There was a line of defensive stakes which were possibly placed by Iron Age Britons along the river bed from Syon Reach to Brentford; one of them can be seen in Syon House. Iron Age Britons certainly lived in the area and seem to have had a settlement at Brentford Eyot which is known locally as Old England. There was a settlement at Brentford by Saxon times and it was important enough for synods to be held on the Hain, now a recreation ground, in AD 780 and 781. It was a scene of battles in 1016 between Edmund Ironside, the son of Ethelred the Unready, and Canute, who both claimed the throne after Ethelred's death.

In 1642 there was another battle at Brentford between the Royalists and Parliamentarians. The king's army marched from Colnbrook in a thick mist, surprised the small Roundhead force who were barracked at Brentford, and drove them from the town. Thousands of Parliamentarian troops marched all night from London, and an army of 24,000 men assembled at Turnham Green under the Earl of Essex but the Royalists did not wait to fight. The people of Brentford suffered so much from Cavalier looting that the ministers in Middlesex took collections in church for the relief of the townsfolk.

Brentford was granted a market charter in 1306 and by Charles II's reign it had an important livestock market. The Magistrates' Court now stands on the site of the Market House. George I would often pass through on his way to Windsor and he always ordered the coachman to drive slowly for the town reminded him of his native Hanover.

Two of the four Anglican churches are no longer used for worship. St Lawrence, at the western end of the High Street, is now closed, and St George's houses a museum. St Lawrence's tower was built in 1480 but the rest of the yellow brick church was added in 1764. In the church are the arms of a 12th century noble, Maurice de Berkeley; he was the son of Robert FitzHarding who was in dispute with Robert de Berkeley over the ownership of Berkeley Castle. They eventually agreed that their children, Maurice FitzHarding and Alice de Berkeley, should marry and that Maurice should succeed to the title when his father-in-law died. Both title and property have remained with their descendants to the present day.

Henry Redman and his wife Jean are buried in the church. He held office as chief master mason at Henry VIII's court and left bequests for candles to be burnt for his soul. The crown seized his estate because of these "superstitious uses" and the bequests were added to the incumbent's living. Redman is said, in Michael Robbins' excellent book on Middlesex, to have helped to design Hampton Court, Lupton's tower at Eton, and parts of St Margaret's, Westminster. Sir William Noy, Charles I's Attorney General, is buried in the chancel. It was he who suggested the extension of the Ship Money Tax and the reintroduction of other unpopular measures, which all helped to bring about the Civil War. It was Noy who prosecuted William Prynne, the Puritan pamphleteer—Prynne was sentenced to imprisonment, had his ears lopped off, and was branded on the cheeks.

In the wall outside the church is a derelict drinking fountain given by the Grand Junction Water Company and inscribed *Let him that is athirst come and whosoever will let him take the water of life freely*.

At the other end of the High Street is St George's, also closed. It stands in the shadow of a huge gas holder and was built by A. W. Blomfield in 1887, its tower being added in 1913. It now houses the privately owned Piano Museum which has an interesting collection of old musical instruments, automatic pianos and violins, orchestrions and nickleodeons. Next door is the church schoolhouse, built in 1786.

St Paul's Church stands just off the High Street, overshadowed by a new block of flats. It was built in 1867 and has an interesting painting by Zoffany of The Last Supper. The faces of the disciples are those of the fishermen who lived near his home at Strand-on-the-Green, and he himself was the model for St Peter; his Negro servant can be seen in the foreground and St John's face is said to have been suggested by that of Zoffany's wife. He had intended to present the painting to Kew Church but changed his mind when someone suggested that Judas was a portrait of one of the churchwardens. Instead it went to St George's, Brentford, and was moved to St Paul's when St George's ceased to be used for worship.

A more obvious landmark than any of the churches are the Gasworks with their huge gas holder, built in 1820 and now scheduled for demolition, and the nearby minaret of the Grand Union Waterworks, built in 1867. Brentford is notable for its industrial architecture. The construction of the Grand Junction Canal began there in 1793 and it took nearly 12 years to build the 143 miles of canal to Braunston in Northamptonshire but when it was finished it provided a link between the Thames and the Oxford Canal, and so with Birmingham and the North. The Grand Union Canal was built in 1813 to link the Grand Junction with the Union Canal at Market Harborough. Brentford Dock has been run down as part of the redevelopment scheme for the waterfront.

A very different style of architecture can be seen in The Butts, a charming tree-lined square lying to the north of the Magistrates Court. The houses around it are of different periods; particularly notable are Beaufort House on the north side, built about 1700; No. 26, rather later and now divided into three houses; Linden House on the east and the end house in Upper Butts. The ground on which the square stands was once used for archery practice but its appearance today is spoiled by its gravel surface and its use as a car-park. Foxe's *Book of Martyrs* tells us that it was on the Butts Common that six men were burnt at the stake in 1558 for their religious convictions. It was also the scene of the notoriously violent county elections when John Wilkes stood as a candidate in 1768 and 1769. Wilkes, who was a member of the Hellfire Club and the founder of a radical newspaper, *The North Briton*, frequently attacked the government. He was arrested for an alleged libel on George III but was released because of his privilege as an MP. He was later outlawed and expelled from the House of Commons for libels in his paper and for his obscene *Essay on Woman*, which he had printed privately for his friends. He went to Paris, returned for the 1768 election, won it, and was deprived of his seat. The elections for Middlesex were held thrice more with growing violence at Brentford and each time Wilkes was re-elected but in the end the voting was annulled. He at last took his seat after another election in 1774, the year in which he became Lord Mayor of London. Middlesex had a far more democratic suffrage than other countries and was probably the only place that would have elected Wilkes.

Gunnersbury House and Park, which lie partly within Brentford have been described elsewhere (see p. 107) but another distinguished house owned by the Borough is Boston Manor, which houses the National Institute for Housecraft. It is a pleasant red-brick building with numerous windows and a Jacobean porch, very like Forty Hall in Enfield. It was built in 1622 or 1623 and has exceptionally fine plaster ceilings and a fireplace with a carving of Abraham which has been attributed, probably without proper evidence, to Grinling Gibbons. The house is open to the public at certain times (it is advisable to write first) but the park with its lake and fine old cedars is always open.

The manor of Boston, which was known as Bordeston or Burston, belonged to the Convent of St Helen's, Bishopsgate, in 1307. Edward VI granted it to the Duke of Somerset and it became crown property again at his execution until Elizabeth I granted it to the Earl of Leicester. He sold it to Sir Thomas Gresham and from him it passed to Sir William Reade, Lady Gresham's son by another marriage, and it was he and his wife who built the house. On the ceiling of the state drawing-room are Lady Reade's initials and the date 1623. In 1670 the house was bought by a Brentford family, the Clitherows, who restored it after a fire, added the north wing and outbuildings and lived there till 1918; the local authority bought it in 1923. Charles I is said to have watched the Battle of Brentford from the grounds of Boston Manor.

The poet, John Gay, wrote over 250 years ago,

> Brentford, tedious town,
> For dirty streets and white-legged chickens known.

The chickens have changed, and the streets are clean today.

To the east of Brentford, at Hounslow's nearest point to London, is **Chiswick**. To anyone travelling along its High Street or arterial roads, Chiswick seems a dreary place of bustle and noise but near to the river are two oases of calm, the old village centre with Chiswick House and the riverside area of Strand-on-the-Green.

Turning off the busy junction of the Cromwell Road and Hogarth Lane, we enter Church Street with its lovely houses, several of which are Georgian: we pass one that has a figurehead, ship's wheel, and anchor on its wall and then we see the church of St Nicholas. It has a 15th century tower some 80 feet tall, but the rest of the church was built in 1882 by J. L. Pearson. Inside it appears square as the Lady Chapel and chancel are parallel, separated only by a side screen. There are richly carved screens, an elaborate wooden reredos in the chapel showing the Last Supper and a stone one in the chancel showing scenes of Gethsemane, the Crucifixion, and the Last Supper. There are a number of stained-glass windows and one of them in vivid colours showing Christ, St John and St James is perhaps 18th century glass from Cologne Cathedral.

The most interesting of the monuments is in the Lady Chapel, to Sir Thomas Chaloner. He was tutor to James I's eldest son, Prince Henry. The memorial shows Sir Thomas and his wife, kneeling facing each other across a prayer-desk, and on either side an attendant holds back a curtain. Above the south door is a monument by Flaxman showing the bust of Thomas Bentley who died in 1780. He was Josiah Wedgwood's partner in the famous pottery firm. Charles II's mistress, Barbara Villiers, Duchess of Cleveland, is buried in the church though the spot is unknown. Two of Cromwell's daughters, Mary, Lady Fauconberg, and his youngest child, Frances, lie here. Frances's life was tragic. She married Robert Rich, the heir to the Earl of Warwick, in 1657 but her husband died nine weeks after the wedding. She married a second time a few years later, but her husband, Sir John Russell, died before their son was born and she remained a widow for more than 50 years. There has always been a legend that Cromwell himself lies in St Nicholas's churchyard. His remains were exhumed and displayed after the Restoration but it is said they were secretly reburied in the vault of his son-in-law, Lord Fauconberg, at St Nicholas's. Certainly his daughter, Mary, Lady Fauconberg, was a devoted worshipper at the church, but there is no real evidence to support the story.

An extraordinary number of exceptional men and women lie in Chiswick churchyard. Hogarth is here; Garrick erected his tomb with its urn and wrote his epitaph:

> *Farewell, great painter of mankind,*
> *Who reached the noblest point of art,*
> *Whose pictured morals charm the mind*
> *And through the eye correct the heart.*

> *If Genius fire thee, Reader, stay;*
> *If Nature touch thee, drop a tear;*
> *If neither move thee, turn away,*
> *For Hogarth's honoured dust lies here.*

Garrick also wrote the epitaph on the memorial inside the church to his fellow actor, Charles Hollond. One of Italy's greatest patriots, Ugo Foscolo, was buried here but his body was returned to Florence in 1871 and only the monument by Marochetti remains. Foscolo was born in 1778, the son of a Greek mother and an Italian father, who died when Ugo was young; his mother brought him up to love freedom and when he was summoned before the Inquisition to answer for his political activities, she said, "Die, my boy, rather than betray the name of a friend." He hoped that Napoleon would liberate Italy and he enlisted in his army, but his fiery eloquence was not well received by the French so he settled in England and

followed his vocation as a writer—his first drama had been successfully produced when he was only 19.

Sir Charles Bright, the engineer who laid the Atlantic cable, is
buried here, as is William Kent, the architect and landscape
gardener. There is a memorial to Sir John Chardin, the jeweller
who travelled through Turkey, Persia, and India in the 1660s; he is
buried in Westminster Abbey. Henry Joy who sounded the charge
at Balaclava, lies here, and so does Frederick Hitch who won the
VC at Rorke's Drift in Zululand—one of the eight VC's won in that
exceptional battle. Two men who beautified St Paul's Cathedral
are here too—Sir James Thornhill who painted the pictures of the
life of St Paul, and Sir William Richmond who spent 40 years
fitting the mosaics. J. M. Whistler, the painter, lies near Hogarth's
tomb; his admiration for Hogarth was so great that he wanted to
be buried near him. William Rose, the schoolmaster, is buried here
too; he knew Dr Johnson and it was he who brought Rousseau to
Chiswick and boarded him with a grocer who let Rousseau sit in his
shop and pick up English.

Along the unembanked river front by St Nicholas is Chiswick
Mall, a road of splendid houses with little gardens lying between
them and the river. They are of different periods but achieve a
harmony. Among them is Walpole House; most of the exterior is a
reconstruction of the late 18th century but inside there is some 16th
century panelling from the original house. Barbara Villiers is said
to have lived here, and Thackeray went to school in Walpole
House—Becky Sharp's school experiences at the beginning of *Vanity
Fair* are said to be based on the author's memories of his youth at
Chiswick. Sir Henry Beerbohm Tree lived here from 1904 to 1910.

Returning along Church Street to Burlington Lane, we reach
Chiswick Square with its late 17th century Boston House. Nearby
is the entrance to Chiswick House and its park. The original
Chiswick House was a Jacobean mansion purchased in 1628 by
the 1st earl of Burlington. His grandson succeeded to the estate
when a child, travelled in Italy in his young manhood, and came
home fired with an enthusiasm for classical architecture. In 1725
he began to build a little villa in his grounds at Chiswick, basing
the designs on those of the Italian architect Palladio for the Villa
Capra near Vicenza. He was assisted by his friend and protégé,
William Kent, whose burial in St Nicholas's we have already
noticed. The house is square with an octagonal central hall, of two
storeys with the main rooms on the upper floor. These are breathtakingly colourful and lavish; their very names give an impression

of their luxury—the Blue Velvet Room with its elaborate blue and gold ceiling, the Red Velvet Room with two marble fireplaces and a painted ceiling designed by Kent, the Red Closet, the Gallery with gilded apses and columns, the Green Velvet Room with paintings by Sebastiano Ricci and gilded beams in the ceiling and the Bedchamber with three decorated doorways. The house is unfurnished but there are a number of fine paintings, and some wonderful ghostly lead-backed mirrors which give a shadowed reflection. The gardens were laid out by Kent and although the design depends on a main avenue and three subsidiary alleyways of trees, they mark a new departure in English landscape gardening, being far less formal and more imaginative than any that had gone before. With small Roman temples and statues, Kent attempted to produce "prospects to excite not only the eye but the imagination", and he succeeded nobly, for two and a half centuries later the gardens have retained their original plan to the delight, refreshment, and stimulation of all who walk in them. The avenue of cedars is adorned with sphinxes, and behind the house is a gateway brought from Beaufort House in Chelsea for which it had been designed by Inigo Jones. When it was moved in 1736, Pope wrote:

> *I was brought from Chelsea last year*
> *Batter'd with wind and weather;*
> *Inigo Jones put me together;*
> *Sir Hans Sloane let me alone;*
> *Burlington brought me hither.*

When Lord Burlington died in 1753, he left an only daughter who married the 4th duke of Devonshire. Their son demolished the original Jacobean house and added wings to the villa. Georgiana, Duchess of Devonshire, entertained superbly here, and her friend Charles James Fox—perhaps the most brilliant politician England has ever produced—died here in 1806. In 1814 and 1844, successive dukes of Devonshire entertained Tsars of Russia here and Edward VII when Prince of Wales used to take the house for the summer. In 1892 the duke removed the art treasures and leased the villa as a private lunatic asylum until in 1928 it was bought by the Middlesex County Council in whose guardianship it remained till after the last war when it was made over to the Ministry of Works. The ministry restored the house beautifully and the spirits of Inigo Jones and Palladio, whose statues by Rysbrack stand at the foot of the double staircase at the front of the building, must smile to see their pupil's work in such good repair.

Alexander Pope and his parents lived at Chiswick; the ground floor of their house has been reconstructed and is now the Fox and Hounds and Mawson Arms at the corner of Mawson Terrace and Chiswick Lane. While Pope was living there, before he moved to Twickenham, he translated the *Iliad*, writing some of it on the backs of letters he had received.

William Hogarth lived here longer and the house in which he spent his last 15 years is now open to the public and houses a splendid collection of his prints. He called it "his little country box at Chiswick" and it stands near the roundabout in Hogarth Lane in its pleasant garden where the artist used to sit with his pipe, his dog, and a piping bullfinch. It is a friendly house built in 1700 with narrow steep stairs and small wood-panelled rooms. Hogarth bought it in 1749 when he was 52. His father was a poor schoolmaster who apprenticed him to a silver plate engraver. Hogarth set up for himself when he was 21 as a copper engraver, and the excellence of his plates was soon recognised though he found it more profitable to paint portraits. His first great success was *The Harlot's Progress*, a series of engravings which showed the unhappy fate of a country girl in London. He followed it with *The Rake's Progress*, *Marriage à la Mode*, and *Industry and Idleness*, as well as many individual prints. He had a gift for portraying the folly, pretence, and vice of his age. Hazlitt said, "Other pictures we see, Hogarth's we read."

Hogarth met his wife when he attended the art school opened by her father, Sir James Thornhill; since he could not get Thornhill's agreement to the marriage, they eloped when Hogarth was 35 and his bride 19. The marriage turned out very happily and Thornhill was at last reconciled to it. More is told about this great artist and reformer under Coram's Hospital (see p. 79).

Strand-on-the-Green is a peaceful riverside row of houses, very similar to the Mall, though more secluded as there is only a traffic-free pathway between the houses and the river. It was a fishing village until about 1770 when it began to become fashionable and some large houses were built among the fishermen's cottages; none of them is on the grand scale of the houses in the Mall. The most interesting are the Georgian group at the Brentford end of the Strand. They include Springfield House and Zoffany House, with its terracotta lion over the doorway. The artist, John Zoffany, lived there; he took the house in 1780, but three years later he went to India, leaving his wife and children at Zoffany House. He spent six years at the court of the Nabob of Oudh, and returned a very rich man, spending the remaining 20 years of his life living extravagantly at Chiswick.

There are three public houses in the Strand. One of them, the City Barge, is named after the boat that was moored by Fulham Bridge, and later by Chiswick Eyot, to inspect barges and collect their dues. Less often, the barge was used to take the Lord Mayor on his official annual journey to see the swan-upping, or the marking of the swans, when the birds on the Thames between the City and Henley are taken up into the boats (hence the name) and ownership of the current year's broods of cygnets is established, and they are marked accordingly. The young are marked in the same way as their father: two nicks on the beak means they belong to the Vintners' Company, one nick and the Dyers' Company owns them, and if they are unmarked they belong to the Monarch, thus giving her the advantage of owning any strays.

The almshouses in the Strand originated in 1724 but have been restored.

At the northern end of Chiswick is Turnham Green, now only a small area of green between the High Street and the former Town Hall. Christ Church, a large Victorian Church, stands on the Green. It was built in 1843 by Scott and Moffat and is of Early English style faced with bath stone. The nearby Roman Catholic church of Our Lady of Grace and St Edward was built in 1904 in red brick and has an attractive gilt and white interior.

To the west of Brentford lie Heston and Cranford. **Heston** is famous in British aircraft history; it had one of the first aerodromes in this country and much experimental flying was done there. The old airfield, which is overshadowed by Heathrow Airport, until recently housed Fairey Aviation Works. Little remains of the old village, once centred around St Leonard's Church which is pleasantly set in a bay off the Heston Road, and is surrounded by a churchyard entered through a lychgate, a restoration of the original 16th century one. There is a fine four-storey 15th century tower, an iron-studded church door, and a little door inside the tower of the same period, but the rest is an unimaginative restoration by Bellamy of 1866.

The interior is dull but there are several interesting monuments saved from the old church. Among them is a white marble monument to Robert Child of Osterley Park who died in 1782. It was designed by Robert Adam and carved by Van Gelder, and it shows two weeping cherubs, one seated, the other standing beside an elegant urn. Fine candlesticks entwined with flowers and leaves, stand at either side of the monument. Let into the chancel floor and usually covered over, is a brass to Mordecai Bownell, who was vicar of St Leonards in 1581. His figure is lost, but we see his wife, Constance, who died in childbed. The wooden font cover is a reconstruction of a 15th century one; it is cupola-shaped, and covered with a tracery of flowers.

Sir Joseph Banks is buried in the churchyard. He died in 1820 at the age of 77. He inherited a fortune at the age of 18 and, in spite of an income of £6000 a year, refused to lead the life of a dilettante. He studied botany and went to Newfoundland in 1766 to study the flowers of the area and the life of the Eskimo. He went round the world with Cook and took with him—in the *Endeavour*'s cramped quarters—a botanist, an assistant naturalist, two painters, two servants, two Negroes (who both died), and two dogs. Botany Bay in Australia was so named because of the number of hitherto unidentified plants that Banks and his colleagues found there. He enjoyed the voyage and wanted to go with Cook on his next journey but the Admiralty refused to let him, partly because he wanted to take 13 helpers with him but largely because of his high-handed attitude. He was one of the creators of Kew Gardens.

The churchyard also contains a memorial to Frederick John White, a private in the 7th Queen's Own Hussars "erected by his comrades as a testimony of their sympathy for his fate and their respect for his memory". White died in 1864; he had been sentenced to 50 lashes by the colonel of his regiment who, incidentally, was related to him. White made some comments while being flogged which caused the colonel to sentence him at once to a further 50 lashes from which he died. There was a public outcry and soon after the number of lashes to which a soldier could be sentenced was reduced from 150 to 50. The colonel was sent to India to command a sepoy regiment; the East India Company had abolished flogging long before.

There is an unexpectedly rural walk from Heston Church across the fields to Osterley Park. They are all that remains of the farmland which once grew such fine wheat that it was used to make Queen Elizabeth I's bread, and which Michael Drayton praised in his *Polyolbion*.

A little farther north along the Heston Road is the very fine

Roman Catholic church of Our Lady Queen of Apostles. It was built in 1963 and has a solid-looking body and a massive square tower and is approached along an avenue of trees. The interior is open and pleasantly unadorned so that all the visitor's attention is focused on the outstandingly fine modern stained glass in the Lady Chapel, which is alive with swirling colours and patterns.

Oliver Cromwell was a frequent visitor to Heston as his favourite daughter Elizabeth lived there with her husband John Claypole, but their home, the White House, has now gone.

The river Crane from which **Cranford** takes its name flows along the eastern edge of Cranford Park and forms the boundary between Hillingdon and Hounslow so the small charming 15th century church of St Dunstan no longer stands in its old parish but in an isolated position in the borough of Hillingdon. It was once a haven of calm but now the traffic roars past on the M4 just behind the church though it is still notable for its splendid setting and design and for its outstanding monuments.

The church on this site once belonged to the Knights Templar who owned the manor but when they were suppressed in 1310 the church was rededicated to St Dunstan and became the parish church. The chancel and lower part of the tower of the present building are 15th century, the middle of the tower is later and the top was added in 1716 when the nave was built to repair damage done by a fire in 1710. It was extensively restored in 1895 and again in 1937. Inside are a number of fine monuments. The earliest is to Sir Roger Aston (d. 1612) and is carved by William Cure, the king's master mason, who worked under Inigo Jones on the Banqueting House at Whitehall. The painted alabaster figures of Sir Roger, his two wives, four daughters, and a baby in swaddling clothes, are nearly life-size and are very finely detailed with beautifully carved lace and drapes and folds. Sir Roger was a Gentleman of the Bedchamber to James I and the owner of Cranford Manor. Opposite his memorial is the white marble effigy of Lady Elizabeth Berkeley, another owner of the manor. The recumbent figure is finely carved by Nicholas Stone the younger who worked in the studio of the great Italian sculptor Bernini. It was this Lady Berkeley who was largely responsible for the restoration of the church in 1716; she subscribed 19 shillings for every shilling the parishioners raised. There are a number of other memorials to the Berkeley family in the church.

An alabaster tablet in the chancel proclaims the memory of Dr

Thomas Fuller, the author of *Worthies of England* and the rector of Cranford from 1658 to 1661. He is described as a tall and handsome man with laughing eyes, too Anglican for the Commonwealth and too Puritan for the Royalists. Born in Northants, he began preaching early down in Dorset where he married and lost his wife. During the Civil War he offended Parliament by a sermon from the text "Yea, let him take all so that my lord the king return in peace," and he was later denounced by the Royalists as little better than a Puritan for pleading for concessions by the king. It was the Parliament which ejected him from his living and he served as a Royalist chaplain, and while moving from place to place with the army gathered the materials for the *Worthies of England*. In it he runs through English counties telling us a little about them and more about their notable people. The volumes are full of wit, and Fuller remains one of the most quoted men of his day. Charles II would have made him a bishop, but Fuller was struck down with a fever from which he died, at 52. He was full of wit and humanity, and bore himself with goodwill to all men, but his book is a great fund of gentle sarcasm. Coleridge loved it and wrote after reading it, "God bless thee, dear old man, may I meet with thee in Heaven."

The memorial to Sir Charles Scarborough, with its arms and cherubs, says that he died of "a gentle and easy decay" at the age of 79 in 1693. He was physician to Charles II, James II, and Queen Mary. One of the doses he prescribed for Charles II on his death-bed was a mixture of topaz, sapphire, ruby, pearl, emerald, amber-gris, and gold. In spite of this, the king died. Dominating the nave is a huge memorial to William Smythe, a son-in-law of the Berkeleys, who died in 1720 at the age of 80. Beneath the inscription is his bust with two cherubs.

On the east wall of the chancel are the remains of a mediaeval fresco of the Virgin Mary, and the floor is of black-and-white Jacobean marble.

Beside the church are the courtyard and remains of the stables of Cranford House; the early 18th century mansion was demolished in 1939. The haha that once separated the grounds of the house from its parkland still exists on the edge of the wood though the parkland is now open space and playing fields. The manor was the property of the Berkeley family from 1618 until the local authority bought it in 1932.

One of the most interesting of the Berkeleys was Mary, the wife of the 5th earl. She and her equally beautiful sister, the daughters of a Gloucester tradesman, came to London where Mary became the mistress of the Earl of Berkeley. She lived openly with him, entertained his visitors and, because she was a very able woman, helped to manage his estates. She bore him four sons before they married in 1796 and then two more. She and the earl later claimed that they had been secretly married in 1785 and that their eldest son was therefore legitimate and the heir to the title, rather than the fifth son. They took their case to the House of Lords and the eldest son, William Fitzhardinge, pleaded his case again in 1810 when his father died, but the case was dismissed, and as there was some feeling that the countess had forged some of the evidence, she felt it wisest to leave the country for a year. The fifth son was regarded as the rightful earl but he lived all his life as Mr Morton Berkeley in a house he had built on the edge of the park. There is a plain marble tablet to him in the north-west corner of St Dunstan's. After his death, the youngest son, Grantley, inherited the title and started a pamphlet war with his elder brothers.

Little of old Cranford remains, though there are a few good houses, such as the 18th century Stansfield House, with its pilastered doorway, and the Round House remains in the High Street. It is a small circular building dating from 1810, used to imprison thieves and known locally as the Highwayman's Cage. On the Bath Road is a curious group of "chateau-style" shops and a public house, built in 1932.

Cranford is not the site of Mrs Gaskell's novel of that name; her Cranford is Knutsford in Cheshire.

Southwards from Cranford are East Bedfont, Feltham, and Hanworth. **East Bedfont** was once a Saxon village but now seems, at first sight, to be a sprawling residential suburb. It has, however, several buildings of note especially its parish church, St Mary's, which stands beside the village green on the busy Staines Road. The nave and chancel of the little church are 12th century though the chancel was lengthened in the 15th; the church has windows of both periods and a fine Norman chancel arch—the only one in Middlesex—carved in zigzags. The nave was lengthened in 1829 and the tower, with its pleasing timbering, was added in 1865. Though the porch is 19th century, the door, with its design of zigzags and trefoils, is Norman. In a 13th century recess which has two bays with pointed arches are two mediaeval wall-paintings; they were discovered in 1865 when the church was being restored. Though they are faint, the paintings are still discernible; one shows the Crucifixion with Our Lady and St John, and the other shows Christ

The Tower of London and Tower Bridge (*Photograph by Aerofilms Ltd.*)

The Tower of London: St John's Chapel in the White Tower

with His hands raised to show His wounds and angels sounding the Last Trump. Both are painted in red outline on a darker red background, and both are impressive. Hanging on a wall is a small oak panel carved in high relief by Flemish craftsmen probably in the 1530s. It is packed with nearly 40 figures and gives an impression of bustle and activity. Dominating the panel are the figures of Christ and the two thieves on their crosses, and in front of them are soldiers, priests, St John, and St Veronica holding her handkerchief with the impression of Christ's face on it. Near the altar are two very good brasses showing Mathew Page (d. 1631) and his mother (d. 1629). They are kneeling facing each other.

Outside the church are two fine yew trees which for some 200 years were cut so that each resembled a peacock and one had the letters JH, JG, and RT (the vicar's and churchwardens' initials) and the other had the date 1704. Thomas Hood's poem tells us that two sisters who lived at Bedfont had disdainfully refused offers of marriage from an influential local man who said that they were as proud as peacocks and had the trees cut accordingly. Another, by Colmer, to the landlord of the Black Dog states:

Harvey, whose inn commands a view
Of Bedfont's church and churchyard too,
Where yew trees into peacocks shorn
In vegetable torture mourn.

The Black Dog was for a time the headquarters of the Bensington Driving Club, a gathering of wealthy men who drove their own vehicles. Harvey was noted for his beefsteaks and his fish sauce; his inn has been demolished, the present Black Dog on the Staines Road is on a different site.

Next to the church is the late 18th century Burlington House, and some 200 yards to the north of the church in Hatton Road is Pates Manor. The house is presumably named after John Pate and his wife Juliana who lived in Bedfont in the early 15th century. The house is basically 16th century but has been modernised a number of times. From 1622 to 1921, it was the property of Christ's Hospital whose arms can still be seen on the cast-iron escutcheon on the gabled wooden porch of the manor. Facing the church on the far side of the Green is Fawns Manor, a timber-framed 17th century house with an unusual buttressed chimney; it is almost completely hidden from the road by trees and bushes.

K

273

To the west along the Staines Road stands the Fairholme Estate, a well-laid-out neo-Georgian group of houses built in 1934 by C. Hewitt. The houses surround a grassy plot which houses a well and there is a community hall at the back of the quadrangle.

The Saxon name for **Feltham** was *Feldham*, meaning a field village or clearing in the forest. Nowadays it presents a sprawl of modern buildings and little of old Feltham remains though the Green is still attractive and the 18th century Feltham House is still in good use as an RAOC Officers' Mess.

At the end of the High Street, set among trees, are the charming little church of St Dunstan's and its 17th century vicarage. The rustic-looking church, with its short embattled tower and shingled spire, was built in 1802 and its "Norman" aisles were added in the 1850s. Its interior is plain and its most interesting feature is the charity inscription painted in elegant script along the front of the gallery. William Wynne Ryland, the last man but one to be hanged at Tyburn, is buried in the graveyard. He was a noted engraver and was so employed by George III, but was executed is 1783 for using his talent to forge false bills of exchange.

Nearer to the town is Manor Lane with the offices of Minimax housed in a rather fine Victorian mansion. Further east is Feltham Green with its small houses and pond, and the Roman Catholic church of St Lawrence, a small, square church built in the Norman style in the late 1930s by Thomas Scott. An earlier church on the site had been burnt down. The doorway has a lintel showing the twelve apostles and above them the figure of Christ. Inside are striking Stations of the Cross cut into the white walls, and the capitals of the pillars are all carved differently, showing foliage, birds and animals. There are several stained-glass windows; the best is flower-shaped in deep reds and blues showing Christ and Our Lady surrounded by cherubs and angels.

Near the Green are an impressive new shopping centre and office blocks. Many more new buildings are scheduled for the High Street.

St Catherine's, near the railway station, was built in the Early English style in 1880 by Carpenter and Ingelow, and its handsome spire—the best thing about it—was added in 1893. Facing St Catherine's is Bridge House, set in an attractive small park. The house is now a local authority office.

Frances Maria Kelly, a famous melodramatic actress who first appeared on the stage at the age of seven, lived in Rose Cottage at

Feltham. She died, aged 90 in 1882. Charles Lamb had wanted to
marry her and it is of her that he wrote:

> *You are not, Kelly, of the common strain,*
> *That stoop their pride and female honour down*
> *To please that many-headed beast the town*
> *And vend their lavish smiles and tricks for gain;*
> *By fortune thrown amid the actors' train,*
> *You keep your native dignity of thought;*
> *The plaudits that attend you come unsought,*
> *As tributes due unto your natural vein.*
> *Your tears have passion in them, and a grace*
> *Of genuine freshness, which our hearts avow;*
> *Your smiles are winds whose ways we cannot trace,*
> *That vanish and return we know not how,*
> *And please the better from a pensive face,*
> *And thoughtful eye, and a reflecting brow.*

She refused his offer, it is said because of the insanity in his family.

Hanworth, which takes its name from the Saxon for a village or
settlement, was Henry VIII's "chief place of pleasure". He loved
hunting and frequently visited his hunting lodge in Hanworth
Park. His widow, Catherine Parr, lived there after his death and
so, for a time, did Princess Elizabeth who was in her stepmother's
care. However, there was a scandal about the 15-year-old princess
and Catherine's new husband, Sir Thomas Seymour, and she was
removed. Seymour wanted to marry the princess after his wife's
death in 1548 and, when he was executed a year later for treason,
Elizabeth said, "There has died a man with plenty of wit and little
judgement." Other notable occupants of the house were the dramatist brothers, William and Thomas Killigrew, who were born there
in 1606 and 1611. Queen Henrietta Maria, Charles I's wife, stayed
there with all her court in 1635, when there was plague in London.
Sir John Berkeley, the Civil War Royalist general, was born there,
as was his brother, Sir William Berkeley, governor of Virginia. John
Bradshaw, who pronounced the sentence of death on Charles I and
signed his death warrant, was given Hanworth House by Parliament.
His body was exhumed at the Restoration, hanged, and reburied
at Tyburn.

The house, which stood beside St George's Church, was burnt
down in 1797 and now only a moat and some few vestiges of the

building remain, the most interesting are two fine terracotta round-els standing high upon the walls. One shows the head of an emperor and the other of Minerva. They strongly resemble those made by Giovanni de Maiano for Wolsey's Hampton Court (see p. 358). Beside them stands Tudor Court, a battlemented building now turned into flats. This was originally the entrance court and stable block for the Tudor Hanworth House but has been extensively altered.

The Duke of St Albans built a new Hanworth Park House after the fire of 1797 but placed it some way away from the old house, on higher ground. It was enlarged in the mid-19th century and is now an old people's home. Its colonnaded entrance and verandahs give it an American colonial look.

Beside Tudor Court stands St George's Church. The church we now see was built in 1865 by S. S. Teulon who drastically altered the church built by James Wyatt in 1812. There had been an older church still on the site and behind the richly carved modern screen we can still find two 15th century windows, showing seraphim, flowers, and a shield. Beside them is the 17th century shield of the Killigrew family.

Longford River flows through the park. It is 11 miles long and was cut by order of Charles I to reinforce the supply of water for the lakes at Hampton Court. When the Civil War broke out, the local people filled it with rubbish and damaged its bridges. Crom-well had it cleaned out and it still fulfils its original purpose. It is sometimes called the Cardinal's, or the Queen's River.

On the other side of the park, in the Uxbridge Road, stands All Saints, a square brick church by Cashmaille Day, with an interesting interior. A small rectangular church, facing east–west, was built in 1951 and in 1956 the middle of one of its walls was knocked down and the church was extended to a squarer shape, refacing north–south. The interior is brick with ribs of concrete supporting the high roof, and has a rotunda set with coloured glass. The altar and the sus-pended cross with its splendid figure of Christ, is set in a vast arched alcove, gilded and painted with the heads and wings of angels. The windows are plain, apart from those in the Lady Chapel. The modern stone font is carved with biblical figures and on the cover is a far older gilded figure of the Virgin.

ISLINGTON

ISLINGTON

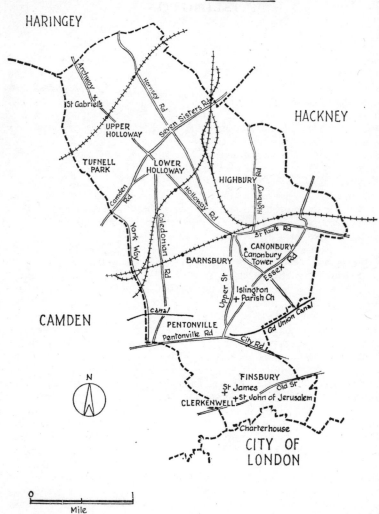

HARINGEY

HACKNEY

Archway

St Gabriels

Hornsey Rd

Seven Sisters Rd

UPPER HOLLOWAY

TUFNELL PARK

LOWER HOLLOWAY

HIGHBURY

Highbury Rd

Camden Rd

Holloway Rd

York Way

Caledonian Rd

St Pauls Rd

CANONBURY
Canonbury Tower

Essex Rd

BARNSBURY

Upper St

Islington Parish Ch

Canal

CAMDEN

PENTONVILLE
Pentonville Rd

Gd Union Canal

City Rd

N

FINSBURY
St James

Old St

CLERKENWELL

St John of Jerusalem

Charterhouse

CITY OF LONDON

0

Mile

ISLINGTON

The new London Borough of Islington consists of the former boroughs of Islington and Finsbury. It lies due north of the City and from the west is bounded by Westminster, Camden, Haringey, and Hackney. There is high ground at Crouch Hill and Highbury; the area is more low-lying near to the City at Clerkenwell and Finsbury. It covers some 3678 acres with a population of just under 300,000. Though the two areas are essentially very different, both were, in a sense, London's recreation grounds in earlier times, and southern Islington and northern Finsbury were built up at the same time. Therefore as far as entertainment and architecture are concerned, that part of Finsbury which lies north of Old Street and south of the Pentonville Road will be described with Islington, and under Finsbury we shall consider only those matters which are peculiarly its own, chiefly its religious institutions, unusual alike in their number and importance.

Until the very end of the 18th century, **Islington** was open countryside, celebrated for its dairy produce. The name appears first in an Anglo-Saxon charter as *Gislandune*, which means Gisla's hill or down. The original village and parish church were at Islington Green where Upper Street now joins the Essex Road, and there were clusters of dwellings at Highbury, Upper and Lower Holloway, Canonbury, Barnsbury, and towards Newington Green. A number of landowners divided the area between them; they included the Canons of St Bartholomew's at Smithfield (hence Canonbury), and the Berners family (hence Barnsbury) whose members included that John, the second baron, who translated Froissart's Chronicles concerning the long wars between England and France, and Dame Juliana who wrote a book on falconry. The de Barowe family gave their land to the Knights of St John of Jerusalem, whose headquarters were in Clerkenwell, and a prior of their Order built a manor house which was burnt down by Jack Straw, one of the ringleaders of Wat Tyler's rebellion of 1381; the ruins lay deserted till the early 19th century.

One great house remains standing, a reminder of 16th century Islington. It is Canonbury Tower, the building of which was probably begun about 1520 by William Bolton, Prior of St Bartholomew's, and which towards the end of the century became the home of a great merchant prince, Sir John Spencer—"Rich Spencer" as he was called. It was from here that his daughter eloped with Lord Compton, later Marquess of Northampton, hidden it is said in a baker's or laundry basket, and it was not till Queen Elizabeth I herself intervened that Sir John would be reconciled with the young couple. From 1616 till 1625, Sir Francis Bacon rented the house and tradition has it that the mulberry tree in the grounds was planted during his tenancy. Canonbury Tower still stands today, the home of the excellent Tavistock Repertory Company, and can be visited by arrangement. There is a fine Jacobean oak staircase, two rooms with Elizabethan panelling, and a third with a handsome plaster ceiling dated 1599. After the Civil War, the house, which consisted in those days of a considerable range of buildings round a courtyard, was let out in apartments. Oliver Goldsmith lived here from 1762 till 1764, and other tenants were Washington Irving, Lord Onslow, and Ephraim Chambers, the compiler of a Cyclopaedia (not the now well-known *Chambers's Encyclopaedia*). John Newbery, the printer and publisher of children's literature, had rooms here and the poor mad poet, Christopher Smart, who will always be remembered for his *Song to David*, was befriended by him.

Apart from such buildings as we have mentioned, Islington was a most countrified place in the 16th century. Gerard speaks in his *Herbal* of the wild orchids that grew there, and hedges that had been planted were levelled on Henry VIII's orders to ensure the practice of archery should continue uninterrupted. A most romantic and true story is told of the sport here. A young woman, Alice Wilkes, sat down to help a country-woman milk a cow. As she rose from the stool, an arrow transfixed her hat and she vowed that if it were ever within her power, she would raise some piece of good works as a thanks-offering for her deliverance. She married Sir Thomas Owen and on his death, founded in 1609 10 almshouses for poor widows and a free school for 24 boys from Islington and six from Clerkenwell. The school is still there, rebuilt in 1840—with 500 pupils today, and a sister foundation for girls was established in 1888 which now has 350 pupils. Its foundation was possible because the original deed said "children", not specifically boys. They stand in Owen Street off the Goswell Road in Finsbury on what used to be Hermitage Fields.

There were a large number of places of entertainment both in Finsbury and Islington, for they lay outside the City boundaries where such places of gathering were forbidden for fear of plague or riot. There were five 17th century theatres, the most important being The Fortune, which stood where Golden Lane now runs, and was built in 1599 for Edward Alleyn and Philip Henslowe. It was burnt down in 1621 but was rebuilt and continued to put on plays till the Puritan rule put an end to such frivolities in 1647/8. So profitable a venture was it that Alleyn was able to found Dulwich College and to build almshouses which were only pulled down in 1964 when the St Luke's Estate was built. Then there was the Red Bull which stood in Woodbridge Street, specialised in putting on comedies, and is said to have been the first English theatre in which an actress performed. Rutland House was a private dwelling near Charterhouse, where the first opera to be seen in England '*The Siege of Rhodes*' was produced by Sir William Davenant in 1656. The Nursery in Golden Lane was a training school run by William Legge for four or five years from 1664. Another theatre, the New Wells in Rosoman Street, Finsbury, opened later, flourishing from 1730 till 1750, but Sadler's Wells, of which we shall have more to say, opened as Sadler's Musick House in 1683.

There were many pleasure gardens in these fields north of London. They were places, centred on an inn or tea-house, where refreshments could be obtained, where the citizens could walk in well-tended gardens, listen to music, play bowls, or otherwise entertain themselves. A quotation from Sir William Davenant's poem, *The Long Vacation in London*, provides the best evocation of what Islington meant to Londoners.

> *Now Damsel young, that dwells in Cheap,*
> *For very joy begins to leap;*
> *Her elbow small she oft doth rub,*
> *Tickled with hopes of Syllabub,*
> *For Mother, (who does gold maintain*
> *On thumb, and keys on silver chain)*
> *In snow-white clout wrapped nook of pye,*
> *Fat capon's wing and rabbit's thigh;*
> *And said to hackney coachman: "Go,*
> *Take shillings six—say Aye or No."*
> *"Whither?" says he—Quoth she, "Thy team*
> *Shall drive to place where groweth cream."*
>
> *But husband grey now comes to stall,*
> *For 'prentice notched he straight doth call.*
> *"Where's Dame?" quoth he—Quoth son of shop*
> *"She's gone her cake in milk to sop."*

> *"Ho! Ho! To Islington! Enough—*
> *Fetch Job my son and our dog Ruffe;*
> *For there, in pond, through mire and muck,*
> *We'll cry Hey duck—there Ruffe—Hey duck!"*

For the most part, only the names remain of these pleasure gardens. There was Highbury Barn and not too far away, near what is now Blackstock Road, Cream Hall, renowned for its syllabub (a delicious mixture of cream beaten with fruit juices), Dobney's Tea Gardens, Busby's Folly, Merlin's Cave, The Peerless Pool, Islington Spa near Sadler's Wells where the Princesses Amelia and Caroline, George II's daughters, used to drink the waters, and the London Spa at the corner of Exmouth Market and Rosoman Street. Couplets written in 1733 describe them thus:

> *Sweethearts with their sweethearts go*
> *To Islington or London Spa;*
> *Some go but just to drink the water,*
> *Some for the ale which they like better.*

There was the Red Lion in St John Street, Clerkenwell, which dated back to 1415 and where Tom Paine may have written his *Rights of Man*, and the Angel which had a galleried courtyard and was known to have been there as early as 1638. It was a place where travellers used to congregate to avoid journeying alone across the last stretch of deserted fields to London, where footpads might be lurking. The inn was rebuilt in 1819, and has now closed, but it has given its name to the area. The Castle Tavern still stands in Cowcross Street; in the bar hangs a pawnbroker's sign for the inn-keeper there lent money to George IV, who had attended a cock-fight at Hockley-in-the-Hole (now Ray Street) and, having lost all he had, borrowed on the security of a royal watch and chain. As a token of his gratitude, the king conferred the double licence on the innkeeper. There is still a White Conduit Inn in Barnsbury Road in Pentonville, though it is not the same alehouse that was built in 1641 opposite the conduit that used to supply thc Charterhouse with water. In 1745, tea-gardens, arbours, and a fishpond were laid out there and in 1782 Thomas Lord founded the cricket club which became the Marylebone Cricket Club and whose ground still flourishes under his name at St John's Wood.

And then there was Sadler's Wells. The well was found by some workmen in 1683 in the grounds of the house of Thomas Sadler, a

Clerkenwell inspector of highways, and it was identified with a well that had once belonged to Clerkenwell Priory and was alleged to have miraculous powers. Sadler made the most of his good fortune, people came to drink the waters and entertainments of all sorts were given. In 1765 a new owner, Thomas Rosoman, made a regular theatre there where Edmund Kean is said to have made early appearances as Master Cary, the boy wonder, and the great clown, Joseph Grimaldi, performed regularly there. He made his first appearance at the age of three as a monkey, lived in Clerkenwell most of his life, became a shareholder of Sadler's Wells, and was buried in St James's, Pentonville Road, in 1837. In 1844, Samuel Phelps became manager and set out to produce Shakespeare's plays, putting on 34 in all over the next 18 years. Later in the century, the theatre fell into disrepair and disrepute till in 1931, Lilian Baylis rebuilt it and reopened it as an "Old Vic" for North London. It became the home of the Sadler's Wells Opera and Ballet Companies, who, though they now perform at the Coliseum in the West End, still use the old theatre for rehearsals, and visiting opera and ballet companies perform there. The original mediaeval well is still there, under a trap-door at the back of the stalls. There is a special Sadler's Wells Collection at Finsbury Library which is well worth a visit.

One other theatre should be mentioned, Samuel Collins' Music Hall in Upper Street beside Islington Green. It opened in 1862 and was known as "The Chapel on the Green". It remained open till it was damaged by fire in 1958. Lily Langtry, Nellie Wallace, George Robey, Sir Harry Lauder, Marie Lloyd, Vesta Tilley, Albert Chevalier, Dan Leno, Gracie Fields, Charlie Chaplin, and Tommy Trinder (it was his first stage appearance) all performed here. A blue plaque marks the converted premises, now a timber warehouse.

The landscape was altered by the completion of Sir Hugh Myddelton's New River in 1613 (see p. 123). Sir Hugh's statue stands on Islington Green, sculpted by John Thomas, looking rather lonely amidst the traffic, and the superb panelling from an older building, erected in 1613 and restored in 1782, has been installed in the new headquarters of the Metropolitan Water Board built in 1920. The wood carving is so fine that it is fairly attributed to Grinling Gibbons, and the plasterwork of the ceiling is equally exquisite.

In 1756, the New Road running from Paddington to Islington was created and the whole area was thereby opened up. A new parish church by Lancelot Dowbiggin had already been built in Upper Street in 1751, and now streets and squares appeared all round, and the Holloway and Hornsey Roads, which had been mere lanes drove northwards as main roads. The development began finely about 1773 under Henry Penton in what became known as Pentonville. Pretty Charlton Place was built, and so were Colebrooke Row and Duncan Terrace, at the end of which Charles and Mary Lamb rented a whole house which, as he said, made him feel like a great lord. It continued well with Cross Street (some fine doorways are there still), elegant Highbury Terrace (1789), beautiful —and once again fashionable—Canonbury Square (c. 1825 by Leroux), and near it, Alwyne Villas, which are enchanting. Thomas Cubitt laid out Barnsbury Square about 1835 agreeably. The Caledonian Asylum for the orphans of Scottish soldiers killed in the Napoleonic wars was established, and Myddelton and Wilmington Squares are pleasant enough. By 1841, a meaner pinched style of building, exemplified in Milner Square, was being erected. The Archway Road had been begun in 1812 (see p. 174) and in 1829, Shillibeer's omnibus began to run from Paddington to the Bank by way of the Angel. Pentonville Prison (1840–42, Caledonian Road) and Holloway Prison (1849–51, Parkhurst Road) disfigured the northern part of the area, and the Metropolitan Cattle Market moved to Copenhagen Fields in 1855. Mr Pooter, George and Weedon Grossmith's humble clerk, took up residence at The Laurels, Holloway, and wrote *The Diary of a Nobody* (a book that is essential reading for all who love London and human nature). The Agricultural Hall opened in 1861, where such displays as Cruft's Dog Show and the Motor Show held London spellbound, till it was taken over by the Post Office for the sorting of overseas parcels. Other Post Office buildings had opened at Mount Pleasant in 1885, first using the buildings of the old prison, the Middlesex House of Correction, and then gradually rebuilding, till the new edifice of 1934 was damaged by fire bombs and was replaced by the present offices.

In addition to those buildings which we have already mentioned, today's visitor to Islington and North Finsbury should seek out the rebuilt Islington parish church. Dowbiggin's St Mary's was bombed, though the tower and robust spire remain, and behind it a new church was constructed by Lord Mottistone and Paul Paget, fine and square with elegantly balanced pulpit and lectern. In the churchyard here lie Thomas Osborne, the impudent bookseller who was knocked down in his shop by Dr Johnson, and, in the same grave, Sir James Stewart and Sir George Wharton who killed each other in a duel and were buried together as an act of sentimental justice on the orders of James I. It was in Islington that the last fatal duel was fought in England, Colonel Fawcett being mortally wounded by Lieutenant Munro in 1843.

Near the church is Camden Passage, a labyrinth of tiny footways, where an antique market is held at weekends. It opened only in 1960 but is now one of the established sights of London. It is most just that there should be such a market here, for the Metropolitan Cattle Market was also London's junk market till the war ended its existence. Many and wonderful are the stories of bargains found or overlooked there. The Caledonian Market has since reopened in Bermondsey, but in its heyday it was the artist Walter Sickert's idea of heaven. He made his home in Islington from 1925 to 1934, painted the streets and music halls here and in Camden Town and St Pancras; Islington Central Reference Library in the Holloway Road has a collection of some drawings by him and of material connected with him. The Caledonian site is now being redeveloped for housing, but the central clock tower is to be retained as are three of the old public houses at the corners.

Behind Camden Passage runs the New River Walk, now a public garden, "like a green finger pointing through Islington", as the late Lord Morrison described it, and facing on to it is Duncan Terrace with the interesting Roman Catholic church of St John the Evangelist (rebuilt in 1870) in the middle of it. Off the Essex Road is Dagmar Passage, where England's only permanent puppet theatre, The Little Angel, regularly delights an audience, both juvenile and adult, with exquisite performances. Ripplevale Grove with the Albion public house, Thornhill Road and Square, Gibson Square, and many other streets around Barnsbury are unusual and rewarding to explore.

There are several interesting churches in the area. We have already mentioned St James's, Pentonville Road, where Grimaldi lies. It is a pretty little chapel built in 1787 by Aaron Hurst who is also buried there, as is Henry Penton. Off Upper Street, in Compton Terrace, is Union Chapel, Islington's chief Non-conformist place of worship. Built in 1876, by James Cubitt, it has a huge red-brick tower topped by a little spire. In the brickwork above the vestry door is a morsel of the Pilgrim Rock, on which the travellers on the *Mayflower* first set foot in 1620. This precious relic was presented in 1883. In Exmouth Market, Clerkenwell, stood Spa Fields Chapel built for the Countess of Huntingdon's Non-conformist services; it was replaced in 1887–88 by the Church of the Holy Redeemer designed by that interesting architect J. D. Sedding, in the Romanesque style. There is a spirited street market here too. Another chapel of the Countess of Huntingdon's connection is now the Roman Catholic church of SS Peter and Paul in Amwell Street. Off the Essex Road, in St Peter's Street, is St Peter's, Sir Charles Barry's first Gothic church, erected very cheaply (£3407) in 1834, and in the Holloway Road, is St Gabriel's, an exciting new Roman Catholic church designed by Gerard Goalen and opened on December 20, 1967.

Northwards towards the Archway a most elaborate road system is being redeveloped. The Whittington Almshouses have gone, removed to Felbridge in Surrey though the hospital still remains, but a statue of Sir Richard's legendary cat can be seen, ensconced on the pavement. It was carved by Jonathan Kenworthy and Tony Southwell and was presented by the actor and writer, Donald Bissett.

To the south of the borough lie **Finsbury** and **Clerkenwell**. Today this is a compact, built-up area with a good deal of light industry but in early times it was separated from the City by the marshy ground of Moorfields. The monk FitzStephen, writing in the 12th century tells us how the apprentices used to skate and disport themselves there:

> *When the great marsh that washes the northern walls of the City is frozen, dense throngs of youths go forth to disport themselves upon the ice. Some gathering speed by a run, glide sideways, with feet set well apart, over a vast space of ice. Others make themselves seats of ice like millstones and are dragged along by a number who run before them holding hands . . . Others there are, more skilled to sport upon the ice, who fit to their feet the shin-bones of beasts, lashing them beneath their ankles, and with iron-shod poles in their hands they strike ever and anon against the ice and are borne along swift as a bird in flight or a bolt shot from a mangonel.*

A causeway was built across the marsh in 1415 by the Lord Mayor, Sir Thomas Falconer, which made things far more comfortable for travellers, but it was not drained till 1527 and later that century was planted out with trees to make a pleasant walk for the citizens. Stow speaks of it as open ground at the end of Queen Elizabeth I's reign, but after the Great Fire in 1666, those who were made homeless camped in the fields and soon dwellings, first temporary and then more durable, were built and the land due north of the City walls was green no longer.

There had of course been permanent buildings there in the Middle Ages, the three chief being religious institutions, the Charterhouse, the Priory of the Knights of St John of Jerusalem, and the Nunnery of St Mary's, Clerkenwell. Little is known of the last of the three, save that it was founded by Jordan de Briset about 1100, stood beside the Clerks' Well (of which we shall say more later), and was dissolved in 1539, but both the Charterhouse and the Priory had great and noble histories.

The Charterhouse was founded in 1371 by Sir Walter de Manny, who was a fulfilment of the mediaeval ideal, being a great soldier and a devout Christian. He fought by land and sea in the wars against France with much distinction, as Froissart tells, and in his old age founded the Carthusian monastery where he was buried a year later (his body was found recently during restoration work after bombing; its position indicates that the monks' chapel was not on the site of the present one). The monastery was renowned and respected for its strictness and it was here that Sir Thomas More lived while he deliberated within himself whether he should, or should not, become a monk. He decided against it and went out into the world to become Lord Chancellor of England till his firm refusal to accept Henry VIII as head of the Church in England brought him to the scaffold. The Prior John Houghton and three other monks similarly refused and suffered an even more horrible fate, for, wearing their monks' habits—which shocked all Europe—they were dragged on hurdles to Tyburn, and were there hung and, still living, drawn and quartered. Their patience and courage amazed all beholders.

In 1545, the buildings of the Charterhouse were granted to Sir Edward North. He demolished much and built himself a mansion where Queen Elizabeth I resided while preparations were made for her coronation. Then it became the residence of the Dukes of Norfolk, and in 1611 was purchased by Thomas Sutton (see p. 145) who established there an almshouse for 80 poor gentlemen and a school for 44 poor boys. A new chapel was built and Sutton was laid there in a sumptuous tomb carved by Nicholas Stone and Nicholas Janssen, and costing £360. It is a tomb-chest with a figure of Sutton lying on it, Corinthian pillars at each corner to support a canopy and allegories carved around and above; the almshouse proved a godsend and the school flourished. Addison, Steele, John Wesley, and Thackeray were educated there. In 1872, the school moved to

Godalming and Merchant Taylors' School occupied and rebuilt the school buildings, till in 1933 they left too and the Medical College of St Bartholomew's now uses the premises. In 1941 the Charterhouse was severely bombed but after an inspired reconstruction by Seeley and Paget, it was made habitable again. The pensioners still eat their meals in the Great Hall, the superb carved staircase is still there, and beyond are courtyards used as domestic offices or let out to institutions, where one can easily think oneself back into the 16th century. The Charterhouse may be seen by appointment; the fee charged goes to the charity. It is well worth seeing.

The Hospital of St John was founded about 1048 in Jerusalem by some merchants of Amalfi. By the next century, it was becoming so difficult to visit the Holy Places that in 1123 the Brethren became a military order for the protection of pilgrims. (They were driven from Jerusalem in 1291, held Rhodes till 1522, and then settled in Malta till driven thence by Napoleon.) In the early 12th century, an English branch was established in Clerkenwell as a receiving and recruiting centre on land given by that generous man, Jordan de Briset. A church was built of which the beautiful crypt remains, but many of the monastic buildings were destroyed or damaged during Wat Tyler's rebellion of 1381. They were eventually rebuilt, the nave of the church and the gatehouse—which still stands—being completed during the priorship of Thomas Docwra, an extremely astute and efficient man.

The House was suppressed in 1540, and Henry VIII's tents and hunting apparatus were stowed there, and the king's master of revels had his offices there as well. Protector Somerset blew up most of the buildings and re-used the materials for old Somerset House. The Order was revived by Queen Mary, suppressed again by Queen Elizabeth I, and the property was owned by a number of people, the church being used as a private, then as a Non-conformist, chapel, till in 1723 it was bought by the crown commissioners and used as the parish church of St John. In 1831 the Order was revived and used the church from 1931 onwards. Although it was burnt out during the war, it has now been most nobly restored. The Order was revived to promote good works, was created a British Order of Chivalry in 1888, and now sponsors the St John's Ambulance Brigade, and the St John's Ophthalmic Hospital in Jerusalem. Its members still wear the distinctive star-like white cross on a black ground of the old Order.

It has its headquarters and museum in the old gatehouse where, from 1731, Edward Cave was editing *The Gentleman's Magazine*, on which he employed Dr Johnson before he became famous. Both gatehouse and crypt can be visited upon application, and should be seen by all who love London, both for their religious and literary associations and for the beauty of the rib-vaulted crypt, where there is a noble tomb brought from Vallidolid on which lies the effigy of Don Juan Ruyz de Vergera, Proctor of the Langue of Castile (d. 1575), with a sleeping boy—perhaps a page, perhaps his son—beside him. The outline of the original church can be traced by those with eyes to see in the cobblestones of Clerkenwell, for the circle which formed it is marked out on them. Like the Templars, this Order built its churches and chapels circular, after the Rotunda of the Anastasis of the Church of the Holy Sepulchre in Jerusalem.

Near St John's is Clerkenwell Green. Nearby is the Clerks' Well, which gave its name to the district, at which the company of Parish Clerks of London used to assemble to perform mystery plays. The well is still there and can be seen under 14–16 Farringdon Road, on personal application to the Branch Librarian at Finsbury Library, 245 St John St, E.C.1, and/or on written application to the Chief Librarian and Curator, Central Library, 68 Holloway Rd. Beside it stood St Mary's Nunnery, a Benedictine house which was suppressed in 1539. The nuns' church served as the parish church of Clerkenwell till a new St James was built between 1788 and 1792 by James Carr. Bishop Gilbert Burnet, that witty and candid chronicler of the court, who ordered that his *History of My Own Times* should not be published till six years after his death in 1715 when it created a considerable stir, was buried here, having lived in St John's Square nearby, and another interesting monument is that of William Wood, Captain of Archers, who died in 1691, and at whose funeral there was an archer's salute, flights of arrows being shot over the grave.

Opposite the church stands the Sessions House, built by a certain Rogers from designs by John Carter and replacing an older house of justice presented by that worthy man, Sir Baptist Hicks, in 1612, which stood in St John Street. The Sessions House is no longer used for its original purpose, being last used on December 23, 1920, but has been converted into offices.

Leaving the Green and walking eastwards towards the City Road, we pass through Charterhouse Square, where several early 18th century houses still stand, and then through the new development of Golden Lane Estate. Off Roscoe Street is a Quaker Garden where George Fox himself lies buried. North of it, in Old Street, are the remains of St Luke's Church and the site of St Luke's Hospital. The church was built under the Fifty New Churches Act of 1711—only 12 were erected in fact—and was designed by Nicholas Hawksmoor and John James, being begun in 1727 and completed in 1733. The steeple is a needle-like obelisk and the weather-vane a dragon. Subsidence was noted in 1959 and the church now stands an empty shell, only its tower and outer walls still existing. The organ which was built in 1754 is safely stored in St Giles's Church, Cripplegate. Caslon the typefounder, Thomas Allen the topographer, and Mark Catesby the author all are buried here. Nearby stood St Luke's Hospital, which opened in 1750 and moved into a noble building by George Dance the Younger in 1787. It was one of London's first two madhouses, the other being Bedlam, and was in its day a model of its kind. In 1916 the inmates were moved into the country and the premises were sold to the Bank of England and used as their printing works. In 1963 it was demolished and a new block stands on the site of a building which Elmes the topographer described with approbation. "There are few buildings in the Metropolis, perhaps in Europe, that, considering the poverty of the material, common English clamp bricks, possess such harmony of proportion, with unity and appropriateness of style."

Southwards in Chiswell Street is Whitbread's Brewery, which moved to this site in 1749. Many of the early brewing buildings remain, notably the Porter Tun Room of 1774, 160 feet long and 60 feet wide with a spectacular timber roof.

Finally we reach Finsbury Pavement and Finsbury Square, laid out by the younger George Dance in 1777. Nothing remains of its Georgian elegance but just north of it, in the City Road, are three remarkable institutions—the Honourable Artillery Company's headquarters, Wesley's house and chapel, and Bunhill Fields. The Honourable Artillery Company is Britain's oldest regiment and traces its origin back to the companies of archers of Edward III's reign. In 1537 it was granted a charter by Henry VIII and in 1641 moved to its present grounds. Armoury House was built in 1735, the embattled gateway is Victorian. In the Great Vellum Book are the signatures of all members from 1611 to 1682, which include Milton, Pepys, and Wren. From these grounds the first balloon ascent in England was made by Lunardi in 1784. The Honourable Artillery Company may march through the City with drums beating, colours flying, and bayonets fixed, and is responsible for firing Royal Salutes from the Tower Battery (see p. 385). The Museum of the Regiment may be visited provided written application is made.

Just beyond it lies Bunhill Fields. The name is a corruption of Bone Hill, for this was a prehistoric burial site. It became a public burial ground for Non-conformists, being opened in 1665 and closed in 1852 by which time 120,000 burials had taken place, among them John Bunyan, Daniel Defoe, William Blake, Isaac Watts, and Susannah Wesley, the formidable mother of John and Charles. Opposite Bunhill Fields is Wesley's chapel and house. In 1739, John Wesley rented an old foundry (which was later used temporarily to house the poor sufferers of St Luke's Hospital) and used it as a makeshift preaching-house and school. A dispensary, a soup-kitchen, an almshouse, and a stable were there too. The congregation was only 426 in 1742 but two years later it had grown to over 2200. The present chapel was built in 1777, a large, oblong, brick building, with galleries supported by pink oval columns which replaced wooden piers which had come from the masts of naval vessels at Deptford Dockyard. Wesley's statue stands in the fore-court and he is buried in the little garden behind. Beside the chapel stands his house where he lived from 1779 till his death on March 2, 1791.

The founder of Methodism was born at Epworth in Lincolnshire on June 28, 1703, the fifteenth of the nineteen children of the Reverend Samuel Wesley and his wife, Susannah, a remarkable and forceful woman. When he was six years old, the rectory was set on fire by some malcontents; one daughter, Hetty, awoke, roused the rest, and they fled into the garden, but when they counted heads, little John was missing and they looked up to see his face at the window. The staircase had fallen in with the flames and there was no ladder to hand, but one man climbed on another's shoulders and managed to lift the child to safety as the roof crashed in. Forever after, Wesley regarded himself literally as a brand snatched from burning, and believed that God had saved him for some special purpose. He went to school at Charterhouse, then to Christ Church at Oxford, and was eventually elected a Fellow at Lincoln College. He was ordained a clergyman of the Church of England and with his brother, Charles, and other like-minded young men such as George Whitfield, he formed a group who planned to deepen their spiritual lives by regular and methodical prayer and Bible study. In 1736, he went to Georgia as chaplain to the state—a not completely successful experience—and then on his return to England, on May 24, 1738, he was attending a prayer meeting when he was suddenly filled with a wonderful sensation of the nearness and love of Christ. He forthwith determined that it was his duty to become an itinerant preacher and this he did for the remaining 52 years of his life. His brother Charles, who remained in the Church of England, contributed his own special gift to the evangelical movement for he composed more than 600 hymns, including "Hark the herald angels sing" and "Lo! He comes with clouds descending".

Wesley's house, now 47 City Road, has been preserved, in all its simplicity and with much of its original furniture, as a museum. It is a tall, narrow house, full of relics. Wesley's christening robe is here, his books, his straddle-chair in which he studied, his tall clock which still keeps good time, and his preacher's gown. It is open daily (not on Sundays) to the public, and should be visited.

The works of mercy and of learning of which there are so many examples in Finsbury are carried on today by two great institutions. The first is Moorfields Eye Hospital or more properly the Royal London Ophthalmic Hospital, which was founded in 1805 in Charterhouse Square. Today it stands in the City Road in a large forbidding building, but the work carried on there is as vital and as humanitarian as ever it was. The second is the City University at Northampton Square which has grown out of the old Northampton Polytechnic Institute founded in 1898, which stands on the site of old Clerkenwell Manor House. In 1957 it became a College of Advanced Technology, engineering, ophthalmic optics, applied physics, mathematics, and industrial chemistry being its main subjects. In 1966 it became the City University and an extensive programme of new buildings is in progress at present. The Gresham Lectures, instituted by Sir Thomas Gresham (see p. 258) in 1579, in music, geometry, rhetoric, astronomy, divinity, physic, and law, are today held here. The City University has, we hope, a long and distinguished future before it.

KENSINGTON

KENSINGTON

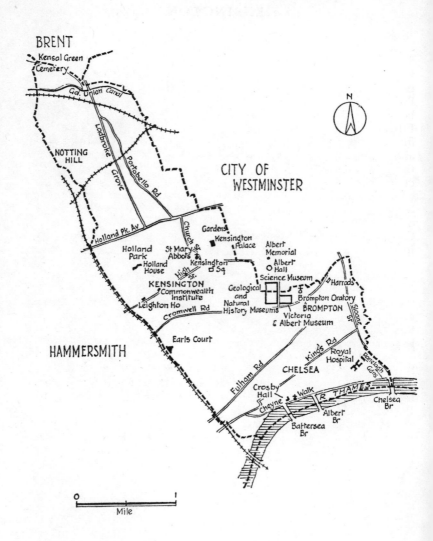

KENSINGTON AND CHELSEA

The Royal Borough of Kensington and Chelsea is a union of the former separate boroughs of Kensington and Chelsea. It lies to the west of London, covers an area of 4·61 square miles, and has a population of 208,480 (1969). Its neighbours are Hammersmith, Brent, and Westminster, with the river Thames on its southern boundary. In 1901, in compliance with the wish of his mother, Edward VII made Kensington a Royal Borough; the honour, confirmed by letters patent on the new borough in 1964, is still proudly and fittingly borne. Until the 19th century, with the exception of the development around Kensington Palace which earned it the charming title of the "old Court suburb", Kensington was open country, market and nursery garden, or farmland, as was Chelsea; both areas were built up in Victorian times though in each several older edifices remain. There is high ground along the ridge of Campden Hill and Notting Hill while the rest is comparatively low-lying.

Kensington probably takes its name from Cynesige, a Saxon landowner; it was his *tun* or place. It is a large area, stretching from the Fulham Road north as far as the Harrow Road, and there are great differences between the rich and the poor who live there, but fortunately the borough has a distinct centre from which we can begin to describe it, travelling first north and then south.

That centre runs along Kensington Gore and Kensington High Street. On the north side is Kensington Palace and Gardens. Although the Gardens are in Westminster, we must describe them briefly here as they are an integral part of the surroundings of the Palace. This had its origins in a house built about 1605 by Sir George Coppins, which later became the property of Sir John Finch, physician and diplomat. It was afterwards conveyed to his brother, Sir Heneage Finch, later Earl of Nottingham, and was known as Nottingham House. In June 1689, William III and Queen Mary purchased it from him for £18,000, infinitely preferring its open airy situation to the old riverside palace of Whitehall, which made William's asthma worse while Mary complained that she could see nothing but "water or wall". Sir Christopher Wren, with Nicholas Hawksmoor as his clerk of works, made hasty additions to it and the court took up residence just before Christmas. Work continued on the house, the Clock Court was built, the Queen's Gallery was added in 1691 and the King's, with its wonderful outlook over the Gardens which were William's delight and relaxation, in 1695–96. Here Mary died suddenly of smallpox in 1694, aged only 33, and here William was brought, at his own wish, after the fall from his horse in 1702 at Hampton Court, which was to prove fatal. He had already spent £11,000 on the gardens, employing the designers London and Wise who had a nursery at Brompton Park, and the work was carried on by the same men when his sister-in-law Anne came to the throne. In 1704 she had built a "Summer Supper House", an orangery designed by Hawksmoor and Vanbrugh. It is an elegant gracious building with a wonderfully tranquil interior, today open to all who care to sit there. She regarded Kensington as a country retreat but when she, the last of the Stuart monarchs, died in 1714, her successor George I had different ideas. Colin Campbell was instructed to turn it from a fine house into a palace. Three staterooms were built, replacing the core of the old Jacobean mansion, and they and the main staircase were decorated by William Kent. New kitchens were built and the Princesses' Courtyard was added, called after the King's granddaughters who lived there with their governess, the Duchess of Portland. When George II succeeded in 1727, he and Queen Caroline made their home there and devoted themselves to the gardens and the rearrangement of furniture and pictures. It was the queen who found a package of drawings by Holbein tucked away in a bureau, which are now one of the prides of the collection at Windsor Castle. The gardens were redesigned, this time by Wise and Charles Bridgeman, the Broad Walk was laid out, the Round Pond was formed, and a group of ponds, part of the Westbourne, were transformed into the Serpentine.

George II was the last monarch to live there, for George III resided at Buckingham House, and Kensington was shut up for 40 years. In the early 19th century it was put in order as apartments for Caroline of Brunswick, George IV's wife (see p. 165) and her daughter Charlotte, for the Duke of Kent, Queen Victoria's father, and for Frederick Augustus, Duke of Sussex. Victoria was born here on May 24, 1819, and grew up in the palace with her widowed mother. She delighted to ride her donkey or to drive in her goat-cart round Kensington Gardens, greeting those whom she met with grave courtesy. It was to Kensington Palace that the Prime Minister and Archbishop of Canterbury came, to awaken the young queen in the middle of the night with news of her accession; her brave and lonely promise, made when a child, "I will be good", echoes through the years. She held her first council there the next day, June 20, 1837, in the room that is at present the entrance hall to the London Museum. Victoria moved to Buckingham Palace but the Duchess of Kent remained at Kensington till her death in 1861, after which her apartments became the home of the Duke and Duchess of Teck, Queen Mary being born there in 1867. Just after Victoria's Diamond Jubilee in 1897, Parliament voted £36,000 for the restoration of the palace and the State Apartments were opened to the public which had, since George II's day, been permitted to enjoy the gardens.

Today we enter the State Apartments by the garden door on the queen's side of the palace. The doorway is hooded by a pediment with a cartouche containing William and Mary's initials surrounded by swirling foliage. It is the work of Thomas Hill, one of Wren's master masons. From it the Queen's Staircase leads to Queen Mary's Gallery and then through several smaller apartments to George III's staterooms, the Privy Chamber, the Cupola Room, and the King's Drawing Room, all with elaborate ceilings by Kent.

From the Privy Chamber can be seen Wren's Clock Court, and in the Cupola Room stands an amazing allegorical clock, made for Augusta, Princess of Wales and George III's mother. It was begun about 1730 by Charles Clay and was completed by John Pyke. There was once a musical box inside it which played tunes by Handel, Corelli, and Geminiani; the silver bas-reliefs on the sides were by Rysbrack and the allegorical figures on the top by Roubiliac himself. It was in this room that Queen Victoria was baptised. The Drawing Room, with a superb chimneypiece carved by James Richards in 1724, contains paintings by Benjamin West, the American artist who was George III's favourite and who became President of the Royal Academy. The windows look out on to the gardens, where three tree-lined avenues radiate from the Round Pond, the central one punctuated by G. F. Watts' bronze equestrian statue, *Physical Energy*. In the Council Chamber beyond is a copy of Sir David Wilkie's painting of Queen Victoria's accession council, and then we reach her own bedroom where she was awakened with the news that she was Queen of England. Her jewel casket is here and so is Prince Albert's inlaid games table, on which chess, cribbage, and backgammon can be played. Beyond it is a little ante-room with Victoria's dolls'-house and some of her dolls and toys and next is the nursery furnished from Queen Mary's collection.

We then return to an older part of the palace, the King's Gallery.

In William's day, his finest paintings were displayed here and the room's most memorable feature is the wind-dial made for the king by Robert Norden in 1694. It shows a map of north-west Europe on which the direction of the prevailing wind is marked by a pointer which is operated by rods connected to a wind-vane on the roof; the mechanism may have been devised by Thomas Tompion. Above the wind-dial is a small painting of the Madonna and Child, probably by Raphael, and the ceiling was decorated by Kent with scenes from the story of Ulysses. Between the windows are busts of eminent scientists and philosophers—Sir Isaac Newton, William Wollaston, John Locke, Robert Boyle, and Samuel Clarke—set on elaborate pedestals, and around the walls are hung paintings of London at various dates.

At the end of the Gallery is the King's Grand Staircase, with a balustrade by Jean Tijou and walls painted by William Kent. On the north and part of the east wall, he depicted a gallery filled with members of George III's court; among them is Peter the Wild Boy who had been found when a child, crawling on all fours in a wood near Hanover and living as a wild animal. He was brought to court as a curiosity, was put in the care of Dr Arbuthnot, and adapted himself quite happily to new ways. To the side of the staircase is the Presence Chamber, built by Wren and decorated by Kent; in it are displayed royal costumes from the London Museum's collection.

The ground floor of part of the Palace is occupied by the London Museum. The collection is concerned with the history and pre-history of the London area and with all aspects of the life of the citizens; it therefore includes an astonishing variety of material. Among the most interesting exhibits are the reconstructions of London and its more important buildings at various periods, the domestic pottery, the exquisite late 16th century jewellery discovered buried in Cheapside, a hand-grip which was once part of a chariot, found at Brentford, entire and fully-equipped shop-fronts, a painting of the Great Fire of 1666, an astonishing wealth of costume—the contrast between Victoria's ball-dresses when she was 17 and the heavy shapeless weeds she wore after Albert's death is pathetic—a 19th century fire-engine, and an abundance of maps, paintings, engravings, and photographs of London from the 16th century onwards. The collection was begun in 1911 and is shortly to be rehoused in less cramped premises,* when the exhibits will cover the city's history right up to the present.

* We hope to describe it more fully in the next volume which will cover the City and Westminster.

On leaving the palace, where the Princesses' and the Prince of Wales' Courtyards are still private apartments, we pass the Sunken Garden, laid out in 1909 as a re-creation of the gardens designed by Queen Anne. Today it is one of the best and most imaginatively tended spots in London. The lime tree tunnels—pleached limes—around three sides are an entrancement to small children, to lovers, and to old people. On the Broad Walk to the right is Princess Louise's statue of her mother, Queen Victoria, and to the right again, before Wren's south front, is a statue of William III by Bauche, presented to Edward VII by Kaiser Wilhelm II in 1907.

To the west of the palace, running due north from the High Street to the Bayswater Road, is Kensington Palace Gardens, a private road with lodges—and lodge-keepers at either end—something rare in London and somehow uncharacteristic—full of great houses, most of them today used as embassies. No. 2, at the south end known as Palace Green, was built for the novelist William Makepeace Thackeray, in 1861 to his own designs. It is a tall Queen Anne house, quite out of sympathy with the architecture of his own Victorian days, and long before the Georgian revival. Here he died in 1863 having lived previously in Young Street and at 36 Onslow Square where he wrote *The Virginians* and planned the *Cornhill Magazine*.

A little way along the High Street is St Mary Abbots Church, built to replace the old parish church in 1869–72 by Sir George Gilbert Scott. It is a dark building approached by a winding cloister which is unusual and mysteriously dramatic. It possesses the highest spire in London—254 feet—modelled on that beautiful landmark, the spire of St Mary Redcliffe in Bristol. The hexagonal pulpit is dated 1697 and may have been the gift of William III; the exceptionally fine plate can be seen in the Victoria and Albert Museum. The most ambitious funeral monument is to Edward, Earl of Warwick and Holland (d. 1721), Addison's stepson; we shall have more to say of him in a moment. St Mary Abbots owes its unusual name to a gift made by Godfrey, son of Aubrey de Vere, Earl of Oxford, who in *c.* 1100 gave land at Kensington to the abbots of Abingdon. It stands at the corner of Church Street, a winding road with many fascinating antique shops. Half-way up it is the Carmelite Church of Our Lady of Mount Carmel and St Simon Stock, designed by Sir Giles Gilbert Scott and opened in 1960.

Beyond the parish church in the High Street is Kensington Town Hall (1878 by R. Walker), and near it, in Old Court Place, stands the fire station, the last in London to use horses. The last fire so attended was at Christmas time in 1921, and on their return the two bay mares, Lucy and Nora, were received in state by the chief of the LCC who gave them sugar and carrots from a silver tray. Behind the High Street in Phillimore Walk is the public library, built in 1960 by E. Vincent Harris. It is a long building with a plain façade and inside is one of the best equipped and most helpful libraries in London. The local history collection is particularly rewarding.

Behind the library, Campden Hill rises sharply. This is an area which repays careful exploration on foot. The many great houses with royal inmates which earned it the title of "The Dukeries" have all gone, but the charm of the houses in Campden Hill Square, the surprise of the sudden view across to St John's, Notting Hill, from the bend in Aubrey Road, the excellence of the design of Holland Park Comprehensive School, and the welcome of the Windsor Castle public house on the corner of Campden Road and Peel Street, make it somewhere that should not be missed. Four houses, one vanished, the others still in existence, are particularly worth remembering. Campden House was built about 1612 by Sir Baptist Hicks, a successful City merchant who became Lord Campden in 1628, and so gave a name to the whole hill. It was occupied by the Parliamentarians during the Civil War but was returned to the Campden family at the Restoration. Anne, while still a princess, lived there from 1691 to 1696 with her precious, delicate son, William Henry, Duke of Gloucester, who died in 1700 at the age of 11, the only one of her 18 children who survived infancy. In the 1840s, it was the home of a Mr Wooley who built a theatre there for amateur productions. One of them was *The Lighthouse*, in which Charles Dickens took part; the back-drop can still be seen at Dickens' house (see p. 80). Campden House was burnt down and a block of flats, Campden House Court, is on the site today.

Holly Lodge, where Macaulay lived from 1856 till his death in 1859, stood on Campden Hill. He was born in 1800 and went to Trinity College, Cambridge where he became a Fellow in 1824. His father's firm failed so he read law, was called to the Bar, and within two years was a Commissioner in Bankruptcy. From 1825 he had been writing for the *Edinburgh Review*, and it was his essay on Milton that opened London society to him and made his extraordinary conversational powers widely known. In 1830 he entered Parliament, was acclaimed as a debater, helped to pass the Reform Bill, and in 1834 became a member of the Supreme Council for

India. He spent four years there, codifying the criminal law and won himself much enmity by his regard for the rights of the Indians. He returned to this country and began to write his *History of England* and *Lays of Ancient Rome*. In 1857 he became Lord Macaulay but by this time his health was failing. He retired to Holly Lodge where he was near his friends, Lord and Lady Holland, at the great house nearby, and there he died, his *History* uncompleted, very quietly in his study on December 28, 1859. He had that morning been reading the instalment of his neighbour Thackeray's novel, *Lovell the Widower*, in the *Cornhill Magazine*.

Nearby in Aubrey Walk is Aubrey House, built in the early 18th century, and once the home of Lady Mary Coke, the diarist (1726–1811). She was a temperamental lady but witty and very beautiful, judging from the painting of her by Allan Ramsay in which she is shown standing, holding a theorbo or bass lute, and wearing a white satin dress. She lived at the house from 1767 to 1788, and from 1873 Aubrey House was the home of the Alexander family. Mr Alexander was a connoisseur of art, and commissioned Whistler to paint his daughter Cecily. The portrait, *An Arrangement in Grey and Green*, is today in the National Gallery. Very occasionally, the grounds of the house are opened for charitable purposes, and a visit at such a time reveals one of the most attractive dwellings in London, one which seems a country house in all save its convenient nearness to town.

One last house should be mentioned—South Lodge, No. 80 Campden Hill Road. It takes its name from Sir James South (1785–1867) who had built an observatory in the grounds of Phillimore House. Here from 1908, Violet Hunt and Ford Madox Ford edited *The English Review* and were visited by all the literary men of their own, and the next, generation; Henry James, Joseph Conrad, H. G. Wells, Arnold Bennett, Ezra Pound, and Wyndham Lewis were among them.

Returning to the High Street, we come to the Commonwealth Institute. This began its existence just off the Exhibition Road as the Imperial Institute; it was a result of the Colonial Exhibition of 1886. The original building was designed by Thomas Collcutt with three copper-topped towers, the tallest 280 feet high; it has been preserved as an achievement of Victorian architecture. The new building on the new site is no less remarkable, and as typical of its own period. It was designed in 1960–62, by Robert Matthew, Johnson-Marshall and Partners, has a hyperbolic paraboloid roof, and houses one of the most fascinating displays possible, depicting every aspect of the life, natural environment, cities, arts, and manufactures of that great Commonwealth of Nations which was once the British Empire. It is an especially rewarding place to which to take children. The displays are so graphically arranged and the different levels connected by ramps afford such freedom of movement that the fatigue which can often set in after a few moments in some museums when accompanied by children is seldom felt here.

Behind the Institute are the remains of Holland House and the beautiful park which has been made from its gardens. Before its almost complete destruction by fire-bombs, this Jacobean house was one of the most astonishing and picturesque survivals so near to the centre of London. It was built between 1605 and 1607 for Sir Walter Cope, who was Chamberlain of the Exchequer, Master of the Court of Wards and Liveries, and Keeper of Hyde Park to James I. These posts were lucrative and Cope's house was ambitious. The house was E-shaped—usual enough at that time, but the central arm of the E is a polygonal porch—while round the courtyard formed by the projecting wings is an arched cloister or loggia. Fleur-de-lys were used everywhere for that was the Cope emblem. This front courtyard is all that remains of the house and has been beautifully restored; in the summer, plays and ballets are performed here under the auspices of the Greater London Council. In 1629, gate piers carved by Nicholas Stone to designs by Inigo Jones, were added; these now stand at the top of a flight of steps leading to the south front, a griffin on top of each, and the Cope and Rich arms displayed. On her father's death, Isabel Cope became mistress of the house and lived there with her husband, Henry Rich, Earl of Holland. They were a gay young couple and decorated the magnificent Gilt Room on the first floor, but their gaiety ended with the Civil War when the earl was executed in 1649 going to the scaffold in a waistcoat of white satin. Lady Holland was allowed to live on in the house but the main part was used by the Parliamentarians and the story goes that Cromwell and Ireton would hold conference in the grounds where they could not be overheard, for Ireton was deaf and the Lord Protector had to shout at him. Isabel's grandson left a widow, Charlotte, who 15 years after her husband's death, in 1711, married Joseph Addison, the poet, essayist, and statesman. Addison died only three years later, summoning his rakish stepson, the 4th earl, to his bedside, to admonish him for the last time and to take leave of him with the famous last words—"See in what peace a Christian can die."

In 1768, the house became the property of Henry Fox, later

Baron Holland, who was Paymaster-General during the Seven Years' War when he amassed himself a fortune. He and his wife, Lady Caroline Lennox, daughter of the Duke and Duchess of Richmond (with whom he had eloped to the utter horror of her parents, for in his youth Henry Fox had been considered a profligate) entertained lavishly and agreeably. Horace Walpole was "excessively amused" in 1761 by a performance of *Jane Shore* given by the young people of the house and their friends. Among the actors was Charles James Fox, who was to become one of the most brilliant debaters and politicians England has ever known, though he was perpetually in debt and often in trouble. But it was his nephew, Henry Richard Vassall Fox (1773–1840) who loved Holland House and it was during his occupation that the house was to show its greatest glory. He and his wife, whom Macaulay described as having the "air of Queen Elizabeth", kept open house. Their home was the centre of the Whig Party; their literary inclinations enabled them to number Sir Walter Scott, Wordsworth, Samuel Rogers, Sydney Smith, Thomas Campbell, Thomas Moore, Washington Irving, Fennimore Cooper, and especially Macaulay among their friends; their political inclinations brought Madame de Staël, Ugo Foscolo, and Talleyrand to the house. When Lord Holland died, his son and daughter-in-law maintained the Holland House circle though on a reduced scale; Panizzi and the artist G. F. Watts were among their friends while Macaulay came to live nearby. At last in 1874 the house was made over to Lord Ilchester and it remained in his family till, after the bombing of 1940, the London County Council bought the ruins from him, restored that which was not totally destroyed, and built on the George VI Youth Hostel for students of all nations. The new buildings are so skilfully designed that, while retaining their integrity to their own day, they harmonise well with the remains of the old.

The grounds are remarkable. Beside the house is a Dutch garden laid out in 1812 by Bonaiuti, the Hollands' librarian, and throughout are avenues of lime trees which perfume the air in spring, while on the lawns peacocks flaunt their tails. The ballroom, detached from the house, and recently severely damaged by fire, is now a restaurant, and the open-air exhibitions of sculpture which are sometimes arranged in the park are among the delights of London.

Just to the west lie Holland Park Road and Melbury Road, both famous for their artistic associations. Leighton House is in Holland Park Road. It was the house of Frederick Leighton, painter and President of the Royal Academy on whom Queen Victoria conferred

303

a barony the day before he died. He was born in 1830, the son and grandson of doctors—his grandfather had been physician to the Empress of Russia—and his family hoped he would follow in the calling. To this end, his father insisted that he should study anatomy, which was of the greatest advantage to him later, but the boy's gift for art was so strong that he was allowed to study under Edward Johann Steile in Frankfort. In 1855 a painting, *Cimabue's Madonna*, was exhibited at the Royal Academy and was bought by Queen Victoria for £600. Characteristically, Leighton immediately bought works from other, less fortunate, artists. He travelled widely and became much interested in Eastern art, so much so that when he settled in London and, with the aid of an architect friend, George Aitchison, built his house, he added an Arab Hall, decorated with 13th to 17th century tiles from Rhodes, Damascus, Cairo, and elsewhere, collected by himself and his friends, Sir C. Purdon Clarke and Sir Richard Burton. Additional tiles were created by William de Morgan who was inspired by the wonderful blues and greens of the old work. The whole hall has a strange, unearthly, underwater quality, which is heightened by the sound of a little fountain which falls into a bowl of black marble, cut from a single block. The stillness of the hall today is deceiving—we should imagine it as it must have been when Leighton was entertaining. In the garden, to which the public have access in the summer, is one of Leighton's rare sculptures, the bronze *Athlete*, and upstairs is his studio, used today for lectures and exhibitions. The house was purpose built, a working home for an artist, and is a complete expression of one man's individual taste. Leighton loved beauty and he loved work, and he surrounded himself with both.

In Little Holland House—Melbury Road covers its site—lived Mr and Mrs Thoby Prinsep, with whom G. F. Watts, the artist and sculptor, made his home for many years. When the house was demolished and the grounds built over, he built himself a new Little Holland House at 6 Melbury Road (Kingfisher House stands there now), and here he created his best-known statue, *Physical Energy*, a memorial to Cecil Rhodes, a copy of which is in Kensington Gardens. He wedded, in middle age, the young Ellen Terry, but the marriage was dissolved after three years. As neighbour, he had Luke Fildes at No. 11 who painted those two passionate and humanitarian statements, *Queuing for Admission to the Casual Wards* (Royal Holloway College) and *The Doctor* (Tate Gallery). At No. 8 was Marcus Stone, another painter and both these houses were designed by Norman Shaw. At No. 2, was Sir William Hamo

Christchurch, Spitalfields, from the west

St Anne's Church, Limehouse, from the west

Hornchurch Church, from the east

Thorneycroft, the sculptor, and Holman Hunt was at No. 18. The most exciting house of all is No. 9, designed as "a model residence of the 15th century" by that extraordinary architect, William Burges, who also designed cathedrals for Cork, Brisbane, and Lille, as well as Cardiff Castle and Harrow School Speech Room.

Beyond Melbury Road is Addison Road, still full of agreeable 19th century villas and with some excellent 20th century development in the streets nearby. In it stands St Barnabas Church (1828 by Lewis Vulliamy), the oldest church building in Kensington. Addison Road leads north to another thoroughfare, variously called Holland Park Avenue, Notting Hill Gate and the Bayswater Road, which runs parallel to Kensington High Street, and north of this, in Notting Hill and Ladbroke Grove, is a very different kind of development. The visitor should not miss the public house, The Hoop, Notting Hill Gate, which has an exceptionally well-designed interior.

Until the 19th century, all this was open country and then in 1837 a race-course, the Hippodrome, was built which attracted a rowdy element to the neighbourhood. It lasted a bare four years before it was closed, but thereafter the land began to be built over along the axis of Ladbroke Grove. The artist Frith had a house among Pembridge Villas; a garage now stands on its site, but there he painted *Derby Day* and *The Railway Station* for which Paddington was a convenient model. Avondale Park is a pleasantly green open space and at its south-east corner, in Walmer Road beside Hippodrome Place, can be found a fascinating industrial survival, a tile kiln, the outer shell of which is built into a wall. The clay soil of the area, which proved too hard for horse-racing and too heavy going in wet weather, was excellent for bricks, drainpipes, and domestic pottery. In *Household Words*, 1850, Dickens refers to this area as "The Potteries". Today the most exciting street is the Portobello Road, where, on Fridays and Saturdays, a market is held. Originally this was a fruit and vegetable market and excellent greengrocery can still be bought here throughout the week, but since the war the Portobello has replaced the Caledonian as one of London's main markets for antiques and curios. The church of St John the Evangelist (1844 by Stevens and Alexander) crowns the rise of Ladbroke Grove and is a focus for the whole area.

Across the northern corner of the borough run the main line from Paddington to the West and the Grand Union Canal beside which there is a most agreeable walk along the towpath. On its further side at the northern tip of Kensington, is Kensal Green

Cemetery. This is one of the seven "hygienic" cemeteries founded between 1832 and 1841; the others were Norwood, Highgate, Abney Park, Brompton, Nunhead, and Tower Hamlets. They were a successful attempt to suppress the churchyard horrors described in Chapter 16 of *Bleak House* or existing in reality beneath Enon Chapel in Clements Lane where the Law Courts now stand. The leading reformer was Dr George Alfred Walker who had made a study of the cemeteries of Paris. In Kensal Green are buried the Duke of Sussex, who had lived in Kensington Palace, Thackeray, Sydney Smith, Blondin the tightrope walker, Wilkie Collins, Anthony Trollope, John Murray, Byron's publisher, Sir Marc Isambard Brunel and his more famous son, Isambard Kingdom, the poet Francis Thompson, and Leigh Hunt, on whose stone is his own famous line—*Write me as one who loves his fellow men.*

We should now return to our starting point, Kensington Palace, and look south. On the far side of Kensington Gore is Hyde Park Gate and at No. 28, Sir Winston Churchill, Prime Minister from 1940 to 1945 and 1951 to 1955, who led Britain through the Second World War with such courage inspiration and eloquence, lived and died. He was accorded a state funeral such as had not been seen since the death of Wellington.

Kensington owes much of its charm to its origin as a court suburb and to its association with the aristocracy and the very rich, but its essence is contained in the 87 acres on which are built an extraordinary group of museums, cultural institutions, and places of learning. Some of this land is in Westminster but no description of Kensington would be complete unless it dealt with the whole area whether or not it is technically within the borough's boundaries.

The origin of this wonderful cultural and academic centre was the Great Exhibition of 1851, held in Hyde Park to display the arts and manufactures of all nations. The exhibition was the idea of Prince Albert and Henry (later Sir Henry) Cole. It was a fantastic success and made a profit of £130,000. With this money, on Prince Albert's advice—he was one of the most sensibly idealistic of men—land was bought south of the park and on it were built the Albert Hall, Imperial College, the Royal Colleges of Arts, Sciences, Music, and Organists, the Royal School of Needlework, the Imperial Institute, the Science, Geological, Natural History, and Victoria and Albert Museums.

After Albert's death, it was felt that this neighbourhood was the most fitting place in which to raise a monument to him, and so the Albert Memorial was built. It was designed by Sir George Gilbert

Scott, cost £120,000, and stands 175 feet high. A huge statue of the prince, reading the catalogue of the Great Exhibition, is seated in the pinnacled Gothic shrine, and round the base is a fascinating frieze of painters, poets, composers, architects, and sculptors. At the inner corners are four groups, Agriculture, Manufacture, Commerce, and Engineering, with four more at the outer corners representing the four continents, Europe, Asia, Africa, and the Americas. The Memorial is so familiar a feature of the London landscape that it is hard to judge it dispassionately. To its own age it was a great work of art, later generations have found it comical or vulgar, but seen at sunset, dark against the sky, it is like something out of a fairy tale, while the frieze at the base is so well thought out and executed that it is easy to spend an hour or more engrossed in the detail.

Opposite it is the Albert Hall designed by Captain Fowke and built between 1867 and 1871. It is an enormous circular brick building, capable of seating 8000, of an immense simplicity (unlike the Memorial), decorated only with a terracotta frieze of the Triumph of the Arts running boldly round the top. Spectacles and entertainments of all kinds are given here, perhaps the most important today being the Promenade Concerts, transferred after the wartime destruction of the Queen's Hall.

To the west of the Hall is the Royal College of Organists, designed by Lieutenant H. H. Cole and weirdly and delightfully decorated in plasterwork by F. W. Moody. Beside it is Sir Hugh Casson's and H. T. Cadbury-Brown's new building for the Royal College of Art (1961/2) made of dark dramatic brick and built round a companionable inner courtyard. Behind the Albert Hall is the Royal College of Music which, in addition to its teaching duties, houses the Donaldson Collection of Musical Instruments which can be seen in term time. The huge bulk of Imperial College (1906, Sir Aston Webb) a complex of buildings, houses schools of Science and Engineering; the standards set here are among the highest in England. On the corner of Exhibition Road stood the Royal School of Needlework (1903, Fairfax B. Wade; now demolished but rehoused in Kensington Gore) where exquisite work is carried out for churches, institutions, and homes, and is often exported to all parts of the world, even as English embroidery has been exported since Norman times.

The Science, Geological, and Natural History Museums form one large group, covering a vast range of scientific knowledge, though they were built at different periods. The excellently designed

Science Museum was erected in 1909 though the collection was started after the Great Exhibition. There are sections devoted to motive power, electricity, transport, technology, astronomy, mining, chemistry, acoustics, aeronautics, and physics. There is a wonderful gallery on the lower ground floor devised to explain scientific and natural phenomena to children. The constant efforts of the museum staff to modernise and improve displays make any detailed description inadvisable, but there are certain exhibits that no visitor should miss seeing, such as the Newcomen Type Atmospheric Engine of 1791, or the Boulton and Watt Rotative Beam Engine of 1788, which greet one on entry. Then there are original Davy safety lamps, the oldest locomotive in existence, the "Puffing Billy" of 1813, and Stephenson's "Rocket" of 1829, an early Bessemer converter for steel-making, Faraday's own chemical chest, Babbage's calculating machine, Sir Frank Whittle's turbo-jet aero-engine, and the Vickers "Vimy" aircraft in which Alcock and Brown made the first Atlantic air-crossing on June 14/15, 1919.

The adjacent Geological Museum teaches us about the structure of the earth and shows us beautiful examples of every mineral to be found on it, while the Natural History Museum is quite simply one of the most wonderful and exciting places in the world. The building itself, designed in 1873–81 by Alfred Waterhouse, is astonishing and yet welcoming—a gentle ramp leads up to an enormous arched portal, and beyond this are a series of halls for displays and a research collection in which examples of every known species of animal and plant life are to be found. The Whale Gallery is a magical place where huge fish float, suspended, but perhaps the most exciting exhibits of all are the fossils, which include such rarities as the earliest known bird, Archaeopteryx, which had a tail and teeth as well as wings, and the remains and reconstructions of such prehistoric monsters as Diplodocus and Tyrannosaurus, and the huge Irish deer with its enormous antlers. Perhaps the most relevant of all to the Londoner, are the remains of two mammoths found at Aveley in Essex, just outside the Greater London boundary, and at Upnor near Rochester.

The museum which has become the Victoria and Albert was the immediate descendant of the Great Exhibition, and its first Director was Sir Henry Cole. In 1856 Sir William Cubitt designed a building of glass and iron on the Cromwell Road to house many of the original exhibits and certain other art collections. It was affectionately known as the "Brompton Boilers" and in 1871 was re-erected at Bethnal Green as an annexe of the Victoria and Albert and an outpost of culture, where its exhibits (see p. 403) have delighted residents and visitors ever since. The four courts of the museum were built from 1862 onwards and the façade was designed by Sir Aston Webb and built between 1891 and 1909. It is adorned with statues of artists and craftsmen and has a huge lanthorn over the main entrance, the whole being in a terracotta brick. Originally, it housed the sciences as well as the arts, but a separate science museum having been established, the Victoria and Albert today concerns itself with the fine and applied arts. There are collections of European, Mediaeval, and Renaissance art, of ceramics, of sculpture and metalwork, and of textiles, furniture, books, and manuscripts. Days can be spent in this museum, and the visitor should be particularly careful not to miss the paintings of John Constable, which are breathtaking, and the Raphael Cartoons bought by Charles I and now on loan from Her Majesty the Queen. Then there is the Great Bed of Ware, made at the end of the 16th century and able to sleep eight people; the Gloucester Candlestick, a miracle of ingenious goldwork, made about 1105; a fine bust of Henry VII, modelled from life by Pietro Torrigiani; miniatures by Holbein and Hilliard; the Armada Jewel portrait of Elizabeth I, and a collection of textiles, embroidery, and costume which is essential study for any woman at all interested in clothing. The new lay-out of the Costume Court is particularly good, as are the displays of musical instruments.

Leaving the museum centre and returning to the south side of Kensington High Street, we pass Young Street which leads into Kensington Square. The square was built during the 1680s by Thomas Young, who gave his name to the street, to house those concerned with Kensington Palace. After George II's reign, when the palace was no longer used by the sovereign and the courtiers left, the square was occupied by successful artists and intellectuals. Archbishop Herring possibly lived at Nos. 11 and 12, and Count Talleyrand the French diplomat may have stayed with him there. John Stuart Mill lived at No. 18 and it was here that his housemaid used the first part of the manuscript of Carlyle's *French Revolution* to light the fire. One shudders at the thought of that careless hearth. Carlyle bore the loss stoically, and rewrote the pages supported by £100 which his publisher advanced him; the contrite Mill added a set of the *Biographie Universelle*. Sir Hubert Parry the composer lived at No. 17, and Mrs Patrick Campbell, the actress who was Shaw's Eliza and Pinero's original Second Mrs Tanqueray, lived at No. 33.

Thackeray lived in Young Street and wrote *Vanity Fair* and *Henry Esmond* here; *Henry Esmond* is a tale of Jacobite intrigue, and part of the plot centres on Lady Castlewood's house in the Square, "over against the Greyhound". The public house still exists though it has been rebuilt. It was here that he gave a party for Charlotte Brontë who was so forbidding in her uncommunicative shyness that Thackeray slipped away to his club and the evening was a dismal failure.

Back in the High Street, we pass several great stores, including Derry and Toms, on the roof of which is a garden. It was created in 1936 by the landscape architect, Ralph Hancock, though the inspiration came from Trevor Bowen, the chairman of Barkers. It has an Italian garden and a Spanish cloister, goldfish and flamingos, rose gardens and pools; it is an enchanting place with a superb view over London on a clear day. The garden is open from Easter to September; an admittance fee is charged and the proceeds from it go to charity. Just behind Derry and Toms in Iverna Gardens is the Armenian Church of St Sarkis built in 1922 by Caloust Sarkis Gulbenkian as a memorial to his parents, and off the far end of the High Street are Edwardes and Pembroke Squares, two of the prettiest places imaginable. Edwardes Square was completed by 1819 and No. 5 is particularly attractive, while Holman Hunt lived at No. 32. In the centre is a garden for the residents, with a little summerhouse called The Temple. Pembroke Square is a little later.

The borough boundary is at the western end of the High Street. Travelling south down Warwick Road, Warwick Gardens, where G. K. Chesterton lived at No. 11, are on the left, and Earls Court Exhibition Centre, built in 1937 to designs by Howard Crane, is on the right. Beyond the exhibition hall is Brompton Cemetery, consecrated in 1840 as part of the same hygienic reformation which created Kensal Green. There is an octagonal chapel with great colonnades designed by Baud, and here lie Sir Henry Cole and Captain Fowke who contributed so much to the development of Kensington. Two monuments are especially sympathetic, those to Robert Coombes and John Jackson. Coombes, who died in 1860, was the champion sculler of the Thames and Tyne and his memorial, with an upturned skiff on top, bears the lines:

> *Then farewell, my trim-built wherry—*
> *Oars, and coat, and badge, farewell.*

They are taken from Dibden's operetta, *The Waterman*, and are most apt.

Jackson—"Gentleman" Jackson—was one of the finest boxers of his day (d. 1845): a large lion sits on his monument, holding his portrait between its paws. Dr John Snow, the anaesthetist and epidemiologist, who saved London from a cholera epidemic in 1854, lies here too. He persuaded the Vestry to remove the handle from the pump in Broad Street, Golden Square, for he realised the contagion was water-borne. His memorial was restored by the Society of Anaesthetists after wartime bombing.

This is the Earls Court area which takes its name from the title of the Earls of Oxford who once held the manor, the line becoming extinct with the 20th earl in 1703. Today the tube station stands near the site of the old Court House. Earls Court House which stood opposite, was the home of the great surgeon John Hunter. West London Air Terminal, built in 1963 to designs by Sir John Burnet, Tait and Partners, is on the Cromwell Road with coaches scurrying between it and Heathrow Airport. South of the Old Brompton Road is a quiet and expensive residential area, centering on The Boltons, an oval made from two crescents of houses. In the middle stands St Mary's Church, built in 1850 by George Gordon. It is shaped like a Greek cross and a high tower rises above the crossing of nave and transepts. The east window created by Margaret Kay in 1954 is very beautiful. Just off The Boltons is Bousfield Primary School, one of the best in the country, built on the site of Beatrix Potter's home, No. 2 Bolton Gardens.

The Old Brompton Road leads back to the Victoria and Albert Museum, having passed such architectural delights as Pelham Crescent, Thurloe Square, and Alexander Square. Beside the museum is a statue of Cardinal Newman by Bodley and Garner, and beyond is Brompton Oratory. The Oratorians were established in England in 1847 largely owing to the support of the cardinal. The church was designed by H. Gribble in 1878, and is fervently Italian, with dramatic decorations by C. T. G. Formilli and huge statues of the Apostles in marble, made about 1680 for Siena Cathedral by G. Mazzuoli. There are several side chapels; in the one dedicated to St Joseph is the altar from the original Oratory which stood in King William Street. Behind the Oratory stands the parish church, Holy Trinity, well set back from the road, with a green churchyard behind it. It was designed in 1826–29 by Professor Donaldson.

At the end of the Brompton road, we reach the eastern boundary of the borough and with it Harrods, the most complete department store in the world. Harrods can arrange a christening, a wedding, or a funeral and can provide its customers with everything they are likely to need, to eat, to use, or to wear, between birth and death. It opened in smaller premises in 1849 and its present terracotta building—Kensington's own colour—was built in 1901-5 from designs by Stevens and Munt. Its façade lit up for Christmas is one of the sights dearest to the small Londoners. Even in the 20th century, it seems one of the stable institutions in life. Behind Harrods, in Pont Street, lies St Columba's Church. The Church of Scotland first erected a building here in 1883-84; it was destroyed by fire-bombs on the night of Saturday, May 10, 1941. A new church, designed by Sir Edward Maufe, was built and consecrated in 1955; it is one of the strongest and most serene churches in all London, of white stone both without and within. Near it are Beauchamp Place and Walton Street with their smaller fascinating shops, and the rebuilt Yeomans Row with its pleasant urban prospect. Opposite Harrods, at 70 Brompton Road, is the Independent Television Authority's Television Gallery, which houses a fascinating display on the history of television. Some of Baird's original equipment is here. The gallery may be visited, free of charge, by previous appointment.

If Kensington owes its inception to the establishment of the palace at the very end of the 17th century, and its inspiration to the Great Exhibition of 1851, many of **Chelsea**'s most vital associations go back to much earlier times. Today it is a narrow triangle of land, bounded by the Thames and the Fulham and Brompton roads on its long sides, by Westminster on the third, shorter one, and bisected by the King's Road which runs through it like a spine. The name is first mentioned in 8th century Saxon charters, and several church councils or synods were held there in those early times, but Chelsea became significant about 1520 when Sir Thomas More, saint, scholar, diplomat, and king's councillor, bought land there on which to build his "poore house". He was born in 1478, the son of Sir John More, a judge. He was educated at St Anthony's School and in Cardinal Morton's household. The cardinal, who was also Archbishop of Canterbury, used to say of him "Whosoever liveth to see it, shall see this child come to an excellent and marvellous proof." More then went to Oxford for two years and then began to study law, living for a while in Charterhouse (see p. 287) while he considered whether or not he had a vocation for religious life. He decided against it and married Jane Colt who bore him three daughters and a son before her death in 1511. Their house was in Bucklersbury in the City where More was much employed by the

City Companies as a most skilful lawyer and negotiator. He was sent to Calais on a commercial embassy in 1516 and was so successful that the king demanded his services and sent him on a diplomatic mission in the following year. Thereafter his promotion at court was rapid; he became Speaker of the House of Commons in 1523, High Steward of both Oxford and Cambridge, and Lord Chancellor in 1529.

More was among the first of the many busy and successful men who have found that they needed a quiet retreat within easy reach of London and yet away from its noise and bustle. He bought land adjacent to the riverside Village of Chelsea, within easy reach of Westminster, the City, or Hampton Court by water, and there built his home, which he shared with his second wife, Alice Middleton, his children and, as they married, their husbands and wives, and their children. His son John married his ward, Anne Cresacre, and she had a necklace of pearls as a wedding gift—she is wearing it in the big family portrait by Holbein in the National Portrait Gallery. His daughters had been as well-educated as his son and here they all made music together, and were visited by Erasmus and Holbein, who probably designed the capitals for the chapel which More built on to the parish church. Here Henry visited More and walked with his chancellor, an arm about his neck, so that all men wondered at the favour the king showed him save Sir Thomas himself, who knew that the royal friendship might well prove fleeting, as indeed it did when he refused to take the oath acknowledging Henry as the Supreme Head of the Church in England. He resigned the Chancellorship in 1532, told his family that they must be content with Lincoln's Inn fare or, if that proved too costly for their resources, must live like the poor scholars of Oxford, and if they could not maintain that humble estate, then they must go begging together. He gave his barge to his successor, found another place for his fool, and settled down to wait quietly for the end which he knew must come. More was too great a man, too well-known throughout Europe, for the king to abide his tacit disapproval, and in 1534 he was arrested, taken to the Tower, and beheaded in the following year (see p. 382). Of all those who have lived in Chelsea and loved the riverside "village of palaces" as it came to be called, there is none more intimately associated with it than Sir Thomas, one of the earliest, and the best, of all its residents.

After his death, his house and property, with the exception of a house he had given to his favourite daughter Margaret and her husband, William Roper, who wrote a life of his father-in-law, was sequestered and passed from hand to hand. In 1627, it was granted by Charles I to George Villiers, Duke of Buckingham, who was murdered, and in 1682 it was sold to Henry, Marquis of Worcester and later Duke of Beaufort. Thereafter it was called Beaufort House and Beaufort Street runs across its site.

Others were swift to follow More's example in preferring Chelsea, and in 1536 Henry VIII purchased the manor and built a house beside the river on a site today covered by Nos. 19–26 Cheyne Walk. Anne of Cleves lived there after her fortunate divorce, and died there peacefully. Catherine Parr settled there as Henry's widow with the young Princess Elizabeth in her charge, but their happy existence was disrupted when Catherine got married again, to Thomas Seymour, younger brother of the Duke of Somerset who was Lord Protector, and the dashing but foolhardy man paid too much attention to the young princess. She was sent to Hatfield and people began to watch Seymour very closely. He ended on the scaffold, charged—fairly—with treason and piracy.

The house that had been the Ropers' was eventually sold in 1623 to Sir John Danvers who built a fine mansion here with sculptures by Nicholas Stone in the garden. He was an exceptionally handsome man who married a widowed lady rather older than himself, Magdalene, Lady Herbert. She was the mother of the poet George Herbert and it was of her that John Donne, who preached her funeral sermon in 1627, wrote:

> *No Spring, nor Summer Beauty hath such grace*
> *As I have seen in one Autumnall face.*

Sir John was one of those who signed Charles I's death warrant, but was fortunate enough to die peacefully in his own home in 1655. The house was pulled down before 1720: Danvers Street and Paulton's Square stand on the site. The gardens had begun to be built over before the house was destroyed; in one of them Dean Swift lodged in 1711 and heard a fellow crying "R-r-r-are Chelsea Buns!"

Sir John had as neighbours Sir Robert Stanley and the physician, Sir Theodore Turquet de Mayerne. Sir Robert built a house at the western extremity of Chelsea—St Mark's College, King's Road, stands in its grounds and the house itself was rebuilt about 1700 and is now the Principal's residence. He married Lady Elizabeth Gorges and they built their house on land sold to them by her mother who possessed another part of the More estate. Sir Robert died in 1632 and is buried in the parish church with a memorial decorated with portrait busts of himself and his two tiny children, Ferdinand and Henrietta. All three carved faces are immensely compelling—Sir Robert's eyes seem to follow the visitor about the church. A central urn is surmounted by an eagle—the Stanley crest—and an eagle comes into the children's epitaph:

> *The Eagle Death greedie of some good prey*
> *With nimble Eyes found where these Infants laye*
> *He truste them in his Tallents and conveyde*
> *There Soules to Heaven & here theire ashes layde.*

Sir Theodore was the utterly dependable French doctor who attended Charles I, Henrietta Maria, the royal children, and as many of the nobility as he had time to see. He lived in what had been the main farmhouse attached to More's estate from about 1639 till his death in 1645. The house was pulled down and rebuilt in the 1670s by the Earl of Lindsay who was visited there by Charles I in 1674 while the ringers at the church sounded a peal for the king and were paid 10 shillings for their pains.

In the 1750s, the house was sold to Count Zinzendorf who headed the Moravian colony in England, and behind the house, to this day, is a burial ground of the members of this quiet, steadfast, and kindly Protestant sect. The house was sub-divided into separate tenements in 1775 and is now Nos. 95–100 Cheyne Walk. No. 98 was from 1811 till 1826 the home of the masterful engineers, Sir Marc Brunel and his young son, Isambard Kingdom, who was to surpass even his father. In the early years of this century Nos. 99 and 100 were united as the home of Sir Hugh Lane, the collector and founder of the Dublin Art Gallery.

Towards the end of the 17th century, there were three significant events in the history of Chelsea. The Society of Apothecaries started a Physic Garden there in 1673, the Royal Hospital was founded in 1684, and in 1698 the manor passed to William, Lord Cheyne. The Physic Garden was established in Chelsea because the healthy air and fertile soil encouraged growth. The apothecaries first rented the ground but were later given the freehold by Sir Hans Sloane on condition that they should annually provide 50 specimens of dried plants for the Royal Society. The garden still flourishes today and can be seen through the railings from Cheyne Walk, Sir Hans' statue by Roubiliac standing in the centre with fragrance all around him. It was from here that cotton seed was sent to America from which the cotton plantations were established.

The Royal Hospital lies in the eastern corner of the borough. It was built in imitation of the Hôtel des Invalides in Paris established by Louis XIV as a home and refuge for soldiers grown old in his service or disabled in his wars. Charles II wished to emulate the French monarch—he had received glowing descriptions of the institution from his son, the Duke of Monmouth, who was visiting Paris—and he founded the Royal Hospital in 1682. The site was that of Chelsea College, a theological college founded by James I in 1609 but which had never thriven. Sir Stephen Fox, the Paymaster-General, bought the site out of his own pocket and gave up his commission of fourpence in the pound on army pay to finance the building and the establishment of the hospital, for the king could only contribute some £7000. John Evelyn was asked to give his advice on the organisation, Sir Christopher Wren was chosen as architect. He planned the buildings around three courtyards— Light Horse Court, Figure Court, and College Court—and their aspect, whether from the river or from Royal Hospital Road, is benign and stalwart. In Figure Court he placed the beautifully panelled council chamber, the chapel and the Great Hall. They are comfortable buildings, fine enough, dignified, but never grandiose. At the one end of the Great Hall is a large mural, begun by Antonio Verrio and completed by Henry Cooke, of Charles II on horseback. Meals are eaten here, the pensioners being served before the officers, as laid down by Sir Christopher Wren, for he wanted to make sure that this was a place where old soldiers would feel honoured and welcomed. It was in this hall that the Duke of Wellington's body lay in state for a week after his death in 1852; the table on which the coffin rested is in the museum attached to the hospital. In the chapel the wainscoting and pews are the work of Sir Charles Hopson, the leading joiner of his day and the Deputy Clerk of Works at the hospital from 1691 till 1698. Between the windows rise pilasters with capitals of cherubs and foliage, and an arched ceiling springs from an elaborate frieze. In the half-dome of the apse is a painting of the Resurrection by Sebastiano Ricci, probably assisted by his nephew Marco, in Queen Anne's day, and below is a magnificent reredos, an arch on two pairs of fluted columns, with a polished panel in the middle, the Star of Bethlehem carved on it. The organ is modern but it is housed in a case by Renatus Harris. The communion plate is exceptionally fine. In the octagonal porch which links the hall and chapel are the staves of trophies captured from the Americans, Dutch, French, Prussians, and Russians, and from various oriental peoples.

On the east and west sides of the Figure Court are the long wards which are the in-pensioners' living quarters. Each man has a berth or cubicle, six feet by nine, wherein, by closing the door and a wooden shutter, he has complete privacy. The upper wards are reached by staircases whose steps have the shallowest of risers, gentle to enfeebled or crippled limbs—Sir Christopher Wren could think of the practical details of a building as well as he could conceive a grand façade, which is one reason why he was probably the greatest architect who has ever lived. There are about 450 in-pensioners who wear scarlet coats and tricorn hats—a modernised version of the service dress of Marlborough's day.

The hall, chapel, and museum, where an astonishing collection of medals won by pensioners is displayed as well as other interesting relics, are open daily; the council chamber can be seen on Sundays only. Visitors may attend morning service on Sundays when the Parade Service is held at 11 a.m. and the chapel looks as if Herkomer's painting, *The Last Muster*, has come to life. On May 29, Oak Apple Day and Founder's Day, the statue of Charles II (by Grinling Gibbons, presented by Tobias Rustat, who also gave £1,000 to the hospital) is wreathed with greenery in memory of his escape after the Battle of Worcester by hiding in Boscobel Oak, and the pensioners parade in his honour.

At the east end of the hospital is the burial ground, where 10,000 pensioners lie, in company with others associated with the hospital, such as William Cheseldon, a wonderful surgeon and the man who attended Sir Isaac Newton on his deathbed, and Dr Charles Burney, organist at the hospital from 1783 till 1814, author of *The General History of Music*, and the father of Fanny Burney, the novelist. Here at their own request lie two women warriors, who joined up as men to search for their husbands, Christiana Davis and Hannah Snell. Adjacent to the hospital in Chelsea Bridge Road, though actually in Westminster, stand Chelsea Barracks, built 1960–62 and designed by Tripe and Wakeham, a building good enough to stand beside Wren's hospital, which is high praise indeed. On the other side of the hospital is the new Army Museum, opened in 1971. It deals with the history of the British Army from the reign of Henry VII to the outbreak of the First World War, when the story is taken up by the Imperial War Museum. It also tells the story of the Indian Army until 1947. In the grounds, on the Thames side, is an obelisk to the memory of those who fell in the Sikh wars, and here the Chelsea Flower Show is held each May so that for a few days all Chelsea seems to have become one vast glorious bouquet.

317

On the landward side of the hospital and belonging to it, is a large green square, Burton's Court. On its far side is St Leonard's Terrace with some pretty 18th century houses. From it runs Royal Avenue, laid out and planted with four rows of limes on the orders of William III to connect the Royal Hospital with the King's Road. The road had been made as a connection between Whitehall and Hampton Court and Charles II had hoped to keep it private, but realising the unpopularity of the move, he wisely opened it to the public. It would be interesting to hear that monarch's comments on today's sartorial extravagances of the King's Road, could he but return to it.

A few years after he inherited Chelsea, Lord Cheyne began to develop his estate by building Cheyne Row in 1708, which was joined by Cheyne Walk, built at right-angles to it, along the river front, beginning about 1717. There is little or nothing left of the original houses today, but the terrace, Nos. 19–26 with several beautiful front doors, was built about 1760 and stands on the site of Henry VIII's manor house. No. 16, Queen's House, is a large and lovely dwelling where Rossetti and Swinburne lived. The walk stretches westward to Cremorne Road and includes Lindsay House, now separate dwellings, with a magnificently carved doorway. The line of the Walk is broken near the church by the recently opened Roper's Gardens, with well-stocked flowerbeds and a pretty statue, *The Awakening*, by Gilbert Ledward.

In 1712, Sir Hans Sloane bought the manor and 30 years later established himself there with his amazing collection of books, manuscripts, coins, gems, fossils, minerals, curiosities, botanical and natural specimens. He was an excellent physician and an ardent natural historian; he was first Secretary and later President of the Royal Society. He was very wealthy, both by his own efforts and by his marriage with the widow of a Jamaican planter—he had been physician to the Governor of Jamaica and had produced a catalogue of the plants of that beautiful island—and he spent his money well and wisely. The last 11 years of his life he passed in Chelsea, dying in 1753 at the age of 92. One great injury he did to Chelsea, for he had Sir Thomas More's old home, Beaufort House, demolished in 1740. The gateway from the house, designed by Inigo Jones, was removed to Chiswick House. After his death, he willed that his collection should go to the nation for £20,000 which he felt was no more than a quarter of its value. It was bought and with the Cottonian and Harleian manuscripts became the nucleus of the British Museum Collections. The rejects from his collection had been carefully preserved by his valet James Salter, who opened a coffee house adorned with them at No. 18 Cheyne Walk. James became known as "Don Saltero", and the coffee house became a popular rendezvous. His estate Sir Hans left to his daughters, Elizabeth, Lady Cadogan, and Mrs Sarah Stanley. Lord Cadogan leased land to the architect, Henry Holland, who built himself a villa, The Pavilion, and laid out Hans Place, Sloane Street, and Cadogan Square.

Memories of all these illustrious landowners and many others are gathered together in All Saints parish church which stands beside the river. The chancel of the church dated from the 13th century and the nave and tower from the 17th, but great damage was done by bombs in 1941. Most of the monuments were saved and re-instated when the church was rebuilt and reconsecrated in 1958. More's own chapel is on the south side of the chancel. It contains a plain recessed tomb with an inscription to his two wives who both lie here. Jane is described as *chara uxorcula*—his dear little wife; Alice is praised for her tenderness to Jane's children. The words are by More himself, who hoped that he would lie here in their company. His body, however, is in the Chapel of St Peter in the Tower and his severed head, snatched by his daughter Margaret from where it was impaled on London Bridge, is in the Roper vault at Canterbury.

There are wall plaques with small kneeling figures to Thomas Hungerford (d. 1581) and Thomas Lawrence (d. 1593) and their wives and children, a good brass to Sir Arthur Gorges (d. 1625) with all his family about him, and a magnificent one to the Duchess of Northumberland who is shown with all her 13 children. Gregory, Lord Dacre, and his wife have a splendid monument, on which their effigies lie, life-sized, Lord Dacre in full armour. There is a free-standing, decorated arch to Richard Jervoise (d. 1563), like a proud triumphal arch. One of the most dramatic monuments is to Sara Colville (d. 1631), whose effigy rises from its shroud, eyes and hands raised to heaven; the work is inspired by Nicholas Stone's memorial to John Donne in St Paul's Cathedral. The Stanley tomb has already been described, but Lady Cheyne's is also very fine with a life-sized recumbent figure of the lady carved by Pietro Bernini, the great sculptor's son. The Hon. William Ashburnham lies here too; one evening he absent-mindedly wandered into the misty Thames and only found his way back to shore by the ringing of the church bells. Dying in 1679, he left money for a bell which was to be rung each evening thereafter and the practice was continued

319

till 1822. In the churchyard lie little Elizabeth Smollett, the writer's adored daughter from whose death he never really recovered, and Sir Hans Sloane whose memorial is an urn by Joseph Wilton. Between the churchyard and the river is a statue of Sir Thomas More, set up in 1970, the work of L. Cubitt Bevis.

This is a church so crowded with memories that the visitor needs to return again and again, but even on a first visit attention should be paid to the hassocks embroidered by the ladies of the parish, each one different and each one with a portrait or symbol in memory of a famous resident. This is an enchanting way of telling Chelsea's history.

Near to the church are Swan Walk and Lawrence Street. The Swan public house, from which the Walk takes its name, was the finishing point of the race between boatmen instituted in 1716 by Robert Doggett in honour of George I's accession; the prize was a coat, cap, and badge. In Lawrence Street stood the Chelsea china works which flourished from about 1745 till 1785, producing exquisite wares. Dr Johnson visited the pottery regularly to try his hand at the work but was most unsuccessful; when he relinquished his attempts, the manufactory presented him with a dinner service.

While Sir Hans Sloane lived in Chelsea, there were gay doings in the eastern corner, just beyond the Royal Hospital. Richard, Earl of Ranelagh, had had a house there; 30 years after his death in 1712, the grounds were opened as a public pleasure garden, much to the annoyance of the hospital. A rotunda, designed by William Jones, was built, masquerades were held which George III and the royal family attended, and Mozart, aged eight, played the harpsichord and organ there in 1764. Horace Walpole wrote enthusiastically of a masquerade there in 1749. It was meant to be in "the Venetian manner"; there was "nothing Venetian in it but was by far the best understood and prettiest spectacle I ever saw: nothing in a fairy tale ever surpassed it." But by the turn of the century, Ranelagh's hey-day was past and a balloon ascent by Garnerin did little to revive it. It was closed in 1805; the grounds are now a park belonging to Chelsea Hospital but open to the public. It had a successor, however, in Cremorne Gardens, these being in the extreme western corner of Chelsea. They opened in 1845 in what had been the grounds of Viscount Cremorne's house, and flourished till 1875. Montgolfier made balloon ascents from here and Madame Genevieve walked a tightrope across the Thames. When they closed, they were replaced by houses and, nearby, Lot's Road Power Station.

By this time, the river had been embanked (1874), thereby much altering the character of Chelsea, and three bridges spanned the Thames. Old Battersea Bridge had been built of wood in 1772 by Earl Spencer, and was a subject for many artists, including Turner, De Wint, Girtin, Varley, and Whistler, but it was pulled down in 1887 and was replaced by the present structure three years later. The Albert Bridge and the present Chelsea Bridge were built in 1873 and 1934 respectively. They are both suspension bridges and an informative comparison in changes of style during 60 years can be made by examining the differences between the two.

Two new churches had been built as well, a new parish church, St Luke's, Sydney Street, and Holy Trinity, Sloane Street. St Luke's was designed by Savage between 1820 and 1824, and is one of the earliest of churches of the Gothic Revival. It is a plain dignified church with Northcote's *Descent from the Cross* over the altar, and a good monument by Chantrey to Lt-Col. Henry Cadogan who fell at the Battle of Vittoria in 1813. The original Holy Trinity was also by Savage but was replaced by another church designed by Sedding in 1890. This is a splendid, lively building by an exceptionally interesting architect. Many other members of the Arts and Crafts Movement contributed to it, and Burne-Jones designed the glass in the huge east windows.

Throughout the 19th century, Chelsea was full of artists and writers. Holbein had been the first, but 300 years later he was followed by Turner who took a house, now 119 Cheyne Walk, during the 1830s and divided his time between that and his finer dwelling in Queen Anne Street, Marylebone, till his death in 1851. Sometimes he painted the river, but more often he drew inspiration from it. John Martin, who painted enormous reconstructions of biblical scenes, was at 4 Lindsey House from 1848 to 1854, Holman Hunt painted *The Light of the World* and *The Hireling Shepherd* at 5 Prospect Place (now replaced by the Children's Hospital, Cheyne Walk) where he lived from 1850 to 1854, and visited Dante Gabriel Rossetti at 16 Cheyne Walk. Rossetti spent the last 21 years of his life there and the poet Algernon Swinburne stayed with him for part of the time. A later Pre-Raphaelite, William de Morgan, had a series of Chelsea addresses, notably 30 Cheyne Row where he lived from 1872 to 1882, renting No. 36, where the Roman Catholic Church of the Holy Redeemer now stands, for his pottery work on his inimitable and lovely lustreware. From 1887 to 1909, he and his artist wife Evelyn were at No. 1 The Vale, and when that was about to be demolished, they gave a house-cooling party when they closed the cul-de-sac, festooned lanterns up and down it, stationed Chelsea Pensioners in their scarlet coats at the entrance to the lane, and gave the visitors access to all the gardens. De Morgan describes it in his autobiography, *The Old Man's Youth*. He died at 127 Church Street where he wrote those wonderful novels of his last years. Philip Wilson Steer, that quiet expressive painter, lived at 109 Cheyne Walk from 1898 till his death in 1942, and was not driven out by the bombs that fell around him. He had had as neighbours Whistler and Sargent who lived at 33 Tite Street. Steer was a founder member of the Chelsea Arts Club which opened in 1891 at 181 King's Road and then moved to 143 Old Church Street where it still flourishes. Whistler had eight Chelsea addresses between 1863 and 1903. He lived in Lindsay House from 1866 to 1878, and then at the studio, The White House, in Tite Street which he and that astonishing architect, Edward William Godwin, designed together. He was there a bare eight months, from October 1878 till May 1879. The costs of his libel action against Ruskin for the critic's comments on his paintings, *Fireworks at Cremorne* and *Old Battersea Bridge*, left him bankrupt and the house was sold.

Despite Ruskin's disapproval, Whistler's paintings of Chelsea were, and are, wonderful, and by his patronage of Walter Greaves, he placed London under still greater obligation to him. Greaves (1848–1930) was the son of a boat-builder who lived at 104 Cheyne Walk. Whistler fascinated the boy and his brother Henry and both of them became painters. Walter's superb *Hammersmith Bridge on Boat Race Day* hangs in the Tate Gallery though the artist was only about 16 when he painted it. He died poor, despite the fame which came to him after an exhibition at the Goupil Gallery in 1911, a pensioner in Charterhouse.

Whistler's fellow American, Sargent, spent part of each year from the 1890s till his death in 1925 at his house, 33 Tite Street, and regularly visited his mother and sister who lived in Carlyle Mansions.

Among writers, Mrs Gaskell was born and George Eliot died in Chelsea. Elizabeth Cleghorn Stevenson was born at 93 Cheyne Walk in 1810, but her mother died within a month of her birth and she was sent to her aunt at Knutsford in Cheshire, which provided the material for her novel *Cranford*. Chelsea can at least claim a little share in this determined lady who would write her novels on scraps of paper at the kitchen table with her family around her, and whose deep sympathies with the industrial poor produced *North and South*, while her love of humanity is displayed in *Ruth* and *Wives and Daughters*. Mary Anne Evans, better known as George Eliot (1819–1880) and author of *The Mill on the Floss* and *Middlemarch*, was an ailing woman when she came to 4 Cheyne Walk. George Henry Lewes with whom she had lived for 24 years and whose love and encouragement had enabled her to realise her genius, had died in 1878, leaving her depressed and alone. In March 1880 she married John Cross, a man much younger than herself, who had been a friend to both her and Lewes, and they moved to London for her health which seemed to improve in the Chelsea air. But she went to a concert at the St James's Hall, caught a chill and was dead in less than three weeks of her arrival in the new house.

The author most deeply associated with Chelsea is Thomas Carlyle (1795–1881). The historian and essayist was born in Ecclefechen in Dumfriesshire. He studied at Edinburgh University, took tutoring posts, and wrote for the *Edinburgh Review*. In 1826 he married Jane Baillie Welsh and soon after they went to live at Craiganputtock where she owned a small property, and he wrote *Sartor Resartus*. In 1834, they decided to move to London, and he came up to find a house. He took 5 (now 24) Cheyne Row and they lived there for the rest of their lives. His letter to Jane about his discovery is endearingly enthusiastic and very practical:

Eminent, antique: wainscotted to the very ceiling and has been all new-painted and repaired; broadish stair, with massive balustrade (in the old style) corniced and as thick as one's thigh; floors firm as a rock, wood of them here and there worm-eaten yet capable of cleanness, and still thrice the strength of a modern floor. And then as to room, Goody! . . . Three storeys beside the sunk storey; in every one of them three apartments in depth . . . then . . . a chinaroom, or pantry, or I know not what, all shelved and fit to hold crockery for the whole Street.

The rent was £35 a year and the Carlyles moved in. Over their doorstep came all literary and intellectual London, and all were influenced by or drew strength from the owner's pessimistic but resolute philosophy. Here Carlyle built himself a sound-proof room on the roof to deaden the noise of the local cocks and hens. What he would say of today's aeroplanes does not bear thought. Here Jane's body was laid on the sofa when she died peacefully driving in her carriage in 1866, and here Carlyle lived on alone till his own death 15 years later. Today the house is a museum to their memory and is owned by the National Trust. It is an interesting example of an 18th century house furnished in the somewhat claustrophobic taste of 100 years later.

During the first seven years of his tenancy, Carlyle had as neighbour Leigh Hunt, writer and editor, who lived at 4 (now 22) Upper Cheyne Row with his wife and seven hungry, noisy children. Leigh Hunt, the friend of Shelley, Byron, Keats, and Lamb, loved Chelsea and was happy there, though it was of Kensington that he wrote in *The Old Court Suburb* when he moved to 32 Edwardes Square in 1840. Curiously enough, he and Carlyle liked each other though temperamentally they were very different. Carlyle wrote in his Journal (September 8, 1834) that Leigh Hunt was "a good man" though he could not approve of his household which displayed "hugger-mugger, *un*thrift and sordid collapse". Carlyle described a visit there:

In his family room where are a sickly large wife and a whole school of well-conditioned wild children, you will find half-a-dozen old rickety chairs gathered from half-a-dozen different hucksters and all seeming engaged, and just pausing, in a violent hornpipe. On these and around them and over the dusty table and ragged carpet lie all kinds of litter—books, papers, eggshells, scissors and last night when I was there, the torn heart of a quartern loaf.

In the middle of it all, Hunt sat in his dressing-gown, discoursing on "philosophy and the prospects of Man". He was a brave man as well as a good one, always able to give encouragement and comfort to others however difficult his own situation might have been.

The turn of the 20th century gave Chelsea another pair of dissimilar authors, Oscar Wilde and Henry James. Wilde lived at 16 Tite Street from his marriage in 1884 till his tragic imprisonment in 1895, but though he wrote his plays and polished his witticisms here, he is less closely associated with Chelsea than the meticulously exact American novelist who spent the last years of his life at 21 Carlyle Mansions, Cheyne Walk, and who at the outbreak of the 1914–18 war became a British subject in order to identify himself more closely with this country's fortunes. He is buried in the parish church and there is a wall-tablet there to his memory.

One other resident of Chelsea must be mentioned—one of the most courageous men who has ever lived—Captain Robert Falcon Scott. He lived at 56 Oakley Street during his short married life and it was from there that he set out on his last expedition to reach the South Pole, an expedition as glorious as it was ill-fated.

The additions of the 20th century may seem insignificant compared with Chelsea's past, but they are none the less worth recording. They include those three distinctions of Sloane Square—the fountain by Gilbert Ledward erected in 1953 and paid for out of the money Lord Leighton left the Royal Academy, the façade and interior of Messrs Peter Jones' store, designed in 1936 by Slater, Crabtree, and Moberly which has one of the most satisfactory shopfronts in London, and the Royal Court Theatre, which the dramatist Harley Granville-Barker managed for some while and which reopened in 1952 after war-damage. Ever since then it has put on a series of plays intended to make the audience think hard. Then there is the kaleidoscope of the King's Road where everything that is new or extreme in fashion can be seen; and the public library in Manresa Road which, opening in 1891, was the first to provide a separate room for children with walls decorated with frescoes by students of the Royal College of Art. There is also the exciting new development planned for World's End, the south-west corner of Chelsea, which, when completed in a few years' time, will be one of the largest public housing schemes in London. The gates of Cremorne Gardens have been preserved and are to be given a place of honour. Finally, there is Crosby Hall.

This had stood in Bishopsgate since 1466 when it was built as the great hall of Sir John Crosby's mansion. He was an exceptionally wealthy and successful merchant and Lord Mayor of London. In 1483, the Duke of Gloucester stayed here while he sought to be offered the crown which he later assumed as Richard III. In 1523–24, the hall was for a few months in the possession of Sir Thomas More, though there is no certain evidence that he ever lived there. He sold the lease early in 1524 to his friend, Antonio Bonvisi, Italian merchant and freeman of the City of London, banker and benefactor of scholars. He left the country in Edward VI's reign and the hall came into the hands of Sir John Spencer, "Rich Spencer" (see p. 280), and afterwards into those of his daughter and her husband, the Earl of Northampton. The family held it till 1678 and thereafter it passed into lesser hands and was put to meaner uses. In 1908 the Chartered Bank of India, Australia, and China bought the site for new offices and with great generosity paid for the hall to be taken down carefully and re-erected on a site near to Chelsea old church provided by the University of London. It is today part of the headquarters of the Federation of University

325

Women and its doors are usually open on Saturday and Sunday afternoons so that all may admire the superb roof and noble proportions of the hall. It is very fitting that history's most recent contribution to Chelsea's topography should be to erect a hall which once, even if for a very short while, belonged to its finest resident, on a corner of Sir Thomas More's own garden.

NEWHAM

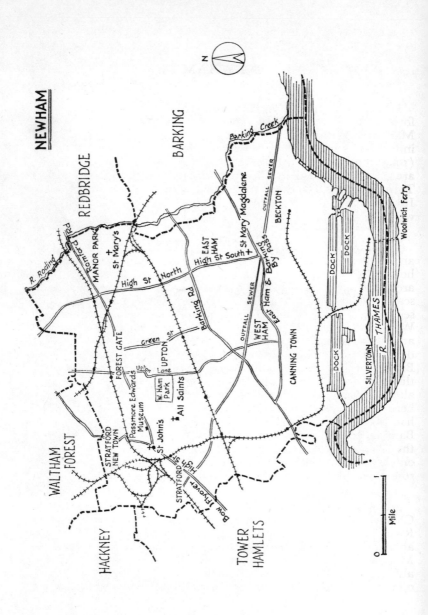

NEWHAM

Newham consists of East Ham and West Ham and includes Stratford, Canning Town, Silver Town, Beckton, Forest Gate, Plashet, Manor Park, and Upton Park. An area largely dockland and industrial, it covers 8986 acres and has a population of 255,130 (1969) though in 1801 there were less than 8000 people in the whole area. It is bounded by the River Thames to the south, and by Tower Hamlets, Hackney, Walthamstow, Redbridge, and Barking. It is level ground, marshy by the Thames and beside the River Lea which forms the boundary with Tower Hamlets.

Until 1965, Newham was part of Essex. The name indicates the antiquity of the area, for it comes from the Anglo-Saxon *ham*—"a homestead". It lies over the Lea and right outside London; it is an area with a real history of its own and a dramatic industrial landscape with cranes stark against the sky and great ships in the docks, seemingly moored inland. During the Blitz of 1940, East Ham and West Ham were most cruelly devastated by bombing, for repeated attacks were made against the docks and 29,000 buildings were damaged in East Ham and 14,000 in West Ham—in one area, Tidal Basin Ward, 85 per cent of the houses were destroyed. After the war the opportunity was taken to clear away remaining slums and, although there are still bombed sites where elderberry bushes, willow herb, and convolvulus flower, by 1969 some 17,768 new dwellings had been built. Viewed from the High Street at Stratford or from Barking Road, Canning Town, this has led to a dramatic change in the skyline, now pierced by many tall blocks of flats where before only cranes, the sides of ships, schools, public buildings, or factories rose above the roofs of terraced dwellings.

Approaching from London, we come first to **Stratford**, not Chaucer's Stratford-atte-Bowe which lies on the London side of the River Lea, but the village which grew up around the Cistercian abbey of Stratford Langthorne, founded about 1135 by Walter de Montfichet, Lord of Ham; the crozier in Newham's arms recalls the abbots and the chevrons the Montfichet family. As we leave London, our eyes are drawn to the graceful arc of Bow Flyover, completed in

1967 and serving the same purpose as the original Bow Bridge, the first arched stone bridge in Essex, which gave a name to the area. It was built by that eminently practical Queen, Matilda, wife to Henry I. She also built the causeway over Stratford Marsh, for she herself had once barely escaped drowning in the Lea, and her bridge continued to be used till it was replaced in 1839. The care of the bridge was the responsibility first of the abbess of Barking, and then of the abbot of Stratford Langthorne. The abbey covered several acres, its gate being in what is now Bakers' Row off Abbey Road, but it has all disappeared with the exception of some window tracery now built into the long south porch of West Ham parish church. Nearby, however, approached by a footpath beside the Channelsea river and now part of Messrs Nicholson's gin distillery, are three 18th century mills, which stand on a site that once belonged to the abbey, and grinding wheels have gone round here since the brethren ground their corn in the middle ages.

The main church in Stratford today is St John's in The Broadway, a large building designed by Teulon in 1834. Near its site was erected the stake at which men and women were burnt for the Protestant faith during the unhappy Marian persecution. Eighteen people suffered in all, 11 men and two women on June 27, 1556, in the same fire which was said to have been the turning point of the Protestant movement in England, so bitter was the feeling that it aroused. Earlier that year, Hugh Laverock and John Apprice, the one blind and the other lame, had died there, jesting at the stake that they would soon be healed of their infirmities. (It is debatable whether the burning took place here or at Stratford-atte-Bowe across the Lea.) A memorial designed by J. T. Newman and erected to them in 1874 stands in the churchyard with a relief of the burning taken from Foxe's *Book of Martyrs* and the names and dates of the victims. The spire is capped with a martyr's crown. At this time, a boy was born in Stratford, the son of that Lord Mayor of London whose ships are said to have begun the slave trade with Africa. His name was Thomas Lodge and he was set to study the law but left it to become a poet and a playwright. While on a long voyage to the Canaries, he wrote a romance called *Rosalynde*, from which Shakespeare is said to have taken the plot of *As You Like It*. Near to the church, at No. 30 Romford Road, is an attractive weatherboarded house, and not far away is a good 18th century terrace. With the coming of the railways the area was abruptly developed. What is today Stratford New Town was built to house the workers, and was then known as Hudson's Town after the "railway king".

Next to Stratford is **West Ham**, whose most important old building is the parish church, dedicated to All Saints. It has a complicated building history for the nave walls are Norman with blocked clerestorey windows—there must have been a great church here once—the pillars in the nave are 13th century but the roof above them has beams which date from Henry VII's or Henry VIII's days, about 1500. The chancel arch and the tower, of stone much patched with brick, date from about 1400, the south chancel chapel with octagonal piers is 15th century, and the handsome north chapel about 1550. This chapel is of red brick with blue brick diapering and has fine three- and four-light windows with brick mullions. There is a long brick cloister to the south porch, near which is set one two-light late mediaeval window from Langthorne Abbey, and from the same source comes a stone carved with a skull, set into the inner north wall of the tower. On the outer south wall is a big square sundial of 1803.

Within the church is an unusual collection of monuments. On the chancel arch is an Elizabethan brass of Thomas Staples faced by four women, beneath are 20 verses, one for every shilling he left as an annuity to the poor. In a round-headed recess in the chancel wall are kneeling figures of John and Frances Faldo who died in 1613 and 1632; they look very small beside the later monuments. In the north chapel is a memorial with rich pilasters framing the armoured figure of Captain Robert Rooke and his two wives with their seven children. Sir Thomas Foote, a Lord Mayor of London in Restoration days, stands, wearing his chain of office, with his wife beside a fine urn. Nearby are cherubs adorning the monument of one of his successors, Sir James Smith, who died in the reign of Queen Anne. William Fawcit and his wife kneel facing each other; the lady's first husband reclines below, comfortably reading a book. Nicholas and Eleanor Buckeridge lost their five children between 1698 and 1710; the whole family cluster together on their memorial. They were related to that Thomas Buckeridge who wished to have his remains mingled with those of his "dear and innocent child" at West Ham Church. He was a friend of Sir Godfrey Kneller and the Duke of Buckingham and wrote *Lives of the English Painters*. There are two exceptionally fine figures of James Cooper (d. 1743) and his wife who stand together in a niche; it would be interesting to know who was the sculptor.

Near to the church is West Ham Park which used to be the grounds of Ham House, now demolished. Samuel Gurney, the Quaker philanthropist, lived at Ham House, and at The Cedars nearby lived his sister Elizabeth Fry with her family (for her story see p. 19). The park was "dedicated to the people" by the City of London Corporation in 1874. There was a large Quaker community in West Ham in the 18th and early 19th centuries and among them were Dr John Fotheringill the botanist who maintained there a garden which in its day ranked second only to Kew, and Joseph Lister, later Lord Lister, who was born at Upton House in Upton Lane in 1827. The house has gone and a block of flats, Lister House, stands on the site, but the man's work lives on and has benefited generations.

Lister took his medical degree at the age of 25, became professor of surgery at Glasgow eight years later, and worked there for many years returning at last to spend the final 16 years of his working life at King's College. It was as a prince of surgeons that he devised the methods associated forever with his name. He worked in hospitals where 80 per cent of those operated upon died from infections following treatment. When Pasteur announced his discovery of infection from germs, Lister realised that these were the cause of the appalling mortality. He sought out sterilising agents and prevented the wounds getting in contact with anything calculated to create septic conditions. Almost at once he reduced mortality by 65 per cent, and today hardly a life is lost after an operation which, little more than 100 years ago, would almost certainly have been fatal.

Half-way along Upton Lane, not far from Lister's birthplace, is a weatherboarded 17th century public house, the Spotted Dog, where it is said that London merchants used to meet in plague times to transact business, and on the far side of West Ham Park, in the Romford Road, is the Public Library, the College of Technology, and the Passmore Edwards Museum. The buildings were designed in 1896–98 by Gibson and Russell with columns and turrets and statues and a cupola. They stand well back from the road and are an exciting and endearing group. The museum, maintained and staffed by the borough, owes much to the Essex Field Club and John Passmore Edwards, the philanthropist, whose bust is in the main hall. The Countess of Warwick performed the opening ceremony in 1900 of this, the only purpose-built museum in the county. The building is therefore of considerable interest to students of late Victorian architecture. The museum also has the distinction of having its functions clearly defined; to quote the lawyer's prose, it should be administered as "a centre of information and study of Biology Zoology Geology Topography Meteorology and Ethnology and kindred studies with particular reference to Essex and of the pre-history antiquities and industries of Essex"! The central feature of the Natural History Gallery is a large pond surrounded by flowers, which contains a selection of local fish. Other exhibitions display the wildlife of Essex, and there is a small gallery for displays of the work of local artists or for loan exhibitions. The upper galleries deal with the history of Essex from the formation of its geological features to the end of the 19th century. There is a particularly good selection of palaeolithic material from the Lea Valley and a small but significant collection of Bow porcelain made within walking distance of the museum. The 19th century exhibits are housed in the very striking Rotunda Gallery and illustrate the growth of population, industry, and transport as well as agriculture and obsolete country crafts. There is also a laboratory, reserve collections such as the Lister Herbarium, and a most helpful and able staff.

The museum is a place of which West Ham is justly very proud, and would have delighted George Edwards who was born here in 1694. He went to a clergyman's school in Leytonstone and read incessantly while he was apprenticed in the City. He travelled in Holland and Scandinavia, where his naturalist pursuits seemed so suspicious that he was arrested as a spy, but he returned home to become Librarian of the Royal College of Physicians. He studied fossils, corresponded with Linnaeus and spent 21 years writing a great *History of Birds*, which was published from 1743 to 1764. In it there are some 500 wonderful paintings of bird scenes, and he worked on till he was an old man and was at last laid to rest in the church-yard at West Ham.

The Bow porcelain in the museum reminds us of a local industry which flourished from 1748/9 till 1776 in premises on the north side of Stratford High Street. Exquisite little figures and trinkets were produced which are today sought after by collectors. Another local industry, which was founded in 1676 by William Sherwin and lasted for 200 years, was calico-printing and there were 80 acres of calico grounds by the Channelsea, a tributary of the Lea, in Stratford. West Ham, being outside the London boundaries with their restrictions on factories and some of the more noisome trades, was a place where industry could flourish, and flourish it did, alongside market-gardening. It was West Ham South that returned the first Labour MP to Westminster, James Keir Hardie, who held the seat from 1892 till 1895, and was, on taking his seat, escorted to Parliament by a brass band. Ships were built in West Ham throughout the 19th century and the Thames Ironworks flourished from 1858 till 1911, when its last ship was the Dreadnought *Thunderer*, which fought at the battle of Jutland, of which engagement we shall have more to say.

But what has really made Newham what it is today are the docks. By the middle of the 19th century, the older docks near London could not accommodate the larger steam vessels which were entering the Thames. Here, at what has become Canning Town, Silvertown, and Beckton, was unencumbered level land, already about 10 feet below high-water mark, and easy to excavate. Furthermore it was linked to London by the Barking Road and the new North Woolwich railway line. The Royal Victoria Dock was constructed between 1850 and 1855. During excavations a pre-Roman canoe was found which is today in the British Museum—surely one of the earliest craft to navigate these waters! The Royal Victoria Dock covers 83 acres of water and was the first dock in the country to use hydraulic machinery. In 1880 the Royal Albert Dock was opened, a mile long and 500 feet wide; it was the first public undertaking in the country to be lit by electricity. But even these docks were too small for some 20th century vessels and in 1921 the King George V Dock was opened with a depth of 38 feet and a lock large enough to admit the *Mauretania* herself when she came up the Thames in 1939. This group of docks is the largest area of impounded dock water in the world. They cover 1000 acres of which 230 are water and can accommodate 50 ocean-going vessels at any one time.

It is a stark landscape. Cranes rear up against the sky, great ships seem to have floated inland, and factories such as Tate and Lyle sugar refinery or Beckton gas works, the largest in Europe, brood over it all. On the east, or Beckton, side of the docks, stretching away to Barking Creek, are flat open marshlands, irrigated by little channels and littered with small prefabricated houses, most of them well-kept. There are two havens, St Mark's Church, Silvertown, and the Royal Victoria Gardens. St Mark's was designed by S. S. Teulon in 1861–82. It is of brick with a comfortable porch, an apse, and a crossing tower with a pyramid roof. It stands near an almost deserted railway and its little well-tended rose garden is wonderfully calm and quiet. The Royal Victoria Gardens (formerly in North Woolwich) are most imaginatively maintained. There is not a scrap of litter to be seen, the flowerbeds are well-stocked, there are plenty of trees including four weeping ash trees clipped into neat umbrellas, and a look-out platform from which young and old can survey the river and the Kentish shore of the Thames.

334

East Ham, which shares the docks with West Ham, is just to the north. Across it runs the hump of the Northern Outfall Sewer, designed by Sir Joseph Bazalgette in 1864; its pumping station at Stratford is one of the glories of Victorian ironwork and should be preserved as such.

The main parish church is St Bartholomew's in the Barking Road. Designed in 1901 by Micklethwaite and Somers Clarke, it was bombed and was rebuilt after the last war. It is a fine big building of red brick. The mediaeval mother church, dedicated to Mary Magdalene, still stands and flourishes, at the far end of the High Street South. It is one of the very few scarcely altered Norman churches to be found in the London area, and there are few more lovely or more lovingly tended. The body of the church dates from about 1130, though there are Roman bricks used in with the Norman pudding-stone, and the upper part of the tower is 16th century. The church consists of a nave, chancel, and apse only, without aisles. The nave is high and wide, the chancel and apse each lower and narrower than the other. The nave has a timber roof, the chancel a vaulted one with intersecting arches decorated with zigzag carving, and the Norman west doorway which now opens into the tower, has chevron carvings too. In the north chancel wall, there is an opening into the cell of a hermit or anchorite, and above it a fragment of a carving, the head and wings of a cherub. Along the same wall are the remains of a lovely interlacing arcade of round arches with zigzag. Four arches are complete but the rest have been cut into for tombs and for a Tudor doorway to the rood-stairs. The apse is entered by a noble, semi-circular arch, and its roof is unique, unaltered and unrepaired since the Normans completed it in 1130. It is held together with wooden pegs and is the greatest treasure the church contains. The apse was once vaulted and the lines of the mural decorations of 1230 show this quite plainly. Within it, there is a 13th century double piscina; another has been uncovered in the nave. There are traces of wall-paintings and the font which has a fine bowl of 1639 balanced on a later stem, was the gift of Sir Richard Heigham, to whose relation, William, there is a lovely wall-stone with two gilt cherubs, one holding a spade, the other a trumpet. There is a brass to Hester Neve in Stuart dress and high on the chancel wall is a brightly painted monument with shields, pilasters, and obelisks giving it an air of dignity; in its arched recesses Charles Breame and his wife have been kneeling since 1621.

In a corner of the apse is an elaborate monument with many armorial bearings, to Edmund Nevill and his wife Jane, a very determined-looking woman. In front of the tomb kneel their sons and daughters. The inscription tells us, with a touch of defiance, that Nevill was truly the 7th earl of Westmorland, descended from kings and princes. He was indeed descended from Ralph Nevill, whose loyalty to Henry IV has so vividly been used by Shakespeare, but since the 6th earl had been attainted for his attempt to release Mary Queen of Scots and not even James I would restore his title, Edmund's claim is sadly worthless. His wife has on her monument the countess's coronet she coveted in life.

But the most famous man who is buried here lies in an unmarked grave. He was Dr William Stukeley, the antiquary (1687–1765). When he was an old man, he wandered here with the vicar, his friend, and asked that he might rest here in a grave without memorial. He was the leading antiquarian of his day and realised how vain are pompous sepulchres. He was born in 1687 at Holbeach in Lincolnshire, and went from the grammar school there to Cambridge, became a doctor and practised, but his heart was in the ancient story of our country and he helped to found the Society of Antiquaries, becoming its secretary. He journied all over England with his friends, observing and noting all that he saw. Historians have used his works ever since. He was fascinated by pre-Roman remains which he recorded with remarkable accuracy and objectiveness. He believed, wrongly, that Stonehenge and Avebury were built by the Druids and his theories are still popularly accredited to this very day, though scholars now know that both monuments are far, far older than the priesthood which the Romans found here. But his errors are as nothing for they can be corrected. What is remembered of Stukeley is his zeal and his intense love of the past. In 1765 they brought him here by the Essex highway and over Bow Bridge and laid him to rest in East Ham churchyard, levelling the grass so that none can point to the spot, and he lies unknown as he wished to lie.

At the other end of the High Street is some excellent civic architecture of various periods. The Town Hall at the junction with Barking Road was designed by Cheers and Smith, 1901–03. It is of plum-coloured brick and yellow stone. The style is that of a Loire chateau adorned with Tudor fancies; it stands well back from the road. Next to it is the library in the same style, and opposite the Technical College built in 1962 by J. W. Taylor and H. C. Macaree. This crossroads of buildings gives East Ham a real town centre, one of strength and poise. Just up the road is Central Park, with a good war memorial.

Because of the devastation of the war years, Newham is a place for

Hampton Court: the main gateway

Hampton Court: the Tudor kitchen

Hampton Court: the Fountain Court

Hampton Court: Tijou ironwork

experimental architecture, and the tower blocks in Freemasons Road, the shopping arcade at Normandy Terrace, and the market which is being developed at Queen Street are particularly worth attention. In the market, there is a nice public house, The Queens, with inn signs of the *Queen Elizabeth* and the *Queen Mary*. At the feet of the tall buildings spread out the original two-storey Victorian dwellings, quite as comfortable in many ways as any modern flat. The builders in this area have always been imaginative—there are many fascinating variations on the acanthus leaf mouldings which adorn the houses in Green Street, and in the Romford Road the houses have keystones with heads—one of them wears a cricketer's cap!

The inhabitants here are served by a great variety of unusual religious sects, but the one old house in the area, Green Street House, has recently gone, to be replaced by a Roman Catholic school. It was a rambling 16th century manor house, with a great hall and a range of kitchen buildings. Henry VIII and Anne Boleyn are dubiously reputed to have stayed here and the house was known as Boleyn Castle. Its grounds backed on to the famous football ground of West Ham United. Nearby in Gladding Road, are the remains of East Ham Burnel Manor House, now part of the London Co-op Dairies, but built in the 18th century. Not far away is the Jewish cemetery where the Rothschild family mausoleum stands.

At the crossing of Station Road and the Romford Road is a grim reminder of war-time—an air-raid warning siren is still in position on its long pole. At the end of the road, cattle graze on Wanstead Flats and nearby are two churches, a spacious modern Catholic one with vaulted roof, dedicated to St Stephen, and opposite it the parish church, dedicated to St Mary. Like the parish churches of East Ham and West Ham, this is an old building, the fabric going back to Norman times, and there is a well-established tradition that there was once a Saxon church on the site. We have already said that the word "ham" comes from the Anglo-Saxon for a homestead, and since excavations at Corbets Tey near Upminster have revealed a large Saxon farm, we may think that the tradition at Manor Park is an acceptable one.

St Mary's Church is tiny. The 12th century nave is only 50 feet long with walls three feet thick. The chancel was rebuilt in the 17th century by the Waldegrave family and the bell-turret was added in the 18th. At about the same time, the Lethieullier family, lords of the manor of Barking, added their own chapel, with a fireplace, on the north side. The memorials in the church are all to members of important local families. Earliest and most interesting is a brass to young Thomas Heron, who died in 1517 and is shown as a schoolboy with pencase and inkhorn. He was the son and heir of Sir John Heron, Henry VIII's treasurer, who owned the manor house of Aldersbrook which stood where the City of London cemetery is today. In the Lethieullier chapel, now the vestry, is an ancient window in one corner of which is a heron, probably a symbol of the family's association with the church. Near Thomas's memorial are two older brasses, to William (d. 1614) and Anne Hyde (d. 1630). William was only a baby and is in swaddling clothes; Anne was in her teens and has a fine lace collar. Up on the north wall of the chancel kneel William Waldegrave and his wife, tiny effigies of their three sons, eldest daughter and twin girls below them. In the Lethieullier chapel is a window made of a medley of ancient glass, including the arms of England with red and white roses for Lancaster and York. On the north wall is an enormous monument to several generations of the family who originally came from Brabant in Belgium and settled here in the 17th century. Christopher Lethieullier and his son, Sir John, both became Sheriffs of London and Sir John's grandson, Smart Lethieullier, was the 18th century antiquarian who revealed the vast foundations of Barking Abbey, and whose epitaph tells us that he was "a gentleman of polite literature and elegant taste, and richly possessed of the curious productions of Nature, but modestly desired no other inscription than what he had made the rule of his life—to do justly, to love mercy, and to walk humbly with his God." There is a tablet to William Fry who died the year before his famous mother.

Nearby, in Manor Park cemetery, lies Jack Cornwell, who met death with a man's courage before he was a man in years. He was born in Leyton, but went to school in Walton Road, Manor Park, joined the Scouts and, despite a great ambition to go to sea, went to work on a tradesman's van. When the war broke out, he was allowed to go into training at Devonport, being then 14, and at 16 he became first class boy on HMS *Chester*, a light cruiser of Admiral Beatty's squadron. He was on this ship at Jutland when the German Navy tried to annihilate the British Fleet. In that great battle on the last day of May in 1916, Jack Cornwell was acting as sight-setter for the gun and in five minutes his gun was out of action and Jack had received a mortal wound. Of the crew of ten round the gun eight were killed or wounded, but the boy would not take shelter. He stood at his post till the end of the fight and was landed at Grimsby the next day and taken to hospital. Except for the officers his was the only name mentioned in the original despatches, and he received the Victoria Cross for an example of fortitude and courage that rang round England. His mother arrived in time to see him, but 48 hours after the battle he died and was buried near his home, though many said he should have been laid in Westminster Abbey. The Scouts named their badge for highest fortitude after him, and while boys love to read or to hear stories of great courage, the endurance of one so young will not be forgotten.*

* Photographs of Cornwell, and the bell of HMS *Chester*, can be seen on board HMS *Belfast*, the cruiser recently moored on the Thames off Tooley Street, as a permanent naval museum.

REDBRIDGE

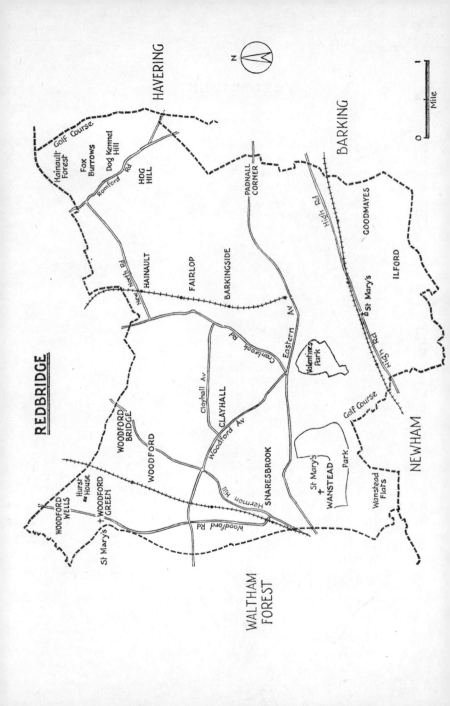

REDBRIDGE

The borough of Redbridge lies to the north-east of the Greater London area and consists of the former boroughs of Woodford and Wanstead and of Ilford, with parts of Chigwell and Dagenham, all formerly in Essex. It is bounded by Havering to the east, Barking and Newham to the south, Waltham Forest to the west, and Essex to the north. It covers an area of nearly 22 square miles and has a population of 242,840 (1970).

Redbridge takes its name from the bridge over the River Roding on what is now Eastern Avenue (A12) just outside Wanstead. The old Red Bridge, which was first recorded on John Rocque's map of 1746 but which was probably a century older, has been replaced by a modern one but it has given its pretty name to a whole new borough. This is a flat country bordered by Epping and Hainault forests, with the three townships of Woodford, Wanstead, and Ilford arranged in a triangle. Even today, as one drives along Hainault Road, there are open ploughed lands on either side. The towns have grown up since the mid-19th century and with the exception of the centre of Ilford and the addition of some new housing estates have changed little since; the network of streets around Thorold Road and Balfour Road in Ilford is Victorian and Edwardian, but with far pleasanter and better-proportioned rooms than the exterior would lead one to expect.

Beginning in the north-west corner with **Woodford**, there is much to see and to admire. The church itself, St Mary's, was built in 1817 by Charles Begon, apart from the tower which was erected in 1708, but it was burnt down in 1969. Its rebuilding is planned but for a long while the aisles stood open to the sky. The monuments, such as that to Rowland Elrington and his wife who lived in Tudor times, and a tall column to the Godfrey family, are undamaged. In an unmarked tomb in the churchyard lies Sir Thomas Roe, one of the most successful ambassadors England ever sent to a foreign land. He came of the London merchant class, his grandfather being a lord mayor. His education was by travel, though he went to Oxford and also had legal studies. When Elizabeth I was old he was a young

343

squire at her court, and James I knighted him, while the Prince of Wales sent him more than once to explore the great South American rivers. His first experience as an ambassador was to the Mogul Emperor of Hindustan, to open up trade, and he succeeded in laying trade foundations in the Bombay region. On his way home he made a successful call in Persia and introduced England there.

After that his journeys abroad were frequent. First he went as ambassador to Turkey, and was so successful that he was kept at Constantinople against his own wishes for seven years. While there he negotiated a peace treaty between Turkey and Poland and liberated hundreds of English captives from Algerian pirates, secured the famous Codex Alexandrinus copy of the Bible now in the British Museum, and collected 29 manuscripts for the Bodleian. His next mission was to mediate on peace between Sweden and Poland, and he was successful in arranging a truce. On the way home he made trade treaties with Danzig and Denmark. James had a gold medal struck in his honour. Again he was sent abroad as the English Ambassador Extraordinary to a conference for settling a general European Peace, and similar visits continued until his death in 1644.

Robert Raikes, the pioneer of education for poor children lies here and a large draped urn in St Mary's churchyard marks the resting place of the father and mother of William Morris. He died in 1847 and she many years later. William was born in 1834 in Waltham-stow (see p. 410 for his story) but his parents moved to Woodford Hall when he was six and he passed his boyhood here. Of Epping Forest which he knew and loved, he wrote: "I knew it yard by yard from Wanstead to the Theydons, and from Hale End to the Fairlop Oak. In those days it had no worse enemies than the gravel stealers and the rolling fence maker, and was always interesting and often very beautiful." An unattractive church hall now stands on the site of his home.

Beside the church is the old vicarage, a beautiful 18th century building now used and well cared-for as the Magistrates' Court and, a little further on, the High Street runs up Salway Hill on the eastern side of which stands Hurst House, a superb mansion built about 1714 for a wealthy brewer. It has giant Corinthian pilasters, a parapet with vases, and a beautiful doorway. In the 19th century it became known as The Naked Beauty, perhaps because of its exposed position; it was seriously damaged by fire in 1936 but was exactly restored. In front of the house is a little obelisk and just beside it, on the southernmost corner of the Green, stands a statue of Sir

Winston Churchill, Member of Parliament for Wanstead and Woodford from 1924 to 1964. The bronze statue by David McFall shows Sir Winston in later life, holding his usual dogged stance.

Further up the hill, just over the boundary into Waltham Forest, is Highams, built in 1768 by Anthony Bacon Esq., and now the Woodford County High School for Girls. It is an imposing creamy-white building standing in fine grounds, a complete contrast with the stalwart Victorian red-brick edifice of Bancroft's School, also on the Green. Nearby in Chigwell Road is Broadmead Baptist Church, designed in 1957 by Denis Hull with an enchanting little aluminium spire and rough-cast walls, sculptured by the architect himself to tell the stories of the Creation and the Crucifixion.

Two interesting men were born in Woodford, though neither was associated with the place in later life. They were the parson and wit, Sydney Smith (1771–1845) and the poet, Coventry Patmore (1823–96). Sydney Smith took orders, but was famous for his excellent conversation and his liberal political views, for he did much to advance Catholic emancipation; he became a canon of St Paul's and inherited a fortune from his brother. Coventry Patmore worked in the Printed Books Department of the British Museum and published between 1854 and 1862 the four poems which make up his masterpiece, *The Angel in the House,* a poetic celebration of married love. In 1864 he entered the Roman Catholic Church and wrote a number of religious meditations. He was a friend of Tennyson and of Ruskin.

Away to the west of the borough, where Snakes Lane (in which there is an excellent new public library) runs into Manor Road, is Dr Barnardo's, and there is also a second centre around Mossford Hall at Barkingside, not far away. It is at Barkingside that Dr Barnardo is buried; his grave is at the end of a little avenue, under a memorial by Sir George Frampton. His portrait is on the pedestal of a mother and child and three children are seated below. The monument is as simple and appealing as the man himself and on it is this proud statement of his faith:

I hope to die as I have lived, in the humble but assured faith of Jesus Christ as my Saviour, my Master, and my King.

John Thomas Barnardo dedicated his life to children, to helping those children whom nobody wanted and who were too desolate or

345

too little to be able to help themselves. He was born in Dublin in 1845; his father was of Jewish origin, his mother Irish. He was a delicate child, so frail that, after a bout of diphtheria at the age of two, he was pronounced dead by the doctor and it was the under-taker himself who perceived that there was a spark of life in the little body. He grew up strong enough and entered his father's fur business but in 1862 he attended some Evangelical meetings and, undergoing a deep religious experience, he decided to go to China as a missionary, after training as a doctor in London so that he might thereby be more useful. While a student, in his spare time, he sold Bibles in the East End and taught in a ragged school in Stepney. He was beaten up by toughs till his pupils formed a bodyguard and then one night, a child, Jim Jarvis, begged to be allowed to sleep in the wretched shed that served as a school-house. Barnardo told him to go home but the boy had no home to which to go. The doctor took the boy back to his lodgings and fed him, for he was starving, and Jim then took him to see where a group of 11 boys lay huddled together on an outhouse roof in the bitter November cold, sleeping there because they had no shelter whatsoever. Barnardo realised that his duty lay in London rather than in China. He interested Lord Shaftesbury in the plight of the children and began to receive them into his own lodgings or to board them out. At first he was careful not to outstrip his resources but after a child, John Somers known as "Carrots", had died of cold and starvation after having been turned away, he nailed a notice to his door in Stepney Cause-way "No destitute child is ever refused admittance" and from that time onwards, Barnardo's was known as "The Ever Open Door".

In 1875 he married Syrie Louise Elmslie who came of a wealthy family but who shared his views and who was as remarkable a person as himself. Their married life was very happy and they had seven children. As a wedding present a wealthy stockbroker gave them a 21-year lease of Mossford Lodge, Barkingside, and there they set up house and started the first home for destitute girls whose plight had been haunting Barnardo ever since, a few months before, a little waif called Martha had tapped at his door and asked, "Please, do you take in little gels too?" She had been admitted and with his wife's aid many more were succoured too. His father-in-law bought him 13 acres of land near Mossford Lodge and in it, with C. Pite as his architect, he built his Village Homes where children were cared for in small family groups—a revolution in child care in those days. Barnardo carried on his work, usually toiling till three in the morning, till the day of his death, September 19, 1905, when he said to his wife, "My head is so heavy. Let me rest it on your face," and quietly passed away.

Today the site of the original home in Stepney Causeway is being redeveloped and the administrative work is centred at Barkingside, but there are centres all over the country and in Africa too. The emphasis is on the small family group and each teenage child has his or her own room. Pioneer work is being undertaken with delinquent and educationally sub-normal children. During the doctor's life-time, a home had been given to 59,384 children; today the number has risen to 188,333. But the force of his example has affected the treatment of millions more. Only a man of exceptional courage and indomitable will could have undertaken such a task; only a man of extraordinary ability could have organised his homes as he did. And only a saint could have loved loveless children so well that he could say, "I have never seen an ugly child."

At Aldborough Hatch near Barkingside stands a small modern church dedicated to St Peter; in its walls are some of the stones from old Westminster Bridge, the bridge on which Wordsworth stood when he wrote his sonnet on London,

Earth hath not anything to show more fair.

Returning to Manor Road, we reach Claybury Hospital. This was the first lunatic asylum built by the London County Council in 1890–93. It is a large forbidding red brick-and-tile building in which wonderful work is done to help those who are mentally unstable. It stands in the grounds of Claybury Hall which was built in 1791 and has a pretty garden front with a colonnade; the Hall is today used as an annexe.

To the east there is open land across to Hainault where there is first some uninspired development and then the splendid open space that was once the forest itself and the air is quite different, fresh and cold. Turning southwards, we cross open farmland and pass boats sailing on Fairlop Lake, till we come to the impressive Goodmayes Asylum opened in 1901 by Councillor Abednigo Bishop, who was mayor of West Ham at the time, and then we reach Goodmayes Park, once the site of a farmhouse belonging to Barking Abbey. It is linked to South Park by Levett Gardens, a fascinating street of bungalows with spiked finials on their roofs, built about 1924. One house, called *Domus Tuliparum*, has the most alluring stained-glass tulips in its porch windows. The street has an endearing and dramatic character, like a very large backdrop for a musical. Nearby is Newbury Park tube station, designed in 1937 by Oliver Hill but not built till after the war, from 1947 onwards. It has a copper-clad parabolic canopy to shelter those arriving or leaving, and is a worthy addition to the excellent architecture of London's tube stations.

In the south corner of the borough is **Ilford**. It is a 19th century place which is trying to turn itself into a 20th century one very fast—a walk the full length of the High Road is instructive, with small shops built out in front up at the east end by St Mary's Church (built in 1831 by James Savage) giving way to new high blocks of shops, down at the west end by the ornate Town Hall, built in 1901 by B. Woolland. But Ilford contains Uphall Camp and St Mary's Hospital, the two oldest things in the borough, and the Fairlop Oak once stood near here (see under Barking, p. 17).

Uphall Camp is the remains of an Iron Age or early Roman encampment. Little remains of it now but it once covered several acres and stood beside the River Roding, commanding the way. It is now within the grounds of Messrs Laporte and Sons, chemical manufacturers. St Mary's Hospital is at the east end of the High Road and one enters its little courtyard through a pretty gateway. It was founded about 1140 as a home for lepers, but after the Reformation it became an almshouse, maintained by the Marquis of Salisbury. There is a tiny chapel and a house on either side of it. Most of the buildings were renewed in the 17th and 19th centuries, but the chancel is mediaeval and in it is a stone figure of a priest, thought to be John Smythe who was Master of the Hospital some 500 years ago. A 20th century church, St Andrew's by Sir Herbert Baker, in The Drive at Ilford is also well worth visiting. The sculpture by Sir Charles Wheeler and the glass by Carl Parsons, are particularly fine.

Half a mile due north of Ilford is Valentines Park, a pretty place in which there still stands the old house, built about 1696 though much altered; it is today used as borough council offices. The house was built in the first half of the 18th century by Mr James Chadwick, son-in-law to Archbishop Tillotson, and in the grounds stood a hot-house in which there grew a marvellous vine, the parent of the famous one at Hampton Court, which was planted from a cutting in 1769. In its heyday, the Ilford vine produced four hundredweight of fruit a year, but at last it died and the stump was thrown away by the gardener. Northwards again at Fullwell Cross is a new public library, built in 1967 by Sir Frederick Gibberd. It is circular with an angular cupola on top and is one of the most attractive and welcoming libraries built in this country since the war. Nearby are the municipal swimming baths, another interesting if less gay design.

Wanstead occupies the south-eastern corner of the borough. Its main interest centres on the church, which still delights us, and around Wanstead House which has vanished. The present church, St Mary's, was completed in 1790 to the designs of Thomas Hardwick. It is a fine rectangular classical building with a lofty porch held up on pairs of Doric pillars and above it a high bell-turret. Inside, it is all white with galleries on either side and high box-pews in the nave. There is a fine three-decker pulpit and the altar is a superb marquetry table, possibly brought from Wanstead House. The pride of the church is its monument to Sir Josiah Child (d. 1699) probably carved by John Van Nost. It is enormous, standing some 20 feet high, and of white marble. Sir Josiah stands in the centre in Roman apparel and wig while his son Bernard lies at his feet. Mourning women grieve on either side and four cherubs blow golden trumpets to acclaim his achievements which, in matters of finance, had been considerable. He was a governor of the East India Company and John Evelyn described him as a "sudden monied man". Of his family we shall say more in a moment.

There had been an earlier smaller Wanstead church which was demolished by the rector, Dr Glasse, when the present building was completed. It stood in what is today the churchyard, near to what looks like a tall sentry-box. This marks the tomb of the Wilton family and is said to be a replica of the entrance to the Holy Sepulchre in Jerusalem but local people will tell you that it is a "watcher's box" in which sentries were posted to frustrate raids on the churchyard by body-snatchers. The list of rectors goes back to 1207 and there is one name, James Pound (rector 1711–25), which is particularly worth remembering. He was a Fellow of the Royal Society and a fine astronomer, indeed so excellent a one that the Royal Society lent him an enormous telescope constructed by Christian Huygens of Holland for his observations. The telescope required a huge pole for its erection. Now it so happened that in 1718 the Maypole in the Strand was about to be taken down since it was in the way of the new church of St Mary-le-Strand (a maypole, 124 feet high, had stood there ever since the Restoration of Charles II in 1660) and Sir Isaac

Newton arranged for it to be sent to Dr Pound to support the largest telescope in Europe. An anonymous poet questioned:

> *What's not destroyed by Time's relentless hand?*
> *Where's Troy? and where the maypole in the Strand?*

and when the telescope was in position, another rhymster welcomed it to Wanstead:

> *Here oft I'm scented with a balmy Dew,*
> *A pleasing Blessing which the Strand ne'er knew.*
> *There stood I only to receive abuse,*
> *But here converted to a nobler use;*
> *So that with me all Passengers will say,*
> *I'm better far than when the Pole of May.*

In 1721, Dr Pound was offered the Savilian Professorship of Astronomy at Oxford but he refused it for it would have meant leaving the country parish he loved, and it was offered to the Reverend James Bradley who was Dr Pound's nephew, curate, and assistant in astronomy. Dr Bradley later became Astronomer Royal in succession to Halley who first observed the comet called after him.

Returning to the Child family, Sir Josiah's son, Sir Richard, built a great house at Wanstead. His architect was Colin Campbell and it was begun in 1715 thus being the first major building in the country of the Palladian revival. Walpole said the house had cost £100,000 and the gardens as much more. It was an immensely broad house, 260 feet long by 70 feet deep, with a portico raised on steps and surmounted by a carved pediment. This Wanstead House replaced a much older one built by Lord Rich who grew wealthy by the Dissolution of the Monasteries, and the house was enlarged by the Earl of Leicester to entertain his royal mistress, Elizabeth, whom he subsequently displeased by marrying, at Wanstead, Lettice Knowles, the widowed Countess of Essex.

When the new house was being built, a Roman tessellated pavement was discovered but was destroyed instead of being preserved as it should have been. The grounds were as magnificent as the dwelling itself, with a huge basin of water, an avenue of trees, a canal and a pretty summerhouse which still beautify the public park which these grounds have become. Hogarth painted the scene at an assembly there—the original of his painting is now in America. All that remains of the house, however, are the stables, just south of St

Mary's Church, which are today used as a golf club, and two massive stone pillars at the end of Overton Drive, which once carried the main gates of the estate for the mansion was demolished tragically in 1824.

These were the circumstances. Sir Josiah's grandson, James, died childless in 1784. He was succeeded by a relative, Sir James Long, from Wiltshire, who died 10 years later leaving an infant son and daughter. The boy did not survive and his sister, Catherine Tylney Long, became the richest heiress in England with an income of £80,000 a year. The poor lady, wearing a wedding dress that cost 700 guineas, foolishly married a dissolute young man, William Pole Wellesley, who within 10 years brought her whole estate to utter ruin, chiefly by his gambling. The house and its contents were sold at auction, the sale lasting 32 days, but the house fetched only £10,000 as builder's materials. It was knocked down in 1824. Poor Catherine died two years later and her three children were made wards in Chancery. Pole Wellesley married again—and ruined his second wife too; she ended her days in the poorhouse. All that remains of the glory that was Wanstead House is the park with its lake where herons used to nest, and its magnificent trees. As we walk here and enjoy the landscape that has been preserved for us, we may think of the pomp of Sir Josiah and Sir Richard, of the architectural skill of Colin Cambell, and of the heartbreak of poor Catherine.

The Green at Wanstead is still agreeable with some fine Spanish chestnut trees. It leads through to the High Street, passing on its way Christ Church, built in 1861 by Sir Gilbert Scott, a sturdy church with a fine spire and a very active community. The High Street is changing fast and is one in which the student must look hard at the upper storeys and the backs of houses, rather than at the shop fronts that have been built on to them. Messrs J. Joliffe, Builders, operate from an old weatherboarded house, and the Conservative Club occupies the manor house. Northwards on Hermon Hill is Wanstead Hospital built to accommodate the Royal Merchant Seamen's Orphanage, in an elaborate pseudo-Venetian style, with a relief of a ship at sea over the doorway and well-laid-out flowerbeds. Nearby on Snaresbrook Road is the Royal Wanstead School which also was originally an orphanage. It was built in 1843 by Sir Gilbert Scott in a Jacobean style, and seen across Eagle Pond it is a rare and impressive sight.

Among the many who have made their homes in Wanstead, finding it to be a pretty village near to London—as indeed, it still was only a generation ago—there were two particularly interesting men

351

—the poet Thomas Hood and the engineer Sir Charles Bright. Hood spent three years at Lake House, from 1832 to 1835, and there his son was born, so weakly an infant that he was hurriedly baptised from water in a pudding basin though he lived to a good old age. Sir Charles Bright was responsible for laying the first telegraphic cable across the Atlantic, and he accomplished this in August 1858 despite great difficulties and threats from storms. The operators tapped out in Morse code across the ocean "Glory to God in the highest!" and on both sides of the water, men rejoiced.

RICHMOND UPON THAMES

RICHMOND UPON THAMES

N

HOUNSLOW

Hammersmith Bridge

Kew Bridge

R. Thames

KEW

CASTELNAU

Royal Botanical Gardens

NORTH SHEEN

BARNES

RICHMOND

Sheen Rd

MORTLAKE

EAST SHEEN

WANDSWORTH

Marble Hill

WHITTON

St Mary's

RICHMOND PARK

Pope's Villa

TWICKENHAM

Petersham Rd

Strawberry Hill

St Alban's

St Mary's

HAMPTON HILL

TEDDINGTON

Bushy House

HAMPTON WICK

HAMPTON

St Mary's

BUSHY PARK

Hampton Court Rd

KINGSTON

Palace

HAMPTON COURT PARK

0   1

Mile

RICHMOND UPON THAMES

The borough of Richmond upon Thames lies to the south-west of London and is composed of Richmond and Barnes on the Surrey side of the Thames and of Twickenham on the north. These boundaries include Hampton Court and Kew Gardens. The borough covers an area of nearly 14,000 acres of which almost one half is open space. It has a population of about 177,000. Here is the most beautiful stretch of the river to be found near London, whether it is viewed from the top of Richmond Hill looking down on Petersham Meadows and across to Marble Hill Park in Twickenham, or whether one looks towards the hill from the riverside walk on the Middlesex bank. We have decided to describe only the Middlesex side in this volume which deals with London north of the Thames but to include the whole borough in a later volume which will deal with London south of the river.

The most important building in the borough—indeed, one of the most important buildings in England—is **Hampton Court**. If Versailles is a spectacular palace, then Hampton Court is lovable and friendly, whether it is seen in summer with the Tudor brickwork glowing warmly in the sunshine and the roses in full bloom against the garden walls, or in winter when the branches of the chestnut avenue stand attentive against the sky. The manor of Hampton originally belonged to the de St Valerie family who, in the early 13th century, presented it to the Knights of St John. Wolsey leased it from them in 1514 and immediately began to build himself a palace there. His career is one of the most meteoric in British history. Born in Ipswich in about 1475, the son of a butcher, he entered the Church and became chaplain to Henry VII in 1507. Henry VIII made him his Almoner and in 1513 he became Dean of York, in 1514 Archbishop, and in 1515 Lord Chancellor and Cardinal. He was ambitious, ruthless, superbly efficient, and lived with a panache and on a scale that made the king, 16 years his junior, long to emulate him. The satirist John Skelton wrote:

> *Why come ye not to Court?*
> *To whyche court?*
> *To the Kynges Courte?*

355

> *Or to Hampton Court?*
> *Nay, to the Kynges Courte,*
> *But Hampton Court*
> *Hath the preeminence.*

At Hampton Court 280 rooms were kept always ready for guests, and when ambassadors came from France in 1528 Wolsey was able to entertain the whole train there in a manner that was, to say the least, regal. It is significant that both Wolsey's town house and his country house became royal palaces. In 1529, hoping to appease his master's jealousy and wrath, Wolsey presented the king with Hampton Court and all its contents but it was too late. He was arrested for high treason and died on his way to the Tower, while Henry seized York Place and turned it into Whitehall Palace.

Wolsey's master mason at Hampton Court was probably Henry Redman who also worked on the Cardinal's College at Oxford, now known as Christ Church. Wolsey built the West Front, the Base Court, the Clock Court, the Chapel and the Master Carpenter's Court, and excavated the moat—probably the last to be dug in England. Henry delighted in his new palace, already the biggest house in England, and spent more money on it than on any of his other dwellings except perhaps Greenwich. His master mason was John Molton. He added the wings to the West Front, a new court where Wren's Fountain Court now is, remodelled the Clock Court and built the Great Hall. Here he brought five of his six queens— Catherine of Aragon had visited it when it was still Wolsey's mansion. We can still see Henry's initials entwined with Anne Boleyn's on the gateway which bears her name, and the royal arms impaling Jane Seymour's have replaced Wolsey's on the chapel doors. Here his son Edward was born, and here his dearest queen, Jane, died, a few days after the baby's birth. Anne of Cleeves and Catherine Parr walked here peacefully, and here Catherine Howard was arrested for her misdemeanours.

After Henry's death, Edward succeeded with his uncle, the Duke of Somerset, as Protector. When the duke's power waned, he fled to Hampton Court with the young king, was arrested there by his envious rivals and was executed. When Mary succeeded her younger brother, she spent her honeymoon with Philip of Spain at Hampton, and here Elizabeth I often came throughout her reign. It is said that Shakespeare acted before her in the Great Hall. When James I summoned a conference of divines to settle what was "amiss with the Church", it met at Hampton Court and, though it failed to solve the Church's troubles, from it came the work that resulted in the Authorised Version of the Bible.

Charles I lived here as king, kept some of his superb art collection here, and returned here as a prisoner in 1647. One night he retired early to his room, slipped out by another door and so down to the riverside where he was met with horses. He fled to the Isle of Wight where he was incarcerated in Carisbrooke Castle and returned to London only for his execution. After his death, his art collection was stripped from the walls and sold, but Hampton Court itself did not go to the highest bidder as did other royal properties, being preserved for the use of the Lord Protector Cromwell. Charles II lived merrily here; he made no alterations to the buildings but busied himself with the laying out of the gardens.

When James II lost his throne to his daughter Mary II and her husband, William of Orange, there were great changes, however. William was asthmatic and could not endure the London air, and from 1689 onwards, Sir Christopher Wren was employed in re-building and extending Hampton Court. At first, the plan was to demolish the whole Tudor palace and to build afresh, but in the end only one of Henry VIII's courtyards disappeared, to be replaced by the Fountain Court, around which the State Rooms were built. This was William's answer to the Versailles of his enemy, Louis XIV of France; there could hardly be a greater contrast. Versailles is overwhelmingly magnificent—fit for a monarch who compared himself to the very sun; William's palace is modest by comparison but always dignified and noble—a thoroughly humane building. When William died in 1702, his horse having thrown its rider after stumbling over a molehill in Hampton Court Park, the work almost ceased. Queen Anne stayed there and so did George I and George II, and the decoration of the State Rooms was completed, but when George III came to the throne in 1760, it ceased to be a royal residence and in 1838 the young and public-spirited Queen Victoria opened the State Rooms and grounds to the public who have delighted in it ever since. Other accommodation was turned into "grace and favour" dwellings for the widows or children of distinguished servants of the Crown.

Although royalty would usually have approached the palace by water in the royal barge, we enter it today from the roadway through the George II Trophy Gates and, crossing the Outer Green Court, come to the moat and West Front. The Gatehouse in the middle was originally two storeys higher—it was, lamentably, reduced in 1771–73—and had gilded weathervanes on top of lead cupolas; to reach it we cross the bridge built by Henry VIII, buried by Charles II, excavated and restored in 1910, and now adorned on either parapet by the Queen's Beasts. Over the main gate is a panel carved with Henry VIII's arms and on each turret is a roundel with the head of a Roman emperor in high relief.

We enter the first or Base Court through the original heavy oak doors of the palace; they are carved with linenfold panelling. This court had not changed much since Wolsey's day when his household and guests lodged here. The buildings are only two storeys high and there are more medallions with Roman emperors' heads. They were designed for Wolsey by Giovanni da Maiano in 1521 and cost £2 6s 8d each; a similar set was designed for the Holbein Gate at Whitehall (see also p. 276) and those on the Great Gate may come from there. The importance of these roundels lies in the fact that they are a sign that the revival of classical learning was reaching England from Italy. Under the Anne Boleyn gateway, so called because it was embellished during the short reign of Henry's second queen, we come to the Clock Court which takes its name from the wonderful astronomical clock made in 1540 for Henry by Nicholas Oursian. It shows the hour, the day, the month, the number of days since New Year, the phases of the moon and the times of high water at London Bridge. Beneath it is a terracotta panel with Wolsey's arms supported by *putti* and surmounted by his cardinal's hat. On the north side, the wall of the Great Hall rises up. There are very small cellar windows at the base, then an expanse of brickwork, then five large, four-light, transomed windows, and above them a battlemented parapet and the roof. The east side of the courtyard is the George II gateway rebuilt in 1732 but still with four Roman emperor medallions, and on the south side is a graceful colonnade added by Sir Christopher Wren.

Before we begin to describe Wren's work, it would be as well to examine the Tudor interiors to the north of the palace. There are two huge beer cellars—the amount consumed by a large household in the 16th century was vast—a wine cellar, and the kitchens, well sited for service to the Great Hall. The huge ovens and spits are still in position, and there is much Tudor kitchen equipment on display —a great deal of time can be spent here. Above the cellars is the Great Hall, built in 1531–36 in place of Wolsey's more modest one. The carpenters and masons worked through the night by candlelight to complete it swiftly. The hall is 106 feet long, 40 feet wide and 60 feet high; it has one of the finest hammerbeam roofs ever created, with carved lantern pendants, probably the work of Richard Rydge of London. At the upper end is a dais where the king sat with his favoured guests, behind them a superb bay window of 48 lights with a stone fan vault; the stained glass in it is now all Victorian. Lesser guests and the household sat at tables down the hall, and at the lower end is an oak screen to support the minstrels' gallery and conceal the service of food from the kitchens which are reached by a staircase at the end of the Screens Passage. Outside the Hall is the Great Watching Chamber, Henry's guard room to his Presence Chamber and State Rooms. These have gone but the Watching Chamber shows the scale on which they were conceived. It is magnificent with a panelled ceiling, the ribs carved down to form pendants and in the spaces between are bosses displaying the Tudor and Seymour arms.

The Watching Chamber is linked to the Chapel Royal by the Haunted Gallery which takes its name from the belief that the spectre of Catherine Howard, Henry's fifth wife, walks there. Only 15 months after her marriage, she was accused of misconduct and was arrested, but she managed to evade her guards and ran down the corridor trying to reach the king who was at mass in the chapel so that she might plead with him. She was dragged back shrieking, and was beheaded three months later.

The passage leads into the Royal Pew which forms a gallery at the west end of the chapel—the household would have occupied the floor of the nave. The present gallery dates from about 1711 when the chapel was redecorated by Wren and Grinling Gibbons for Queen Anne, but the building itself with its magnificent fan-vaulted ceiling, is of Henry's time.

Two groups of rooms bear Wolsey's name and are all that is left of the Tudor state accommodation. Three of them are on the south side of the Clock Court, behind Wren's colonnade. There is some fine linenfold panelling and one and a half original ceilings adorned with plasterwork of the first importance since it is a very early example of the technique which was later to become one of the glories of 16th century architecture; here, the composition is quite simple, merely lozenges, stars, and bands entwined together. The other two rooms are on the east side of the same court, near the head of the Queen's Staircase. One of them, only 12 feet square, is known as Wolsey's Closet. Its walls are covered with much-restored linenfold panelling, and its ceiling is a miracle of blue and gold interlaced octagons and squares centred round bosses with Tudor roses and Prince of Wales feathers. This is the finest early Renaissance ceiling in England.

The moulded frieze with mermen, dolphins, and other emblems and devices is exquisite, and below it runs Wolsey's motto, repeated again and again, *Dominus mihi adjutor*, "The Lord is my helper." Below that is a series of somewhat later 16th century Italian paintings depicting The Last Supper, the Scourging of Christ, the Bearing of the Cross, and the Resurrection. This room gives some inkling of the magnificence of Wolsey's own apartments. The student of Tudor architecture will spend a long time here, and when he leaves he should be watchful for the amazing forest of Tudor chimneypots to be seen at Hampton, with their variety of patterned brickwork.

When Wren began the rebuilding for William and Mary, he pulled down all the Tudor State Rooms and replaced them with the Fountain Court. The ground floor is a cloister built round a fountain—a wonderfully cool place in summer and a mysterious one in winter. Above the cloister run two suites of State Apartments, the King's Side overlooking the gardens to the south, and the Queen's Side overlooking the Long Water and the park to the east. We enter today from the Colonnade in the Clock Court and ascend by the King's Staircase with its magnificent wrought-iron balustrade designed by Tijou. The walls are decorated by Verrio. At the top is the Guard Room and then the four State Rooms—the First Presence Chamber, the Second Presence Chamber, the Audience Room, and the King's Drawing Room. They contain wonderful woodcarving by Grinling Gibbons and William III's great chair of state. Beyond are the king's private rooms and behind, facing on to the Fountain Court, is the Cartoon Gallery completed in 1695 to house the seven Raphael cartoons which Charles had bought in 1632 and which are now in the Victoria and Albert Museum. In their place hang tapestries copied from Raphael's paintings during the 17th century.

Along the east front runs the Queen's Gallery with an enchanting fireplace sculpted by John van Nost. This leads to the Queen's State Rooms. (The approach should be made by the Queen's Staircase on the north side of the Fountain Court but this description necessarily follows the prescribed course of today's tour.) We enter the Bedroom first which was decorated by Sir James Thornhill for the future George II when he was still Prince of Wales. There are medallion portraits of George I, the Prince and Princess of Wales and their son, Frederick, who died before he could come to the throne. The Drawing Room was decorated by Verrio for Queen Anne, showing her as Justice and depicting her power over the four corners of the globe. Her husband, Prince George of Denmark, is shown backed by the British Fleet. There is a huge red canopy above the chair of state in the Audience Room, and the Public Dining Room and Queen's Presence Chamber were decorated by William Kent for George II. In the Guards' Chamber on the north side of the court-yard and in the Communication Gallery are two famous sets of paintings, the Hampton Court Beauties by Sir Godfrey Kneller and the Windsor Beauties by Sir Peter Lely; portraits of the great ladies at the courts of William III and Charles II who still smile down at us. Behind the State Rooms on the East Front are seven small private rooms for the royal family, cosy by comparison with the great halls of state; the Queen's Privy Chamber and Closet are fitted with marble washbasins installed for Caroline, George II's queen.

Leaving the palace by the Queen's Staircase—once again the balustrade was designed by Tijou—we walk through the Fountain Court and out to Wren's East Front. It is 23 windows wide, ap-parently three storeys high (a fourth storey is hidden behind a balustrade) and quite plain except for a carved pediment above a frieze and pilasters in the centre; it creates its impression not by magnificence but by dignity and good manners. Beyond the gardens stretch away, laid out by Charles II's orders in the 1660s when the mile-long canal, ending in a semi-circular sweep of water, was dug through the Home Park. Three avenues of trees run to meet it and a fountain plays in an oval basin. The Broad Walk stretches out for a quarter of a mile on either side of the palace and along it runs one of the finest and most varied herbaceous borders to be seen in England. To the south of the palace are the formal privy gardens, terminating in Tijou's wonderful iron screen along the river front. Near the palace is a slightly sunken garden laid out on Tudor lines and then known as the Pond Garden. It is enchanting at all times with its meticulous arrangements of flowers, and a 20th century replanting of a Tudor knot garden, created by Mr Ernest Law, the historian of Hampton Court. Here also are William III's Banqueting House, the main room prettily decorated by Verrio about 1700, the Great Vine planted in 1769 from a slip taken from one at Ilford in Essex (see p. 348), and the Orangery which houses the famous cartoons of the Triumph of Caesar. Mantegna painted them between 1485 and 1494, and Charles I purchased them from the Duke of Mantua in 1629; today they are among the most valuable pictures owned by the Crown.

To the north of the palace, beyond Tennis Court Lane, lies Henry

VIII's Tennis Court much altered by Charles II but still the oldest in England, and then we come to The Wilderness where William III planned a vast forecourt which happily was never executed. It is now a pleasant tree-filled area, criss-crossed with paths leading to the Maze which was laid out in Queen Anne's day and in which thousands of people have delighted to lose themselves ever since. Tijou's superb Lion Gates open to the Hampton Court Road and beyond is the Chestnut Avenue planted by William III and his gardeners, George London and Henry Wise, in 1689. Subsidiary lime avenues stretch away to west and east. The chestnuts, flanked by rows of lime trees, march for a mile across Bushy Park, broken only by a large circular lake in the middle of which stands a bronze statue of Diana (or Venus or Arethusa) by Fanelli; according to Evelyn, Charles I had intended it for the Privy Garden. The Avenue, as planned by William and Wren, was to have been a magnificent approach road to the completely new palace which they planned but never built; what we have today is only the shadow of a dream compared with what they intended. Perhaps we are lucky; the palace might have been more imposing but would have been far less friendly. West of the Wilderness lies Henry VIII's Tiltyard, now planted out with rose beds, where spectators could once have watched the jousting and equitation from four high towers. The king delighted in such sports and this part of the grounds was well-used.

The greatness of Hampton Court tends to detract the visitor's attention from the charm of **Hampton** itself, but the little town is well worth a visit on its own merits. The finest houses cluster around the Green; they are Crown property and were built in the time of William and Mary and Anne for people associated with the court. The best is the Old Court House where Wren lived from 1708 till his death which took place quietly in his chair at his other house in St James's Street, one evening in 1723. He was 90 years old. He had begun his life in 1632 when Charles I was still on the throne, had grown up during the Civil War, had become Professor of Astronomy at Gresham College in London when he was 25 and Savilian Professor of Astronomy at Oxford when he was 29. He had become an architect almost by chance, had seen four-fifths of London destroyed by fire in 1666, and had done more to rebuild it than any other man. He designed St Paul's Cathedral and the rebuilt City churches, Hampton Court and Kensington Palace, Greenwich Hospital and Chelsea Hospital, the Sheldonian Theatre at Oxford, and the Library of Trinity College at Cambridge. He was one of the greatest Englishmen and most incomparable architects who has ever lived.

Near Wren's house are the Royal Mews which include a magnificent barn, dated 1570, with a ringpost roof. The bridge across the river was rebuilt in 1933 by Sir Edwin Lutyens, and on the Hampton side is the stately 19th century Mitre Hotel. A fair is held on the green at bank holidays which can vie with the one on Hampstead Heath. The village itself is separated from the green by half a mile of road running along the Thames beside Ash Island, Tagg's Island, and Platt's Ait. Hampton itself clusters around St Mary's Church, built in 1831 by E. Lapidge who also designed St John the Baptist at Hampton Wyck. This building is of plain brick but there was certainly a church on the site in 1342 when it came into the possession of the Priory of Takeley in Essex, and there may have been one much earlier. There are a number of interesting monuments, notably that of Dame Sibel Penn, Edward VI's nurse, whose effigy lies in the south porch. Until her death from small pox in 1562, she lived nearby at Penn's Place, Church Street. There is a wall-monument to Edmund Pigeon and his son Nicholas who served their kings and queens from Henry VIII to James I. Edmund attended Henry at Boulogne and may have been with him on the Field of the Cloth of Gold. Susanna Thomas and her mother have a fine monument. Susanna died in 1731, the only daughter and heiress of Sir Dalby Thomas, governor of the African Company's Settlements. His lady reclines at her daughter's feet, and Susanna leans her elbow on an urn, a book on her knee which she is about to read to her mother. The monument was designed by William Archer and executed by Sir William Henry Powell; the conception is perhaps more successful than the execution. It was this memorial that Harris in Jerome K. Jerome's *Three Men in a Boat* wanted to come ashore to see (see Chapter 7).

Two other memorials should be mentioned. On the floor of the nave is a slab recording the death of Edward Progers Esq., page of honour to Charles I, Member of Parliament for Brecknockshire, and groom of the bed chamber to Charles II. He distinguished himself during the Civil War and died at Upper Lodge, Bushey Park, on December 31, 1713, aged 96, "of the anguish of cutting teeth, having cut four new teeth, and had several ready to cut, which so inflamed his gums he died". On the south wall of the south aisle is a portion of a monument to Huntingdon Shaw, the smith who executed much of the wrought-iron work at Hampton Court. He died in 1710 and lies in the churchyard, where also lie Lady Roberts, Earl Roberts' mother, and Thomas Rosoman who built Sadler's Wells. There is a curious pyramid tomb which encloses John and Catherine Greg of Dominica who died in 1795 and 1819 respectively and who expressed a wish to be "buried" above ground.

In the north gallery there used to be a royal pew, for William IV used to attend the church and presented the organ. The royal coat of arms is now over the west door, around which is an impressive mural by the Reverend Geoffrey M. Fraser depicting Hampton parishioners past and present; Henry VIII and Anne Boleyn are there and so are Edward VI and Dame Sibel and Charles II.

Near the church is David Garrick's villa, now converted, very skilfully, into elegant flats. Its grounds are now covered with a neo-Georgian development of town houses. If such building must take place, this is an exceptionally successful example. The great actor lived at Hampton for a quarter of a century before his death in 1779, and his widow continued to live there till her death 43 years later. The river front, with stone portico and pilasters, was designed by Adam who also enlarged the house. Garrick had come up to London, wretchedly poor, in 1737, in company with his school-master, Samuel Johnson. Both men became famous and remained friends throughout their lives. Johnson often visited Hampton and when asked how he liked it, said, "Ah, David, it is the leaving of such places that makes a death-bed terrible." The house is linked by a tunnel running under the road to a garden beside the river in which stands Garrick's Temple, a summerhouse with dome and projecting porch. It was designed by Adam to house Roubiliac's statue of Shakespeare for which Garrick was the model. The statue is now in the British Museum and the Temple is the property of the borough council; the garden is open to everyone.

In Roy Grove is the cannon buried upright in 1791 by General William Roy to mark the end of the base line begun on Hounslow Heath for the first of the triangles into which he divided the South of England when he mapped it. We tell the story at Hounslow (see p. 251).

Teddington lies due north of Hampton Court, on the far side of Bushey Park, crossed by the avenue of chestnut trees which we have already described. In the park stands Bushey House, originally built as Upper Lodge by Edward Progers in the late 17th century and largely rebuilt by Charles Montagu, Earl of Halifax in the first half of the 18th. He was also Ranger of Bushey Park, and the next three holders of the house and the office were all his relatives. The Duke of Clarence, later William IV, lived there with his beloved and generous-hearted mistress, Dorothea Jordan the actress, and seven of their children were born there. After William's death, in 1837, the house was granted to his consort, Queen Adelaide, who used it till her death in 1849. It was afterwards lent by Queen Victoria to Louis, Duc de Nemours, who lived there intermittently till 1896. Today it is the headquarters of the National Physical Laboratory, which opened in 1902 as the national standardising laboratory; its objectives are "to bring scientific knowledge to bear practically on our everyday industrial and commercial life; to break down the barrier between theory and practice; to effect a union between science and commerce." It is responsible for the basic standards of measurement and does all sorts of scientific testing, with particular attention to methods of transport and to computer usage. To assist in these researches, it has at Feltham a huge tank for trying out designs of ships and hovercraft, and a wind tunnel for testing aeroplanes. Electricity, metal fatigue, optical meteorology, and radiation are all studied here and all humanity benefits from the work carried out by the experts at the National Physical Laboratory.

It is at Teddington that the Thames' tide turns—indeed it has been suggested that the very name derives from "Tide-end-town" though philologists consider that the *tun* (place or farm) of Tuda's people is more likely. The biggest lock on the Thames is here, 650 feet long and 25 feet wide, able to take a tug and 6 barges. High-water mark is reached here one and a half hours later than at London Bridge, 18 miles away. It is here that the Thames Conservancy Board's water-clocks check the flow in the river and are ready to warn Londoners when precautions must be taken in time of drought.

Teddington has always somehow been more important for the people who have lived there than for the buildings they have erected, but the two parish churches which stand facing each other are both interesting and a great contrast. They are typical of Teddington's growth from a village of 1200 folk 100 years ago to the sizeable town which it is today—the modesty of St Mary's, which served the old place, enhanced by the striking contrast with its ambitious companion, St Alban's, begun in 1889–96 and not yet complete. The newer church was designed by W. Niven. It is so large as to be bewildering, with a light green copper roof which is a landmark when seen from Richmond Hill. It is known as the cathedral of the Thames Valley and has seven silver altar lamps which once hung in

365

the Church of the Holy Sepulchre in Jerusalem. They each bear a Greek inscription, of which one means "sent by the bounty of the patriarch Nicodemus to the Church in Teddington, from the Treasures of the Temple of the Resurrection, 1888". Six of the lamps appear to have been made in Russia and the seventh the Crusaders probably took to Jerusalem from Venice. The carving throughout the church is unusually fine—the pulpit with the saints Columba, Aidan, Oswald, Augustine, and Wilfred is particularly worth attention.

The old parish church is dedicated to St Mary. The south aisle of patterned brickwork is early 16th century and the rest, excepting for the 19th century chancel, dates from 1753–54 and is a miniature copy of John James' church at Twickenham. There is a little embattled tower and some good Victorian glass in the south aisle. There is a little brass to John Goodyere (d. 1506), a civilian with a big purse at his waist, and to Thomasyne, his wife, who wears a kennel headdress. Sir Orlando Bridgeman has an elaborate monument with Corinthian capitals and a pediment; he was the Lord Keeper who tried the men who had tried their king, Charles I, and he retired to Teddington in 1672 after refusing to sign James II's Declaration of Indulgence, granting freedom of religious worship. Son of a Wigan rector who became Bishop of Chester, Orlando, born soon after the death of Elizabeth I, passed from Cambridge to the Bar, and supported the king in the Short and Long Parliaments, for which he was knighted. During the Civil War he joined Charles at Oxford, but under the Protectorate, though compelled to withdraw from the Bar, his reputation for moderation and his skill in law were such that Cromwell permitted him to continue in practice. Royalists and Cromwellians consulted him with equal confidence. He became Lord Keeper in 1667, but found that he was not the keeper of the king's secrets, being tricked over the secret treaty with France in which Charles avowed himself a Roman Catholic and a pensioner of Louis XIV. He resisted the closing of the Exchequer, the threat of armed force, the so-called Declaration of Indulgence, and lost his position through refusing to fix the Great Seal to secret grants for the king's favourites. After his deposition he retired to his Teddington estate, where in 1674 he died and was buried. The Earls of Bradford are his descendants.

Sir Orlando Bridgeman had as his chaplain Thomas Traherne, a shoemaker's son who had a mind like William Blake. He lived through the Civil War and would often preach in this church, where he now lies. He left behind much poetry and prose, much of it fascinating to read, full of dreamings and imaginings. He imagined himself crowned with glory at his birth:

> *How like an angel came I down!*
> *How bright are all things here!*

His best work is to be found in *Centuries of Meditation*.

Six other notable persons lie here, the greatest of them perhaps being Stephen Hales who became vicar here in 1709 when he was 32 and remained until his death in 1761. He is buried under the tower. He was a pioneer of physiology and an inventor. In 1727, he published *Vegetable Staticks*, the most important 18th century contribution to the study of the physiology of plants, and his *Statical Essays* on animal physiology are second only to the work of Harvey. He discovered a means of obtaining fresh water from sea water; he invented a method of freeing corn from weevils by fumigation and of keeping meat fresh for long periods. He also designed a ventilator, a sort of modified organ bellows worked by hand which forced air under pressure wherever it was needed. It was applied to the Navy, to slave-ships, and to prisons with extraordinary success. A captain reported that his ship was perfectly healthy when becalmed for four months at sea, whereas ships without the ventilator had a serious sick list. Newgate's mortality was reduced by half and gaol fever was virtually banished, though its ravages had been so terrible that sweet herbs were placed in the courts in an attempt to ward off the deadly infection from the Bench and Bar. Hales was chaplain to George III and a monument to him was placed in Westminster Abbey, but he rightly lies in Teddington, in the parish he served so long and so lovingly.

In the chancel is a memorial adorned with cherubim and a skull, to Margaret Woffington, the Polly of John Gay's *Beggar's Opera*. One of the most gifted and popular actresses of her day, she was only 39 when she died and was buried here. Some say she built the house called Peg Woffington's Cottage for an almshouse; others say she lived in it; it is more probable that the name is just a link with her, a memory left behind in a part of the world she knew well. On the lower half of her memorial is an inscription to her little nephew, Horace, who died at the age of six months, and was the son of her sister and of the Hon. Robert Cholmondeley who became an earl and who built Cholmondeley House, later known as Queensberry Villa, in Richmond in 1708.

The satirist Paul Whitehead (1710–74) is buried here too. He did much of his writing in the debtors' prison, the Fleet, and later became a hanger-on of politicians, being rewarded with a subordinate post in the Treasury. He was one of the wild group, the Monks of Medmenham, who centred on Sir Francis Dashwood, and his heart is buried in Sir Francis's mausoleum in West Wycombe. Here also lies Henry Flitcroft, son of a Hampton Court gardener, who began his career as an architect by working on a volume of Inigo Jones' designs, became a clerk of works in Whitehall, and was finally Controller of Works for England till he was buried here in 1769.

In 1812, John Walter, the coal merchant who founded *The Times* in 1785, was buried here, in the church where he had often worshipped. He also insured ships and he was made bankrupt by the American War of Independence. Happily he had the respect and confidence of his creditors, who, when the estate was wound up, presented him with a little fund of money enabling him to start afresh. His premises in Printing House Square occupied the historic site on which stood the Blackfriars Theatre in which Shakespeare acted and produced his own plays. The printing press was not a success by itself, so on the first day of 1785 Walter launched the *Daily Universal Register*, whose title was altered three years later to *The Times, or Daily Universal Register*.

Walter merely hoped that his paper would advertise and feed his printing works. As a newspaper proprietor he stooped at times to the worst traditions of Grub Street, accepted Treasury subsidies, and published personal paragraphs which he was paid to contradict. That was typical 18th century journalism. The candour with which his paper assailed George III's sons led at last to his being fined, imprisoned, and sentenced to the pillory. To his credit it has to be added that his information was received from a reliable source, which he had the magnanimity not to reveal. He was succeeded by his son and his grandson, and his newspaper flourishes to this day.

Finally, Richard Dodderidge Blackmore the author of *Lorna Doone*, is buried here, after living and running a market garden for more than 40 years in Teddington. He had been trained for the law but gave this up through ill health and instead wrote 15 novels. *Lorna Doone* is probably the only one still read today, but they are all worthwhile and *The Maid of Sker*, the author's favourite, is good. He had great sympathy with Nature and tried to do for Devonshire what Scott had done for the Highlands.

Twickenham, to the north of Teddington, is one of the prettiest places alongside the Thames and one which takes several days to

St Jude's Church, Hampstead Garden Suburb, from the north-west

The Old Church, Greenford

Forty Hall, Enfield, from the south

Swakeleys, Ickenham: the east front

explore, so many and so interesting are the buildings there. It is perhaps best known today for its football ground. It is not mentioned in Domesday Book for it was a part of the manor of Isleworth and probably takes its name from a Saxon named Tuicca who had his homestead there. It was an obscure rural community till the end of the 17th century but from then onwards a series of fine houses were built there, to be lived in by interesting people.

The first of them was York House. It stands on the site of Yorke's Farm—hence the name—and was granted to Edward Hyde, Earl of Clarendon and Lord Chancellor, in 1666. He probably built the house which was much altered in 1700. It was most conveniently near to Hampton Court and he was glad to be able to retire each night to "my own house in Twickenham" after waiting on the king who spent much time at Hampton. It is a fine plain building of brick dressed with stone, three storeys high and seven windows wide. It is said that Clarendon, who wrote that wonderful history of the Civil War, *The History of the Great Rebellion*, lent the house to his son-in-law, the future James II, and that the little princesses, Mary and Anne, both played here. After Clarendon's fall from power, it passed to his son, the Earl of Rochester, and later, in 1816, became the property of the Hon. Mrs Damer, the sculptress and feminist. She was visited here by such distinguished ladies as the Hampstead poetess, Joanna Baillie, by Mrs Siddons and by Mrs Garrick. The Comte de Paris, the claimant to the throne of France, resided here in the 1860s and '70s, and the house then became the property of the Right Hon. Mountstuart Grant-Duff whose visitors included Gladstone, Benjamin Jowett, Lord Morley, and Ernest Renan. The last private occupant was the Indian merchant prince, Sir Ratan Tata, who modernised the building and installed in the grounds an astonishing group of statuary—eight marble nereides clustering round a cascade of water. In 1924 York House became the property of the borough council and the grounds, linked to the riverside terrace by an ingenious bridge which spans the road, are now open to the public so that everyone can enjoy the gardens and admire the nymphs. Inside the house, the staircase, ceilings, marble fireplaces, and fleur-de-lys fire-backs are unusual furnishings for borough council offices, but perhaps are all the more delightful for that.

Beside York House are the grounds of Orleans House and of Marble Hill. Orleans House was built in the 1710s by James Johnstone, the Secretary of State for Scotland. About 1720, he had an octagonal room built in the garden and it was often visited by George II's Queen, Caroline. The house became known as Orleans

N

House after the Duke of Orleans, the future King Louis-Philippe of France, lived there. The house has gone but the octagonal room remains, and was bequeathed with the grounds and adjacent Riverside House, to the council by the Hon. Mrs Nellie Ionides in 1956. The octagonal room has recently been opened as a municipal art gallery.

Marble Hill House is one of the loveliest and most intriguing houses near London. It was built between 1723 and 1734 for Henrietta Howard, the Countess of Suffolk, George II's mistress. The architects were Henry Herbert, the 9th Earl of Pembroke who was a brilliant architect, and Roger Morris. It is a severely plain house, adorned only with restrained pilasters and a pediment on the riverside front, but inside is a superb mahogany staircase, the wood for which was virtually stolen by the Navy from Honduras and nearly caused a war with Spain. The Countess retired from court in 1734 and settled herself at Twickenham. In the following year, the Earl of Suffolk being dead, she married an old friend, the Hon. George Berkeley. They had an idyllic life together and Henrietta kept her own little court, surrounded by all that was most intelligent in society. Pope, Arbuthnot, Dean Swift, and John Gay, the composer of the *Beggar's Opera*, all came. Gay was often in trouble for debt but he always had a refuge at Marble Hill. When Henrietta was a very old woman indeed, the young Horace Walpole used to come over from his house at Strawberry Hill, to gossip with her, and he preserved many of her reminiscences in his *Memoirs*. Perhaps the lady's excellent qualities are best summed up in Pope's characteristic verses about her:

> *I know a thing that's most uncommon*
> *(Envy, be silent and attend!)*
> *I know a reasonable woman,*
> *Handsome and witty, yet a friend.*

> *Not warp'd by passion, awed by rumour;*
> *Not grave through pride, nor gay through folly;*
> *An equal mixture of good humour*
> *And sensible soft melancholy.*

> *Has she no faults then (Envy says) Sir?*
> *Yes, she has one, I must aver:*
> *When all the world conspires to praise her,*
> *The woman's deaf, and does not hear.*

Some while after Henrietta's death in 1767, the house was rented for a year, 1795, by Mrs FitzHerbert and then passed through various hands in the 19th century till the London County Council, most courageously, bought it in 1902 to preserve the view from Richmond Hill. During the 1960s the house was expertly restored and redecorated and is now open to the public. Marble Hill and Kenwood are, to your editor's mind, the two loveliest 18th century houses in the surrounds of London.

Just on the edge of Marble Hill Park is a beautiful terrace of early 18th century houses, Montpelier Row. Here Tennyson lived for a while and here another great poet, Walter de la Mare, spent the last years of his life. Val Prinsep, the Victorian Academician whose work is undervalued today, lived here too. Earlier literary associations cling to Fielding Cottages in Holly Road where Henry Fielding had a now vanished wooden cottage in which he wrote *Tom Jones*, and to No. 2 Ailsa Park Villas, St Margaret's, where Dickens lived in 1838–39 and where he wrote *Oliver Twist*. Amateurs of 18th century architecture should also admire Sion Row, an elegant terrace of 12 houses, just beside York House.

St Mary's Church is best seen from the Riverside Walk, that charming promenade which leads us past nearly all that is most agreeable in Twickenham. On the churchyard wall is a tablet recording an exceptionally high tide in 1774; it is eight feet above the road. This is a pretty church, designed in 1714–15 by John James, with a much older embattled tower of stone which dates from a 15th century building, possibly undertaken on the orders of William of Wykeham, who endowed Winchester College with the living of Twickenham. After the Reformation, the patronage of the living became the right of the Dean and Canons of St George at Windsor, who hold it to this day.

There are a number of interesting monuments in the church. They include a brass to Robert Burton with the royal arms of Lancaster upon it. He died on July 24, 1443, having been cook to Henry VI. There are two fine figures of Francis Poulton (d. 1642) and his wife, who clasp hands across a skull, and Sir Chaloner Ogle who trounced pirates off the Barbary Coast, has a striking monument by Rysbrack. There is another good piece of sculpture by John Bacon the younger to the memory of George and Anne Gostling; it shows a weeping woman. In the tower is a monument to the Berkeley family, including that Sir William who was governor of Virginia in 1676 when the colony was inflamed into a state of insurrection by Nathaniel Bacon, an aristocratic demagogue and the governor's cousin by marriage. Bacon died, probably of typhus and Berkeley regained control, but he was recalled home and died in retirement—having in all probability suffered great injustice.

Sir Godfrey Kneller has a memorial here, and another in Westminster Abbey; he was buried on his estate at Whitton. The poet Pope visited him two days before his death at Kneller Hall and found him looking at plans for his monument. Since he could not get the space he needed for it at Twickenham, he left money for its erection in the Abbey. Pope wrote the epitaph, as he did for another Twickenham inhabitant, the lawyer Nathaniel Pigott: "Many he assisted in the law; more he kept from it." Sir Godfrey had been much concerned with the church; the nave fell down during the night of April 9, 1713, but the artist was churchwarden and busied himself so vigorously in the matter that money was soon raised and the church rebuilt. Kitty Clive, the actress for whom Horace Walpole found a home in her old age at Little Strawberry Hill, lies in the churchyard and so does Thomas Twining who built the Dial House which is now the vicarage and founded a tea and coffee house and business whose brands of beverages still refresh us today. The poet Alexander Pope lies in the nave, having spent a great part of his life in Twickenham.

Pope was born in 1688. A delicate child but extraordinarily clever, he was virtually self-educated. His first poems were published when he was very young and in 1712 he wrote *The Rape of the Lock* which made him famous. Thereafter his life was one of uninterrupted success. His translation of the *Iliad* made him a small fortune and in 1719 after his father's death he settled at Twickenham with his mother and old nurse to look after him and continued to write poetry there for the rest of his life. His publications included a translation of the *Odyssey* and a bitter and vehement satire, *The Dunciad*, directed against an unfortunate and otherwise forgotten poet, Lewis Theobald. Pope's frame and health were not strong and he made his home the centre of his world. His great delight was to receive guests and to adorn his grounds, in which he built a grotto to link the house on the riverbank with the garden on the other side of the road. He adorned it with all kinds of spars and glittering minerals and this grotto alone remains, for his villa was demolished in the last century and replaced by another which in its turn gave way to a convent school. The grounds are well maintained but, in spite of all the nuns can do, the grotto needs restoration. Pope died at his villa and was buried in the nave of the parish church though he was a Roman Catholic, near the memorial he had raised to his father and mother, while in the churchyard lies his old nurse, Mary Beach, who served him for 38 years. Pope would not be buried in Westminster Abbey but was borne to his grave by six of the poorest men in Twickenham, each of whom was given a grey woollen suit for his pains. He wrote his own epitaph which runs:

> *Heroes and kings, your distance keep:*
> *In peace let one poor poet sleep;*
> *Who never flattered folks like you;*
> *Let Horace blush and Virgil too.*

Near to where Pope's villa stood is a fine early 18th century house, Crossdeep, and near the church are the remains of the old manor house which legend associates with Catherine of Aragon and Catherine of Braganza, Charles II's queen. Opposite the church, in the river, where the ferry celebrated in a Victorian drawing-room ballad used to ply to and fro, is Eel Pie Island, which has always been a pleasure resort—the Kenwigs family, in *Nicholas Nickleby*, came here and had "a cold collation of bottled beer, shrub [a mixture of fruit-juice and alchohol] and shrimps". The little Duke of Gloucester, the only one of Queen Anne's 17 children to survive as long as the age of 11, used to drill his regiment of boys here. One's heart aches for that poor queen who had to bear so much sorrow and who never seemed romantic or tragic, just a very sad, kind, forbearing woman.

Along the riverside, just beyond the site of Pope's Villa, droop three glorious willow trees whose colour and movement are a sheer delight to watch. They are all that remains of the Earl of Radnor's fine house and grounds; the house was bombed and the grounds became an agreeable public park. To the north of the borough, at Whitton, another open space, Murray Park, covers the site where the Duke of Argyll's mansion once stood, and nearby is Kneller Hall where Sir Godfrey lived. His house however has been enlarged and altered beyond recognition and is now the Royal Military School of Music. On the Chertsey bypass is All Hallows, a modern church designed by Robert Atkinson but with the tower of Wren's church which stood in Lombard Street and was moved here stone by stone in the 1930s. An excellent peal of 10 bells came too, along with some fine pews and panelling and a pulpit from which John Wesley once preached.

Finally we come to Strawberry Hill, the home and the creation of Horace Walpole, and now well-preserved by the Vincentian Order as St Mary's Teachers' Training College. Horace Walpole (1717–97)

373

was the youngest son of Sir Robert, Prime Minister to George I and George II. Although Sir Robert took little interest in the boy, his mother cherished him. He went to Eton and Cambridge where he became friends with the poet Thomas Gray, and the two young men set out to make the Grand Tour in Europe. They journeyed all over Italy and Walpole then returned home to take up a rather dilettante career in politics. In 1747 he bought from Mrs Chenevix, who kept a wonderful toyshop near Charing Cross, a little cottage which had been the home of the dramatist, Colley Cibber. Walpole was enchanted with his purchase—he wrote about the house in lyrical manner:

It is a little play-thing-house that I got out of Mrs Chenevix's shop, and it is the prettiest bauble you ever saw. It is set in enamelled meadows, with filigree hedges . . . Two delightful roads, that you would call dusty, supply me continually with coaches and chaises; barges as solemn as Barons of the Exchequer move under my window; Richmond Hill and Ham walks bound my prospect . . . I have enough land about to keep such a farm as Noah's when he set up in the ark with a pair of each kind, but my cottage is rather cleaner than I believe his was after they had been cooped up together forty days.

Here he spent the rest of his life adding to the house and adorning it in a Gothic manner. Here he wrote his books—*The Castle of Otranto*, the forerunner of Mrs Radclyffe's and "Monk" Lewis's romances of terror, a tragedy called *The Mysterious Mother, Anecdotes of Painting*, a *Catalogue of Engravers*, an *Essay on Modern Gardening, Memoirs of the Last Ten Years of George II*, and *Memoirs of the Reign of George III*. From here he sent out thousands of letters, witty, vivacious, often malicious, always brilliant, and he set up a printing press to publish his own works and those of his friends, such as Gray. Here he received everyone of interest or importance, here he was looked after by the two charming sisters, Mary and Agnes Berry, whom he used to call his twin wives, though he never married. From here he would set out to visit his neighbour, the Countess of Suffolk, to join in London society, or to cross the Channel to talk to that venerable and delightful lady, Madame du Deffand.

In the designs of his house he was aided by a series of architects— John Chute, Richard Bentley the son of the great philologist, Thomas Pitt later Lord Camelford, and finally James Essex. He quarrelled with them all. The house became larger and larger as a long gallery was added with a ceiling fan-vaulted like that of Henry VII's Chapel in Westminster Abbey, a door copied from the north door of St Alban's Abbey, and gilt fretwork and mirrors on the walls. The Staircase Hall was covered with "a paper painted in perspective to represent Gothic fretwork" and Walpole thought it "so pretty and so small that I am inclined to wrap it up and send it to you in my letter", while his library has bookcases copied from the side doors to the screen of Old St Paul's, and a chimneypiece inspired by John of Eltham's tomb in Westminster Abbey. When he died, an old man of 80, at his house in Berkeley Square, he left the house to his cousin, the sculptress Mrs Damer, for her lifetime and thereafter to his great-niece, the Countess of Waldegrave who left Walpole's fantasies intact and unmolested, and so they have passed on to delight us today, for the house is open once a year when a Strawberry Fair is held to raise money for charity, and it can be seen at any reasonable time provided permission is sought in writing first. It should be seen, for Strawberry Hill is one of the most original literary and architectural monuments in all England, and the harbinger of the Gothic revival in building that was to sweep England in the 19th century.

TOWER HAMLETS

TOWER HAMLETS

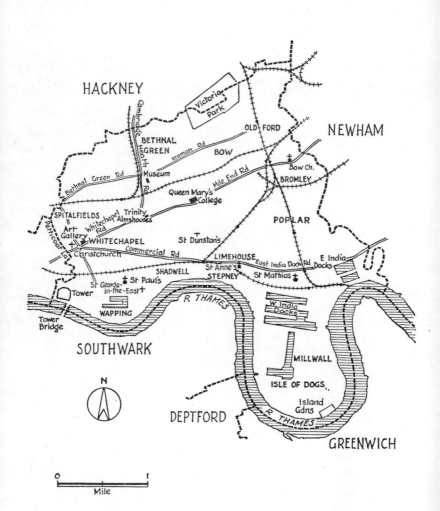

TOWER HAMLETS

The London Borough of Tower Hamlets consists of the former boroughs of Stepney, Poplar, and Bethnal Green, and includes most of the area known as the East End of London. Its southern boundary is the Thames and on the west lies the City of London while to the north is Hackney and to the east Newham, which was formerly in Essex. It is an area of immense character and individuality, quite unlike any other part of London and with an astonishingly large share of the city's finest churches. It covers an area of 7·8 square miles and has a population of 192,000.

The East End of London stretches out, a flat, low-lying land, from the City walls to the River Lea. Throughout the Middle Ages, the greater part of what is now Tower Hamlets belonged to the Bishop of London's huge manor of Stepney. It was agricultural land and, apart from farm buildings, the main dwellings were the monasteries which were established there—the Hospital of St Mary (Spital Square), the Hospital of St Katharine (St Katharine's Dock), the Nunnery of Poor Clares or Minorites (Holy Trinity, Minorites bombed and demolished) and the Convent of St Leonards at Bromley-by-Bow. Its pattern of existence was defined early—it was a place where foreigners tended to settle since outside the City walls they could be free of guild restrictions, and where those trades which, because of their dirt, noise, or stench, were unfitted for practice within the city, tended to congregate. Once the monasteries had been dissolved in Henry VIII's reign, their sites were swiftly converted into tenements or rows of small cottages to accommodate London's increasing population, and no edict that Elizabeth I or James I might promulgate could restrain the building. John Stow, London's greatest historian, lamented the change; he wrote of Hog Lane, now Middlesex Street (where the Petticoat Lane Market is held today):

This Hog Lane stretched north towards St Mary Spitle without Bishops-gate, and within these forty years had on both sides fair hedgerows of elm trees, with bridges and easy stiles to pass over into the pleasant fields, very commodious for citizens therein to walk, shoot and otherwise recreate and refresh their dull spirits in the sweet and wholesome air, which is now within a few years made a continual building throughout, of garden-houses and small cottages, and the fields on either side be turned into garden-plots, tenter yards, bowling alleys, and such like, from Houndes Ditch in the west, as far as White Chappell, and further towards the east.

When in the late 18th and early 19th centuries the docks were created along the Thames to accommodate the vast increase of trade, the East End as we know it was established—a heavily over-built area, with an intense dock life, many small factories and businesses and an extremely mixed population.

Stepney takes its name from Stybba's *hythe* or landing place, showing that even in Saxon times its development was closely linked with ships and their movements. In its south-west corner are a group of buildings whose history really belongs to the general history of London and these we will examine first. The most important of all is the Tower of London, the massive fortification which guards City and river, and asserts the royal authority over both. It was begun in 1067 as an earthwork within the eastern angle of the Roman city wall, thrown up by William's men to overawe "the vast and fierce populace" of London. A more permanent building was begun about 1078 under the direction of Gundulf, a monk of Bec in Normandy who became Bishop of Rochester. This was of Caen stone, specially imported and, since the walls were whitewashed, was known as the White Tower. It was not completed till 1097, well after the Conqueror's death and is one of the few hall-keeps, both palace and fortress, left in Europe. Its walls are 90 feet high and 15 feet thick at the base. On the second floor is the Chapel of St John, a perfect Norman chapel, virtually unaltered and un-spoiled, with tunnel-vaulted nave and gallery and groin-vaulted aisles. The pillars—round in the aisles, square in the gallery—are thick and squat with rough carving on the capitals. The royal pews are at the west end so that the monarch and his family, knowing themselves to be surrounded by a hostile populace, need not fear a knife in the back when kneeling at prayer. In the other rooms of the keep is the magnificent collection of armour, assembled here by Charles II. In the Tudor Room on the top floor is the personal armour of the kings of England, and here is the headsman's block and axe, and the cloak which wrapped Wolfe's wounded body at the taking of Quebec.

Today, when the Tower is considered as little more than a tourist attraction, its importance in English history cannot be overstressed.

It was the monarch's last stronghold, his refuge when all else failed, his secure prison, his treasure-house, his arsenal. It was the Tower that was given in pledge for the completion of Magna Carta, it was here that the child king, Richard II, took refuge from Wat Tyler's men, and it was here that the same monarch, when a man himself, resigned his crown to his cousin Bolingbroke, later Henry IV, in 1399; it was here, during the long wars with France, that David, King of Scots, John, King of France, Charles, Duke of Blois, and John de Vienne, the governor of Calais with his 12 brave burgesses, were lodged, and it was here that Henry VII greeted his future queen, Elizabeth of York, their marriage ending the Wars of the Roses.

Around the White Tower, two roughly concentric lines of defence were built during the long reign of Henry III and his son, Edward I, and beyond them a moat was dug. Henry spent close on £10,000 and built the first chapel of St Peter ad Vincula to the west of the White Tower. Edward completed his father's work which indeed, as by far the better soldier of the two, he may have planned during the previous reign, and rebuilt St Peter's Chapel. By the time of his death in 1307 the defences of the Tower were effectually complete.

The attention of the visitor, who enters over the drawbridge and under the Middle Tower, attaches itself to the towers around the inner line of defence—Bell Tower, Beauchamp Tower, Devereux Tower, Flint, Bowyer, Brick and Martin Towers, Constable Tower, Broad Arrow, Salt and Lanthorn Towers, Wakefield Tower, and Bloody Tower. It was in the towers, more especially the first and last pairs, that that series of royal and noble prisoners were lodged, whose fates go to make up the history of England. Poor saintly unsuccessful Henry VI was struck down by an assassin while he knelt in the oratory of the Wakefield Tower. His rival, Edward IV, had secured the throne by his victory at Barnet (see p. 26) and wanted Henry out of the way. Every year on May 21, representatives of Eton College and King's College, Cambridge, lay lilies and roses on the spot where Henry's body was discovered, for the unfortunate monarch was the founder of these two great educational institutions. Some years later, his death was most brutally revenged when Edward's sons, the young King Edward V, aged 13, and his little brother, the Duke of York, aged 8, were suffocated; whether the orders were given by their uncle, who was to become Richard III, or by his successor, Henry VII, is debatable. The little bodies were buried under a staircase on the south side of the White Tower where they remained till they were discovered in 1674 and were reburied in Westminster Abbey on Charles II's orders. Sir Thomas More, once Chancellor of England and the king's friend, was confined for 15 months in the Bell Tower for his refusal to accept Henry VIII as Head of the Church of England. His friend John Fisher, Bishop of Rochester, was imprisoned in the room above him for the same cause. Fisher was beheaded on June 19, More on July 6, 1535, on Tower Hill. So great was More's courage, so complete his self-control, that he was able to jest as he ascended the scaffold. The bodies of those two saints were buried in the chapel of St Peter ad Vincula.

In the angle of the Bell Tower is the Queen's House, an L-shaped building which is the residence of the Lieutenant of the Tower. Here Anne Boleyn, accused of infidelity to Henry VIII, was confined for the last 18 days of her life before being executed on Tower Green by the Executioner of Calais who skilfully used a sword rather than the customary axe. Her body was placed in an arrow-chest and buried in St Peter's Chapel. Her cousin, Catherine Howard, suffered the same accusation and the same fate; on the night before her death, she sent for the block to be brought to her room so that she could rehearse the next morning's ordeal and conduct herself as a member of the Howard family and as a queen on the scaffold.

Lady Jane Grey, the tragic Nine Days' Queen, stayed here, and watched from the window her young husband, Lord Guildford Dudley, go to the scaffold on Tower Hill, and later saw his body, headless, carried back on a cart. He had been confined in the Beauchamp Tower and carved her name—JANE—on the wall there, an eternal love-letter never delivered. The next day the poor child— she was only 17—was herself beheaded on Tower Green. The princess Elizabeth, Anne Boleyn's daughter, was lodged in the Bell Tower but took her meals in the Lieutenant's lodgings during 1554, when she was confined on her sister's orders on suspicion of complicity in Sir Thomas Wyatt's rebellion. She was brought by river to the grim entrance at Traitor's Gate and refused to go ashore, vehemently asserting that she was no traitor. A downpour of rain and the entreaties of the Lieutenant, Sir James Brydges, brought her to land. She was allowed to walk along the ramparts and to this day the stretch of wall is called Elizabeth's Walk.

At the very end of her reign, Elizabeth signed the warrant for the execution of her favourite, the Earl of Essex, for his abortive rising against her; he died on Tower Green. In James I's reign, the most distinguished prisoners were his poor innocent cousin, Lady Arabella Stuart, whom he feared as a possible rival for the throne, and who died mad after four years of confinement, and the noble Sir Walter Raleigh who was imprisoned in the Tower on three separate occasions for a sum of nearly 13 years. He lodged in the Bloody Tower, ate his meals in the Lieutenant's lodgings, and had a small laboratory for his experiments on Tower Green. While in captivity, he wrote many books, including the *History of the World*; "Only my father would keep such a bird in such a cave," protested Prince Henry, James I's eldest son. Raleigh was beheaded on October 28, 1618, in the Palace Yard at Westminster and was buried in St Margaret's, Westminster.

The Earl of Strafford and Archbishop Laud were incarcerated and executed as scapegoats for Charles I; as Strafford went out to the scaffold on Tower Hill, the aged prelate thrust his hands between the bars of his window to bless the sufferer. Vile Judge Jeffereys, responsible for the Bloody Assizes at Dorchester after the Duke of Monmouth's unsuccessful rebellion against his uncle, James II, ended his days in the Tower. A more fortunate prisoner was Lord Nithsdale, imprisoned for his part in the 1715 Rising in Scotland against George I. His brave wife smuggled him out disguised as a woman. Three other Scottish noblemen, Lords Kilmarnock, Balmerino, and Lovat, were less fortunate; they were all executed in 1746 and 1747 for supporting Prince Charles Edward Stuart, the Young Pretender. Simon Fraser, Lord Lovat, was the last man to be beheaded in England; he died on April 9, 1747. During the First World War, Sir Roger Casement was imprisoned in the Tower; during the Second, Rudolf Hess spent a few days there. Today, the place of the scaffold on Tower Hill is a meeting place for street orators, while the Tower ravens strut around the site of the block on Tower Green.

The longest queues in summer are always to visit the Crown Jewels which glitter in their Aladdin's Cave of splendour in the Wakefield Tower. The original regalia, amassed by six centuries of monarchy since the days of Edward the Confessor, were sold or melted down by Cromwell. A copy of St Edward's Crown was made for Charles II. The Imperial State Crown was made for the coronation of Queen Victoria in 1838, and in it is set one ancient jewel, the ruby said to have been given to the Black Prince by Pedro the Cruel after the Battle of Navarette in 1367, and later worn by Henry V in the coronet surrounding his helmet at the Battle of Agincourt in 1415. The crown later had added to it the second largest of the Stars of Africa, cut from the Cullinan diamond; the largest Star is in the Sceptre. Only two ancient pieces survive, the anointing spoon which may have been made for John's coronation in 1199, and the Ampulla, a vessel for holding the oil, shaped like an eagle, which was probably made in Henry IV's day (1399–1413). The orbs and sceptres and swords of state are also here, and much fine plate besides.

The chapel of St Peter ad Vincula, where so many illustrous sufferers are buried, is the third chapel with that dedication, having been rebuilt again early in the 16th century, after a fire in 1512. Here, in Stow's words, there lie before the high altar "two dukes between two queens, to wit, the Duke of Somerset and the Duke of Northumberland, between Queen Anne and Queen Catharine, all four beheaded". There are several interesting monuments here, the earliest being the tomb of John, Duke of Exeter (d. 1447), originally in the chapel of St Katharine's Hospital. It is a tomb-chest with an elaborate canopy over three recumbent figures. In the sanctuary are two recessed tombs with finely carved figures of members of the Blount family, two of them Lieutenants of the Tower. Sir Richard is in armour kneeling with his wife and their four children under two arches on a grand wall monument richly adorned; and his father Sir Michael kneels with his wife and their three sons. A curious 17th century wall monument has busts of George Payler and his wife in oval recesses, their little son sleeping in a recess between them, and below them two other sleeping children are supported by cherubs. A monument to Sir Alan Apsley, a 17th century Lieutenant of the Tower, has a sleeping baby holding an hourglass; one to Captain Valentine Pyne, Master Gunner of England in the 17th century, has a tablet with a plaque of a man of war; and on an altar tomb of 1544 are figures of Sir Richard Cholmondeley in armour, with his feet on a lion and his wife supported by angels with two small dogs at her feet. The font is 16th century. To the north of the nave stands the empty tomb of Sir Richard Cholmondeley, who, preparing his tomb in advance, fell from favour after serving Henry VIII, and is buried elsewhere. During restorations last century the 14th century font, which had been missing since Stuart days, was found in the empty tomb.

Beside the chapel are the Waterloo Barracks and beyond them the Museum of the Royal Fusiliers. A great attraction at the Tower are the Yeomen Warders, originally appointed by Henry VII and popularly known as Beefeaters, in their magnificent scarlet Tudor uniforms. In addition to assisting and controlling visitors, they take part nightly in the Ceremony of the Keys when the Tower is locked up for the night. (Permission to attend may be granted on written application; it is well worth making such application.) Every third year on Ascension Day the Yeoman Warders help to beat the bounds of Tower Liberty. Royal Salutes are fired from the Tower on appropriate occasions by the Honourable Artillery Company.

The Tower is the most important mediaeval secular building left in London, but it stands in an area very much of the 20th century. The Port of London Authority and Trinity House, which was founded by a Stepney man, Sir Thomas Spert, are both here though just inside the City boundary, but the Memorial of the 36,000 merchant seamen who lost their lives in the two World Wars is in Trinity Square Gardens which is in Stepney. The First World War memorial is an arcade or cloister designed by Sir Edward Lutyens, PRA, who also designed the Cenotaph in Whitehall; that for the Second World War is a horseshoe-shaped wall with alcoves, surrounding a lawn, with the names of the dead and their ships inscribed on bronze plaques around the walls. A memorial to sailors could not be in a more fitting place than Tower Hamlets, so much is the borough concerned with ships and the sea.

A piece of the old Roman city wall stood in Trinity Place and in a bastion there was found embedded part of a Roman tombstone, now in the British Museum. It was raised to the memory of Julius Classicianus by his sorrowing wife, Julia Pacata. He was that courageous administrator who dared brave the authority of his general, Suetonius Paulinus, when too harsh a retribution was being exacted from the Britons after Boadicea's rebellion. Suetonius was recalled to Rome and Classicianus was put in charge of the province which he ruled by milder means. He died in the city which he had fostered, one of the first and greatest of Londoners.

Behind the Tower is the Royal Mint. Coin has been struck in London since Roman times, and continuously so since Alfred's reign. The Mint was established within the walls of the Tower in 1300, and was removed to its present building in 1811. The plans were by James Johnson and were completed after his death in 1807 by Robert Smirke; the new machinery was designed by Boulton, Watt, and Rennie. In addition to producing the coinage of the United Kingdom, the Mint supplies coinage for most of the Commonwealth countries and for many foreign ones. It may be that it will soon leave its historic site and remove to Glamorganshire, leaving London the poorer, both literally and metaphorically, thereby.

On the river side is Tower Bridge, which was opened on June 30, 1894, by the Prince of Wales, later Edward VII. It was designed by Sir Horace Jones and built by Sir Wolfe Barry; it cost one and a quarter million pounds. The twin steel towers inside the masonry rise 200 feet high. The gloomy arches of the towers are approached by suspended spans 90 yards long, and the 70 yards of the middle span are divided into two parts weighing 1000 tons each, which can be raised by hydraulic machinery in one minute. They are locked by massive bolts, which are withdrawn for the raising of the bridge, enabling the two leaves to rise to a vertical position against the tower. The average time of the raising and lowering of the roadway is five minutes. When closed the central span is nearly 30 feet above high-water mark. The weight of iron and steel in the bridge is nearly 12,000 tons. Between high-water mark and the depth where the foundations rest is 60 feet.

The bridge is one of the best loved monuments of London and its footbridge gives one of the finest views of the City and the Thames. There are few more dramatic and moving sights than to come up river in a cargo boat and to see in the dawn the arms of the bridge open as if in welcome to admit the ship into the Upper Pool.

Stepney divides itself into several distinct areas, which are indeed the direct descendants of those hamlets near to the Tower which give the modern borough its name. Along the river lie Wapping and Ratcliffe (the Red Cliff), Shadwell and Limehouse. Then, where the Whitechapel/Mile End Road forms a fork with the Commercial Road, is Whitechapel. Between the arms of the fork lies Stepney itself and north of Whitechapel is Spitalfields. We will describe first the parent village, Stepney, which gave its name to the whole of the former metropolitan borough.

On Stepney Green, St Dunstan's Church still stands, reposed and dignified, surrounded by seven acres of churchyard. There was probably a church here in Saxon times and the chancel walls are of the 13th century though most of the present building dates from the 15th century. It is of Kentish rag with stone dressings, with a stalwart tower. The parishioners have recently removed much 19th century clutter from the interior and the beauty of the church can be seen. There is a broad nave with aisles, seven bays long. The chancel has a fine east window with excellent modern glass by Hugh Easton; a huge figure of Christ, crucified but reigning from the Tree, rises above bombed Stepney. Below it, on the wall, is St Dunstan's greatest treasure, a Saxon rood-stone; Our Lady and St John stand beside the Cross. Though the stone is much worn, the wonderfully fluid line of arms and draperies is still visible. On the north wall of the chancel hangs a little 14th or 15th century stone carving showing the Annunciation, and near it is the tomb-chest of Sir Henry Colet, twice Lord Mayor of London, whose son John was rector here before he left to become Dean of St Paul's and founder of St Paul's School. The parish he administered was so large that it was split into 66 parishes in later times. Near the tomb is a squint and opposite it a triple sedilia with 13th century carved foliage. Near to Sir Henry lies Richard Pace, who became Dean of St Paul's soon after John Colet, who rose high in favour at court and from Stepney vicarage went out as ambassador to Venice with tragic consequences for, failing in his efforts to secure the Papacy for Cardinal Wolsey, he fell into disgrace and his misfortunes affected his brain. In the end he died here, neglected and forgotten.

A lofty wall monument to Joseph Somes tells us that he was a seafaring man of the last century and that "by the sedulous application of a powerful mind he raised himself to the position of the most extensive shipowner in this great commercial country". A fine relief below has on it two sailing ships, one entering dock and one leaving. There is another ship carved on a 17th century stone in memory of Sir Thomas Spert, who founded Trinity House 400 years ago and was the proud commander of the ship which bore Henry VIII to the Field of the Cloth of Gold.

High on the chancel wall, gay with gilding and colour, kneels Robert Clarke in a black cloak, with his daughter Frances wearing a high starched collar as in Stuart days; and in the nave kneels Elizabeth Startute with a daughter and her husband, ruffs framing their shining faces. In a niche is an 18th century bust of John Berry, wearing a lace cravat and a long wig falling over his shoulders; and in the sanctuary is a relief of the Good Samaritan in memory of old Benjamin Kenton, who has lain beneath since 1800, having done much to help hospitals for the poor.

In the churchyard under a fine tomb lies the Commander-in-Chief of Queen Anne's fleet, the "brave and fortunate" Sir John Leake. We read that he destroyed scores of ships, seized all the French settlements in Newfoundland, destroyed their fisheries, and took a fleet of 90 cornships to the relief of Barcelona when the French were besieging it. Queen Anne rewarded him with diamond rings. On another tomb here is an odd epitaph to Betsey Harris, "who died suddenly while contemplating the beauties of the moon in 1831".

Alongside them in the churchyard lies Roger Crab, though his tomb is now unmarked. He was a 17th century vegetarian, when such views were rare. Pamphlets were published about him and his

387

way of life was a matter for wonder. In two other unmarked graves lie a father and son, Matthew and Richard Mead. Matthew succeeded William Greenhill, who had been vicar of Stepney during the Commonwealth period, as minister at Stepney Meeting House; his son Richard grew up to become physician at St Thomas's Hospital and a member of the Royal Society.

Stepney Meeting House still flourishes in Stepney Way. The first minister, William Greenhill, was chaplain to the Parliamentary army and was given charge of Charles I's children after the king's execution. He dedicated one of his volumes to little Princess Elizabeth for he found her a "most hopeful lady" as a pupil.

At the south end of the Green are Lady Mico's Almshouses which were founded in 1691 and rebuilt by the Mercers' Company in 1859. They are of grey brick with a garden in front and unusual projecting front parlours. At No. 29, a fine house built about 1710, is Roland House, the headquarters of the East London Scouts, named after the Hon. Roland Philipps, son of Lord St Davids, who was killed at the Battle of the Somme. Before the war, he had been determined to live and work in the East End and to help those less fortunate than himself and he had bought No. 29 for this purpose; after his death, his friends carried on his work. His sword, his Military Cross, and the wooden cross from his grave in France are all here, as is his scout staff with the proficiency badges he had won, for he would always pass a test himself before examining a boy.

To the west of Stepney Green is the huge Ocean Estate of GLC flats, a brave if rather turgid attempt at mass housing. Here a blue plaque reminds us that nearby, at 18 Stepney Causeway, Dr Barnardo began his great work (see p. 346). Nearby in Tower Hamlets Cemetery lies Will Crooks who was born in Poplar workhouse in 1852 and trained as a cooper but found time to hold open-air meetings, and such was his power as a speaker that these meetings were known as Crooks's College. After the age of 40, he was supported by the voluntary subscriptions of workmen, never receiving more than £4 a week. In 1901, he became Mayor of Poplar, the first Labour mayor in London, and he made his way to Parliament and became a Privy-Councillor, G. K. Chesterton calls him "Very like a poor man in Dickens", and his epitaph rightly says: "He lived and died a servant of the people."

Back in the noble width of the Mile End Road, where shops and stalls and small factories crowd in on remains of 18th century terraces, such as Coburn Terrace, there is much of interest. Very early in the morning mists, one can imagine the buildings gone and try to see the road as Mile End Waste where Wat Tyler's men gathered in 1381 on their way to Smithfield to demand the abolition of serfdom and fairer taxation from their young king, Richard II. They had already demonstrated their earnestness by dragging Archbishop Simon Sudbury from the Tower and beheading him. Young Richard spoke to them soothingly but Wat Tyler laid his hand on the royal bridle and was struck down by the dagger of the Lord Mayor of London, Sir William Walworth. The dagger has appeared on the City arms ever since. A great cry went up from Tyler's men and it looked as if they would overwhelm the royal party but Richard urged his horse forward, crying that he himself would be their leader and that all their demands should be met. The people dispersed to their homes, the king broke his word, and savage retribution was meted out, but the peasants had made themselves felt and the rising was remembered uneasily by those in command.

By the time it is fully daylight, the Mile End Road is alive with traffic and with bargaining, for all sorts of commodities—fruit, china, materials, and net curtains foaming out from baskets—are offered for sale along the pavements. At Nos. 153–175 is Booth House, the Salvation Army's Working Men's Hostel, quite close to where, in the disused Quaker burial ground in Thomas (later Fulbourne) Street, on Sunday, July 2, 1865, William Booth preached the first sermon which was to lead to the formation of that great and wonderful body, the Salvation Army, which is known all over the world today for its noble work in saving both the souls and bodies of men. A few minutes before he began to speak, Boot watched a boy hanging naphtha lamps to light the tent on a length of rope. "One of these days," he said, "they will be hanging lights like that all round the world," and his prophecy has come true.

Nearby is Queen Mary College which nourishes men's intellects. It grew out of the East London College known as the People's Palace and although fires have destroyed the old buildings, the work goes on today with 2500 students who take degrees in any of the vast range of studies offered by London University, of which Queen Mary College is a part. Beside the college, St Benet's Church which was bombed has been rebuilt as a small domed chapel, designed by Messrs Playne and Lacey, and behind it lies a burial ground which has a great place in English history for it is the graveyard which Cromwell allowed the Jews to buy when he gave them permission to enter England. In it lies Benjamin Disraeli, the grandfather of the Prime Minister.

389

No. 88 and No. 401 Mile End Road are both worth remembering for at the former house lived Captain James Cook, the wonderful navigator and explorer who claimed Australia for England, with his wife and sons, and it was from here that he set off on his last voyage from which he never returned for he was killed by the natives of Hawaii (see also p. 13), while 401 was the home and workshop of C. R. Ashbee who founded the Art Workers' Guild. Around here are many of London's great breweries—Truman's in Brick Lane, Charrington's in the Mile End Road, and Watney Mann's in Whitechapel Road—and then, almost at the fork with Cambridge Heath Road, are Trinity Almshouses. They were built in 1694–95, probably to the designs of William Ogbourne by the Trinity House Corporation for "28 decayed masters and commanders of ships, or the widows of such". Between the two rows of almshouses stood a pretty chapel. They were severely bombed during the war and stood derelict till they were acquired by the London County Council, and restored as a training centre for disabled people, and as flats for social workers. The principal room has been panelled with some fine deal panelling from Bradmore House, Hammersmith, which was demolished in 1913, and it now looks as if the old almshouses have a long and useful life in front of them again.

Right against the City wall but beyond the City's ancient entrance, Aldgate, is **Whitechapel**. Roman remains have been found here for this has always been the main road between the two Roman cities of London and Colchester, though the line of it, as we shall see, has varied over the centuries. Whitechapel takes its name from the white stone chapel of St Mary Matfelon (Matfelon is a family name) which was built as a chapel of ease to St Dunstan's in the mid-13th century, became a parish church about 1338, was destroyed by a tempest in 1362 and was rebuilt from the offerings of those who made a special pilgrimage there for the remission of their sins. The church was rebuilt in the late 17th century and again in 1877. It was bombed on December 29, 1940, and was demolished in 1952, six centuries of history disappearing without a trace, save the name of the district. In the churchyard here was buried Richard Brandon, the executioner who lopped off Charles I's head. Brandon always declared that he had not wished to do the work, but was forced to do it when "fetched out of bed by a troop of horse", receiving £30 for his pains, all paid in half-crowns within an hour. He also said that he had an orange stuck full of cloves and a handkerchief out of the king's pocket, which he sold for ten shillings; and that he returned home and gave his wife the money, saying it was the dearest he had ever earned, for it would cost him his life. When he died, full of remorse, in that same year, a great crowd of Whitechapel people waited to see his coffin, some crying "Hang him, rogue!" and others "Bury him in the dunghill"; but at last he was carried to this churchyard with a branch of rosemary at each end of the coffin.

Somewhere near him lies the mutineer of the *Nore*, Richard Parker, who was hanged on board the flagship. His wife having secretly moved the body from Sheerness burial ground, the mob prevented its burial in Aldgate, and it was laid secure here in a vault, this church being then the first country church out of London.

Whitechapel has been a desperately poor area. The French artist, Gustave Doré, recorded its horrors, and many novelists and writers—Charles Dickens, *Our Mutual Friend*, Sir Walter Besant, *All Sorts and Conditions of Men* (which was directly responsible for the founding of the People's Palace, see p. 389), Arthur Morrison, *A Child of the Jago*, Jack London, *The People of the Abyss*, Israel Zangwill, *The King of Schnorrers* and *Children of the Ghetto*, have written of it with indignation. Many great philanthropic undertakings have begun here, and today there are no barefoot children and the young women with their bouffant hairstyles and skirts—mini, midi, or maxi, as fashion decrees—are elegant, but the older faces still show how hard conditions have been within their lifetimes.

The London Hospital was built here in 1752–59 (architect Boulton Mainwaring), and in 1884 Canon Barnett founded the first University Settlement, Toynbee Hall. Here, undergraduates from Oxford and Cambridge were brought into contact with people from the East End. Toynbee Hall is still there today, helping both old and young, and people with every sort of problem and of every colour. Near it is the Whitechapel Art Gallery which had its beginnings in exhibitions organised by the Barnetts. It opened in 1901, having been designed by Townsend; it is one of the most interesting Art Nouveau buildings in London. It has no permanent collection of its own but mounts about five important exhibitions yearly. The range is wide—George Stubbs, Piet Mondrian, or very abstract sculpture being equally well displayed.

Near here is the turning officially known as Middlesex Street—which was once Stow's Hog Lane—but which is famous all the world over as the site of the Petticoat Lane Market on Sunday mornings, with its bustle and bargaining and excitement. There are clothes for sale, new and second-hand, excellent fruit and all sorts of china. The stalls line the streets and customers throng the road between them as if it were the nave of a church, while the pavements are the aisles.

The bell foundry of Messrs Mears and Stainbank is at Nos. 33 and 34 Whitechapel Road; it started in premises on the opposite side in 1570 and moved to the present site about 100 years later. Bells from this foundry ring up and down the land—and indeed all over the world; when Big Ben, made at Stockton-on-Tees, had to be recast, the work was done here. At No. 47 Aldgate High Street is the Hoop and Grapes, a late 17th century inn which is well worth visiting. South of the Whitechapel Road is Alie Street where David Garrick made his debut as Richard III in 1741, and on the corner of the Commercial Road is the Proof House of the Gunmakers' Company, which has been in continuous use since 1757.

North of Whitechapel lies **Spitalfields**. It was famous first for its hospital founded in 1197 by Walter and Rosia Brune, citizens of London. In the churchyard was a pulpit cross like the one at St Paul's. Sermons preached here had a particular significance and it was here that riots among the apprentices broke out on Evil May Day in 1517 against the Flemish weavers who had settled in the area, it being beyond the restrictions of the city guilds. Casualties and damage were heavy and Henry VIII hanged 12 young men for their part in it and also informed the Flemings that in future they might not take on apprentices. More than a century and a half later, in 1685 when Louis XIV revoked the Edict of Nantes granting freedom of worship in France, French Protestants, the Huguenots, arrived in this country in thousands, and those who were skilled silk-weavers settled in Spitalfields. For a century and a half they produced superb fabrics—lustrous examples can be seen in the Bethnal Green Museum.

Today the site of the hospital is covered by Spitalfields Market where flowers and fruit are sold, and the prosperous houses the weavers were able to build for themselves have all vanished, but the area has one great architectural glory, Christchurch, built by Nicholas Hawksmoor between 1715 and 1729. The tower rises from the portico of four huge Tuscan columns, immensely broad and most emphatic. The roof was found to be unsafe in 1958 and the church has been closed since for restoration. Nearby are three buildings of particular interest. No. 71 Spital Yard, Spital Square, was the birthplace of Susannah Annesley, the future mother of John and

Charles Wesley. She was her mother's 25th child and grew up to be the mother of 19 so in her two homes there were 44 children. She would whip her own children to teach them to cry softly and she gave them one day each in which to learn the alphabet. One day she crept out of her sick-bed to escape from the burning rectory at Epworth where she and her husband lived, and looking back saw John's little pale face pressed against the window. The child was safely rescued and grew up to be the great religious reformer. At the corner of Fournier Street and Brick Lane stands the Great Synagogue and in Artillery Lane is a superb mid-18th century shop front which is worth walking a long way to admire.

Moving south to the river, we come to **Wapping**. The docks begin at Wapping, for here are St Katharine's and the London Dock, dug in 1828 and 1805 respectively. St Katharine's takes its name from the Hospital of St Katharine, a religious foundation and charity founded in 1148, as an offshoot of the Augustinian Priors at Aldgate, by Matilda, Stephen's queen, refounded by Queen Eleanor, and which has always been under the especial patronage of the queens of England, thus escaping disbanding at the Dissolution of the monasteries. When the dock took its place, a new church with ecclesiastical grace and favour houses was built in the newly laid-out Regent's Park. The memorials from the old church, and especially the elaborate tomb of John Holland, Duke of Exeter, were moved there too. After the 1939–45 War, the houses passed into secular hands, and the church became the Danish church in London, while the Duke of Exeter's tomb was moved to St Peter's Chapel in the Tower, a stone's throw from where he was originally buried. St Katharine's was re-established by the river in the churchyard of the bombed St James's Ratcliffe, by Queen Mary. The William and Mary Vicarage serves the community which acts as a spiritual centre for Tower Hamlets, and is run as a conference and retreat house. The modern chapel was built by Messrs Enthoven. The building is immensely plain with a free-standing altar, perhaps the first in England in modern times, but the furnishings are mostly pre-reformation and include such treasures as contemporary statues of Edward III and his queen, Philippa of Hainault, the 12 chapter stalls that were Queen Philippa's gift with the best preserved misericords in England and an astonishing pulpit with carved views of the original St Katharine's. The chapel is open daily and is one of the most exciting churches in London.

The dock was designed by Telford with splendid warehouses with

Doric colonnades. Later accommodation by Hardwick was given a similar arcading. Now both St Katharine's and the London docks have been closed and are being drained as they are too small and too shallow for the heavy ships of today and they are to be redeveloped as housing areas. It is hoped that the warehouses and their colonnades may be saved and incorporated in the new scheme. Those visiting the area should not miss the Prospect of Whitby public house on the river front; the view of the Thames from its terrace at night is quite magical.

Wapping's associations are almost all maritime, whether grim or cheerful. It was here in the grisly Execution Dock that the bodies of pirates and other malefactors hung as a dreadful warning till three tides had passed over them. More hospitably, there are many clubs and hostels here to welcome sailors, such as the Sailors' Home and Red Ensign Club in Dock Street. Beside it is St Paul's, built in 1846 by H. Roberts and known as the Sailors' Church. There is a golden ship as a weather vane and inside is a striking window showing Admiral Parry's ship, the *Hecla* held fast in the ice of the North-West Passage. The memorials around the walls are an epitome of the dangers of the sea—"Fell to the deck—Lost with all hands"— they lament. The street-names—Cable Street, Cannon Street, Dock Street, Ensign Street, Betts Street for Captain Cook's patient lonely wife, and Ropemakers' Fields—all tell of the sea and the ships that sail thereon.

Just east of Dock Street stood two churches, both of which have disappeared. They were the Danish Church in London, built in 1696 in Wellclose Square, and the Swedish Church, built in 1728 in Princess (later Swedenborg) Square. It was said that the Scandinavians warmed their hands at the Fire of London, so great was the amount of timber imported to rebuild the city. The Danish and Swedish merchants built themselves comfortable houses and imposing places of worship. The Danish Church was designed by Caius Cibber, a Dane who had settled in London and had made a name for himself here; he refused all payment for his work and carved in addition statues of St Peter and St Paul for the church. They are superb and dramatic. The church itself has disappeared and the last of the houses are being bulldozed down at this moment, to be replaced by large blocks of flats, but the statues are lovingly housed in the new Danish Church at 649 Commercial Road. This church, designed by Holger Jensen in 1958, is one of the best pieces of modern architecture in London, and other churchbuilders in the capital should make the pilgrimage to the East End to learn from it.

394

The Swedish Church, which has disappeared, too, was the burial place of the mystic, Count Swedenborg, and had as pastor Dr Solander, the botanist. Both men are commemorated in nearby street-names.

Just beyond Swedenborg Square stands St George-in-the-East. It was designed by Nicholas Hawksmoor and built 1715–26. It was one of the 50 new churches which were planned for London in Queen Anne's day to calm and combat the obstreperousness of the growing population; in the end, only 12 churches were built of which three—perhaps the most interesting three—were all by Hawksmoor and all in the East End. Christ Church we have already mentioned, St Anne's Limehouse will be described soon. The original St George's was in the form of a Greek cross with an enormous square tower topped by an octagonal lantern with four turrets behind it surmounted by cupolas and finials. Even today it is an unmistakable landmark from the river. In May 1941 St George's was gutted by incendiary bombs. A prefabricated church was erected and dedicated, and carried on its work for 17 years. Under the inspired direction of the architect, Arthur Bailey, the church was built anew, with a parish hall in the crypt, and a plain glass west window which is one of the most breathtakingly beautiful things in London. The church is smaller than it was in Hawksmoor's day; one enters it under his tower and across a courtyard. The interior is all honey-coloured and warm with five 19th century Venetian glass mosaics of scenes from the Life of Our Lord which serves as a reredos in the apse. In the churchyard is an elaborate monument to Henry Raine who was a great benefactor to Wapping in the 18th century and who founded Raine's School which still flourishes in a new building in Arbour Square.

Down by the river, running from Wapping High Street to Rotherhithe is the Thames Tunnel, constructed by the two Brunels between 1825 and 1843. The tunnel was one of the bravest engineering feats of all time. A 90-ton shield, impelled by screw-jacks, was driven forward. In it were 36 compartments, in each of which a man worked with pick and shovel, tunnelling away. A twin-arch lining of brick was built behind the shield. All sorts of emergencies occurred and the work was often held up for lack of money but the Brunels never gave up till at last the work was complete and the elder man was knighted for his great achievement.

Next door to Wapping is **Shadwell**. In the Highway is the sole remaining church by John Walters, an architect who died young but whose talent promised great things. He drew his inspiration from the work of Sir Christopher Wren and St Paul's graceful spire recalls the City churches, though it is a copy of none of them. Beside it is King Edward's Memorial Garden, a smooth pleasant green space with a wonderful view of the river. In it is a ventilation shaft of the Rotherhithe Tunnel under the Thames and against the shaft is a boulder inscribed with the names of Sir Hugh Willoughby, Richard Chancellor, William Borough, and Sir Martin Frobisher, who set sail from this reach of the river, known as Ratcliffe Cross, on voyages of exploration and discovery in "tall ships of the city of London" as Hakluyt puts it in his wonderful account of 16th century maritime adventures. Sir Hugh Willoughby and Richard Chancellor set off in 1553 to discover the north-west passage to India; Sir Hugh and his ship perished on the Lapland coast of Norway, but Chancellor in the *Edward Bonaventure* held on his course and reached Russia, thereby establishing trade with that country. The brothers, William and Stephen Borough, both served on the *Edward Bonaventure*, and William rose to become Comptroller of the Navy, vice-admiral under Drake at his attack on Cadiz, and commander of a vessel in the fleet which went to meet the Armada. Frobisher made two expeditions in search of the north-west passage to India and got as far as Frobisher's Bay; he commanded a squadron against the Armada and was knighted for his services.

Just beside King Edward's Park is Glamis Road, and in it stood the East London Hospital which closed in 1963. This started as a dispensary for sick women and children opened in 1868 with 10 beds in a disused factory by Nathan Heckford and his wife. Charles Dickens visited them and wrote of their work in *All the Year Round* and readers—even children—sent gifts spontaneously. A committee was formed to build a hospital but before it could be begun, Heckford died at the age of 29. His work goes on today.

Beyond Shadwell lies **Limehouse,** taking its name from the lime burning which used to go on in the area. It is transversed by London's oldest canal, Limehouse Cut, constructed about 1770 to link the Lea at Bow with the Thames at Limehouse, thereby saving the heavy barge traffic the passage of the double hairpin bend of the Lea near Blackwall and round the Isle of Dogs to reach the Pool of London. The Regent's Canal Dock is here too but is closed to shipping. The Canal, nearly nine miles long, links the Grand Union Canal at Paddington with the Thames. It was the idea of Thomas Homer, but was carried through by the enthusiasm and support of the architect, John Nash. It was completed, after

...cely indispensable
...ep baking tin into
...to about half th...
...than adequate.

is more ... adequate.

used to call such an
an many a powered and
a tremendous saving in
progressive" - I am mer...
ng the little bits and
ttery of gleaming *Keep-u...*

from Imperial to Metric
ch specifications are n...
is very unlikely to ca...

many mishaps, in 1820. Near it, in Narrow Street, is The Grapes public house, a characterful 18th century building.

But the pride of Limehouse is St Anne's Church, again by Hawksmoor and possibly his masterpiece. It was begun in 1712, dedicated in honour of Queen Anne, and completed in 1730. It was gutted by fire on Good Friday 1850; restoration was carried out under Philip Hardwick who did not try to improve on the older architect's work. It has an apsidal west entrance and above it the enormous tower rides proudly, a landmark to all those on the river. It is in three stages, the top one surmounted by four finials like pepperpots, and the church clock is probably the highest in London.

Eastwards again from Limehouse the East India Dock Road reaches **Poplar**, which takes its name from the trees which used to abound here. The Thames loops sharply here, leaving a peninsula, the Isle of Dogs (the origin of the name is unknown), on which the India and Millwall Docks have been dug. Throughout the Middle Ages, retaining walls had been built around the peninsula to prevent the Thames from encroachment; the west wall was the Millwall—at one time seven windmills stood on it—and the east wall was the Bleak or Blackwall. Here about 1660, the East India Company, which had been founded about 60 years earlier, built a small wet dock for fitting out their ships. This was London's first proper dock and Pepys visited it on January 15, 1661. Goods were not handled there since they had to be landed at one of the legal quays between London Bridge and the Tower. By the 17th century these were already inadequate to deal with the traffic and trade and sufferance wharfs were opened with restricted privileges. But the commerce in the port nearly doubled between 1700 and 1770, and again between 1770 and 1795. The space in the Upper Pool was sufficient to moor some 545 vessels; as many as 1775 might try to use it at any one time. The thieving of the "River Pirates, Night Plunderers, Light Horsemen, Heavy Horsemen, Scuffle Hunters, and Mudlarks" was insufferable and in 1799, a Bill was passed authorising the building of the West India Dock. Two docks were constructed with a range of splendid five-storey warehouses and an armed watch of 100 men was provided reinforced by 100 special constables. The docks were opened with much ceremony by the Prime Minister, Henry Addington, on August 22, 1802. A third dock was added in 1829 when the City Canal, dug in 1805 from Limehouse Reach to Blackwall Reach, was taken over and enlarged. The advantages of the enclosed docks were immediately obvious, and others were constructed, the London Dock opening in 1805, the East India Docks in 1806, St Katharine's in 1828, and Millwall in 1868. Only the Millwall and the West India Docks are now active, the others having been closed. Shipbuilding still goes on along the Thames in a limited way; lighters, barges, and tugs are still built but great ships were once constructed on the south bank at Woolwich and Deptford in Henry VIII's day and fast clippers were built at Blackwall Yard for the East India Company for the tea trade and the Australian wool runs. In 1858, the *Great Eastern* was launched—with difficulty, for she was more than 600 feet long—at Millwall, and the last big ship to be built was the Dreadnought, the *Thunderer*, launched in 1912 (see p. 19).

It was from Blackwall that Captain John Smith sailed with 104 other brave men on December 19, 1606, in three small ships, the *Sarah Constant* of 100 tons, the *Godspeed* of 40 tons, and the *Discovery* of a mere 20 tons, to found the first permanent British colony in America. They landed at Cape Henry in Virginia, on May 13, 1607. Smith opened trade with the natives, was taken prisoner by them and was only saved by the intercession of the chieftain's daughter, Princess Pocahontas, who later married another Englishman, John Rolfe, founder of the tobacco industry in America. Near here is the entrance to the Blackwall Tunnel, originally designed by Sir Alexander Binnie at the end of the last century; it is nearly a mile long and runs under the river for a quarter of a mile. The inside diameter is 24 feet and there was just room for two lanes of traffic. Traffic is now carried in a new tunnel, opened August 1967, which runs parallel to the old.

The best method of viewing the Isle of Dogs is to drive round the perimeter by way of West Ferry Road on the Millwall side and Manchester Road along Blackwall Reach. Admission to the Docks is rightly restricted but quite a lot can be seen from the road and a glorious smell of timber is everywhere. One can also examine the various GLC housing estates in the area. They range through the pleasant Barley Mow Estate, sink to the forbidding desert of the Manchester Estate, all built of cold white bricks and as bitterly miserable as any Victorian Peabody Buildings, and rise to the lovely achievement of Plevna Street and Castalia Square where houses are on a human scale, traffic is restricted and the whole effect is friendly. The Manchester Estate has in part replaced Cubitt Town, built to house the employees of the great builder during the last half of the 18th century, and provided with a masterful place of worship, Christ Church, designed in 1852 by William Cubitt himself with an asymmetrical spire. By turning up East Ferry Road at the junction of West Ferry and Manchester Roads, one comes to some 1910–20 development around Thermopylae Gate and Chapel Street (the chapel commemorated was one that stood here in the Middle Ages to serve the marshland folk). The style is that of the Hampstead Garden Suburb or Welwyn Garden City, the standard at least as high as at Castalia Square, and one looks around with pleasure and then remembers with an awful certainty that we shall be judged as the generation that ruined London with unbearable tower blocks. Nearby is Millwall Park crossed by a jolly viaduct and well lined with trees.

At the very tip of the Isle of Dogs is a public garden—Island Gardens—with one of the most spectacular views in London. It looks across to Greenwich and one can see the superb composition of the Royal Naval College, the Queen's House, and the Royal Observatory. The *Cutty Sark*, with her spars and rigging silhouetted against the sky, is moored beside them. A good case can be made for regarding this as the finest group of buildings in all Europe. An icy-clad, cupola'd entrance leads down to the Greenwich Footway Tunnel, a very exciting place to explore, especially for small boys.

One leaves the Isle of Dogs by way of Preston's Road. In a small turning off it, cruelly named Coldharbour, is a public house, The Gun, with a superb view of the river from its back garden. The Gun should be visited with those public houses already named—The Prospect of Whitby, The Grapes, and The Hoop and Grapes (this is now just inside the city boundary but used to stand on the boundary itself)—though possibly not all in the same evening. Rejoining the East India Dock Road and travelling westwards, we come to four interesting churches, All Saints, St Matthias, Trinity Church, and St Mary and St Joseph. All Saints was designed by C. Hollis in 1817–20, with a tower and a tall obelisk spire, 161 feet high, huge fluted Ionic pillars as a portico, and two pairs of enormous Corinthian pillars holding a canopy over the altar. Near to it in a large park where a stone angel stands as memorial to 18 little children, most of them only five years old, who were blown to pieces by a German bomb on June 13, 1917, is St Matthias' Church. A chapel was built here by the East India Company in 1654 and was largely rebuilt in 1776, plain, dignified, and gracious, with the masts of ships as columns along the nave. George Steevens, the Shakespearean scholar, has a memorial here by Flaxman; it shows him seated comfortably looking at a bust of the dramatist. Between 1867 and 1870, the Victorians encased the chapel in a winding-sheet of

399

Kentish ragstone, added a bell-turret of more than ordinary ugliness and inserted quite hideous glass in the windows. The vicarage behind the church is unspoiled, with a charming pediment and coat of arms over the door. Farther west, on the opposite side of the road, is Trinity Church with a united congregation of Presbyterians and Congregationalists. The original church was destroyed by one of the last flying bombs of the war, and the present one was designed by Cecil C. Handisyde and D. Rogers Stark. It is a pleasant church with a fine tower and lantern, with excellent parish amenities and some outstandingly good engraved glass. In a small park beside it stands *The Docker*, a massive, impressive sculpture by Sydney Harpley. Behind it in Upper North Street is the Roman Catholic church of St Mary and St Joseph, designed in 1954 by Adrian Gilbert Scott. It is in the shape of a broad Greek Cross with an enormous central lantern which lights the interior. The pulpit is most uncommon and beautiful, being a little gallery by itself, and over the altar is a canopy.

North of the church, in the angle made by the East India Dock Road and Limehouse Cut is Lansbury, the GLC estate developed in part for the Festival of Britain in 1951. It is a good piece of development with buildings of different scales and a charming public house, The Festive Briton, and a good shopping centre.

Northwards from Lansbury we regain the main London to Colchester Road which by this time has become the Bow Road. The road was realigned in the 11th century when Queen Matilda, Henry I's wife, had Bow Bridge built over the Lea. The right angle in Old Ford Road probably indicates the original crossing place of the river. St Leonard's Convent lay near here, from which Chaucer's Prioress came. She must have been a very sweet lady:

> And she was cleped madame Eglantyne.
> Full weel she soong the service dyvyne,
> Entuned in her nose ful semely,
> And Frenssh she spak ful faire and fetishly,
> After the scole of Stratford atte Bowe,
> For Frenssh of Paris was to hire unknowe.

James I built a comely palace here which was destroyed only in 1894–95 though one magnificent panelled room was saved and can be seen today in the Victoria and Albert Museum.

On an island in the middle of the Bow Road, shaken by the traffic which has necessitated double glazing of the windows, stands the

Pitshanger House, Ealing

Wanstead Hospital

Hornsey Town Hall

Newbury Park tube stati[on]

church of St Mary, Stratford, Bow. It is basically a 14th century building with a fine chancel roof but it was heavily damaged in the Second World War and the top of the 15th century stone tower has had to be repaired with brickwork, thus making clear its honourable battle scars. The other St Mary's Church, of Bromley St Leonard, was a 12th century foundation which was rebuilt in 1842–43. The monuments from the old church were retained, however, and when the church was bombed out of existence, one of the most charming of all English funeral effigies was lost to us. It was to William Ferrars (d. 1625) and his wife Jane; it showed them half-length under arches and below them a full-length figure of their baby son, wearing a bonnet and a ruff and holding a rose. Beneath him was this verse:

> As nurses strive their babes in bed to lay
> When they too liberally the wanton play,
> So to prevent his farther growing crimes
> Nature his nurse got him to bed betimes.

But if Bromley has lost St Mary's Church, it has gained St Paul's on Bow Common, which was built on the corner of Burdett Road and St Paul's Way between 1958 and 1960 to the designs of Robert Maguire and Keith Murray. It is utterly modern and completely successful. Built of purple brick with a superb lantern, it should be visited by all those who are interested in the Church of England or in modern architecture.

In the streets just behind St Mary's, is the Theatre Royal, Stratford. An old music hall, it reopened as a theatre in 1953 with the Theatre Workshop Company directed by Miss Joan Littlewood, who has been a revolutionary influence in the theatre ever since.

Fairfield Road runs north from Bow Road and passes Bromley recreation ground, where the gateway of old Northumberland House still stands in St Leonards Street. In this road is the factory of Messrs Bryant and May, makers of matches, and it was here that the first successful strike was organised when, inspired by Annie Besant, the match girls demanded—and won—from the management proper safety precautions in their dangerous work. Their example fired the dockers to emulate them and the results were the great dock strikes of 1889 and 1911, which achieved sorely needed better conditions for the dock-labourers. Messrs Bryant and May are also responsible for the remarkable collection of fire-lighting appliances in the Science Museum.

At the northern edge of the borough is Victoria Park which is shared with Hackney. It was laid out in 1842–45 by James Pennethorne, the adopted son and pupil of John Nash, who was responsible for that other fine London garden, Regent's Park. Its 217 acres were laid out on the site of Bonner Fields where Wesley used to preach. It was called after the young queen who, when she at last visited it in 1873, was so delighted with the welcome she received that she presented a peal of bells to St Mark's Church. The park has broad walks, fine trees, a lake, two stone alcoves from old London Bridge, and a huge drinking-fountain given by Baroness Burdett-Coutts.

The Baroness began life as Miss Angela Burdett-Coutts. Her father was Sir Francis Burdett, the Radical politician, and she inherited a large share of the banking millions. Armed with a fortune, with the kindest of hearts, and with unlimited determination, she set to work to relieve the miserable condition of the London poor and succeeded so well that Queen Victoria created her a peeress in her own right. In **Bethnal Green**, she bought up and demolished a terrible slum, Nova Scotia Gardens, and built on the site Columbia Market, designed by Henry Darbishire. It opened in 1869 and was intended as a market where food and wares of good quality were to be sold to the poor at fair prices. It was a failure from the start, although the baroness hired her own fleet of fishing boats, made arrangements with the railways and transferred the market to the City Corporation. Vested interests were too strong, even for her. In 1960 the wonderful cathedral-like building was demolished and the site redeveloped.

Bethnal Green is a place with a real centre, a true heart, to it. At the junction of Old Ford Road and Cambridge Heath Road are the remains of the Green, and grouped around it are various civic buildings, including the former Town Hall in whose council chamber windows is glass depicting that legendary figure, the Blind Beggar of Bethnal Green. A fine 17th century dwelling, Netteswell House, is still here. Just east of the Green stood Bethnal House or Kirby's Castle, built for a merchant John Kirby in Queen Elizabeth I's day. It was here, when it was Sir William Rider's home, that Pepys came with his diary and plate during the Fire of London, arriving at four in the morning, "riding in my nightgowne in the cart".

On the Green is St John's Church, designed by Sir John Soane in 1825–28, with a fine spire and cupola. Beside it is Bethnal Green

Museum, one of the most delightful places in London. It opened in 1872, a branch of the Victoria and Albert Museum, and is housed in that museum's original buildings, made of iron and glass and of so utilitarian a design that they were known as "The Brompton Boilers". Since the destruction of the Crystal Palace, they are probably the most important examples left in this country of this type of prefabricated building. The museum contains all sorts of interesting exhibits—silver, china, Japanese armour, Victorian sculptures such as *The Eagle Slayer* by John Bell (which stands outside the museum), and a good collection of English water-colours, especially by Rowlandson, bequeathed by Joshua Dixon, a poor East End boy who made his fortune in America, but pride of place goes to the fine display of costume and the wonderful collection of toys. The costumes are particularly interesting as many of the exhibits are of Spitalfields silk and show what magnificent work was being done by the Huguenot weavers. There is also a group of wedding-dresses, dating from 1782 to 1963. The toys are quite wonderful. There are dolls of every description, rocking-horses, tops, puzzles, card games, sets of picture bricks, puppets, model theatres and optical toys, and, above all, doll's-houses. The earliest came from Nuremburg in 1673 and there is a huge one made in Dorset in 1760 with a flight of steps and balustraded roof, another made for Queen Victoria and a fourth furnished by Queen Mary. Children of all ages can delight in a visit to Bethnal Green.

WALTHAM FOREST

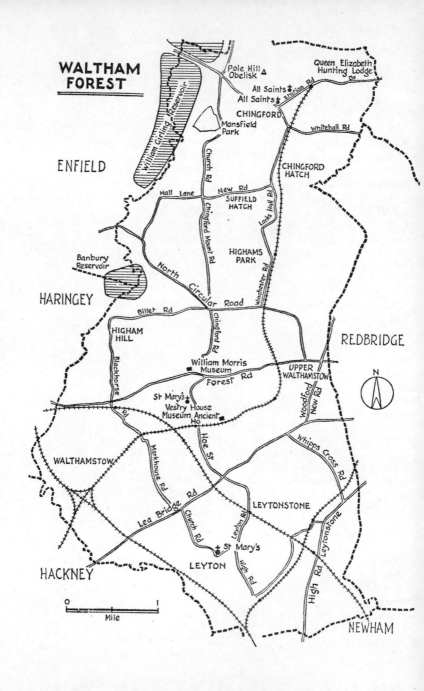

WALTHAM FOREST

The London Borough of Waltham Forest consists of the former boroughs of Chingford, Walthamstow, and Leyton. It is a thin strip of land stretching from the high ground at Chingford on the outskirts of Epping Forest to the low-lying Leyton marshes. Along the eastern boundary a chain of reservoirs spreads out, all of which are to be incorporated in the Greater London Council's exciting plan for the Lee Valley Regional Park (see Enfield, p. 123). To the north is Waltham Holy Cross and, travelling clockwise, the borough is surrounded by Chigwell, Redbridge, Newham, Hackney, Haringey, and Enfield. It covers an area of $15\frac{1}{3}$ square miles (9805 acres) and has a population of 239,520. All three boroughs were formerly in Essex.

Chingford itself is set on a hill overlooking the Lea Valley. It has two churches, an old and a new; they are linked together by The Ridgeway which runs along the spine of the high ground. The old church, dedicated to All Saints, has had a chequered history for it flourished from Norman times till the middle of the 19th century and then fell into almost complete disrepair, only to be restored again in 1929–30. Today it is a second parish centre, as beautiful and as vital as it has ever been in all its history. The doorway on the south side has a 13th century arch and inside are circular pillars, exact copies of the 13th century piers which used to stand there, the old stone having been re-used where possible. The tower was added about 1400, the chancel and part of the north wall of the nave were rebuilt about 60 years later, and the brick south porch was built on in the 16th century. The south wall of the aisle was heightened in the late 17th century, increasing the weight of the brickwork by 52 tons, and this additional load, combined with the undermining of the walls by graves being dug close to the church, reduced the building to such decay that it was judged unsafe and a new church, dedicated to St Peter and St Paul, was built a mile away on Chingford Green. The old church was left to become a ruin. A creeper so entwined the building that it was known as "The Green Church" and artists came from far and near to paint it, as many as six having been observed at work all at one time depicting the same scene. In 1928, Miss Boothby-Heathcote, daughter of the rector who had built St Peter and St Paul, financed the reclamation of All Saints by the architect C. C. Winmill, and the work was carried out with astonishing success. The condition of the building was such that the stones of the 13th century arch in the south wall had to be fitted together like a jigsaw puzzle, but at last all the puzzles were solved, and the church stands, splendid and useful, today.

In the church and churchyard are several memorials to the Heathcote family and to the Leighs. In the chancel there is a tiny carving of Mary Leigh, who died in childbed in 1602. Her baby is beside her and nearby are her relations, Sir Robert (d. 1612) and Margaret Leigh (d. 1624), each of whom has a kneeling effigy. In the wall to the south side of the chancel arch is a partially blocked squint, and on the beam under the tower arch is a 13th century foliated cross, probably originally a gable-finial. In the tower hang three bells, of 1626, 1657, and 1835. They had been removed to the new church but were restored to the old in 1929.

Along the Ridgeway which links the two churches are several interesting buildings and a spectacular view. Beside All Saints stands the modern Baptist church built of unusual white bricks. In the window facing the road is a flask of water—a simple but arresting allegory of the help that faith can give. A little further on is Mansfield Park with neat flowerbeds and a vista across the William Girling reservoir which is quite extraordinary, especially when seen early on a summer's morning when there is still a little mist. The Ridgeway bears eastward at this point and one notices a traditional signpost which reads "Hertford 16 miles", before passing the former Chingford Town Hall, now council offices, the Magistrates' Court, and the Social Services Centre, an exceptionally successful group of civic buildings erected between 1929 and the 1960s. The standard of lettering used on civic property in Waltham Forest, from buildings to litter bins, is very high.

The new church, built in 1844 by Lewis Vulliamy, stands on the Green. The exterior is a bold chequer-board of flush work, and there is a fine high spire. The nave is broad with aisles and in the south aisle is the St Elizabeth chapel with a good modern embroidered frontal and some pleasant glass, portraying St Francis, St Christopher, and St Hubert. The main object to note is the 12th century square font of Purbeck marble, brought here from the old church.

Across the Green is a splendid Victorian public house, The Bull and Crown, and west of the church is King's Head Hill where stands the early 18th century King's Head public house with the remains of a fine stabling block. Behind it Pole Hill rises up; on its summit is an obelisk erected in 1824 by the Reverend John Pound, the Astronomer Royal, to mark the north when sighted from Greenwich Observatory. The meridian was adjusted in 1884 and the true north line is now 19 feet to the east of the obelisk.

Beyond the hill, to the north, are the borders of Epping Forest. The Forest was placed under the protection of the City of London in 1882 and is the largest open space under the guardianship of a public body in England. It is a magnificent stretch of forest and common land, spreading from Epping to Wanstead Flats 12 miles away to the south—in all an area of some 9 square miles of which 300 acres lie in Chingford. Houses come up to its very edge, houses of such a period and design that they look like those on the front at Eastbourne or at Frinton. Their windows gaze out on to the Forest as if its greenness were the waves of the sea. Indeed, this part of Chingford is like a pleasant seaside resort—every dwelling in Woodberry Way or Eglington Road has a pretty porch that would be ideal for hanging up seaweed to dry, and Bryn-Coed in Crescent Road is as fantastic an Edwardian creeper-covered façade as can be found anywhere. On the outskirts of the Forest, near to the beautiful lake known as Connaught Water, stands Queen Elizabeth's Hunting Lodge. This is an astonishing survival, an early 16th century hunting standing which has been well maintained throughout its existence. In Tudor times, the giver of a hunt and his guests took their places in a platform or standing and shot at the deer which were driven in front of them by a pack of hounds. This lodge was unusually elaborate with two storeys with open sides for shooting and underneath living quarters. William Morris wrote of the rooms with faded green hangings—his imagination must have been coloured by it for ever. It is today an excellent local history museum, open daily, except Mondays and Tuesdays, from 2 p.m. till 6 p.m.

Near to the hunting lodge is the East Essex Golf Club, whose members all wear red shirts when playing in order to show up against the intense green, and very picturesque they look. On the other side of Chingford is a council nursery garden where Pimp Hall, a 16th century farmhouse, used to stand. Everything has gone except one fine brick and timber barn, the walls a little derelict but the roof-beams still apparently sound, and beside it the remains of an enormous dovecote, the roof and footings still intact but the walls patched up with slabs of concrete pargetting. The borough council has here the opportunity of saving and preserving two interesting examples of early domestic architecture. Nearby is Friday Hill, a large house built for the Boothby-Heathcote family by Vulliamy, whom they had employed to build the new parish church. It is of slate-coloured brick, ornate, a little forbidding, with some fine carving in the panelled hall and a good staircase. The house is now a community centre. The grounds must have been impressive—a cedar felled by a member of the family served to make a new altar-table for the old church—but except for the lawns near the house they are now largely built over with council housing, some of it good and well-designed, some less so. Some well-planned accommodation for the old and infirm is included and nearby, in Whitehall Road, is Heathcote Secondary School, an exceptionally good design by H. Connolly.

Southwards lies **Walthamstow**, a very ancient place indeed. When the Maynard reservoir was being dug in 1869, an Iron Age pile dwelling or *crannog* was discovered and flint instruments found in the area showed that man had been here in even earlier times. When the Lockwood reservoir was dug in 1900, a Bronze Age canoe was found, hollowed out of solid oak with a flat bottom and straight sides. It is today in the British Museum. In the same reservoir a ship, formerly regarded as Viking, but now believed to be a Saxon barge, was found as well, a clinker-built boat about 45 feet long, keel upwards and a man's skeleton underneath.

When the railways came in 1870, Walthamstow began to grow. In 1851, there had been under 5000 people. In 1871, there were 11,092, in 1901, 96,720, and the peak was not reached till 1931, when there were 132,972. Since then, numbers have, fortunately, been falling. Today, Walthamstow has two centres of interest, one on Forest Road and the other to the south of it, around or near the old church. In the main road stands the Town Hall and the big Technical College, the fine building of the Sir George Monoux School, and Water House in Lloyds Park. This house was one of the boyhood homes of William Morris (1834–96) who so changed and improved English taste in the 19th century. He was an artist, a poet, a Socialist reformer, a printer, a manufacturer, and a very great man. His father was a bill-broker in the City, his mother a member of a musical family. It was a lucky parentage for William for he inherited his mother's gifts and his father's business instincts, and to them he added immeasurable gifts of his own. He had a happy childhood, running wild in Epping Forest and grounding himself in that passionate love of flowers that never left him. He went to Marl-borough and then to Oxford, where he formed a friendship with a group of undergraduates which was broken only by death. They included Edward Burne-Jones the artist, and Charles Faulkner a mathematician who became Morris's business partner. They were young men with great ideals, both in art and culture, and in responsibility towards society.

Morris developed a great love for art and history, particularly that of the Middle Ages. He read everything by Ruskin and Carlyle that he could lay his hand on, and he travelled. He took up architecture, became the articled pupil of G. E. Street, and soon another influence came into his life, that of Dante Gabriel Rossetti, who persuaded Morris that he would be much better as an artist than as an architect. All the while, in his spare time he was writing poetry. It was as well for him that he had money behind him, while he was deliberating between professions. A poor man could not have taken such a course. It was Morris's fate to be a jack-of-all-arts—and master of them all.

He lived at first at 17 Red Lion Square and then, when he was 25 and about to marry the beautiful Jane Burden, he wanted a better home and set to work to build a palace of art of his own at Bexley in Kent. It was called the Red House and was designed for him by his friend Philip Webb. Morris himself designed most of the furniture and decorations for he could find nothing in the shops that was fit to be put in his home. In 1861, he formed a company with his friends—Ford Madox Brown, Edward Burne-Jones, C. J. Faulkner, Arthur Hughes, P. P. Marshall, Rossetti and Philip Webb, and they began to produce furniture, wall-paintings, stained glass, metal and glass work, artistic tiles, tapestries, printed materials, jewellery, and embroideries. More than a century later, Morris's designs are still in production as wallpapers and furnishing materials, as satisfying and as beautiful as they were when they were first produced.

Morris later lived at Hammersmith and at Kelmscott Manor in Oxfordshire—he used to delight in the fact that the same River Thames flowed past both his front doors. At Kelmscott he set up a printing press, and produced books for which he designed the typefaces and Burne-Jones provided woodcuts as illustrations. He also found time to illuminate manuscripts, and all the time was actively concerned with the Socialist movement for he longed intensely to improve the lot of his fellow men in all ways. He died when only 62, worn out by all he had done, but recognised as one of the greatest creative geniuses and most perfect craftsmen that modern England has known.

The borough of Waltham Forest has taken his words "Fellowship is Life" as its motto and at Water House a Morris Museum has been set up. On the ground floor can be seen rooms furnished entirely with decorations and furniture designed by Morris. The dresses he designed for his daughters, the herbals from which he took the flower motifs that are the glory of so many of his designs, are here, and upstairs is a collection of paintings by Sir Frank Brangwyn. Temporary exhibitions are often arranged, and the grounds of Lloyd Park, in which the house stands, are beautifully laid out. Morris would approve of the use to which his childhood home had been put, could he see it.

Old Walthamstow is centred around the church. Various houses in the neighbouring streets—The Chestnuts in Hoe Street, built in 1745–47 by Thomas Allen and later an annexe of the Waltham Forest Technical College (now part of the North-East London Polytechnic), or Thorpe Coombe in Forest Road, built in 1770 by George Wombwell and now a maternity hospital, or Walthamstow House built in 1772 and in 1784 belonging to Sir Robert Wigram an East India merchant with 23 children (it is said that the cannon used as bollards outside the main gates came from one of his ships)—make us suspect the excitements that lie there, but the busy approach from Hoe Street, (off which, in the High Street, the largest open market near London is held), though timeless in the buying and selling that goes on, is very much of today, so that the five or six acres of peacefulness around the church come as a surprise when one enters the oasis. The church itself, dedicated to St Mary and first mentioned in the 12th century was considerably rebuilt in 1535—though there had been a church here since the 12th century—and the tower, aisles, and chancel chapels are all of that date. The church was enlarged in 1818 and 1843, and the galleries and roof date from 1876. The chancel was enlarged and extended, and a new east window inserted in 1938. On a pillar near to the chancel is a fine brass of Sir George Monoux wearing his chain of office as Mayor of London, and beside him is his wife. He was a successful Bristol merchant who came to London in 1502 and by 1514 was mayor. About 1507 he built himself a house, Moons, whose site is marked by Monoux Grove in Billet Road. He was the founder of the group of almshouses on the north side of the churchyard. Lady Lucy Stanley kneels in a cloak and coronet under a kind of triumphal arch with four daughters dressed as in Stuart days; there is magnificent heraldry on her tomb. A monument by the great sculptor Nicholas Stone has busts of Sir Thomas Merry (d. 1654) and his wife with richly detailed portraits of their four children. An elaborate wall-monument with fine ironwork in front of it shows Sigismund

Trafford (d. 1723) in Roman dress with his wife similarly attired and their little daughter. The figures are life-size. Both Sir Thomas and Trafford had their memorials prepared many years before their actual deaths, and sat in church, Sunday after Sunday, regarding these reminders of their mortality. In the churchyard lies Lady Penn, mother of the Quaker. Her husband, Sir William, was sent by Cromwell to take Guiana but in fact captured Jamaica.

Opposite the church is the Ancient House, a 15th century timber framed building with wings. It is still virtually intact and probably stands on the site of the original manor house, replacing it after a new manor house had been built in what is now Shernhall Street. The Ancient House is today a shop selling excellent furniture, china, and kitchen equipment. Beside the church is St Mary's Infant School, a gracious building of 1828, still used for its original purpose. Round the corner from it are Squires' Almshouses, founded in 1795 by Mrs Mary Squires for "six decayed tradesmen's widows", and near it is the Vestry House Museum, one of the best local history museums to be found anywhere near London.

The building was originally erected as a workhouse in 1730, one room being reserved for vestry meetings. The house was enlarged three times during the century, and when the paupers were removed to Stratford, their premises were used as a police station and by the Walthamstow Volunteers as an armoury. From 1892 till 1930, the Vestry House became a private dwelling and was then equipped as a museum. It is an ideal place for children to visit with excellent displays of local archaeology and history, illustrated by dioramas. It is also an archives respository for the advanced student, with material ranging from court rolls to paintings and photographs of the area. Perhaps its most famous exhibit is the Bremer Car, built between 1892 and 1895 by Mr Frederick Bremer of Walthamstow; it is proudly claimed to be the first British car with an internal combustion engine. It was still able to join in the Veteran Car Rally to Brighton in 1964 and 1965. Those visiting the house should look carefully at the beautiful side door and should observe a splendid and superbly incongruous piece of sculpture on the pavement outside the museum. It is a capital from St Martin-le-Grand Post Office, built in 1829 and demolished in 1913. Mr Frank Mortimer, a local builder, bought the capital and presented it to the borough, which must surely rejoice to have such an original possession.

Opposite the museum is the Spiritualist Church, built as the National Schools in 1819. It is a graceful building, and well cared for. Two great houses, Salisbury Hall and Essex Hall, have disappeared altogether, Salisbury Hall being demolished in 1952 and Essex Hall in 1933. Salisbury Hall was the home of that Countess of Salisbury who was so cruelly executed, or rather butchered, on Henry VIII's orders. Roger Ascham, beloved tutor to Lady Jane Grey, lived there from 1557 till his death in 1568. Essex Hall, having been the property of the Rowe family, became a school about 1801, run by the Reverend Eliezer Cogan, who numbered among his pupils the young Benjamin Disraeli, Florence Nightingale's father, and Samuel Lister, the future pioneer of antiseptic medicine (see p. 332). A modern block of flats stands on the site, marked with a blue plaque. Two other buildings in Walthamstow should be mentioned—the Coppermill and Highams. In the 17th and 18th centuries, it was usual to coin tokens for all sorts of private concerns, and they were used in place of money or to establish a claim to some benefit or privilege. A coppermill was set up on the marshes near Walthamstow to strike copper coins to relieve distress during the Napoleonic wars; it is today a storehouse for the Water Board. Highams was built in 1768 for Anthony Bacon, lord of the manor of Higham Benstead, by William Newton, architect of the interior of the chapel of Greenwich Hospital and assistant to James "Athenian" Stuart, and the grounds were laid out in 1793 by Humphrey Repton, the great landscape gardener. It is today Woodford County High School for Girls.

Southwards again is **Leyton**, a more crowded area, much in need of such open spaces as it has, such as the pleasant Coronation Gardens. Jack Cornwell was born here (for his story see p. 338) and went to the same school as another future VC, George Mitchell, after whom the school is now named. Housing has been a problem here and Leyton has responded gallantly with such outstanding pieces of design as John Strype Court on the site of the Old Vicarage in High Road, Leyton, and Leving Road.

The church is a storehouse of Old Leyton, with many names which were famous long before Jack Cornwell, and with views and manuscripts and portraits displayed in the galleries. Domesday tells us that there were two priests in Leyton in the 11th century and one of them very probably served a church on this site; there was certainly a church here in 1182 when it was presented to Stratford Langthorpe Abbey (see p. 330) and in 1327 we have the first name recorded for a vicar, Simon of Sudbury. The oldest object in the church is one of the nine bells, which was cast by Dawe about 1400; there is another of 1694 and a second 17th century bell in the cupola while the rest are all of the 20th century. The tower and north aisle date from Oliver Cromwell's time, the south aisle and west end from the last century and it was enlarged and remodelled in the 1930s. There are two interesting brasses—to Ursula Gasper (d. 1493), and to Elizabeth Wood which shows her with her husband Toby and their 12 children. At the base of the tower is the Hickes chapel with five life-size effigies—Sir Michael (d. 1612), and his wife, Dame Elizabeth (d. 1635), their son, Sir William (d. 1680), his son, another Sir William (d. 1702) and his wife, Lady Marthagnes. Sir Michael, secretary to Lord Burghley and to Robert Cecil, is in full armour though he was essentially a man of peace; Dame Elizabeth wears widow's weeds. Sir Michael's epitaph reads:

Those things I desired in life I attained; pledges lately deemed the sweetest, a dear wife and a fortune. I was happy in my family; two sons and a daughter call me father. I began to long for Christ, therefore I willingly yield to death; willingly I leave wife, fortune, sons, and daughter.

The eldest Sir William reclines in 17th century dress, the younger stands, in Roman armour, with a full curled wig.

There are several other interesting monuments beside, two of them by John Flaxman. The finer of the pair is in memory of John Hillerson and shows a girl reading a book. The other is for William Bosanquet (d. 1818) and bears a relief of the Good Samaritan. Along the west wall, in the north-west corner, are memorials to two William Bowyers (d. 1737 and 1777), both of them famous printers, with others to their relatives, Ichabod and Sarah Dawkes. On the north wall is a monument sculptured by Sir Henry Cheere, to Sir John Strange, (d. 1754). He sat in Parliament, was one of those who enquired into the conduct of Sir Robert Walpole, and took part in the impeachment of Lord Lovat.

Then there is a tablet to John Lane (d. 1852) of Leyton Grange— a descendant of that family which helped Charles II to escape after the Battle of Worcester in 1652 when he was still an uncrowned king. Two important merchants are commemorated in the south aisle; Sir Robert Beachcroft (d. 1721), Alderman and Lord Mayor of London, who has a carved stone with his mayoral fur cape, sword, and mace, and Sir Edward Holmden (d. 1616), Alderman and Sheriff of London, Master of the Grocers' Company and East India merchant, who has a plain slab on the floor. There is an interesting collection of old maps in the gallery and prints of now lost memorials to Sir William Ryder, the 16th century haberdasher who introduced woollen stockings into England from Italy and of Samuel Keme or Kemp who was incumbent here in 1639. In the Civil War he led a troop of Parliamentary horse. The Royalists said "that he would preach in the morning and plunder in the afternoon, was looked upon as a saint in the pulpit and a devil out of it". The description is possibly prejudiced.

The church also has an old communion bench, called a housling bench, an hour-glass marking the quarters, made in Munich in 1693, a 17th century almsbox and an old beadle's staff dated 1824. The font is probably of the 15th century.

In the churchyard lie a soldier and in the church a vicar with astonishing records of service. The soldier was William O'Brian who served 60 years in the army, dying at last in 1733. Four ye rs later died old John Strype, aged 94, having been vicar here for 68 years, during which time he became famous as an antiquarian, wrote lives of Cranmer and other archbishops, and built Leyton its church house with a handsome doorway, now unfortunately destroyed by bombs. His father came to London as a refugee and his son John was born in Houndsditch, went to St Paul's School and on to Cambridge, and grew up to divide his time between preaching and writing, becoming vicar of Leyton in 1669. He annotated and enlarged Stowe's history of London and when his works were reprinted in the 19th century they filled 19 learned volumes. He outlived his wife and all his children died lamenting that he had left so much work undone, and wrote his own Latin epitaph.

Joseph Cotton is buried in the churchyard too. He entered the navy in 1760 at the age of 15 and then transferred to the marine service of the East India Company of which he became a director. He was Deputy Master of Trinity House from 1803 till 1825 and wrote a book about our coastal lights at the time. He brought from the East a grass of remarkable fineness and strength known as Rhea or China Grass. His son William who lies in St John's churchyard at Leytonstone, was a director of the Bank of England and invented an automatic weighing machine for sovereigns; it could weigh 23 a minute, accurate to the ten-thousandth part of a grain. He was the first man to stop the iniquitous practice of paying men's wages by orders on a public house and, though not very rich, was a great philanthropist who advocated more schooling, and who delighted in building churches, St John's among them.

That part of Leyton which is known as Leytonstone is believed to take its name from a Roman milestone, now long vanished. There were indeed traces of a Roman camp near Ruckholt House, but the site is now covered by Temple Mills Marshalling Yards.

416

INDEX